BRITISH CHIEF RABBIS,

For the grandchildren:
Evie, Jacob, Ellie, Jonah, Theo, Joshie,
Angus, Benji, Constance, Sam, Joe and Finn.
It's up to you now.

BRITISH CHIEF RABBIS
1664–2006

DEREK TAYLOR

With a Foreword by
Rabbi Dr Abraham Levy, OBE

VALLENTINE MITCHELL
LONDON • PORTLAND, OR

First published in 2007 in Great Britain by
VALLENTINE MITCHELL
Suite 314, Premier House, 112–114 Station Road, Edgware, Middlesex
HA8 7BJ

and in the United States of America by
VALLENTINE MITCHELL
c/o ISBS, 920 NE 58th Avenue, Suite 300, Portland, OR 97213 3786
Portland, Oregon, 97213-3644

Website www.vmbooks.com

British Library Cataloguing in Publication Data:

Taylor, Derek
  British chief rabbis, 1664–2006
  1. Chief Rabbinate – Great Britain – History 2. Rabbis –
  Great Britain – Biography 3. Judaism – Great Britain – History
  I. Title
  296'.0922

ISBN 0 85303 610 1 (cloth)
ISBN 978 0 85303 610 4 (cloth)
ISBN 0 85303 611 X (paper)
ISBN 978 0 85303 611 1 (paper)

Library of Congress Cataloging-in-Publication Data:
A catalogue record for this book has been applied for

Typeset by FiSH Books, Enfield, Middx
Printed in Great Britain by MPG Books Ltd, Bodmin, Cornwall

Contents

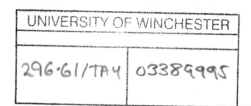

Foreword

It has been my pleasure to help and guide Derek Taylor while researching and writing this fascinating story of the Chief Rabbis and Hahamim of England.

Historically, Anglo-Jewry is a unique community and it was the Chief Rabbinate and the Hahamate who largely fashioned its character and determined its attitudes.

Sadly, the lay leadership of the Spanish and Portuguese congregations developed a sophisticated structure of rules (*ascamot*) which, on many occasions, made the work of the Hahamate much more difficult that it need have been. Hence the many arguments that developed throughout their history. In a similar way, albeit to a lesser extent, the independence of the Ashkenazi Chief Rabbinate often had to be maintained in spite of, rather than because of, the system of by-laws set out by its lay leadership.

What is a little surprising in reading the story of the successive Chief Rabbis is the fact that on one or two occasions the Ashkenazim were prepared to be influenced by the views of the English government in the development of the Chief Rabbinate. This is surprising because, historically, Ashkenazim had a natural aversion to any government involvement in rabbinic duties and appointments – often suffering from such involvement on the Continent. It was, however, seen as quite normal in Sephardi and Oriental countries.

Derek Taylor has told an important and fascinating story. I hope it will encourage the younger generation to feel pride in the community to which they belong.

Rabbi Dr Abraham Levy, OBE
September 2006

Preface

The caricature of the poor Jew in Britain in the eighteenth and nineteenth centuries is of the pedlar pushing his cart along country roads. He sold what he could to the locals and was back home in time for the Sabbath. My maternal great-grandfather, Joseph Freedman, was a pedlar in Wales in about 1880.

When the pogroms were at their height in Russia at the end of the nineteenth century, the refugees who came to London almost took over the tailoring trades, because they would work for less money than the English workers. My paternal grandfather, Albert Taylor (originally Schneider) came from the small village of Vitgifnoie in Poland and set up a tailoring workshop just off Bond Street in London. His son, my father, Philip Taylor, left school to learn his trade in the workshop at the age of 14 in 1910.

Both sides of the family were members of the United Synagogue. Once, when interviewing the Dean of Westminster for an article I was writing, he asked me 'What is *your* religious position?' I told him 'I'm one of the Chief Rabbi's PBIs.' In army terms, that stands for Poor Bloody Infantry. And so I am, just another foot slogger, carrying on the battle for Jewish Orthodox survival as, I hope, will my four children, my four children-in-law and my 12 grandchildren, to whom this book is fondly dedicated. Anyone who writes history has their own opinions and beliefs, but to write good history, these personal views have to be sublimated to the facts and not distorted to make fact support prejudice. I hope I have managed consistently to do that.

It is certainly odd that no history of the Chief Rabbis of England has been written thus far. There have, of course, been monographs on many of them and even books on individuals. Overall, however, they have been relegated to supporting acts in the pageant of British Jewish life since the Resettlement.

There were two major communities in England over the period; the Sephardim and the Ashkenazim. The sage of the Sephardim was called the Haham (pl. Hahamim), and the spiritual leader of the Ashkenazim came to be called the Chief Rabbi. So this book examines the influence of both the Hahamim and the Chief Rabbis over the period from the first haham, Jacob Sasportas in 1664, up to the retirement of the Ashkenazi Chief Rabbi, Immanuel Jakobovits, in 1990, and on to the present Chief Rabbi, Sir Jonathan Sacks.

Jewish history in England has been written by two groups of authors. The majority have been enthusiastic amateurs but, in recent years, professional historians have taken an interest in the field. The professionals tend mildly to denigrate the efforts of the amateurs, many of whom have produced excellent work through the aegis of the Jewish Historical Society of England. The members of this body have been studying Jewish history and then publishing their proceedings since 1892.

There are many people to thank: Rabbi Abraham Levy, the senior rabbi of the Spanish and Portuguese Community, whose advice was invaluable but who left me to make up my own mind on the events of his own years in the community; then Ezra Kahn, former head librarian at Jews College, a guide whenever I was perplexed; Dahlia Tracz at the Mocatta Library at University College, London, who was always helpful; and the experts at the British Library, the Bodleian Library at Oxford and Cambridge University Library. I am also indebted to my wife, Diane, for once again putting up with an endless discussion on a single topic for months on end, my sister, Valerie, ever ready to delve into the research and to Miss Miriam Rodriguez-Pereira, the archivist of the Spanish and Portuguese Community. I should also like to thank the British Library Sound Archive, Rabbi Raymond Apple, Neil Benson, Dayan Ivan Binstock, Gordon and Gillian Burr, Zaki Cooper, Ben Elton, Tamar Eisenstat, Judge Israel Finestein, Dr Miri Freud-Kandel, Rabbi Helen Freeman, Peter Gilles, Stanley Green, Lucien Gubbay, Rabbi Dr Louis Jacobs, Lady Amélie Jakobovits, Lord Janner, Lord Kalms, Elkan Levy, Rabbi Reuben Livingstone, Professor Raphael Loewe, Jack Lopian, Stephen Moss, Hedvah Niculescu, Meir Persoff, Kenneth Rubens, Jeremy Schonfeld, Jonathan Schonfeld, David and Jackie Slesenger, Lionel Swift, Oliver Westall, Professor H.G.M. Williamson and Erla Zimmels. I have given both the West London Synagogue of Progressive Jews and a senior representative of the Right Wing the opportunity to comment on the chapters on their movements but, on a subject as potentially contentious as the Chief Rabbis, I'd like to make it absolutely clear that I am responsible for all the views expressed in this book. Finally, I'd like to thank my son, Simon, for suggesting the idea of the book in the first place.

Glossary

Ab Beth Din	the head of the Jewish Religious court
aliyah	honour of taking a special role in the synagogue service
Amidah	key prayer in the Sabbath service
ascamot (sing. *ascama*)	Sephardi congregational rules
Ba'ale batim	member of the Beth Hamedresh
Baraita	collection of Jewish traditions dating back to the second century CE
barmitzvah	a form of confirmation service held when a boy reaches the age of 13
bassista	bass singer
batmitzvah	a form of confirmation service held when a girl reaches the age of 12
Beth Din	Jewish court of law
Beth Hamedresh	scholarly gatherings for prayer and the study of the Talmud
bima	podium from which the synagogue service is conducted
bodek (pl. bodkim)	the judge of whether animals are fit for Jews to eat
briogas (Yiddish)	aggravation/disruption
briss	circumcision
bubermasser	old wives' tale
carreira	regular row of graves
chevra	small congregation
conversos	forcibly converted
Dayan (pl. Dayanim)	senior rabbi or judge in a Jewish religious court
Din	Jewish religious law
drosha	religious discourse
duchaning	blessings of the priests
eruv	enclosing wall or fence within which it is permitted to carry things on the Sabbath

escaba	prayer for the dead
ethrog	large lemon used in an important prayer at the Festival of Sukkot
finta	voluntary synagogue tax on the earnings of richer members
frum	observant
Gemara	commentary on the Mishnah
genizah	room in a synagogue for keeping Hebrew documents once they have become unnecessary or unusable
Get	when a husband agrees to divorce his wife
haftorah	extract from the Books of the Prophets, read on Sabbath or festival mornings
Haham (pl. Hahamim)	sage of the Sephardim
halacha (adj. halachic)	the legal element in the Talmud
Hazan (pl. hazanim)	the principal leader of a synagogue service
hebra	small, highly orthodox congregation
herem	excommunication from the community
Heskath ha Kehillah	full member of the synagogue
kahal	congregation/community – any of the Jewish communites scattered across Europe, or the local governing body of any of these communities
ketubah (pl. *ketubot*)	marriage certificate
kiddush	Jewish blessing uttered over wine and bread on holy days
kolel	postgraduate college for scholars who are already rabbis
loshen kodesh	holy language, i.e. Hebrew
magid (pl. maggidim)	travelling preacher
Mahamad (pl. Mahamadim)	honorary officers of the Sephardi community
meshorrer	a tenor
mezuzah	parchment scroll containing the *shema* prayer, which is placed in a case and fixed to the doorpost in Jewish houses
Midrash	Hebrew exposition of the Old Testament
mikveh	bath used for ritual purification

minhag	tradition
minyan	group of 10 men needed for a full service
mi sheberech	a blessing
Mishnah	Jewish Oral Law
mitzvah (pl. *mitzvoth*)	good deed (literally commandment)
mohel (pl. mohelim)	experts who perform circumcision on male babies
Parnas (pl. parnassim)	Jewish lay leader
pasken	lay down religious law
Posek	a rabbi who can be consulted on what the law is; a Posek is more eminent than a Dayan
Sefer Torah	scroll on which the Torah is written
semicha	rabbinical diploma
shadchan	marriage broker
shammes	caretaker of a synagogue with a similar role to that of a sexton
Shavuot	spring harvest festival
shechita	ritual slaughtering of animals
shiur (pl. *shiurim*)	learned lecture followed by a discussion
Shiva	seven-day mourning period for the dead
shnodering	auctioning of synagogue privileges to raise money for charity
shochet (pl. shochetim)	ritual butcher
Shtiebl	small group of orthodox Jews gathered together for study and prayer
shul	synagogue
sukkah	flimsy outdoor shelter to be slept in during the festival of Sukkot
tallith	Jewish prayer shawl
Talmud	Jewish sacred writings
tashlich	casting away sins in a river on Rosh Hashanah
trefa	non-kosher (as in non-kosher meat)
Vestry	Ashkenazi equivalent of the Mahamad
Yahid (pl. Yehidim)	member of the Sephardi community
yarmulke	skullcap worn by Jewish males
yeshiva	Jewish religious academy
Yomtov	a festival

Chief Rabbi Solomon Hirschell

Haham Dr Solomon Gaon, Haham of the Spanish and Portuguese
Jews' Congregation, London, 1949–77
© Spanish and Portuguese Jews' Congregation, London

1 Setting the Scene

Ring a ring o'roses.
A pocket full of posies.
Atishoo, atishoo,
We all fall down.

In my imagination, Abe Nunez watched the handcart trundling by outside his window, piled high with the dead. It was 1665 or, according to the Jewish calendar, 5425. He could avoid the overwhelming stench of the sewage in the gutters by sniffing at the posy of flowers he held in his hand. There was no dreaded red rash on his face and he wasn't sneezing, so he was all right for the time being, but he couldn't help wondering if he had been destined to survive the Inquisition only to be killed by the Great Plague in London.

Even the stink in the streets, though, was better than that ghastly smell of human flesh burning at the Auto da Fé in Lisbon. The Catholic Inquisition were patient and thorough at rooting out Marranos, those who still tried to practice their Judaism in secret at home. They had practically eliminated them in Spain and Grandpa Abe had fled Portugal for Amsterdam when they got too close to his family. Uncle Judah, the doctor, hadn't been so lucky. He was still in their dungeons; if he was lucky, he'd get time in the galleys or working as a labourer in the disease-ridden marshes. If he wasn't, the pyre would be set alight, though if the family paid the executioners enough, they might be merciful and strangle him first.

London was different. The king's brother might be a Catholic but the government was staunchly Protestant. They hated the Catholics almost as much as he did. Ever since 1497 in Portugal when the Jews had been forcibly converted, the authorities had been after the Jews to finally pack it in. They'd kidnapped all the kids and refused to give them back until the parents converted. What a lot of suicides that had led to. And yet to stop the persecution all they had to do was admit that Jesus was the true Messiah and that Judaism was finished.

Well, not on his life. It might be alright for some of his old friends and even by members of his family, but the church authorities weren't going to win as far as he was concerned. Whatever it took, they weren't going to win. He might have to earn a living in a foreign country, grovel to the powerful and be constantly on guard against the mob, but he wasn't going to give in. The survival of Judaism owed a great deal to being bloody-minded as well as devout.

Admittedly, he hardly knew any longer what it was he wouldn't give up. He spoke no Hebrew, he had not been circumcised and his father had only been able to pass on to him the scraps of knowledge of Judaism he himself possessed. For over 100 years the memories had been handed down from father to son, as they walked through the fields or talked quietly in their homes where they couldn't be overheard. Abe's friends in London at the synagogue in Creechurch Lane were hardly any the wiser. They'd been given permission to have a synagogue by Oliver Cromwell when he was Lord Protector, the head of state, but the elected Board of Management, the Mahamad, had still thought it sensible to install no less than three lockable doors, back to back, before you could get into the shul proper. From bitter experience they knew that rulers couldn't always control spontaneous anti-Jewish riots quickly enough to save the intended victims.

How would he survive? Well, he had one advantage; he was street-smart. When one mistake could cost you your life, you learned to be street-smart. He was also into the Brazilian diamond trade and the rich loved his stones. He was known outside the synagogue as Antonio Garcia, so that the spies of the Inquisition couldn't learn his true identity and take it out on the family back in Portugal. He'd get by; the Jews stuck together because there was a lot more safety in numbers than there was safety as an individual against the state. He was almost indistinguishable from his neighbours anyway. A bit darker than them, perhaps, but he dressed the same way, as did Sarah, his wife. He visited the same coffee-houses and nobody cared about his broken English as long as the jewellery was perfect.

The Plague hadn't affected the inhabitants of the Jewish streets very much. Goodness knows why, he thought. What's that banging? Oh, it's only Sarah cleaning the house again. He liked that. His home was so much tidier and sweeter smelling than the houses of the rich he visited with his samples. Sarah had been taught to keep everything spotless by her mother, and he seemed to remember there was some sort of rule in Judaism that you had to do it regularly.

He dropped off in front of the fire. He'd got this far, he thought, and please God, the plague would overlook him and his loved ones.

A few streets away Joe Levy was hoping much the same thing. Those Portuguese Sephardim weren't such a bad lot, he thought. Much they knew about what they were doing in the synagogue, but they were tolerant enough with their Ashkenazi brethren. He was from Hamburg, a survivor of the terrible Thirty Years' War. What an awful time that had been. If you weren't a victim of a massacre, you were likely to go down in some epidemic. It was said that two-thirds of the population had perished in those thirty dreadful years. Mind you, 10 per cent of the English had died in the time of the Civil War, and now the plague had hit London, although nobody knew why. Probably something to do with the mice. Well, that's what the Bible said in 1 Samuel, Chapter 6, Verse 4, when the Philistines went down with it. It would probably take hundreds of years to find out the truth.

Thank goodness he'd made the move – what a fabulous country it was. Rich and powerful in Europe and Protestant to boot. The Protestants wanted to get back to the Bible, as it was originally. The Jews knew the way home. When the news had reached Hamburg that England was letting the Jews back into the country after 350 years, he could hardly believe his luck. He knew they'd be under the protection of the king, just like in the ghetto, and that the English, as far as he could see, were reasonably indifferent to the presence of a small group of Jews in London. A whole boatload of them had come over from Poland in 1649 and that had passed off alright.

It was strange not living in a ghetto. Of course, the London Jews voluntarily lived in a small enclave of the City. They'd all found homes within a mile or so of the synagogue, so that it was easy to walk there to *shul* on the Sabbath, but no English rules dictated that you had to stay in the area – you were free to go where you liked when you liked. He missed the Beth Hamedresh at home in Germany; the gatherings of scholars to study the Talmud, the sacred writings. The Sephardim were hopelessly ignorant compared to the members of an Ashkenazi ghetto. It was very obvious that they knew so little about the faith that the Rabbi had to teach them even the basics. In fairness, though, nobody had tried to stop him studying in Hamburg, as they had the Marranos in Portugal.

He hadn't got much of a job. He helped out around the synagogue; the rich Portuguese Sephardim used the Tedescos, the poor German Jews, for the menial tasks. Sometimes he peddled laces in the streets but it was a hard life. At least the community didn't have to pay the government additional taxes, as they had back in the old country. What he earned he could keep.

How Leah managed to make a home for him and the six children was a wonder. His youngest, Jacob, was a weak child but the synagogue's doctor was a good man and did his best. He'd like to have a blessing said for the child to recover, but Tedescos didn't get a chance to participate in the services. That was restricted to the Sephardi members. Still, the Sabbath was coming; he'd be able to get out his books and study the Torah. He spoke fluent Hebrew as well as Yiddish; that polyglot mixture of primarily German and Hebrew in which Ashkenazi Jews all over Europe could talk to each other.

Perhaps one day they could have their own *shul* – their own synagogue – their own melodies and pronunciation. The tune that came into his mind was the prayer for the dead. It was said that Rabbi Athias was very ill with the plague. Please God it wouldn't come to his house.

2 The Story so Far

So there are two main kinds of Orthodox Jew; the Sephardim and the Ashkenazim. They only differ in minor matters, although one of these is that they have different melodies for their prayers, which makes it extremely difficult to join in if you're from a synagogue of the other side. When the Jews were thrown out of the Holy Land by the Romans in 132 they spread to many parts of the world. It is generally agreed that the Sephardim originate in the Jewish communities which laid down their foundations after that in North Africa, Spain and Portugal. The Ashkenazim come from northern Europe, from Russia, Germany and Poland. The two communities in Britain have normally got on harmoniously, but as cousins rather than brothers and sisters.

The religious head of a Jewish community is the rabbi. The word simply means 'teacher' and Judaism holds that the rabbi has no power to intercede on your behalf with the Almighty. This runs counter to the position of a Catholic priest, for example, who has the power to grant absolution. The divine relationship, according to Judaism, is a matter for each individual Jew. The Protestants look at it the same way. No rabbi has the power to absolve a member of his congregation from sin and the process of the confessional is not part of Judaism. The rabbi is – each congregation hopes – a sage (Haham). The word originally applied to the rabbi of any specifically Sephardi synagogue, but as a title was needed for the acknowledged spiritual head of all the Sephardi communities in an area, it became restricted in Britain to the Sephardi rabbi who held that position. Thus in considering the Chief Rabbis of Britain since the Jews returned in numbers to the country after 1658, it's Chief Rabbi for the Ashkenazi and Haham for the Sephardi communities. Strangely, there was no equivalent to a Chief Rabbi anywhere else in the world when it came to be accepted in England; it was a purely English concept that a rabbi could have authority over other rabbis.

Elsewhere, a rabbi might become a Dayan and be one of the judges in a Beth Din – a court of Jewish law. A rabbi might be so learned that his advice was sought when the local rabbi or community were in doubt on a technical point. Outside England, however, all this was voluntary. In England – and without the state demanding it – the role's authority just quietly emerged. How do you become a rabbi? You study with an existing rabbi whose judgement of scholarship is generally considered to be of a high quality. When he is satisfied with your level of expertise, he will grant you the title.

The Jews had been expelled from Britain in 1290. It was a good way to get rid of an unpopular minority and to avoid repaying the very substantial debts that many aristocratic families had incurred by borrowing from Jewish moneylenders. In mediaeval times the laws of Christianity forbade charging interest on a loan, so the Jews filled the gap in the economic framework. They were labelled moneylenders, an occupation with unpleasant overtones, and consequently were not popular – if you have a serious overdraft you'll appreciate why – and the appellation 'moneylender' hasn't the positive spin of 'banker'. In fact, Jews weren't just moneylenders. Because, as a faith, they trusted their co-religionists, they could be recommended to each other – Relationship Marketing in today's terms – and they could move funds safely from country to country, just like banks. The term 'banker' was seldom used at the time, however, and, over the centuries, they have come down to us as moneylenders.

Another reason the Jews lent money was because they weren't allowed to do much else. They were forbidden to own land or to join the mediaeval guilds and become manufacturers. When William Cobett, the nineteenth-century journalist who championed the cause of the underprivileged, attacked the Jews in Parliament in the 1830s, he said that: 'usury is the only pursuit for which they are fit'. Thomas Macauley, the great historian, got up and buried him: 'Such, sir, has been in every age the reasoning of bigots. They never fail to plead in justification of persecution the vices which persecution has engendered.'

To make life more difficult for the mediaeval English Jews, the Church was, of course, intent on converting them by every available means, and if persuasion was unsuccessful, expulsion was always an alternative. Massacre was another, often preceded by torture. No story was too ludicrous to be believed and acted upon. One English Christian commentator during the Napoleonic Wars reviewed just some of the calumnies of the past:

> Because a King of France happened to be more insane than some of his predecessors, all Jews were expelled from their

native country: for the royal lunatic was declared by an archbishop to be so, in consequence of Jewish witchcraft... Was there a plague? The waters were poisoned by the Jews! Was there a famine? The harvests were bewitched by the synagogue ... Was a king crowned? The royal ceremony was attended with the splendid destruction of his unhappy subjects; the Jews.[1]

The Blood Libel reared its extremely ugly head in mediaeval England. In 1255 the English chronicler, Matthew Paris, explained a murder by saying that the Jews had killed the victim because they needed his blood to make matzo – unleavened bread – for Passover. This inflamed the mob against the Jews to Paris' satisfaction and his anti-Semitic successors kept the old canard alive over the centuries. There would be many Jewish deaths in Syria in 1841 because of a similar allegation. Accusations of international Jewish conspiracies to conquer the world would culminate in a twentieth-century publication entitled *The Protocols of the Elders of Zion*, which remains a bestseller in the Arab world today. It has been shown to be a Tsarist secret police piece of disinformation to justify the pogroms, but when enough mud is thrown, some of it will stick.

Consequently in 1290 those Jews who refused to convert left Britain. Over the next 350 years a few were occasionally to return, often surreptitiously, sometimes to set up the British branch office of a trading company they had established in another country. After 132 the Jews thought internationally; for example, in the tenth century, they were already trading regularly between Cairo and China. There was a Jewish community in China, which had arrived from Persia in about 1000. Sometimes Jews came to England because they produced good doctors – Queen Elizabeth's doctor for some years was Dr Roberto Ridolfi. He of the Ridolfi plot of 1571, which would have resulted in his summary execution had he not been back in his native Italy at the time. There were two other famous Jewish medics in England; Dr Roderigo Lopes and Dr Hector Nunes, who were both Queen Elizabeth's doctors as well. Lopes, unlike Ridolfi, didn't get out quickly enough, and was executed in 1594 for allegedly plotting to murder the Queen. The records show that: 'an overwhelmingly large proportion of the eminent Spanish and Portuguese practitioners, from the sixteenth century onwards, are known to have been of Jewish extraction'.[2] According to Spanish Inquisition records there were almost 100 Jews in England in Elizabethan times.[3]

When complaints were made about the existence of tiny cadres of

Jews in English towns, they were often expelled again. Many did convert to Christianity, of whom one of the most famous in England was Sir Edward Brampton, later a Yorkist general, who had started life as Duarte Brando. One Jew, Joachim Ganz, was to be found in Keswick in the Lake District in 1581, helping with advice on how to smelt lead and iron ores. A nineteenth-century Chief Rabbi commented dryly: 'He would have remained in this country if he had not committed the indiscretion of endeavouring to prove to a Christian friend that there was but one God, who had neither wife nor child.'[4]

The Jews in the mid-seventeenth century were still in desperate need of more countries who would let them in to live in peace. Those who had converted, rather than leave Spain after the expulsion of 1492, were known as Marranos, meaning 'pigs' or 'filthy' in Spanish. Most thought that the expulsion was a phase they had to get through and that everything would eventually return to normal. It did, but not until nearly 500 years later. If the Marranos tried to continue to practise Judaism, they could be caught by the Inquisition – an organization set up by the Pope to keep the faithful in line. There had been a Papal Bull in 1478 ordering the Church to root out heretics, including the converts who were still following Jewish practices. Autos da Fé – which included the burning to death of heretics – were major public events and the gracious and impressive Plaza Mayor in Madrid is still an evil place for the Jews who visit it and know its history. The Inquisition was efficient; the Spanish Marranos were, effectively, wiped out over the next 50 years.

Of the 100,000 Jews who chose to leave Spain in 1492, 60,000 crossed the border to Portugal; they were a great help to the Portuguese economy. Portugal needed international merchants following the Papal Donation of Pope Alexander VI in 1493. His Holiness had graciously given everything east of Rome to Portugal and everything west of Rome to Spain. Hence the Portuguese in Asia and the Spaniards in the Americas, though the Portuguese also ran Brazil.

King Manuel the Fortunate, however, wanted to marry Isabella of Castile and she wouldn't agree unless all the Jews in Portugal were converted. To encourage the Jews to come on board, Manuel had all the Jewish children aged between 4 and 14 arrested at Passover in 1497 and forcibly converted. If their parents wanted them back, they had to convert too. When the adults still resisted, Manuel had them forcibly converted anyway. Even then the Marranos continued to practice Judaism in their homes, and so Manuel called on the Pope to deploy the Inquisition in Portugal. This eventually was the subject of a Papal Bull in 1531 and then came the usual witch-hunt. Over the next couple of hundred years 1,500 Jews were executed and ten times that number finished up in dungeons, the galleys, or working as labourers in the disease-infested marshes. As many as 226 were burnt at the stake between 1637 and 1653 alone. A few continued practising what Judaism they could remember until modern times. As late as 1926 the Lisbon Jewish community launched an appeal to raise money for schools to teach Marrano children the religion their families had never entirely given up.

Many of the Marranos went on their travels again and moved north, setting up home in Belgium, France, Germany, Greece and Holland. The people of the Low Countries had been ruled by the Spanish but had fought hard against the occupying power and the seven northern Protestant provinces got rid of them in 1581, at which point they declared themselves the United Provinces. The southern part of the country remained under Spanish rule until Napoleon. Some, though not all, United Provinces towns now welcomed the influx of Jews. Those who did were attracted by the ability of the Sephardim to help their international trade and would have taken the view that any enemy of the Spanish was likely to be a friend of the Dutch. If they were anti-Catholic as well, so much the better.

The relatives of the immigrants, however, might well have remained in Portugal where their lives were constantly in danger if they continued secretly to practise Judaism. In addition, the Inquisition would try to identify members of other European Jewish communities so that they could investigate their relatives at home for crypto-Jewish practices, or arrest the overseas Jews if they ever went home to see their families.

Many Jews countered this by adopting two names; one within the religion and another when mixing with the rest of the world, such as Duarte Brando becoming Edward Brampton as well. When Richard Chapman got a pass to go to Italy in 1696, his real name was Isaac Fernandez, but the ship was calling at Spanish ports, so it was wise to use his alias.[5]

The Marranos were the first Jews to adopt surnames. A Jew's Hebrew name is his own followed by the name of his father; for instance, Jacob ben Joseph, Jacob son of Joseph. Now the Jews of Spain often took the names of noble Spanish families. The Jews of Italy mostly adopted the surnames of the cities in which they lived; Model, Pepperoni, Perugia, etc. When the Ashkenazi Jews adopted surnames, they either designated their city of origin, for example Hamburger, or what they did for a living – Goldsmid for goldsmiths or Schneider for tailors.

Even after migrating to London: 'Most of them who were now living in London feared that it was not yet safe for them to cast off the cloak of Christianity.'[6] The fear was sensible but the Marranos had also picked up a fierce pride from the Spanish over the centuries. As Haham Solomon Gaon wrote: 'rugged and uncompromising individualism was evident among the Spanish exiles when they settled in different communities'.[7]

If the Jews were in trouble, even if they weren't family, they were still Jews and that was enough for the Jewish communities elsewhere. They would be given help wherever possible. For example, one of the more lucrative ways of amassing a fortune in the seafaring world of the Mediterranean at the time was to kidnap travelling merchants – including Jews – and hold them to ransom. The money to get them back would often come through collections taken up throughout the Jewish world.

So the search for safe havens was always pressing, but it had hit one of its regular panic buttons in the 1650s. The ravages of the Thirty Years' War of 1618–48 had killed some 50 per cent of the German population, through warfare and disease. By 1648 Germany was on its knees. So there were Jewish Ashkenazi refugees coming from Germany. In 1648 a Cossack called Bogdan Chmielnicki started a revolt in the Ukraine against Polish landowners, Catholic clergy and Jews. One contemporary source claims that 744 Jewish communities were wiped out. Certainly tens – if not hundreds – of thousands of Jews were butchered, which meant more refugees streaming westwards. Often they had spent their lives confined to the town ghetto – a poor section of the town designated only for Jews. Thus the Ashkenazim, as a whole, were less exposed to European culture than the nominally Christian Marranos.

There was another problem for the stable communities. The refugees were often destitute and there was a limit to the help any single city could give them. If, however, you could straighten out the refugees and then ship them off to another town or even another country, you would have done your job and be relieved of any further burden; so that often became the objective. Even the resident Amsterdam community looked for better opportunities elsewhere. About 25 per cent of them emigrated to Brazil in the seventeenth century because there were fortunes to be made trading in diamonds and sugar. It was an earlier version of the Gold Rush.

It was their international network of co-religionists which enabled the Jews to become great traders. It's difficult to appreciate in our world of mass travel and tourism that in the seventeenth century most people were born and died in the same village, without ever seeing any part of the rest of the world. Persecution ensured that the Jews were different, so they tended to have communities in the large trading ports; in Italy in Leghorn and Venice, natural entrepôt ports between east and west, in Germany in Hamburg, in Holland in Amsterdam. And where there was a settled community, there often grew up a school of religious scholars; Leghorn and Hamburg were typical examples of these yeshivas (religious academies). The congregations also kept in touch with each other in case money for ransoms was needed – or qualified religious officials, expert spiritual and legal advice, suitable marriage partners or help with the Building Fund.

In the 1650s the 3,000 Sephardi Jews in Amsterdam wondered – not for the first time – whether England, which had London as its great trading centre, might be another port in a storm. The inhabitants of London made up at least one-twelfth of the population of England in the seventeenth century. By contrast, only one in 40 French citizens lived in Paris. Well, it was certainly worth trying. After all, though it might have been difficult for Jews to live in England under the Stuarts, many had managed it. In 1613 a playwright called Thomas Dekker had written the *Will of the Devil*: 'My Will is that all the Brokers in Long Lane be sent to me...and for their brethren (the rest of their Jewish tribe in the synagogue of Houns-ditch) let them be assured they will not be forgotten.'[8] The Jews may have been thrown out by Edward I in 1290 but it was obviously fairly common knowledge in the seventeenth century that they still provided merchants in the City of London. The Spanish plundered the gold in South America from the Incas but they needed to sell it on in Europe, and for this they often used Jewish bullion merchants.

The thinking was that, as the last king had had his head chopped off in 1649, maybe the new rulers would be sympathetic. Was it possible to get back? The Jews had a foothold because Antonio Fernando Carvajal had quietly moved to London in 1633 and a few Jews met at his house for prayers. He was a rich ship-owner and bullion merchant and not only supplied grain to Oliver Cromwell, but also spied for him; nevertheless, Carvajal's public behaviour included attending Mass in the chapel attached to the Spanish embassy. He became highly regarded by Cromwell, who made him an English citizen in 1655. Samuel Pepys, the diarist, was only a young clerk in 1659, but when Carvajal died, Pepys came to the synagogue for the memorial service. Did he know what Carvajal had done for the navy for which he worked? It was Carvajal's contacts in Holland who enabled him to tell Cromwell some of the details of Charles II's attempt to mount an invasion of England in 1656 with the help of the Spanish:

> When, ultimately, the Commonwealth frigates saved England from a renewal of the civil war by the seizure of the Royalist shipping at Ostend, there can be little doubt that the information purveyed by Carvajal…was a factor of some importance in the success of that enterprise.[9]

There was also the point that Cromwell, the effective ruler of the new Commonwealth after the Civil War, had approved the Navigation Act in 1651; this meant that all goods imported into England now had to arrive in British ships. This was ruinous for the Jewish merchants in Amsterdam who were in the West Indies sugar market. They wanted to refine the sugar in Amsterdam before exporting it to England; better now to run it in a British vessel from a British colony direct to London. The Jamaican Jewish community was actually formed in 1655 and Barbados was the first British possession to remove all political restrictions from the Jews. In the West Indies the Jews were deeply involved in the sugar, vanilla, tobacco and dyestuffs trades.

From Oliver Cromwell's point of view, there were at least five good reasons for letting the Jews return. First, they would be able to help in the export drive; they had connections in so many parts of the world. The great explorers, such as Drake and Raleigh, had made the full extent of the world better known back home, but that didn't make them merchants. Jewish traders could buy and sell almost anywhere. If it had been discovered, they would be trying to trade there. Rabbis could also be relied on to pass on money or receive it and send it back across the oceans and along trade routes. Rabbis could be in business. They weren't usually full-time ministers. The new creed of Puritanism saw eye-to-eye with the Jews in trying to improve their lot. They embraced the work ethic and regarded the self-made man as a hero.

Second, Cromwell wanted the Jews for their creativity. In 1655, Solomon Dormido, a Jewish broker in London, was already offering insurance on cargoes; typical rates were 2.5 per cent of the value if it was a trade with Lisbon and 3.5 per cent if the port was Barbados. The regulations for such insurance were covered in the Talmud in biblical times. There is a Baraita, a collection of traditions, which dates back to the second century CE, which covers the field (BK 116b). So the idea wasn't that new, but few non-Jewish brokers studied the Talmud. Jewish merchants also developed such essential instruments of international trade as letters of credit and bearer bonds.

Dormido couldn't, in fact, legally be a broker because all brokers had to be Freemen of the City of London. This was impossible for Jews who wouldn't take the required entry oath as a 'true Christian', which Dormido wasn't about to do. So the City ignored the need to be a Freeman. For the same reason Dormido couldn't be elected to the City's Court of Aldermen, so they ignored that as well and gave him the appointment. Dormido must have been a popular character, and anyway, the City Fathers, like many modern international traders, disliked the law getting in the way of business. In 1657, however, it was agreed that there could only be 12 Jew Brokers, and they would have to pay the Lord Mayor of London handsomely for the privilege. The last recorded instance of this fee being charged took place as late as 1826 when J.B. Montefiore paid £1,575 to Sir William Magnay, the Lord Mayor, for the medal which was the title deed for the position.

'Broker' here constitutes what today would be termed a commodity broker. Someone who sells goods – often imported – in quantity on behalf of the owners. This developed into selling government bonds and the shares of companies as well, but there was no official Stock Exchange until the late eighteenth century. Most of the negotiations were done in the City's coffee houses or around the Royal Exchange building. Messengers were used to take communications between the two. They were rewarded for their speed; hence TIP – To Insure Promptitude. The Jews were certainly among the first Stock Jobbers in England.

Dormido was always looked after by Cromwell. When he wanted to get some of his property returned to him in Portugal, the Protector wrote personally to the King of Portugal on his behalf. The letter, in Latin, was written by one of his officials, John Milton, the poet, and signed by Cromwell. The king made the necessary arrangements.

Third, Cromwell was particularly keen to get the Brazilian trade away from the Dutch. Brazil was, legally, a Portuguese colony but the Dutch dominated the seas around it, so there were rich pickings for patriots/pirates – depending on your viewpoint – and it was relatively easy to get away with murder.

Fourth, Cromwell needed spies in Spain and Portugal as well as in Holland. Valuable information could come from Marranos – after all Hector Nunes had tipped off the English that Philip II was building an Armada in 1587.[10] Lord Orrery told Bishop Burnet that he had seen a Jew tell Cromwell of the sailing of a Spanish ship carrying the pay for the Spanish army in Holland. The ship had been stopped and the bullion confiscated.[11] In any conflict with Spain – and war broke out in 1655 – Cromwell would remember that the Jews had told him that it was their opinion that: 'Spain was Antichrist and the Inquisition the Harlot of Babylon.' And that, they no doubt considered, was on a good day. What the expulsion of 1492 had created was a Fifth Column of Jews who had good cause to hate Spain and who would do all they could to undermine its interests. Cromwell wanted to take advantage of that.

Furthermore, it was now fashionable to take a deep interest in the Bible, even to the point of comparing current events with biblical highlights; for example, the execution of Charles I with that of a biblical tyrant. Cromwell was very religious but he also believed fervently in total religious toleration. Anyway, he knew he would be able to trust the Jews because of their common hatred of the Catholics. Puritanism was immensely important in England and if it was a simpler form of Christianity, aimed at purifying the Church of Catholicism, it looked to the Jews as representative of those early days of the religion. Puritans considered it elevating rather than demeaning to refer to themselves as a Second Israel.

A number of English pamphleteers started to call for the Jews to return. Some said it was to try to apologize for the treatment they had received in 1290. Some because it was believed that the Messiah wouldn't come until there were Jews in every country. Some pointed out, with unassailable logic, that it was difficult to convert the Jews if there were no Jews to convert.

Cromwell was convinced and Rabbi Manasseh ben Israel, the insurance Jew Broker's uncle, came over from Holland in 1655 to try to reach an agreement with the Protector. Manasseh ben Israel's father had tangled with the Inquisition in Lisbon, and the family had decided to get out after the Auto da Fé in 1603. Manasseh was born in La Rochelle and then the family went on to Amsterdam. The boy was, effectively, brought up by Rabbi Isaac Uzziel, who had been the rabbi of Fez in Morocco. Manasseh was something of a prodigy, and when Uzziel died in 1620, Manasseh took over from him, even though he was only 16. He became a very famous printer and, though he was only the third most senior rabbi in Amsterdam, he was acknowledged to be an able diplomat.

The English secretary of state, John Thurlow, had deliberately met with Rabbi Manasseh in Amsterdam in 1651. The subject of a possible return to England would have been very much in both men's minds. Rabbi Manasseh was kindly received by Cromwell, who promised to do his best to get the government to agree. An official council considered the proposal and the law officers said there was nothing to stop the Jews living in England. In fact, they said there hadn't been a problem since Edward I died in 1307. The decision to banish the Jews had been entirely his prerogative and the prohibition ended with his death. They pointed out that Edward II and his successors hadn't renewed it. The salient point that nobody had taken that view for 350 years was conveniently overlooked.

In the end the rabbi didn't get his law passed at the Whitehall Conference in 1655. The residual prejudice against Jews was still strong. Cromwell, though, wasn't really into democracy by this time; so he told the authorities that, even if they didn't approve, they weren't to make a fuss if the Jews returned.

When the Marranos arrived, they were clearly understood to be under Cromwell's personal protection and brought with them a vast £1.5 million of capital (roughly £400 million in today's money). They were soon responsible for one twelfth of England's trade. Cromwell had also created a financial problem in passing the Navigation Act, which meant that England now had to finance all the West Indies trade. That meant an increase in the amount of bullion in circulation and that had to come from Spain. The Jews arranged for Cromwell to import the bullion. Carvajal, himself, imported £200,000-worth. This was, naturally, exceptionally useful when England and Spain were at war.

At the end of 1656 it was agreed with the churchwardens of St Katherine's Creechurch that Carvajal could have 5, Creechurch Lane for a synagogue at a rent of £40 a year and a lease of 21 years. Carvajal signed the lease on 19 December 1656 and the community also leased land for a cemetery in February 1657. Although the negotiations were done through an agent – Jews couldn't own property – the churchwardens knew what Carvajal wanted the house for, even though no law had been passed to allow the Jews back into England. In the churchwarden's list of payments for 1656 it says: 'paid for warning the workmen before the Court of Alderman that were Imployed in building the Jews Synagogue'.[12]

Services started in January 1657. A vital Sefer Torah (the scroll of the first five books of the Bible) had arrived from Amsterdam earlier on. The Jews were almost all Sephardim and they were, nationally, a mixed lot, coming from both Holland and Portugal. Four of the members were converts. Some of the merchants had been rivals, each hoping for the country where they lived to dominate the Brazilian trade. England was comfortable with an alliance with anything Portuguese, because the English knew that the Portuguese would dislike Spain as well. The Portuguese had been great explorers and traders in the times of intrepid sailors like Vasco da Gama in the fifteenth century, but Portugal had lost its independence to Spain in 1580 and didn't get it back until 1640.

Manasseh ben Israel took the precaution of penning a prayer for the ruler, to be said in the synagogue on the Sabbath and Festivals, and a similar prayer for the royal family would be recognized in any British Orthodox synagogue today:

> He that giveth salvation unto Kings and dominion unto Lords, he that delivereth his servant, David, from the sword of the enemy, he that make a way in the sea and a path in the strange waters, bless and keep, preserve and rescue, exalt and magnify, and lift up higher and higher, our Lord [the ruler's name]. The King of Kings defend him in his mercy, making him joyful, and free him from all dangers and distress. The King of Kings, for his goodness sake, raise up and exalt his planetary star and multiply his days over his kingdom. The King of Kings, for his mercies sake, put into his heart and into the hearts of his Counsellors, and those who attend and minister to him, that he may show mercy unto us and unto all the people of Israel. In his days and in our days, let Judah be safe and Israel dwell securely, and let the Redeemer come to Israel and so may it please God, amen.

The joy of being safe in a free country was overwhelming, but would it last? As the Jews knew to their cost, regime change was always likely. That possibility lay in the future, though, and there is a contemporary account of the Jews one autumn taking themselves to the south side of the Thames and living in booths for the duration of the Festival of Sukkot, as Jewish law instructed. It was a brief, high-profile moment before they got their heads down below the parapet again.

What the Christians felt about this strange behaviour is not recorded, though when Pepys visited the synagogue at the same time of the year in 1663, he was amazed at the service. Sukkot is a very joyous festival and there is a lot of singing and jollification. To an outsider the result may appear distinctly odd:

> the disorder, laughing, sporting, and no attention, but confusion in all their service, more like brutes than people knowing the true

God, would make a man forswear ever seeing them more: and indeed I never did see so much, or could have imagined there had been any religion in the whole world so absurdly performed as this.

Well, it is a happy time and not all synagogue services are 100 per cent solemn.

There had been a lot of wild rumours about the future if the Jews were allowed to return. In December 1657 the Earl of Monmouth wrote to a friend: 'The Jews' mouths, though not their eyes, are to be opened; who I do hear, are to have two sinagogs allowed them in London, whereof St Paellas to be one!'[13] This *bubermasser* (old wives' tale) that St Paul's was going to be converted resurfaced on more than one occasion in the ensuing centuries.

Such a rumour, if widely believed, could have led to riots against the Jews and worse. Far less had led to far greater oppression in times gone by. The Jews were scared of the majority community wherever they lived. They were unarmed, outnumbered by thousands to one and easy prey for persecutors. Most of them would remain apprehensive until the present day. Not only did they have every right to be afraid because of their experiences, there was also the fact that wherever and whenever there was oppression of the Jews, the news reached almost every Jewish community. They were regularly fed a diet of terrible events and needed to be if they were to respond to the cries for help, which could come after long periods of time living tranquilly in a country, or simply be the latest in a series of anti-Semitic outbreaks. Jews carried the umbrella of awareness in case it rained oppression – and so often they seemed to find themselves in a potentially wet political and religious climate.

Over the next 350 years in Britain, there would be no anti-Semitic outrages on anything like the scale found in the rest of Europe; but we have the benefit of hindsight, though most Jews always stayed scared. After the Holocaust it would often be said in private that something equally appalling could happen in Britain. It was totally unfair if you considered the British record, but totally understandable if you considered the performance of so many cultivated, civilized French, Poles or Austrians who would help the Nazis with enthusiasm to carry out the Final Solution. The fear has been interwoven into the panorama of Jewish history since the Romans expelled them.

In the 1650s in Amsterdam, Charles II was trying to regain his throne. In 1649 when Parliament had executed his father, he had fled to Amsterdam just ahead of Cromwell's posse. In the Dutch capital he plotted his restoration, but he needed a lot of help to make the attempt and wondered whether the rich Jewish merchants could be brought onside.

The Jews didn't know who was going to come out on top in England; the parliamentarians or the king? If possible, the safest course would surely be to back both runners. While Rabbi Manasseh went over to England to plead with Cromwell, the Jews were pleased to receive an indirect approach from Charles in September 1656. He sent his emissary, General Middleton, to open negotiations and he gave him a clear brief:

> to assure them that if they shall in the coniuncture be ready by any contribution of money, ARMs or ammunicion to advance that service which wee have intrusted you, they shall find that when God shall restore us to the possession of our right and to that power which of right doth belonge to us, wee shall extende that protection to them which they can reasonably expecte, and abate that rigour of the lawes which is against them in our severall dominions.[14]

Who backed the king and by how much is not known. The wealthy Sephardim knew that their investment in his success could turn out to be a losing bet, but then the Jews had become great gamblers over the centuries too; if you're likely to lose everything through a massacre tomorrow, you might just as well try to make a fortune today. It was perfectly possible that Charles would die in exile, as would his brother, James II, and his nephew and great-nephew: James Edward Stuart, the Old Pretender and Charles Edward Stuart, Bonnie Prince Charlie, the Young Pretender. On the other hand, he might recover the throne, in which case not only were the loans safe, but the other promised advantages might well provide additional dividends.

Charles had also given Middleton further instructions: 'If the Amsterdam Jews do nothing for the cause beyond expressing general goodwill, he is not to make them any specific promises.' 15 From the king's subsequent support after 1660, it would seem that they did more than offer general goodwill. Certainly Augustin Coronel, the agent for the king of Portugal, was a conduit for funds for Charles and it was he who suggested that the future monarch marry Catherine of Braganza, when he was discussing the king's financial situation with the king-maker, General Monck. When Charles did marry Catherine in 1662, it not only cemented an Anglo-Portuguese alliance, but it brought Charles a very large dowry. The royal court also received more Jewish retainers. Catherine had contracted erysipelas – which, before penicillin, could kill you – on her way to England. Her father, John IV of Portugal, had sent his own doctor post-haste to look after her. He was a Marrano called Antonio Mendes and it was not surprising that the king had chosen a converted Jew:

> The Pope of Rome and the Queen of England: the Doge of Venice and the Stadtholder of the Netherlands: the Kings of France, Spain, Portugal and Denmark: the Czar of Russia and the Sultan of Turkey: all had at one time or another Jewish medical attendants of Marrano birth.[16]

When Catherine recovered, she asked Mendes to be her permanent doctor and also appointed his brother, Andrea, her chamberlain. When they reached the safety of London they both took a deep breath, announced they still considered themselves Jews and were welcomed by the Sephardi community. Catherine kept them in her retinue, even though they would have been regarded as heretics at home in Portugal. They later adopted another surname – da Costa – and the Mendes da Costa clan were stalwarts of the Sephardi community for centuries afterwards. Mendes became one of Charles' doctors as well. He was rewarded by being made a fellow of the Royal College of Physicians in 1687.

When Charles was restored to the throne in 1660, thanks to Cromwell's instructions, he found the small Jewish community, with 35 heads of families, living in the City of London: 'A small community of Jews was already established in London and that Cromwell had employed some of them as army contractors and loan-mongers.'[17]

For the Jews, the failure to pass a Commonwealth law allowing them back into England was a stroke of luck because, when Charles regained the throne, he abolished every law that the Protector had passed. It was a way of showing who was in charge now. The return of the Jews, fortuitously, didn't need to involve that process. The discussions between Cromwell and Manasseh ben Israel were played down. As Carvajal had died recently, his betrayal of Charles' earlier invasion plans could be forgotten.

There was still, however, a lot of opposition to their admission for both spiritual and economic reasons. Spiritually, because many Christian authorities considered them blind to the gospel truth at best and, economically, because some of them were already competing successfully with a lot of important mercantile interests in the City. In the time of Richard Cromwell, who took over from his father, there was already a petition from some London merchants asking for the expulsion of the Jews – and the confiscation of their goods before they left! Richard didn't pay the request much attention because he was too busy deciding if he wanted his new job. Within a year, he had decided he didn't and was gone.

The coronation banquet for Charles had hardly been cleared away before the Corporation of the City of London approached the king officially and asked him, in no uncertain terms, to throw the Jews out again. Now it could well be that, once Charles II had given his word, he would never go back on it. The original document instructing General Middleton existed and a king's promise was not lightly broken. There was, however, another consideration that could not have escaped Charles. What if his restoration to the throne didn't work? There were still powerful republican forces in Britain; Cromwell had been popular as the man who had helped defeat what was perceived by large numbers of the good and the great to have been a tyrannical regime.

Charles had, at least partially, been brought back to fill the vacuum when Richard Cromwell abdicated and took himself off to France to avoid his creditors. But what, though, was going to happen if Charles ceased to be the flavour of the month? What if he had to go on his travels again? It would be back to Amsterdam and he might well need the financial help of members of the Jewish community there once again. Admittedly, the Jews could be irritating. Augustin Coronel had converted to Christianity but he then went bankrupt in 1662. Charles was not best pleased at this disruption to his financial arrangements. He declared emphatically: 'If the bankrupts do not make full restitution I will have not more Jews.'

If the King was serious at the time, he soon got over his paddy. He asked Parliament for its advice on the Corporation's request. While they were thinking what to reply, he moved the goal posts. Now he wanted their guidance on how to protect the Jews. Parliament took the hint and said that the situation established under Cromwell should continue. Another crisis had been overcome, but would it be the last? It never had been over several millennia.

The Marrano community started to put down roots. The community needed lay officers and, like Amsterdam, they were elected by the members. The honorary officers were called the Mahamad and the members were called the Yehidim. There were four wardens, a treasurer and a number of other members. If a vacancy occurred, an electoral committee decided, by lot, which member could nominate the replacement. It led to an oligarchy but only one member of a family could serve. If you were on the Mahamad, your son, grandson, son-in-law, stepson, brother, brother-in-law, nephew or cousin couldn't be. If you were under 25 you couldn't be treasurer and no one under the age of 40 could be a warden.

After a few years, it was agreed that the congregation should employ a permanent Haham. Their first rabbi was also a merchant, called Samuel Levy. Then there was Moses Athias, who worked for Carvajal and had been a hazan in Hamburg. The hazan conducts the services and is usually known more for his fine voice than his talmudic erudition. Many members, though, were rich, they had expensive tastes and they wanted a full-time spiritual leader who would lend brilliance to their new body. They signed Rabbi Jacob Sasportas from Amsterdam as the spiritual head of the Sephardi community. It was agreed that the few Ashkenazim who were also in London could attend the synagogue, but couldn't be elected as officials or take a leading part in the service. They were almost all poor and were treated as second-class citizens.

There were to be 21 more Chief Rabbis over the next 350 years. As you would expect, they had mixed abilities and characteristics. As beatification is not part of Judaism, the Chief Rabbis were never going to make saints. Some were brilliant scholars, others brilliant leaders and occasionally they were both. What all but one of them had in common was total commitment to the faith, whatever the tempta-tion to listen to the siren calls of fashionable alternatives; we'll talk about the exception, Solomon Ayllon, later.

For those who support the existence and continuation of Anglo-Jewry as a traditional Orthodox community, they have all been key players. Their place in British Jewish history, however, does bear something in common with supporting Arsenal in recent years – the club may be English but the team are normally from abroad.

Only three Chief Rabbis since Sasportas in 1664 have been born in Britain; Solomon Hirschell (1802–42) in London, Israel Brodie (1948–65) in Newcastle and Jonathan Sacks (1991–) in London again. The others have come from Germany, Greece, Hungary, Italy, North Africa, Poland, Rumania, Spain and Yugoslavia. The rationale for the continual signing of foreign Chief Rabbis has been exactly the same as Arsenal's thinking – they were very likely to be better at the job than their English counterparts, and in the beginning this was to be expected. For over a century the Marranos had been unable to study the practices of Judaism together for fear of betrayal. The laws, passed down in secret from father to son had become like dog Latin – a poor imitation of the original. Many of the Marranos who settled in London hadn't even been circumcised – the biblical covenant with the Almighty. The theological intellectual level of the community was inevitably pathetic compared to the great Jewish religious centres in Europe.

To make matters worse – and it was usually possible in the world of that time for things to get worse for the Jews – there was enormous internal dissension within the faith. This came about because it is a fundamental belief in Judaism that there will be peace in the world when the Messiah comes. All will be well on that great day. Indeed, during the Seder service at the Jewish festival of Passover – the oldest religious service in the world – there is a part in the proceedings when the front door is opened to see if the Messiah is waiting outside. A cup of wine is even filled for him in advance in case he arrives. For 3,500 years the Jews have repeated the ritual at the Seder service – that was the reason for the Last Supper Jesus was celebrating – and the disastrous events of the first half of the seventeenth century had led them to hope for his coming with even more fervour than usual.

Then, in 1665, in the depths of their despair, it was reported that the Messiah had come! A Turkish rabbi publicly announced that, as a matter of fact, he was the Messiah. His name was Sabbatai Tzevi (1626–76). There was consternation and an outpouring of overwhelming joy. At about the same time rumours of other great happenings started to spread like wildfire. At their most extreme, it was reported that the Lost Tribes of Israel had reappeared from the east and an army of over 1 million Jews was winning battles against Christians and Moslems. The rumour mill worked overtime. Nevertheless, a famous rabbi in the Holy Land, Nathan of Gaza, decided that Tzevi was genuine and started to publicize his views. The movement spread like wildfire.

Amazingly, amidst all the hype, only one highly regarded rabbi, Jacob Sasportas, remained firmly of the opinion that Tzevi was a fake. He spent the rest of his life fighting the Sabbateian movement and drumming up support for his view within all the Jewish communities he could reach.

Tzevi raised Orthodox hackles sky-high in many of his teachings. For example, the second saddest day in the Jewish calendar is Tisha B'av, the ninth day of the month of Av when, in biblical times, the destruction of both the first and the second Temples took place. As, however, Tzevi was born on Tisha B'av, he told his followers to celebrate on that day instead.

Tzevi eventually went too far when he decided, single-handed, to overthrow the sultan in Turkey! Arriving for that purpose in Istanbul from the Holy Land, he was, not surprisingly, immediately arrested. When it became a question of saving his life, he quickly agreed to become a Moslem. Not even this apostasy destroyed his movement, however. It lost him a great deal of support, but the Sabbateians continued, as they do to this day, a small community in Istanbul, a mixture of Judaism and Mohammedanism, called the Donme.

The growing threat of Sabbateianism was taking place while Sasportas was serving as Haham in London.

There was one other internal movement threatening Orthodox Jewish thinking at the time, which was created by Benedict Spinoza. Now here was a good Jewish lad from a nice Marrano family, whose kinfolk had escaped from Portugal and become leaders of the Amsterdam community. Manasseh ben Israel had been one of his teachers and yet Spinoza rocked the boat violently by demanding to know where was the proof in the Bible that God has no body, or for the existence of an immortal soul or angels? Among a lot of other things. Overall, his view was that there were other major factors, such as nature, in the creation of the world besides the Almighty.

The Mahamad in Amsterdam unsuccessfully tried to wean him from these ideas. So it excommunicated him in 1660. Its reasoning was partly that, in attacking the Jewish concept of God, he was also attacking the Christian concept – which could well not be good news if you wanted to be allowed to stay in Holland. Excommunicated or not, the influence of Spinozist thought would still become powerful in the development of many future philosophies. Sabbatai Tzevi and Benedict Spinoza; two thinkers the Jewish authorities, trying to keep the Marranos on-message, could have done without.

The whole process of the Reformation and the Renaissance produced a lot of new thinking. More was being discovered about science and in 1662 the Royal Society of London was incorporated from a number of smaller scientific associations. Charles had seen what religious fanaticism could do and it wasn't for him. He was much more interested in the development of science and this he encouraged. The problem scientists had always had was to communicate their findings to others but now, with the development of printing, it was much easier. In 1665 the Royal Society produced its *Philosophical Transactions*. Science was going to start to take its place in intellectual life as a major force, a fact that Judaism would also have to take on board.

Over the next three and a half centuries, for their community to survive, the English Chief Rabbis would have to overcome the most incredible list of threats – a positively Himalayan range of mountainous obstacles from both outside and within the religion. From outside they would have to deal with discriminatory laws, they would be opposed by substantial sections of the Church of England and they knew that the Catholic Church was after their blood. Furthermore, they were always conscious that if anything happened to England, the alternative European governments were almost all going to be far worse. Within the religion they would have to deal with the Sabbateians and then adjust to the new challenges of science, the Enlightenment and Zionism. They would have to survive the attacks on the Oral and then the Written Law – the two major planks of Orthodox Judaism – by the future Reform and Liberal movements. They would also have to do it with a large drain on the community as members became Christians or left the Orthodox ranks. Finally, they had to make the faith more attractive than secular and materialist societies.

Had they been able, in the seventeenth century, to see the assault course stretching in front of them, the chances of the community surviving would have appeared negligible. How the Chief Rabbis, the spiritual leaders, managed it is what this book is all about.

Which brings us to the first of them, Haham Jacob Sasportas.

NOTES

1   *Jewish Chronicle*, 15 May 1874.
2   Cecil Roth, *Jewish Contribution to Civilization*, Macmillan, 1938.
3   Lucien Wolf, *The First English Jew*, Jewish Historical Society of England, 1895.
4   Chief Rabbi Hermann Adler, Jewish Historical Society of England, 1898.
5   Jewish Historical Society of England, Miscellany 1, p. 24.
6   L.D. Barnett, *Bevis Marks Records*, Oxford University Press, 1940.
7   Solomon Gaon, 'The Sephardi character and outlook', in *Essays Presented to Chief Rabbi Israel Brodie*, Soncino, 1967.
8   Thomas Dekker, *A Strange Horse Race*, 1613.

9   Lucien Wolf, 'Cromwell's Jewish Intelligencers', in *Essays in Jewish History*, ed. Cecil Roth, Jewish Historical Society of England, 1934.

10 Jewish Historical Society of England, 1902–5.

11 Judith Samuel, *Jews in Bristol*, Redcliffe, 1997.

12 Wilfred S. Samuel, *First London Synagogue of the Resettlement*, Spottiswoode Ballantyne, 1924.

13 *Times Literary Supplement*, 8 September 1921.

14 Wilfred S. Samuel, Jewish Historical Society of England, 1936.

15 Ibid.

16 Roth, *Jewish Contribution to Civilization*.

17 Wolf, 'Cromwell's Jewish Intelligencers'.

3   Jacob Sasportas 1664–65

The first Haham of the Sephardi community was Rabbi Jacob Sasportas from Amsterdam. Sasportas is probably a corruption of Seisportas – Six Gates, to mark their home. He came from a distinguished Spanish family of clerics who had been living in Algeria in the sixteenth century, and the family could trace their ancestry back ten generations, to Nachmanides (Rabbi Moses ben Nahman), the great Spanish talmudist, known as The Ramban for short. The two most distinguished Jewish families in Morocco were Sasportas and Toledano.

Sasportas was born in Oran in 1610, so he was already a mature 54 years old when he received the call to Kzeh Ha-aretz – the end of the earth – which was the Jewish name for England in the Middle Ages. He had first been the community rabbi in Tlemcen in Morocco at the age of 24 and then served the communities in Fez and Sali. At the time: 'all goods imported to Morocco from England . . . as well as sugar exported to England from Morocco, passed through Jewish hands'.[1]

The Jews acted on behalf of the rulers and were never safe from the vagaries of their tempers. When Sasportas was 34 years old the king tried to extort money from him and he was forced to escape from subsequent imprisonment after a couple of years. He managed to reach Amsterdam and he might have been part of Manasseh ben Israel's delegation to Cromwell.[2] The pendulum then swung back and he was recalled by Prince Benbukar. The prince appointed him ambassador to the Spanish court in about 1659, to try to secure their help to put down a rebellion in Morocco. This in spite of the fact that he was living in Amsterdam – Sasportas was a man of the world.

The Sephardim knew they needed to keep an umbilical cord intact to the community in Amsterdam as the Dutch Jews, in their turn, organized their community much along the lines of the Venice congregation. In London the Sephardim were delighted to have attracted as distinguished a talmudist as Sasportas: 'The most eminent rabbi of the age on technical questions of religious observance.'[3]

Holland was the nearest country where the Sephardim could find the necessary rabbinical knowledge and Sasportas, having been born and brought up in North Africa, rather than in Portugal, had been able to study all he wanted. When the London Mahamad wanted to justify their dicta, they would often say *combo se Estelle em Amsterdam* – if it was all right back home, it was all right for them.

What the Mahamad must also have known, however, was that Sasportas was ferociously controversial. From the time he arrived in Amsterdam in 1644 he had been arguing for traditional practices, even against rabbis who were prepared to adjust them in order to soften the discipline for their Marrano *conversos* (forcibly converted) congregation. It is significant that, although he was much respected for his learning, he was never given a rabbinic office in the 15 or so years he lived in Holland:

> he coveted the power and status of rabbinic office, and his thwarted ambition merely added to his bitterness and frustration ... he was petulant and touchy and sensitive about his honour. His colleagues when writing to him exercised the utmost caution, for the slightest hint of criticism made him fly into a towering rage. His irascibility and contentiousness show in all his letters.[4]

You still could not question his expertise. He worked for Manasseh ben Israel as a proof-reader and there was no room for the slightest error in that role. He was an author as well; in 1652 he had written a highly regarded book called *Toledot Ya'acob*.

The Amsterdam community probably weren't too sorry to see Sasportas go. The Haham's qualifications as a seasoned diplomat, however, would have been a major attraction to the London Sephardi community, trying gingerly to settle into a new country. He was appointed in 1663 when he was teaching at the De Pinto Yeshiva in Amsterdam. When he arrived in London in 1664 he was given a home in the fashionable Strand and a relatively handsome salary of £50 a year. Sasportas was engaged to state the Din (lay down the religious law), preach on every Sabbath and festival and officiate as hazan, conducting the synagogue services. This might well have resulted in an improvement in the manner in which decorum was kept up in the synagogue. In 1662 a Christian visitor had reported that, if there was talking, the Parnas (lay leader) of the community: 'Did call aloud with a barbarous thundering voice and knocked upon the high desk with his fist, yet all sounded again.'[5] As was the custom in Amsterdam, Sasportas would, annually, give over

50 sermons. A hundred years later, Ashkenazi Chief Rabbis in England would only give a handful.

Sasportas was also to be in charge of *shechita* (the ritual slaughtering of animals). This latter responsibility he was to delegate to his son, Samuel, who had come with him primarily to arrange for the provision of kosher meat to the community. His grown-up sons, Abraham and Isaac, had chosen to stay in Amsterdam.

What Jews may and may not eat is laid down in the Bible. There are many prohibited foods and it's up to each Jew to decide whether to obey the laws. Eating forbidden food was, of course, a sin. There is, however, a crucial area where Jews rely on others for the level of their observance; that's in the way the animals are killed and in making sure the animals are fit for consumption, which is the job of the shochet and bodek, respectively. As serious rows over how well they do their job spring up from time to time over the centuries, it's important to realize that the standard of butchery is no minor matter for the observant. Admittedly, it is true that if they sin inadvertently, their actions can be excused. Nevertheless, they'd rather not sin in the first place.

Preparing the meat and selling it to the community is also a business and there's usually a profit in it, which can go to the individual butcher or to good causes if the synagogue runs the *shechita* operation for itself. There can, on occasions, be accusations of malpractice. They may be true, they may be malicious and the argument can end up in court, as it did in 1904 in the time of Chief Rabbi Hermann Adler. As the rules are complicated, the area is a minefield and, in the background, is always the concern that the Biblical method of killing animals may be made illegal; that fear syndrome again. *Shechita* has always been a favourite target of anti-Semites, even though the Jewish method of slaughter causes the animal the minimum of suffering, as the most eminent veterinary surgeons agree. Furthermore, shochetim undergo rigorous training.

Sasportas' £50 salary had to cover both himself and his son but the Haham soon found that he couldn't manage. Almost as soon as he arrived in 1664, he asked the Mahamad for an increase:

> pointing to the outlays which he had made and the expensiveness of the country, he requested that kind consideration should be shown to him and his family in order that he might be able to maintain himself, inasmuch as it is his nature not to be troublesome nor to disturb anyone with other sufficient reasons.[6]

The Mahamad gave him another £20 a year from the spring of 1664. This brought him up from the pay of a Church of England curate into line with a well-established clergyman.[7]

When Sasportas reached England, he found the community very much on edge. Many of them still preferred to live their double lives and retain their two names. Within the community they were Jews. Outside it they were still, legally, Spanish or Portuguese citizens. In other words, they might have been allowed to *live* in Holland but that didn't make them Dutch.

In the event, both Cromwell and Charles II were personally prepared to accept the unique and extraordinary position that the Jews were neither Spanish nor Portuguese citizens, but instead they had *Jewish* nationality – a concept for which there was absolutely no legal justification – and could become English citizens after a period of time by paying the king's ransom for endenizment – citizenship. Nelson wasn't the first Englishman to put his reasoning telescope to his blind eye to avoid seeing the obvious. Through this stratagem it had already been possible for Cromwell to prevent the goods of Jewish merchants from being confiscated when the country was actually at war with Spain in 1656.

For the Jews, however, these were flimsy foundations on which to build their security, and they were always aware that their very lives might be in danger if the king withdrew his support. If they had to return to Amsterdam, if the Spanish reconquered Holland, their former membership of the Sephardi community in London would be accepted as amply sufficient evidence to justify the Inquisition having them sentenced to death.

By the time Sasportas arrived in London the Mahamad had already issued its congregation's rules; the 42 *ascamot*. These had been drawn up by laymen, sometimes in the exact words used in Amsterdam, with the overriding intention of avoiding upsetting the government and risking expulsion again. The Mahamad kept in close touch with the court. Delegations could go and see the king when it was felt to be necessary. Indeed the king had said that he looked to the Mahamad: 'to enforce obedience to the laws of the realm'.[8] Thus it had royal authority for its authority. Not surprisingly under these circumstances, another *ascama* was that nobody could join a political party 'which any of the people may form against the government, the ministry, or the judicial administration of the kingdom'.

It was essential to make sure that the members of the congregation did nothing as individuals to adversely affect the community's position; if there was one thing the Sephardim didn't need it was any loose cannons, and the Jews weren't alone in this – the Quakers' rules were, in many ways, similar.

So the *ascamot* were rigid and it was laid down that succeeding Mahamadim had no right to change the original regulations, though they subsequently did. *Ascamot* specifically forbade the creation of any other congregation within miles of the synagogue, or the holding of services even in your own home, unless it was on the occasion of a wedding or during shiva, the mourning period for the dead.

Among other things, nobody could get into an argument with a Christian minister. You couldn't settle a business dispute in court unless you had taken it to the Mahamad for arbitration and that had proved unsuccessful; the good name of the community had to be maintained at all costs. You couldn't publish a book on any subject unless you had the Mahamad's permission first: 'The Mahamad shall have authority and supremacy over everything, and no person shall rise in the Synagogue to reprobate the decisions which they may take, nor shall they draw up papers concerning it, and they who shall do so shall be subject to the penalty of Herem.'[9]

Herem was, effectively, excommunication from the community. If applied, you would not be allowed to takeany part in the service of the synagogue and you couldn't be buried in the Jewish cemetery. You would be branded an outcast in the Jewish world. Your friends would desert you. It was an extremely serious penalty, particularly as the only friends a Jew could definitely rely on were likely to be his co-religionists. Even to be fined for breaking an *ascama* could be embarrassing as you had to go on the bima (the podium from which the synagogue service is conducted) on the Sabbath and repent 'in an audible voice'.

As far as the *ascamot* were concerned, the Mahamad could point to precedents by copying much of the phrasing that was already in force in the communities in Venice and Amsterdam. Venice was significant because it was in Venice that Isaac Abravanel, a major leader of the Jews who left Spain, had finally settled. It was to be significant that, among the *ascamot*, were also prohibitions which applied to the Haham.

Sasportas couldn't criticize the decisions of the Mahamad from the pulpit and he couldn't choose the recipients of *aliyahs* (the honour of taking special roles in the synagogue service). Without the approval of the Mahamad he couldn't grant a divorce, nor could he order either circumcision or a *mikveh* (ritual bath) for those seeking conversion to Judaism, both of which were prerequisites. Like the rest of the congregation he needed permission to print a book and he couldn't argue against Christianity outside the community. Some of Chief Rabbi Hermann Adler's sermons in the early twentieth century would certainly not have passed the seventeenth-century censor. The Haham couldn't set the times of services either.

Sasportas signed the document, binding himself to the rules and giving them his imprimatur as the Haham. He was accustomed to serving a superior secular authority in Amsterdam, and the Venice precedents would also have carried weight with him. Nevertheless, he established the rules for his successors and the constraints were to be the source of conflict on many future occasions. The only 'out' was that the Haham could say that what he was doing was for the spiritual good of a congregant or the community and that it was in his bailiwick.

On occasions, the Mahamad might argue back that it was they who were the ultimate authority even on divorce; in cases where the religious status of those wanting to get married was in doubt, or where if the marriage took place, it would be without the consent of a parent. The Haham was not invited to attend the meetings of the Mahamad, nor did he get a copy of the minutes – a situation which remains unchanged to this day.

Criticism of the Mahamad and of its Ashkenazi equivalent, the Vestry, was like grumbling at the performance of your football club's management; everybody did it. Among other accusations, the Boards were too rigid/too lax, they favoured the rich season ticket holders rather than the plebs on the terraces and they were a self-perpetuating oligarchy. In a twenty-first-century, democratic society such a set-up could be denounced, but democracy as we know it didn't exist in the seventeenth century. In a country where only a tiny minority of the population had the vote – and even that generosity was exceptional in European terms – the control exercised by small committees was the rule rather than the exception. It is, indeed, from the time of Charles II that we get the word 'cabal' – a mnemonic for Charles' five ministers – Clifford, Ashley, Buckingham, Arlington and Lauderdale.

Then again, the name of the game for the Mahamad was to keep the community together. If you alienate the members, eventually they don't come to your synagogue, which is how breakaway synagogues were to emerge in the future. So you don't set out to annoy them. If, however, you want to pay your bills – and a synagogue is a business in that respect – you particularly don't want to upset the rich members. They're the ones who are going to contribute most to the refurbishing of the building, or find the funds if some Jewish community overseas has its synagogue burnt down in a riot. They're the main supporters of the synagogue charities – and most of the Jewish community over the next 200 years would range from poverty-stricken, to poor, to at best lower-middle-class, and would need help. So as, in reality, money does talk in almost any society, it was pragmatic to pay a lot of attention to looking after your main financial contributors and trying to make sure that they didn't move to another community.

It was in Sasportas' time, in the spring of 1665 that the first Sephardi charity was created. This was the Hebra de Bikun Holim e Guemilut Hasadim – a society for taking care of the sick and burying the impoverished dead.

The community had its own surgeon, who also acted as the shammes (beadle) during services. This was Solomon Lopes whose fee for bloodletting was 5p and every spring he also supervised the making of matzo for Passover. Lopes was nothing if not helpful. If you were going abroad, he would even take the matzo down to the port of Gravesend for you.

Jews have the well-earned reputation for being brilliant at raising money for charity. The reason is that charity is absolutely central to the tenets of the religion. On the most solemn day of the year, the fast of Yom Kippur, it is believed that the Almighty makes the final decision on what happens to you during the coming year. The key prayer on that subject, spelling out the possibilities in some stark detail, ends with the sentence, 'But penitence, prayer and charity avert the severe decree.' The Haham would regularly appeal to the members to repent their sins and attend more synagogue services, but giving money for charity was every bit as important – it was seen as the ultimate in life insurance.

The control of the Jewish community in many European countries was, again, different from England in the 1660s. Usually the continental ruler wanted just one Jewish representative on whom he could load demands for special taxes which would only apply to the Jewish community. It would be up to that individual – the Court Jew – to raise the money or suffer the consequences. So just as he raised money for the ruler, so he could tax the community for general purposes. This was not the case in England after the Restoration, except once, for a short period, in the 1690s. Otherwise there were no special Jewish taxes, so any money raised from the members of the congregation was purely voluntary.

If you needed the rich, what could you offer them in return for their bounty? Well, you could start with a better view of the proceedings in synagogue; the rich had seats at the front. When the poor were put at the back, it wasn't disdain. It was pragmatic; they couldn't afford the front seats, just as the front stalls in a theatre are more expensive than those at the rear. The rich could also be given more synagogue honours; letting them hold up the sefer torah or open the Ark (in which the sefer torahs were kept). In Jewish law the wise are to be more admired than the rich and it seems unlikely that any of the honours would influence the Almighty. Nevertheless, those who tried to balance the synagogue accounts had nothing else to offer. So it was fortunate that these honours were highly prized. For years they would be auctioned – it was known as *shnodering*. Not a very dignified procedure – but the money went to any number of deserving causes, and there were always plenty of those.

Many of the Sephardim who made up the original community were seriously rich. They needed to be. There was a call for members to serve the community as honorary officers every year. If you were asked and didn't feel you had the time, you had to pay a fine of £10 if you wanted to be excused. Now putting that figure into modern money isn't a perfect science because some items go up more than others over the years. With mass production techniques, tulip bulbs today haven't gone up as much as, say, houses. As a rough guide, though, you could multiply by 100. Which means that if you turned down an appointment, you had to pay a fine of £1,000.

That the synagogue authorities were self-perpetuating oligarchies was true until at least the nineteenth century. This, however, kept the rich involved and everything was strictly voluntary – apart from the fines. To run the synagogue took a lot of time and effort. In the twentieth century the multimillionaire Sir Isaac Wolfson, president of the United Synagogue and a warden at the Central Synagogue, had been in office at the *shul* for over ten years. His son suggested that his father should let someone younger take his place. The great man looked at his son kindly. 'It doesn't pay very well', he reflected, 'but it's regular work!' So it always had been; lots of meetings, often thankless effort, but, as far as the wealthy were concerned, they were taught from birth that it was their privilege to serve their community.

Of course there would always be the Haham working behind the scenes; persuading and advising the honorary officers and the Yehidim on the correct behaviour for Orthodox Jews. There were few instances when the spiritual leader wasn't allowed the last word, but only in the area of religious matters.

It is significant, for example, that the community would have

nothing to do with the City's slave trade. There had been slavery in
the Holy Land in biblical times but it was strictly controlled. The
London Sephardi members only had to consult the rules between
slave and master, codified in Joseph Caro's *Shulchan Aruch* (The
Prepared Table) 100 years earlier, to know where Judaism stood on
the subject. In Jewish law, to kill a slave was murder and hurting him
badly resulted in his immediate freedom. You couldn't hand an
escaped slave back to his master and, if he reached the Holy Land,
he was released from bondage. After seven years a slave had to be
offered his freedom by his master. In the year after the 49th year –
the Jubilee Year – he had to accept freedom.

Modern historians have pointed out that the trade in slaves was a
major plank in creating the economic powerhouse of the British
Empire; a factor that tended to be shoved under the historical
account table when slavery became unfashionable. Yet the Jews in
the City, heavy investors in the East India Company and the new
Bank of England, would have nothing to do with the Royal
Adventurers Company, later the Royal Africa Company, which had
the monopoly of the West African slave trade. There was nothing to
stop them buying the shares but, with very rare exceptions, they
didn't. Which also turned out to be a commercially sensible idea as
the company moved 90,000 African slaves to the Caribbean between
1673 and 1711 and still managed to go broke.

The Jews didn't own any of the slave ships, nor did they own any
of the cargoes of slaves. They didn't have slaves when they lived in
Spain and Portugal and nobody brought a slave to London. That
was the English community experience. In Amsterdam in 1614,
however, it had been decided that the slaves of Jewish masters should
be allowed to be buried in the Sephardi cemetery.[10] In the eighteenth
century there were very occasional Jewish investor exceptions, but
the basic inhumanity of the slave trade was fully recognized by the
London Sephardim.

Sasportas might work behind the scenes but there had been *two*
public authoritative voices in Biblical times. One was that of the
kings and the other was that of the prophets. When they disagreed
on moral and ethical grounds, the prophet would frequently
denounce the king in front of his people. Often the king showed
remorse and was punished by the prophet. The prophets practised
freedom of speech in biblical times where you seldom find it in
dictatorships today. In the rules of the *ascamot*, however, the public
voice of the prophet was designed to be stilled if his views went
contrary to the lay rulers of the community.

If there were many rich Jews in the Carolingian Sephardi community, there were a large number of poor Jews as well; mostly Ashkenazim. If the former considered themselves superior to the latter in every way – which they did – in terms of material wealth the Sephardim certainly were. What was more, the two sides were mutually suspicious of each other, having developed separately over the last 1,000 years. They met again as strangers, and it took many years to break down the barriers. The Portuguese Jews were more likely to remain in touch with members of their family and friends back home, than to have much to do with the Ashkenazim.

The community lived, as Jews always try to do, in the streets around the synagogue. You cannot ride on the Sabbath – it's making animals work, which is forbidden in the fourth of the Ten Commandments. The invention of the car didn't help. The internal combustion engine involves starting a fire, which is also forbidden, so you have to walk to synagogue. The Jews, therefore, lived in the East End of London. Like so many other migrant communities before them, they arrived at the docks and never ventured much further. As far as the merchants were concerned, they liked to be near their business centre and the financiers were in the City where the broking firms plied their trade.

To the outside world Sasportas' position as Haham made him, officially, the spiritual head of the community and when, somewhat belatedly, the Sephardim decided to make a Loyal Address to Charles II, it was Sasportas who led them. He also represented the community in the synagogue when Christians came to see their first Jewish service. Looking back over the history of the period in 1873, the *Jewish Chronicle* reported:

> The synagogue became a kind of show place whereto resorted substantial citizens, gay gallants and fashionable ladies, who visited thither just as they went to see the handsome Kynaston at the Cockpit Playhouse in Drury Lane or to hear the dignified Betterton at the Dukes Theatre in Lincolns Inn...[The] presence of a concourse of curious sightseers was not at all likely to promote the religious feelings of the congregants.[11]

So the Mahamad stopped members inviting them, but as anybody can visit a synagogue if they want to, the Mahamad couldn't stop them coming of their own volition.

One Christian schoolteacher who ventured in was the Reverend John Greenhalgh, who was very impressed by the large assembly of 100 worshippers in the synagogue and the literacy of the congregation. Except for the academics and the rich, most of the native British population couldn't read or write English. Yet he found the Jewish children could read Hebrew, 'and were as ready and nimble in it . . . as the men'. Greenhalgh would have stood out like a sore thumb in synagogue because in those days nobody suggested that a non-Jew should cover their head and nor do they wear a *tallith* (prayer shawl).

Another who kept a close eye on the synagogue was an Inquisition informer called Don Alonso de Mailona. He told the authorities back in Portugal about two Marranos he recognized:

> I have often seen them accompanied by other Jews and dressed in holiday attire on Saturdays, with fine bands (valises) and shoes and white breeches and with their beards trimmed on Friday, which is the chief sign by which they are to be told and recognized in the City of London and never have I seen them on Saturdays attending the Exchange or carrying on business and never on Sundays or Saints Days have I seen them attend Mass in the Chapel or other place of worship.

The community had, therefore, to be constantly on its guard. One of the problems Sasportas had to consider almost immediately he arrived was the effect of the Conventicle Act in 1664, which was designed to prevent the spread of Nonconformist practices. Such non-Church of England meetings of more than five participants were forbidden on pain of substantial fines for anybody who took part in them. The law officially applied equally to the Jews, who had to have a quorum of ten to say the most important prayers. So the Earl of Berkshire offered to arrange for them to be able to avoid the Act – if he was given sufficient money to go to work on their behalf. Faced with, effectively, blackmail, the Mahamad just arranged for a delegation to call on the king in Whitehall to ask for his protection from the effect of the legislation. This Charles II readily gave, 'laughing and spitting' that they shouldn't worry and should come to him if there was any problem.

The document confirming that position was returned to them, and there is a hand-written comment alongside the paper which reads:

> Whitehall, August 22nd 1664. His Majesty having considered this petition has been graciously pleased to declare that he has not given any particular order for the molesting or disquieting of the petitioners, either in their persons or estates, and they

may promise themselves the effects of the same favour as formerly they have had, so long as they demean themselves peacably and quietly with due obedience to his Majesty's laws and without scandal to his government. Signed Henry Bennett.

Henry Bennett was the secretary of state – and later the Lord Arlington in cabal – and he put it in writing. They could have the same agreement which had been reached with Oliver Cromwell. In the petition the Sephardim had pointed out that the petitioners: 'are ignorant of any laws now in force which should hinder their residence in this kingdom.' Since the king didn't comment on that, they considered that he accepted it. Now they felt themselves quite safe – temporarily. They knew it would all have to be renegotiated when the king died.

Having seen the comparative ease with which the community avoided the penalties of the Conventicle Act, Sasportas became very impressed with the treatment of the English Jews. As he wrote to his friend, Rabbi Josiah Pardo:

> We live at a time in which God has seen fit greatly to ameliorate the condition of his people, bringing them forth from the general condition of serfdom into freedom ... specifically, in that we are free to practice our own true religion ... a written statement was issued from him (Charles II), duly signed, affirming that no untoward measures had been or would be initiated against us, and that 'they should not look forward towards any protector other than his Majesty: during the continuance of whose lifetime they need feel no trepidation because of any sect that might oppose them, inasmuch as he himself would be their advocate and assist them with all his power.'

Politically they were home and dry – which wasn't true of other dissenting communities – but when Sasportas arrived in London he soon discovered another challenge. The level of religious observance of his own community was well below the standard he expected. While the former Catholic converts were happy to shelter under the agreement for their return, many of them were less happy about actually observing Jewish religious precepts.

One serious problem was that many of them had not been circumcised. Sasportas insisted they should be, but that wasn't as simple an issue as it might appear. You could insist that the pain – severe for an adult in an age before anaesthetics – was worth bearing, but what if the congregants wanted to visit their families at home in Spain or Portugal afterwards? To have been circumcised was as good as a death warrant if the Inquisition found out. It proved you were still practising Judaism. It was some years before many families would even have their children circumcised.

Sasportas would have told them not to go back then and, feeling on firm ground with the Mahamad, took a stand and banished a considerable proportion of the members from the community.[12] A figure as high as 50 per cent of the community is quite feasible. As was to be expected, since the banished had friends in high places, disagreements with individual members of the Mahamad were immediate. The problem for them was that, even though Sasportas had signed the *ascamot*, he was still no lightweight figure who could safely be overruled on spiritual matters, as could one or two of his successors. With his long white spade beard, substantial skullcap, great knowledge and a readiness to stand his ground, Sasportas presented an imposing figure.

On the education front Sasportas worked hard. Twelve Jewish children were born in London in 1663 to swell the numbers of the younger generation, and the community started the Gates of Hope School for boys as early as 1664. On the curriculum was not just Hebrew, but Arithmetic, English and Reading and Writing. Sasportas taught the advanced studies himself while his son, Samuel, undertook the teaching of 'such students as may be.'

Samuel agreed originally to teach for six hours a day, so there was obviously keen interest among the *conversos* in learning more about their faith. A number of them hadn't decided which religion they would eventually follow, and some, according to Sasportas, remained members of the Church as well as the synagogue. A number of the Jews had to flee the Inquisition only because the Inquisition thought they were heretics, whereas, in reality, they were practising Christians. Most of the new members tried hard to conform; 50 per cent of the community went to synagogue on the Sabbath and 70 per cent of the men. That compares with 5 per cent overall of a far larger Jewish population in 1974![13]

Samuel went on to become an official broker on the London Exchange in 1670 – the oath was ignored as usual – though he started as an unofficial broker. As such, he was temporarily imprisoned in Newgate for not having the required status.

One problem Sasportas did not have was to agree a common language in which he and his pupils could converse. The very similar Spanish and Portuguese languages were those of most of the Sephardim. They might learn English for their business lives but

Portuguese became almost a second *loshen kodesh* for synagogue; a second holy language alongside Hebrew. As Abraham Pimental, an eighteenth-century member, explained: 'Our brethren who have fled from Spanish and Portuguese persecution hither to London were compelled to pray in Spanish because of their ignorance of the Hebrew.'[14]

Unfortunately, while Sasportas' pupils would have understood him in Portuguese, future pupils, born in England, would be likely to have more difficulty. Any sermons Sasportas gave would have been in Spanish or Portuguese and future sermons in Ashkenazi synagogues would be given in Yiddish as a common language for their congregation.

Underlying a lot of the problems Sasportas had with individual members was that many of them hadn't imagined Judaism was anything like the religion they found outside Portugal. For 100 years the Latin Bible was the only religious book they could read at home. For example, they thought the Apocrypha was as valid as the Old Testament and that what was in the Old Testament was the entire religion. All many of them had was: 'a pastiche of fragments, inherited from parents, gleaned haphazardly from books, disorganized, with significant gaps, sometimes distorted'.[15]

When they got to London they found that the Written Law in the Pentateuch had been massively expanded over the centuries by the addition of rabbinic views on the implications of what was in the Bible – this was the Oral Law.

For example, the third of the Ten Commandments says you can't work on the Sabbath. The only problem with that is to identify what constitutes work, because the word isn't defined in the Bible. What is, however, set out is what must be done to build a Tabernacle. That, obviously, involves work. So it was decided that anything you did to build a Tabernacle you couldn't do on the Sabbath.

It wasn't always that easy, however. For instance, all the Oral Laws on keeping milk and meat separate in kosher meals is based on the single instruction in the Bible not 'to seethe the kid in its mother's milk'. Having said that, *kashrut*, as a whole, has a great deal going for it. For example, you might enjoy oysters but any decent restaurateur will tell you that you'll be on your back for two weeks if you eat a bad one. Orthodox Jews don't have to worry; they are forbidden to eat any shellfish.

It wasn't that Sasportas' community was ignorant in other areas. Many had had an education in such intellectual subjects as logic, philosophy, metaphysics and medicine. They disliked appearing theologically ignorant and so a number of them argued on the subject. As Isaac de Castro, a contemporary in Amsterdam, had written: 'They parade great learning in contradicting that which they do not understand.'[16]

A few of them even decided they knew enough to tangle with Sasportas, who took on Orthodox critics as well. Rabbi Solomon Franco was one who was outshone by the arrival of the new Haham. Sasportas dismissed him with the scathing comment that: 'He'll die without morals, as a blasphemer of God. I, unlike my adversary, am innocent, and I will refuse to apologize against his charges, since it is below my dignity to reply.'[17]

Franco went on to convert to Christianity in 1668 which tended to prove Sasportas' point of view. Those who converted were rewarded by the Church at the expense of their original congregation. So the Sephardim were forced to give Franco £12 a year until his death in 1675. After that they had to reach agreement on a pension with his widow, and that was done in front of the Privy Council with the king present.

Rabbinical Judaism – the Oral Law – came under fire from many of the newcomers. Although the *conversos* had stuck to their faith as far as possible, they had also been forced to study the New Testament to keep up appearances. There were considerable differences of interpretation between the two. For example, while in the Gospels the Pharisees are the villains of the piece, from the Jewish point of view they kept the flag of rabbinic Judaism flying. The Marranos had to make a big mental adjustment.

By contrast with the hundreds of laws which had emerged over the centuries, based on the words in the Bible, many Marranos found the Protestant attitude more appealing – a belief that faith was what mattered and not so much ritual. If the Marranos joined the Protestants they wouldn't have to learn and observe so many Judaic rules and they'd be freed from any kind of discrimination; a fact which every Haham and Chief Rabbi has recognized. In England, it was a good offer, and their job was to make sure it wasn't taken up. The Haham didn't try to compromise, however: 'Sasportas saw the religious health of his congregants as his own responsibility and told the leaders in no uncertain terms to desist from interfering.'[18] Either the Yehidim were going to conform to the basics of the religion or they would have to go. Sasportas reported: 'Since I came here they have decreased their evil actions and I constantly bombard them with my sermons on every single Sabbath advising them...to lovingly accept the yoke of heavenly rule.'[19]

Both the Mahamad and Sasportas saw one non-spiritual danger in the failure of many of the Marranos to keep the Sabbath. If the Jews had asked to come back to England in order to practice their religion, their opponents could query why so many of them didn't, in fact, do so.

It was around the time of Sasportas' term of office in London that Sabbatai Tzevi said that he was the Messiah. Depending on one's point of view, Tsevi either was the Messiah or he was a madman or a mountebank. In 1665 the hero-worship of Tsevi had been slowly growing in the Middle East for years. Now the number of believers was growing much faster: 'The pilgrims who had come to Gaza to see Nathan were so numerous that "the people slept in the streets and bazaars because the houses and courtyards could not contain all of them".'[20]

Tzevi was a rabbi and an expert on the Kabbalah, that mystical strain in Judaism that, again depending on one's point of view, either illuminates deep spiritual truths or is very difficult to appreciate. In 1665 the Sabbateian movement was, for most oppressed Jews, as unexpected a craze as Harry Potter and just as attractive. As the support for it grew, a number of Orthodox rabbis realized that this movement could become a serious threat to the survival of the faith in its traditional form.

Sasportas wrote extensively on the subject after he had left London for Hamburg. He was a kabbalist, like Tzevi,[21] but considered that Tzevi had usurped the kabbalistic throne. 'Almost the only prominent Jewish leader in the whole of Europe to preserve his sanity was Jacob Sasportas who, from his refuge in Hamburg, poured scorn on the pretender's Messianic claims, and in the end succeeded in restoring a sense of proportion to the Jewish world.'[22]

There was only one occasion when Sasportas wavered. It came in 1666. Respected rabbis in the Holy Land wrote to Hamburg confirming the standing of Rabbi Nathan and what he said about Tzevi. This so impressed Sasportas that, for a short time, he also became convinced of Tzevi's authenticity. It was only when a report came through from Izmir in Turkey, where Tzevi was well known, saying that the rabbis there had their doubts, that Sasportas switched back to out-and-out opposition. In his own written account of his opposition to Tzevi, Sasportas was not afraid to suggest he had always been consistent: 'One cannot but admire the editorial skill with which he could transform, by a few deft touches, expressions of cautious hesitancy into fierce denunciations.'[23]

It was a dangerous stance. Sasportas wrote about Abraham de Souza, one of the most prominent merchants in Amsterdam but a man who did not believe in Tzevi as the Messiah: 'He suffered indescribable abuse and harassment because of this and they would have killed him, but for the Grace of God which protected him, for many a time they were lying in wait to get hold of him.'[24]

Nor was everybody in London convinced of Tzevi's messianic qualification. The doubters ranged from the Haham himself, to the Jew who was mentioned in Pepys' Diary on 19 February 1666:

> of a Jew in town, that in the name of the rest, doth offer to give any man £10 to be paid £100 if a certain person now in Smirna be within these two years owned by all the princes of the East … as the King of the world … A friend says … that the Jew hath disposed of £1,100 in this manner.'

They drew up formal Bills of Exchange when they made their bets too. Apparently, the bookies were alive and well and living in London in 1666.

The stories about Tzevi multiplied, but they weren't the only ones. There was also that supposed reappearance of the Lost Tribes of Israel. As Sasportas wrote:

> multitudes of Israel had come by way of the desert to Mecca, the burial place of the prophet of the Muslims, which they had despoiled. When the Grand Turk marched against them with a mighty army, they wrought vengeance on him … these rumours were accepted even by Christians in England![25]

Sightings of Martians in space ships were about as likely as a successful Jewish army in 1665, but without the BBC on the spot anything was credible. What was undeniable was that in 1665, when Sasportas had only been Haham for a year, the Great Plague broke out and his colleague, Rabbi Athias died. Sasportas panicked. He announced he was going back to Amsterdam: 'from fear of the destroying hand of the Lord, which was against our community in London'.

This was hardly a courageous stance and he could well have mistaken the intentions of the Almighty. Although 68,000 Londoners died in the Great Plague, only about 15 Jews perished; a much smaller percentage of the community. The explanation was that the majority of the victims lived outside the walls of the City in very unsanitary conditions. The Jews lived inside the walls and they would have carried out the demanding hygienic conditions laid down by Judaism. The plague carriers – the rats – would have found a larger menu available in non-Jewish homes.

The Mahamad feared that visitors to the synagogue might bring the disease with them. In 1665 it was ordered that no member should bring a lady, rise for a lady or make room for a lady, nor introduce any man without the Mahamad's permission.

It is possible that if Sasportas hadn't gone, the Yehidim would have tried to throw him out, as his insistence on circumcision continued to split the community. Still, although Sasportas never came back to London, the Mahamad bore him no ill will. It appointed his pupils as later Hahamim, it wrote to him to ask his advice on thorny spiritual problems, it gave his son, Samuel, £5 when he wanted to emigrate to Barbados, and Sasportas kept in touch with three of his successors, Hahamim Da Silva, Abendana and Ayllon. On his death in 1698 there was general mourning in his former congregation.

What had Sasportas achieved, as the first Chief Rabbi in Restoration England? He could point to many successes. The congregation had been set on the right road, the synagogue services were taking place in their full and majestic array, and the community had been guided away from the heresies of the false Messiah. Sasportas had done a lot of teaching, enabling many of his brave congregants who had fought to remain Jews to understand more of their religious heritage. Many of those who would have proposed the abandonment of much of the Oral Law had been eliminated from the congregation. They might have easily swayed other members and it had to be established at the beginning that there was no arguing with the law. The Orthodox would never shift on this point. Sasportas had also set a standard of dignity and talmudic knowledge which others would attempt to emulate. In matters of detail, he had ensured that proper arrangements had been made for kosher meat.

The umbilical cord to the Amsterdam brethren was in place, and this was important too. London was a daughter community and Amsterdam could provide help of many kinds if it were needed. There were 7,500 Jews in Amsterdam, as against a few hundred in London. The Dutch Jews made up 7.5 per cent of the population of Amsterdam but they were 13 per cent of the depositors in the Amsterdam Bank. They had powerful commercial connections too. It was good news that relations remained so friendly. Overall, while Sasportas didn't stay in London long, he certainly made his mark.

NOTES

1   J.W. Hirschberg, 'Jews and Jewish affairs in the relations between Great Britain and Morocco in the 18th century', in *Essays Presented to Chief Rabbi Israel Brodie*, Soncino, 1967.

2   David Franco Mendes, *Ha-Meassef*, 1788, and Hyamson, *A History of the Jews in England 1951*, though Roth disagrees, Jewish Historical Society of England. Vol. II, p. 119.

3   Cecil Roth, Jewish Historical Society of England, Vol. II. p. 121.

4   Gershom Scholem, *Sabbatai Sevi*, Routledge & Kegan Paul, 1973.

5   Elkan Nathan Adler, *History of the Jews in London*, Jewish Publications Society of America, 1930.

6   *El Libro de los Acuerdos*, Records of the Spanish & Portuguese Synagogue of London, 1663–1681, translated by Lionel Barnett, Oxford University Press, 1931.

7   Gregory King, [1648–1712]. *Natural & Political Observations and Conclusions Upon the State and Condition of England, 1696*, 1801.

8   *Studies and Essays in Honour of Abraham A. Neuman. Isidore Epstein – the Story of Escama 1*. Dropsie College, USA, 1962.

9   *El Libro de los Acuerdos*.

10 Eli Faber, Jews, *Slaves and the Slave Trade*, NYU Publishing, 1998.

11 *Jewish Chronicle*, 5 September 1873.

12 Porter and Harel Hoshen, *Odyssey of the Exiles*, Beth Hatefutsoth, 1992, p. 61.

13 Matt Goldrich, *Journal of Jewish Studies*, Vol, 45, No. 2, Autumn 1994.

14 Simeon Singer, Jewish Historical Society of England, 1896.

15 Todd Endelman, *Radical Assimilation in English Jewish History, 1656–1945*, Indiana University Press, 1990.

16 Jakob Petuchowski, *The Theology of* Haham *David Nieto*, Ktav Publishing, 1954.

17 Goldrich, *Journal of Jewish Studies*, Vol. 45, No. 2, Autumn 1994.

18 Ibid.

19 Ibid.

20 John Freely, *The Lost Messiah*, Penguin, 2001.

21 Ibid.

22 Cecil Roth, *History of the Jews in England*, John Trotter 1964, p. 176.

23 Gershom Scholem, *Sabbatai Sevi*, Routledge & Kegan Paul 1973.
24 Moshe Carmilly-Weinberger, *Censorship and Freedom of Expression in Jewish History*, Sepher-Hermon Press, 1977.
25 A.S. Diamond, Jewish Historical Society of England, Vol. 24, p. 137.

4 Joshua da Silva 1670–79

The departure of Haham Sasportas at the beginning of the Great Plague took the Mahamad somewhat by surprise. After all, it is quite common for spiritual leaders to stay with their flocks in times of trouble. Reaching the conclusion that if the Almighty seems to have deserted the congregation, it might be as well to do the same is, at best, pragmatic but, overall, unhelpful for your community. The Mahamad would have been justified in expecting Sasportas to tough it out, no matter how rough the going got.

Certainly, the members of the Mahamad had their hands full after Sasportas left, what with the ongoing effects of the Great Plague and then the outbreak of the Great Fire. The calls on the charity given to the dependants of poor members were much greater. Thus Jane Monday saw her 25p a week pension reduced to 23p in 1666 after she lost her husband in the plague. The adverse effects on economic activity during the plague reduced the level of money donated by the members in return for synagogue honours. *Shnodering* in 1665 dropped from £82 to £63. The voluntary synagogue tax on earnings the richer members paid (the *finta*), dropped from £135 to £90. Even the poor pedlars suffered financially as they were no longer welcome when they travelled. Any newcomer from a plague area was automatically suspected of being a potential carrier.

Quite logically, however, 1666 was still considered an *annus mirabilis* in the Sephardi community. First, the fire didn't reach the Jewish quarter in general or the site of the synagogue in particular. The firebreaks created by the Duke of York, blowing up houses with gunpowder, stopped the fire at the Exchange a few streets away:

> Long before the fire, the Jews had drifted East from the neighbourhood to which in Mediaeval times they had given the name that survives in Old Jewry and in the church of St. Lawrence Jewry, and their residential quarter and the synagogues in Leadenhall Street and St. Helens were beyond the area reached by the flames.[1]

The fact that two synagogues are specified proves the existence of at least one group of Jews who were not part of the main Sephardi community. But then ten Jews in any room could be said to constitute a community.

So nobody in the congregation saw their businesses or homes go up in smoke; which was fortunate because the devastation was such that three new Debtors Prisons had to be opened within a few years, as creditors tried to get their money back and pursued those the fire had ruined. On the other hand, the fire got rid of the rats, which had carried the plague bacillus, which then ended. Admittedly, nobody knew at the time that was why the plague stopped. They would not discover that until the twentieth century, unless they had bothered to look at the first book of Samuel in the Bible, where it was clearly laid out, when the Philistines had the plague and were commanded to produce golden images of 'emerods' (haemorrhoids, a symptom of plague) and mice: 'images of your mice that mar the land'.[2]

Another important factor for the Jews was Charles II's leadership during the fire. While Parliament dithered, the king issued proclamations to look after the homeless and to ameliorate the disaster. This went down very well with the man in the street and the Jews needed the king's proclamations to carry weight.

Obviously a scapegoat had to be found for the outbreak of the conflagration and the Catholics were, as usual, the prime suspects. When a crippled Catholic youth, who had been on a ship miles away for the first two days of the fire, decided to confess, he was hung at Tyburn and everybody was satisfied they had found the cause. In the seventeenth century a perfectly ordinary fire at the bakery in Pudding Lane was not likely to emerge as a probable explanation for the conflagration.

The Sephardim now needed to replace Sasportas, which would take time. It wasn't until just after the Fast of Av in 1670 that Joshua da Silva arrived from Amsterdam. He was a friend of Sasportas and had a fine reputation as a Portuguese-speaking preacher in Amsterdam. He had been born and trained in the city and served as both hazan and teacher there. Unfortunately for the graduates of the Etz Haim Yeshiva, there were only a limited number of top jobs available in Amsterdam, the best of which were obviously likely to go to the older and more eminent rabbis. So if others wanted to make a reasonable living, they had to look for posts abroad. When da Silva was offered the same £50 a year as Sasportas, he accepted but, unlike his predecessor, he didn't get a rise during his term of office.

Still, he also had a three-room flat 'below the synagogue' free of taxes, 100 florins to help him relocate, and he would get £1 with which to buy matzo at Passover besides four pieces of gold at the festival of Purim. He found that Sasportas' son Isaac was now in London. Isaac was later to become a famous talmudist as well in Amsterdam although, like his father, he never held rabbinic office. Sasportas dropped a note to da Silva asking him to keep an eye on the young man.

What da Silva didn't have to do was bother himself with the supply of meat to the congregation. The Ashkenazi, Benjamin Levy, who was doing it before Samuel Sasportas, paid the Mahamad £20 a year for the privilege of being the official shochet once again. While they were without a Haham, Levy had also acted as hazan and so it was agreed that he would now share that responsibility with da Silva. The Haham also agreed to preach every fortnight and teach the boys Gemara, which is a commentary on the Mishnah and, at the same time, a supplement to it.

At this point a brief word of explanation about the way Jewish law developed. The first five books of the Bible are called the Torah which, as Moses wrote them all down, are also called the Written Law. The Greek word for them is Pentateuch (*pentateuchos* – five-volumed – *penta*, five, and *teuchos*, a tool, later meaning a book). 'Synagogue' is also a Greek word, for that matter, deriving from *syn* (together) and *agoge* (a bringing), so literally 'a bringing together'. The meaning of the books was subsequently analysed by the biblical sages, prophets and future eminent rabbis. The conclusions they reached are called the Oral Law, which was originally handed down by word of mouth.

After the Jews came back from exile in Babylon in biblical times, their Governor, Nehemiah, and the prophet, Ezra, together with his disciples, gathered all the Oral and Written Law together and wrote everything down; that's called the Midrash. There were two kinds of Midrash; if it had a legal connotation, it was a Midrash Halachah. If it involved a spiritual or moral lesson, it was a Midrash Aggadah.

As civilization developed, more decisions became necessary. More lengthy discussions took place and, after the Romans threw the Jews out of the Holy Land, most of the work was done in Babylon. The head of the yeshiva there, Rabbi Judah Ha Nasi, started producing a new compilation, including almost all the latest work up to his time, which is called the Mishnah.

The only problem with the Mishnah was that Ha Nasi hadn't included many of the opinions of other rabbis. So that material was produced separately and called the Baraita. There were further lengthy discussions and by the time the dust had settled around AD 600 we had the Babylonian Talmud.

Everything is in the Talmud – Oral Law, Written Law, Midrash and Mishnah – but not in very good order, so it needed to be codified. Rambam (Rabbi Moses Maimonides) wrote 1,000 chapters on the subject in the twelfth century in Egypt. There were further codifications by other rabbis and in the sixteenth century, as we've seen, Caro put all the additional material together with the Talmud, and came up with his own codification, the Shulchan Aruch. But Caro was Sephardi and he didn't include any of the differing Ashkenazi views, so Rabbi Moses Isserles wrote the Ashkenazi interpretations, which came to be known as the Mappah. Put the Shulchan Aruch and Mappah together and you've got the up-to-date position in the seventeenth century.

From all these sources came the laws. Originally, there were 613 identified in the Pentateuch, but these had been augmented as their implications had been exhaustively studied. For example, the law on keeping the Sabbath day holy had been compartmentalized into 39 areas where rules applied for the correct performance of the commandment. General speaking, the laws were equally important, but you had to differentiate between those laid down in the Bible and those promulgated by the rabbis. Breaking the former was more to be regretted than breaking the latter. If you were prevented from obeying a law because of the intervention of non-Jews, that was less serious again.

Protestant scholars wanted to study all the Jewish material. They believed that Catholic accretions over the centuries had altered the original meanings in the Old Testament, and they wanted to get back to basics. There was another problem, however – two languages. Some of the material was in Hebrew – the Mishnah, for example – but some was written in the language of the country in which it was first produced. The Babylonian Talmud, for instance, was in Aramaic. Scholars who didn't know both languages were at a serious disadvantage. Men like da Silva were at home in both tongues. Christians and their ministers came in considerable numbers to the synagogue – the chance to actually see the ancient Jews of the Old Testament at prayer was like discovering Tutankhamun's tomb and wondering at its survival.

As da Silva, the new Haham, was a friend and admirer of Sasportas, he would ask for his judgement if there was a particularly knotty Jewish legal problem where he wasn't sure of the answer.

Sasportas would delve into the books and his final answer would be considered definitive because of his reputation as an expert.[3] This was the way in which the widely dispersed communities of Jewry made sure that they weren't deviating from the law. The sage – having earned that reputation with his peers – would lay down the law, and this was known as a responsum. In years to come, one justification for nineteenth-century American Reform rabbis making up their own minds about what was the law, was that they might be 1,000 miles away from the next expert. It's not the soundest of arguments because the Responsa of Rashi or Rambam went all over Europe hundreds of years earlier, and many nineteenth century American Orthodox communities would ask for a Responsa from the Chief Rabbi or Haham in London, 3,500 miles away.

The Jewish communities kept in touch. There was the current excitement about Sabbatei Tzevi and whether the end of the world really was at hand, now that the Messiah was said to have come. Sasportas led the opposition and circularised his rabbinic colleagues when he felt it necessary, warning da Silva in London in 1673 of a Sabbateian propagandist called Benjamin ben Immanuel Mussafia.

The Mahamad were delighted to have a new Haham and did their best to make him comfortable. It cost them nearly £4.50 to repaint his flat and £1.75 for the rent of his lodgings for seven weeks while the work was being done. Manuel Mocata, the landlord, was not expensive. The Building Committee themselves spent 70p in the tavern when they drew up plans for a new synagogue.

Da Silva took his responsibilities towards his pupils seriously. The cost of the books he bought for them was £2 and to keep them warm in 1675 cost £3.65p for coals.[4] To help with the school children, the Mahamad created the position of Parnass de Talmud Torah and that official had to maintain order among the children in the synagogue.

Da Silva's years at the synagogue were certainly not without incident, as far as the position of the Jews was concerned. In the same year he arrived there was concern when the House of Commons directed that an enquiry should be made to see how many Jews there were in England and on what terms they had been allowed to settle. Was there going to be another effort to get rid of the community? At the end of the day, the report was never published.

It was sometimes necessary to try bribery to stop adverse legislation. In the Sephardi accounts for 1670–71 there is an item for £22: 'for various expenses on solicitors and various goings and comings to the Parliament and on bottles of wine that were presented'.[5]

In 1673 an indictment was laid against the Jewish community at the City of London's Court in the Guildhall under the Conventicle Act. It was for Riotous Assembly and the alleged riot was the habit of praying in the synagogue! Organized crowds were forbidden and a True Bill was found by the Grand Jury considering the case. Once again the community had to appeal to Charles II and this time:

> His Majesty in Council taking this matter into consideration was this day pleased to order, and it is hereby ordered, that Mr. Attorney General, do stop all proceedings that were against the Petitioners who had been indicted as aforesaid, and to provide that they may receive no further trouble in this behalf.

Da Silva and the congregation could breathe again. That was another problem out of the way, but the behaviour of the congregation was obviously under constant scrutiny by its enemies. For example, civil marriages before a Justice of the Peace were abolished in Charles II's time. Now the marriage had to be before a clergyman of the Church of England. Most Jews chose to pay the resulting fine they incurred rather than obey the regulation. The Mahamad also became concerned if the Yehidim were not observant in following Jewish practice. This, they realised, could be held against them all. The Mahamad adopted another *ascama* in 1678: 'Any Jew... may not go to the Post Office and take messages of any kind from there on the Sabbath, whether for pay or not for pay, and anyone who violates this decision will be banned from the community and excommunicated.'⁶

The primary ongoing religious row in England, however, continued to be between the Anglicans and the Catholics, with the Popish Plot providing a particularly unpleasant interlude of hysteria at the end of da Silva's ministry in 1678.

A rogue called Titus Oates swore before a judge, Sir Edmund Berry Godfrey, that the Jesuits were plotting to assassinate Charles II in order to put his Catholic brother, James, on the throne. Shortly thereafter, Godfrey was found dead in Parliament Hill Fields near Hampstead. He had, in fact, been killed by a member of the aristocracy to whom he had delivered some harsh words when finding him guilty of murder a few years before. The noble Lord had pleaded Benefit of Clergy, which meant that the civil courts couldn't try him and he got away with the killing, but he was determined to get his revenge on Godfrey.

The death of the judge was put down to the alleged Catholic plot, so there were riots, 24 perfectly innocent Catholics were unfairly hanged for the crime, and the country looked even harder for Catholic plotters under the bed. The Jews were well out of it but it triggered even more popular ill will against Dissenters of any kind.[7]

There had been other progress as well. In 1677 it had been agreed that a Jew could swear in court on the Old Testament rather than the New, and could cover his head while doing so. In the same year a case destined for the London Sessions was moved to Middlesex because London Sessions convened on Saturday and the court recognized that a Jewish witness wasn't going to turn up on the Sabbath.

The main political and economic challenge was the fact that the king couldn't pay his way. In 1672 his budget deficit became unsustainable and there was a stop placed on the Exchequer; the government couldn't come up with the interest on its gilt-edged stock. The shares became junk bonds and five major bankers went bottom up. It was, not surprisingly, very difficult to raise funds thereafter.

As the financial crisis rumbled on and the law went on a witch-hunt for Catholic scapegoats, in 1680 the Bishop of London and Sir Peter Pett came up with what they considered a super idea to alleviate both problems. Why not put the Jews into a ghetto, as had happened in Europe, and in England before the expulsion in 1290, with a non-Jewish justiciar to oversee collecting their imposts? Then they could be mulcted for additional taxes as a community and that would improve the state of the Exchequer considerably. This cunning plan had the added attraction that it was bound to be a popular measure in the country as a whole. The two proponents went to see Charles II and he gave them a lengthy audience on the subject. Subsequently they discussed it with him again. The king gave it thought but, even with the Popish Plot upheaval in full swing and everybody knowing that his brother, James II, was a devout Catholic, Charles decided that he was not prepared to alienate an important potential sector of his personal financial backers. The Jewish community were off the hook again and this was the last time there was any official suggestion that English Jewry should be put into a ghetto.

Naturally, the tolerance, the freedom and the opportunities to make a career in England ensured that the country was extremely attractive to continental Jews, particularly young ones. The influx of substantial numbers of Jews from Germany started. They were known as Dutch Jews – a corruption of Deutsch (German).

The arrival of teachers, hazanim and bodkim from the Amsterdam community kept the London administration going. The Sephardim took a different view of other newcomers, who were often poor and needed handouts. These Tedescos – literally Germans – could spoil the image the Sephardim were carefully constructing of a responsible middle-class group of harmless patriots. Consequently, the Sephardim did their best to give the Tedescos enough money to leave the country again, but still the numbers increased. The community even got the City's Court of Aldermen to prohibit indigent Jews from living in the City but it didn't stop the influx. The Mahamad fumed, but helping poor Sephardi members was another matter. This was far easier to tackle. Abraham Rodrigues Marques, for example, took it upon himself to provide money for dowries for poor girls.

Financially, the synagogue balanced its books. Twenty members paid as much as £20 each to the *finta*, and the richest, Solomon de Medina, paid £28 or more. He had a turnover of £32,000 in 1677 and a colossal £80,000 in 1678. He went on to help finance Marlborough's campaigns in the wars against the French at the end of the century. From 1675–79 Jewish merchants imported 800 and exported 500 cargoes. Of these, 700 of the imports and 400 of the exports were handled by just seven firms. The importance of the custom of the Jewish merchants was such that the great East India Company didn't hold cloth sales on Jewish festivals. When it was decided to build a new synagogue, it was possible to agree to ask for five years of the impost to be paid in advance to defray the cost.

The new synagogue opened in 1676. The synagogue's safety was ensured by the employment of watchmen and they weren't confined to calling for help in an emergency. Among the items of expenditure in 1676 were: 'By cost of two muskets and bandoliers, powder and bullets for the watchmen who offered themselves: £1.10.8. [£1.54].'[8] If the security guards who protect synagogues nowadays had a regiment, they would be just about as old as the most ancient in the British army, the Coldstream Guards, which were raised in circa 1650.

The first recasting of the *ascamot* took place during da Silva's time in 1677: 'To avoid causing scandal to the natives of this city, as we are recommended by His Majesty, whom God preserves.'[9] It was agreed that a majority of two-thirds of the Yehidim present would be necessary to pass any amendments in future. The behaviour of the Mahamad towards the Ashkenazim certainly reflected the views of the members, who felt very superior to the poor Tedesco congregants. In 1678 it passed a regulation that the Ashkenazim couldn't be given any synagogue aliyahs or even recite Kaddish (the prayers for the dead). The only Ashkenazim excluded from the prohibitions were Mayer Levy, Benjamin Levy, the shochet, and Samuel Levy, the shammes, who had all worked well within the Sephardi community. Many of the less important tasks about the synagogue were usually carried out by Ashkenazim. Da Silva went along with this but excluding a whole section of Jewry on such a flimsy basis goes against the Din. Within a few years, the Mahamad had to retract.

One of the more interesting *ascamot* had to do with accepting converts. The only regulation was that the Mahamad had to be told in advance. Isaac Abendana lived for a number of years in Oxford and Cambridge. Not the easiest cities in which to find a prospective Jewish wife in the mid-seventeenth century. So he married a Christian girl, but he married her under the Sephardi auspices. As he was a distinguished academic, the marriage was an event. The conversion of his prospective bride did not seem to worry anybody overmuch. One of the most distinguished members of the community – Joshua Gomes Serra – was even a witness. Furthermore, the *ascamot* pointed out that the Mahamad's need to know was not due to any 'want of love of God or out of a desire to prevent the Gentiles from joining the sacred faith, but only out of consideration for their preservation and as a compliment to the King'.[10] Which could well be another way of saying that the Mahamad always liked to be aware of what was going on, as the king wouldn't seem to be interested.

This appears to be another example of the law of the country being flouted. As the marriage could hardly have been kept a secret, it was either that, or its performance throws doubt on the suggestion that Manasseh ben Israel had agreed with Cromwell that the community would not accept converts.

Unfortunately, no portrait of da Silva has survived, so we don't know what he looked like. We know he died in 1679. His widow, Sara, was granted a pension of £16 a year by the Mahamad, plus 15 sacks of coal for the winter and £1 a month for her lodgings. She left the house in 1682 and probably went back to Amsterdam. Certainly she reprinted some of her husband's sermons in Amsterdam in 1688 through the publishing house of Isaac Hezekiah ben Jacob Cordova.[11] Amsterdam was the Rolls-Royce of Jewish printing at the time. Manasseh ben Israel had published 60 books between 1627 and 1647, many of them his own, and 'Defus Amsterdam' was the manufacturing accolade any author wanted, to match the excellence of his scholarship. In the same way, 'Italic' is a compliment to Italian printing technology.

Discursos Predacaveys is a large book and it says much for the erudition of its author that it was worth reprinting. We know of an earlier edition because the will of Ishack de Matatia Aboab in Amsterdam in 1677 advises his sons on the religious books they should master. Among these are volumes by the finest Amsterdam rabbis and Aboab said: 'and especially, you should read at least each of the following twice: ... sermons of Jeosua da Silva (his Discursos predacaveys)'.

When da Silva died in 1679, the Haham of Amsterdam, Isaac Aboab, came over to London to give the address. Unless Aboab was already in London or was warned that da Silva hadn't long to live, this would have been at a memorial service, rather than at the funeral. Jews have to be buried within 24 hours of their demise and Aboab could hardly have learned of da Silva's death and then got to London in that kind of time frame.

Aboab was a great scholar and would have known da Silva from his time in Amsterdam. The little we know of da Silva's early life does include the fact that he was a corrector for a publisher in the city from 1666–69. Now, checking that a manuscript doesn't have errors in it cannot be described as a very distinguished occupation, even in a city which could pride itself on the quality of its printing. Da Silva would have considered himself fortunate under those circumstances to get a prestigious job as Haham in London.

During da Silva's time the process of making Jews into British citizens started in earnest. It was called endenizment – you bought your citizenship from the king. Normally, approval meant that the applicant agreed to live in England but it was accepted that, in their cases, they could live anywhere in the British dominions. Charles recognized that the best way to improve the export trade was not to sit in your office in London and wait for it to come to you. Between 1673 and 1689 there were 104 endenizments.[12]

Joshua da Silva was only in office for nine years and his main contribution was that he was a safe pair of hands. He worked well in the team which was settling the Sephardi community into its English context and there were no major disasters or scandals during his tenure. In view of what would come, on occasions, in the next 300 years, that was an achievement in itself.

NOTES

1   Walter G. Bell, *The Great Fire of London in 1666*. Greenwood Publishing, 1971.
2   *Samuel 1*, Chapter 6, Verse 5.

3   Jacob Sasportas, Responsa 46 & 66 in *Debar Shemuel* 265.
4   *El Libro de los Acuerdos*, Records of the Spanish & Portuguese Synagogue of London, 1663–1681, translated by Lionel Barnett, Oxford University Press, 1931.
5   Ibid.
6   Ibid.
7   John Dickson Carr, *The Murder of Sir Edmund Berry Godfrey*, Longmans, 1936.
8   *El Libro de los Acuerdos*.
9   Israel Epstein, 'Story of Ascamot 1 of the Spanish and Portuguese Jews of London', in *Studies and Essays in Honour of Abraham A. Neumann*, E.J. Brill, 1962.
10 Moses Gaster, *Jewish Chronicle*, July 1901.
11 Joshua da Silva, *Discursos Predacaveys*, Amsterdam, 1688.
12 Elkan, Adler, *History of Jews in London*, Jewish Publication Society of America, 1930.

5 Jacob Abendana 1681–85

Sometimes it is a little difficult to know where the Mahamads of old were coming from. They were well aware of the minefield which arguing about Old Testament theology with Christian academics and clergy represented. Even talking to a Christian clergyman about religion was out of bounds, according to the Sephardi *ascamot*. Then in 1681 they appointed Jacob Abendana to be Haham; one of the most eminent Jewish theologians of his time. The man who was famous for spending years translating the Mishnah into Spanish; the first time anybody had attempted the task. To make it even less likely that biblical heads would be kept below the parapet, Jacob's brother, Isaac, was equally hard at work translating the Mishnah into Latin and was doing so in the heart of English academic life in Cambridge, lecturing in Hebrew and Kabbalistic Literature as early as 1664 when in his mid-twenties. Although the Jews had been expelled in 1290, the Regius Professor's Chairs in Hebrew at Cambridge and Oxford had been founded in 1540 and were well endowed. No Jew had ever occupied the Chair – and indeed none has yet – but with interest in the Bible becoming ever more fashionable, a string of dons were all waiting impatiently for Jacob and Isaac to finish their work, as were any number of hebraists in Europe.

The Mahamad was, as it always would be, a law unto itself and after a respectful interregnum to mark the demise of Joshua da Silva, Jacob Abendana was appointed Haham in the spring of 1681. He accepted Sasportas' original salary of £50 a year, plus the flat, moving expenses and the expectation of occasional gifts. He was just over 50 years old and there was an age difference of about 10 years between the brothers. They had always been scholars, though Jacob held religious office as well, whereas Isaac was purely an academic. Isaac was born in 1638 and, after Cambridge, he went on to Oxford in later years under the patronage of the Master of University College. He wrote on the *Ecclesiastical and Civil Polity of the Jews* in 1706 and passed away in 1722 at the exceptional age, for the time, of 84.

Although Jews couldn't be students at Oxford or Cambridge for another 200 years because they had to be Christians to get in, Isaac Abendana was given a doctorate in recognition of his excellent work. At the time, and for centuries thereafter, Oxford and Cambridge were: 'closely controlled by the Anglican Church and were chiefly seminaries for Anglican clergymen'.[1]

Jacob Abendana was born in 1630, into a Moroccan family of rabbis and scholars. Like the Sasportas clan from Oran, the family were not Marranos and had always been able to study Judaism. Jacob had been taken to Hamburg as a child, and then he went to Holland to De Los Pintos, the rabbinical academy in Rotterdam. At the age of 25 he became Haham of the charitable Maskil el Dal fraternity in Amsterdam. His memorial address for Abraham Nunez Bernal, burnt at the stake by the Inquisition in Cordoba, was widely admired and disseminated in non-Catholic circles, helping to make his reputation as a: 'Rabbi of great industry and learning'.[2]

In 1660 the two brothers published Solomon ben Melek's Bible commentary with a super-commentary on the Pentateuch. In addition, Jacob added his own thoughts, modestly entitling them *Leket Shikhah* (gleanings). Printing was so expensive at the time that authors would often try to sell their books in advance. Those who wanted a copy would take out a subscription and, when the book was published, they would get their copy.

Authors also sought critical support from well-known individuals in their field. These were known as approbations and, instead of book critics dissecting the work after publication, it would be warmly praised in advance by such endorsements. This list of those who approved would be in the front of the book. It was also possible to get books financed by rich patrons and the Melek book was underwritten by Jacob Fidanque, who we'll meet again at daggers drawn with the next Haham, Solomon Ayllon. It was published by subscription in 1660, and a second edition appeared in 1685.

Abendana, whose name was originally Ibn Danon (the son of Danon), made many Christian friends as he travelled to the University of Leyden to sell the family's books. The Abendanas were the first Jewish authors to gain the admiration of contemporary Christian scholars. Jacob helped one of them, Professor Antonius Hulsius, with his oriental studies and then had a lengthy correspondence with him on the meaning of the biblical verse: 'The latter splendour of this house shall be greater than the former' (Haggai ii:9). This, Christian clerics held, was a forecast that the Church would be greater than the synagogue. Would it not then be a good idea, suggested Hulsius, for Abendana to recognize that Christianity was preordained to be superior, and join the flock?

Abendana made it clear that he was not a candidate for apostasy, though it would not have, by any means, been the first time that rabbis had converted to Christianity. For example, to the Church's satisfaction in London, Rabbi Moses Scialitti converted in 1663. Abendana went to work to produce counter-arguments against Hulsius' thesis and these included the translation of Judah Halevi's philosophical work, *Kuzari*, into Spanish, which he published in Amsterdam in 1663.

The book was dedicated to a British merchant-diplomat, Sir William Davidson, who had been a stalwart benefactor of Charles II in exile and proved a good friend to the Jews. In the dedication, Abendana laid on the flattery with a trowel:

> Your Worship has shown your glorious fidelity and constant loyalty towards the most Serene King of Great Britain, who, absent from his majestic throne through various accidents, and withdrawn in foreign kingdoms from his opulent provinces, has experienced in Your Worship the height to which Royal felicity can reach, in finding a vassal who by continued help has considerably relieved the cares of an offended majesty.[3]

'Various accidents', of course, included chopping off the head of Charles' father but, in fairness, if the level of adulation seems a little excessive, most of the facts bore it out pretty well. At one time, Davidson was just about the only rich supporter Charles had left in Amsterdam. Among other contributions, he bought him a frigate and paid for secret information and for the transport of soldiers.

In 1675, when the new Amsterdam Synagogue was dedicated, Abendana was sufficiently highly regarded to be asked to give one of the addresses. Nevertheless, making ends meet in Holland was not an easy task, and when he was invited to London as Haham, he took the job. Abendana had been introduced to the community in 1667–68 when he had preached in the synagogue and been given a present of £10 to mark his visit. He was probably on his way to see his brother in Cambridge but he took the opportunity to visit Henry Oldenburg, the secretary of the Royal Society, to ask him to write to his friends to buy the Abendana books as well. This Oldenburg was happy to do for him – Abendana was that well-connected.

The brothers also sold other Hebrew books. In 1668 the Bodleian Library in Oxford paid the Abendanas £37 for Hebrew manuscripts. Jacob was regarded as 'a man of profound learning'. He was, however, also described as a polemicist; he was not afraid to stand his ground in controversial discussions. Accepting that possibility, he was unanimously elected by the Yehidim.

Jacob Abendana translated the Mishnah into Spanish for his *conversos* brethren, to tackle the problem that most of them didn't know Hebrew. He included the commentaries of Maimonides and of Obadiah of Bertinoro, a famous fifteenth-century commentator, who had run a distinguished yeshiva in the Holy Land. It took Obadiah two and a half years to reach the land no longer flowing with milk and honey, and his travel book on the journey made him a mediaeval Bill Bryson.

The Abendana Mishnah translation was a fairly mammoth task, but, unfortunately, producing as large a work as the Mishnah was a much more expensive exercise than the Melek. It wasn't possible to sell enough subscriptions and, presumably, Fidanque wouldn't help again. So the book wasn't published, though the manuscript could be studied. When William Surenhoys published a work on the subject at the end of the century in Amsterdam, he certainly used the manuscript as background material. Presumably, he would have had to come to England from Amsterdam to study it.

When Isaac went to Cambridge in 1664 to produce his Latin Mishnah, the Puritan hebraists were testing the Catholic translations of the Bible to see if any mistakes had been made. They were trying to trip up the Catholics as one way of undermining their influence. The hebraists claimed to understand the Old Testament better than the Jewish scholars but this was an impossible argument to sustain, if only because of the scarcity of those who could translate Hebrew or Aramaic. If an academic only knew Hebrew, he was at a serious disadvantage. The Jewish scholars gritted their teeth and didn't argue in public, but behind the scenes, the hebraists were very anxious to get the ammunition against the Catholics, which only the Sephardi Jews were really likely to be able to supply. Where the Ashkenazim in the ghettos of Europe had long since lost any profound knowledge of Latin, the Sephardim, integrated into Western culture, whether they liked it or not, had maintained their understanding of the language.

Isaac Abendana was given a subsistence allowance of £6 a year by Trinity College to keep him going and eventually he got a written agreement from them in 1668. From 1668–73 he was paid £89.12p for the work he did. Each tractate segment he translated, together with the indexing, was worth £1. As there were 63 tractates, that would have accounted for two-thirds of the money. Isaac was hardly well paid and he was not a happy man. He told his friends that: 'but for his desire to complete his translation of the Mishnah, he would long ago have left England'.

To make matters worse, when the work was completed in 1675, it was found that there was no Hebrew type font in Cambridge. Though the translation was in Latin, it obviously included many Hebrew words in the notes, when comparing the texts. So the material was used thereafter by Christian scholars but also only in manuscript. It is now to be found in the Cambridge University Library and remains a valuable work of reference.

Isaac went to Oxford in 1676 and Dr Burrows, the vice-chancellor of Cambridge, gave him a £10 going-away present out of university funds. In addition to the research work he did at Oxford, Isaac became a lecturer in Hebrew at the University in 1689 at a salary of £2 a year, compared to Jacob's £50 plus. The woman who cleaned the synagogue got £2 a year as well, which says something for the status of academics at the time. Or of good cleaners. Isaac now became well known to all the Hebrew scholars at both universities and was held in high regard. Eventually, for a number of years, he produced the *Oxford Almanac and Jewish Calendar* which settled a lot more dates: 'Isaac Abendana's Oxford diaries, with small essays on topics of Jewish interest, became outstanding bestsellers'.[4] So it might have proved worthwhile staying on in the end.

As Haham, one of Jacob Abendana's main responsibilities was teaching. From Passover to the New Year he taught from 11 till 2 during the day and then from 5 till 7 in the evening. For the rest of the year he only taught from 11 to 1.30, but there was no excuse for members to say they couldn't make up for the years of neglect of their Hebrew studies.

The school was primarily for children, of course. The rule was that they had to be sent to their classes washed and combed, and they had to wash their feet once a week. In the seventeenth century a school for poor as well as rich children, with such standards of hygiene, indicated very advanced thinking.

The London community was still in close touch with Amsterdam and Abendana would have corresponded with his old colleagues in the city. Sasportas, for example, would have been concerned about his son, Samuel, now one of the Jew Brokers. The source of the large sum of money which enabled him to buy his seat from the Lord Mayor is not known, but he obviously did well in the West Indies. No former shochet had that sort of money. In 1681, however, he was dismissed from the exchange: 'for trading and merchanting in his owne account',[5] and he only reappears in 1684, forming part of a 'ring' of diamond merchants forcing down prices at an East India Company auction.[6]

In the London community there was still concern about the precarious nature of the Jewish position in England. In those early days their political antenna had to be constantly tuned to sweeping the government horizon. Abendana's ministry included its fair share of alarms. In 1683 an Act was passed to forbid people using blasphemous language against God or the Trinity. While the members of the synagogue were highly unlikely to rail against the Almighty, the Mahamad were glad to have the *ascamot* which forbade discussing Christianity, including the Trinity. Abendana, himself, was treading a tightrope, though the Act was aimed at Dissenters rather than Jews. It was eventually decided that you had to have been a Christian at some time in your life to be subject to the new legislation, which let almost everybody in the community off the hook.

It was another example of the Jews being more fortunate than they were in most of Europe. Calls for help came regularly to the London community; in 1682, for instance, 100 marks was sent to the Gluckstadt congregation at the mouth of the Elbe in Germany, to help restore the synagogue. Members of the two communities probably had trade links. In England the Jews were simply insignificant. After 1685: 'there is no trace in the law reports of the Statutes directed against non-conformists ... being enforced against Jews'.[6]

And there were going to be plenty of them: the Act of Uniformity; the Test Act; the Corporation Act; the Papist's Disabling Bill; the Act of Settlement; and many others. In the name of religion, wars still broke out. So trying to get converts could be conceived as trying to make people potential traitors to the state. Try it, and the least of your many sins, as far as the Church was concerned, would have been to point out to the convert that Jews didn't actually believe in the Trinity.

In 1684 another problem cropped up. Could a Jew sue a Christian in a court of law? The case in point came up before Chief Justice George Jefferys, the judge who was to preside over the Bloody Assizes in 1685 which tried those who had supported the Monmouth Rebellion against James II. They received short shrift from Jefferys, 'the Hanging Judge', who was notorious for his cruelty and corruption. The Christian defendant must, therefore, have felt himself on pretty safe ground when the plaintiff came to court and was denounced by his opponent as a Jew. Jefferys, however, was having an on-day and, having identified that the defendant had no other case, said: 'a Jew may recover as well as a villein' (an ordinary citizen). He said it didn't matter if the plaintiff was a Jew as everybody deserved justice.

Numbers were increasing too. In the same year the Lord Mayor of London asked the Mahamad for a register of the families in the congregation and the final total came to 414, though not all the Jews included were full members of the synagogue. There were 92 heads of families. The list included information on whether the members had been circumcised or not and a lot still hadn't. After the departure of Sasportas, the Mahamad may have prevailed upon da Silva to be more lenient on the subject.

The court stayed in touch. In 1681 Princess Anne, the daughter of the future James II, visited the synagogue to see for herself this new phenomenon. She was able to compare it to the one she had seen some years before in Amsterdam and she came again in 1685 at Passover.

In 1685 Charles II died, treated to the end by his Jewish doctor. As James II came to the throne, yet another problem arose for members of the community. Jews had been given the right to trade as Englishmen under Charles II. Now they were not allowed to do so unless they were naturalized. Many had been, but if they had not, then they had to pay the import duties applied to foreigners. The way to get round this problem on many occasions was to find a co-religionist who was in the import business and who had been endenizened, and then have him import the goods for you.

The Sephardim had reason to call on James II five times in the first few months of his reign. Nobody thought that unusual for this tiny group of his subjects. The Jews had always belonged to the ruler where they lived in Europe, so they were accustomed to that system. James II would have recognized their financial help to his brother and would have wanted to maintain the same relationship. He might have ruefully reflected that it was partially the fault of the Jews that English kings had to share power with Parliament in the first place; when Edward I threw them out in 1290, he lost the opportunity to raise any more money from the community. As early as 1294 he had had to call the Model Parliament into session to raise cash.

In what turned out to be another storm in a teacup, Thomas Beaumont thought he'd test the strength of the Jewish position now that there was a new king. He took out writs against 48 Jews for not going to church or chapel. Of these, 37 were arrested at the Stock Exchange. Eventually the community appealed to James II. The king told the attorney general not to do anything more about the case, though, as usual, there was no real defence against the charge. James said: 'His Majesty's intention being that they should not be troubled upon this account, but quietly enjoy the free exercise of their religion, whilst they behaved themselves dutifully and obediently to his government.' When Beaumont refused to stop the proceedings, he was summoned to appear before the king. That ended the matter, but the case had cost the community £288 to defend.

In France the Revocation of the Edict of Nantes also took place in 1685. Louis XIV had decided that he was not going to tolerate Protestants any longer and they would either convert to Catholicism or be evicted. As a consequence 50,000–100,000 came to England over the next few years – the Huguenots – and the foreign Jewish community became even less conspicuous.

The Abendanas had no children and when the Haham died, he was buried in the Mile End cemetery. Just as he started his tenure of office at the start of the Jewish New Year, on Rosh Hashona in 1681, so he died on Rosh Hashona in 1685. His wife, Sarah, was given a pension of £12 a year and she died in 1697.

Abendana wasn't around for long enough to make any major impression on the Sephardi community but he was the first rabbi in England to work on a basis of equality with Christian clerics. Having friends at an ecclesiastical court meant building valuable bridges in the attempt to reduce the hostility Jews had so often experienced from the church.

NOTES

1   W.D. Rubinstein, *A History of the Jews in the English-Speaking World: Great Britain*, Macmillan, 1996.
2   William S. Samuel, Jewish Historical Society of England, 1936.
3   Ibid.
4   Matt Goldrich, *Journal of Jewish Studies*, Vol. 45, No. 2, Autumn 1994.
5   Wilfred Samuels, Jewish Historical Society of England, 1937.
6   Edgar Samuel, *At the End of the Earth*, Jewish Historical Society of England, 2004.
7   H.S.Q. Henriques, *The Jews and English Law*, Oxford University Press, 1908.

6   Solomon Ayllon 1689–1700

Not to put too fine a point on it, there were a lot of people in Solomon Ayllon's time in London who thought he was a pretty nasty piece of work. On the other hand, when he died in Amsterdam, 'it was decided to inscribe his tombstone with an epitaph emphasizing his perfect wisdom, piety, modesty, his capacity to provide justice and his profound knowledge of Kabbalah'.[1]

Many Jews in Holland wouldn't have gone along with that either. The problem, again, was the schism caused by Sabbatai Tzevi. When Tzevi said that he was the Messiah, a great many Jews came to believe him because they wanted to. Tzevi and his supporters and detractors split the Jews into two major factions. In 1665 he was both hailed as the Messiah by Nathan of Gaza and excommunicated by the rabbis of Jerusalem. Even after he converted and became a Muslim – behaviour which would seem inappropriate for the true Jewish Messiah – the arguments continued to rage about his authenticity and the validity of the teachings which sprang up within the circles of his followers. He died in 1676 but the influence of his pronouncements continued to be very strong.

About 1660 Solomon ben Jacob Ayllon (Ayllon is a town in Segovia in Spain) was born and grew up amid all the competing claims in Salonika, which was the European centre of the Sabbateians after Tzevi's death. Nathan of Gaza had made many converts in the city, Tzevi's wife had retired there and the faithful had gathered round. So Ayllon was influenced by Sabbateianism from his very early days. Nathan, Isaac Hanan and Solomon Florentin were the best teachers in situ but Ayllon wasn't a very good scholar and didn't become a great Talmudist. His responsa in later life, quoted in works such as Rabbi Samuel Aboab's *Debar Shemuel*, illustrate this quite clearly; he made mistakes.

Ayllon went on to Safed, one of the sacred cities in the Holy Land, and another centre for both Kabbalistic and Sabbatean thought. The Kabbalists, as we've seen, were a movement which believed in mysticism. They were strictly Orthodox but they read esoteric meanings into Hebrew words and letters. They created magical formulae for healing the sick and they endeavoured to create a more intense relationship for themselves with God. It was an old movement – its origins could be dated to the first century – but it was at this time that it started to blossom and become more popular. To some extent Tzevi tried to hijack the principles of Kabbalism to support his own claims.

Ayllon was reported to have married a woman who was not divorced from her first husband and who then left him for a third man. It was not the best curriculum vitae for a future Haham and Ayllon came to be seen by many as a man with a distinctly shady past. He did get married officially, however, and imbued with Sabbatean ideas, he came to Europe to raise money for the poor in the Holy Land. He was just under 30 and, initially, he left his wife and children at home.

In 1688 he went to Leghorn which was a nondescript port in Italy but one which the local rulers, the Medicis, wanted to expand. So they encouraged foreigners to come to the city by giving them religious freedom, among other privileges. The city became a centre for the best of Jewish rabbinic scholarship. It was a natural stopping-off place for Ayllon, who collected for his charity and then moved on to another five Italian cities, plus Amsterdam, and then London for more fund-raising.

Ayllon had only been in London for a few months when he was approached to become Haham by the Sephardim. A good fund-raiser needs to be charming and a persuasive speaker. Ayllon obviously used both skills effectively. The Sephardim had been without a Haham since the death of Jacob Abendana in 1685 and young Ayllon seemed a likely replacement. In his fashionable periwig he cut a dashing figure. It was known that he had mixed in Sabbatean circles in Safed, but he assured the Mahamad that he had given up such heretical beliefs. He was appointed in June 1689 and the benefits package was generous. He got an advance of £18 on his salary before he came to London and £22.50 to bring his family over from Safed. He was offered £80 a year and that was soon raised to £100. Plus he got £10 at Purim, the three-room flat in the synagogue and £15 to help fit it out. Ayllon was to serve the community for a very uncomfortable 11 years.

Initially, the congregation had high hopes of him. In 1689, Judge Sewell related in his diary: 'This 29 July the Jews have great joy by reason of a Priest come to town in the Harwich Coach, they not having had one a long time.'[2] It had not been an easy journey, however, and Ayllon was reported to be weak when he arrived and to have lost his books.

Ayllon was often in correspondence with Sasportas, who didn't know of his Sabbateian leanings. All he knew was that Ayllon was a Kabbalist and, therefore, a man who held the same beliefs as himself – often unpopular but not heretical. As Kabbalists they were two of a kind. Ayllon told the old Haham early on what he wanted to achieve – he was 'interested in establishing a halachic-abiding, traditional Jewish Kehillah [congregation]' (or *kahal*).

The reuniting of the Ashkenazi and Sephardi communities in Amsterdam after many centuries had meant that there was a need to marry the different religious practices which had grown up in the interim, even though these were usually only on small details. The Sephardi community had actually appointed an Ashkenazi as their Haham in 1616 – Saul Levi Morteira – because they had nobody as qualified on their side. It was in this spirit that Sasportas responded to Ayllon when the young Haham wanted to make a change in the London community liturgy. Sasportas said that the change would be in line with the Sephardi traditions but as Morteira had introduced the original prayer because it was the Ashkenazi custom, it shouldn't be altered. As very different liturgies emerged with radical new movements in the nineteenth century, a later Haham commented on the Sasportas ruling: 'No one dreamed to isolate himself in matters of religious import ... In those days they tried to keep in close touch with the centre of Jewish life, wherever it may have shifted for the time being.'[3]

The atmosphere in the congregation seemed remarkably convivial to Reverend Robert Kirk of Aberfoyle who visited the synagogue in 1690 soon after Ayllon arrived and commented on the reading of the *sedra* – the portion from the Pentateuch: 'When the rabbi (who looked not like a grave, learned man, for he and many Jews would have laughed and talked when they ended a paragraph).' Now this would have looked distinctly odd to a vicar but the service does, temporarily, come to a halt several times during the reading of the weekly portion. In the pause before another congregant comes to continue the service, the rabbi may congratulate the last participant on the birth of a child, his forthcoming wedding or many other happy events. There is time for quiet conversation at such points.

Not that the Mahamad was unconcerned about the decorum in the synagogue services. It issued a decree in 1696 'prohibiting discordant voices' when the congregation responded in the prayer for the dead. The prayer is said by all those who are in mourning or on the anniversary of the death of a close member of the family. There are two versions and one is longer than the other. During the long one, with everybody going at their own speed, there certainly would have been a babble. So the Mahamad stopped the congregation saying the long one for anyone except their parents.

They were equally concerned not to upset the neighbours. During the Festival of Purim, the children would dress up as characters in the story that unfolds in the biblical Book of Esther, and adults would, traditionally, wear character masks. The Mahamad put a stop to keeping the masks on in the street and any rowdiness. Mind you, masks were illegal anyway as they were much favoured by highwaymen and footpads.

Poor Ashkenazim were arriving in greater numbers all the time. In 1695 a census established that there were 778 Jews in London living outside the City walls in the cheaper parts of town, including 250 Ashkenazim. Only 75 lived within the walls. The Ashkenazim were tolerated in the synagogue but not much more. They still weren't allowed to hold office, vote or take part in the service, nor could they officially say the longer prayer for the dead, which was mean. They might say it under their breath, but the responses of the congregation are an integral part of the prayer and these would be denied the Ashkenazi mourner. Agreed, they weren't asked to contribute financially to the synagogue funds but it was still mean.

The problem for many of the Marranos remained their ignorance of Hebrew. To help them further, the hazan, David Pardo, translated the rules on the more important ritual laws into Spanish. *Compendio de dinim que todo Israel deve Saber y observar*, was the first attempt to do this in the community's familiar tongue.

In judging observance, the Mahamad had become more lenient since the time of Sasportas. They were not so keen to throw out members they suspected of not being 'one of us'. The marginal *conversos* were tolerated although they were not given any honours in synagogue. What was difficult to handle was the lack of Sabbath observance of many members. There were a lot of Jews who opened their businesses on Saturday but closed on Sunday. The Mahamad were prepared to go to draconian extremes to prevent this, as Ayllon told Sasportas. There was now a regulation that the cemetery officials were: 'only to bring [bury] those people, their wives and children, at a distance of four cubits from the graves of Jews.' It's a bit like the Duke and Duchess of Windsor, buried at Windsor, but on the other side of the cemetery from the rest of the Royals.

Ayllon was particularly incensed with a family that had a

circumcision on Saturday. As he reported to Sasportas, the ceremony was in the morning: 'But it soon becomes apparent that they have not repented, and on the very day of the circumcision, the store was open just like a weekday, the same as they do every other Sabbath.'

The Mahamad did its best to correct inappropriate behaviour among its members. In 1687, just before Ayllon arrived, it had temporarily excluded one member who had sent his non-Jewish servant to the shops to buy kosher meat. Who knew whether the non-Jew had touched something non-kosher before he put his hands on the counter? The Mahamad would do whatever was necessary to uphold the laws.

The Ashkenazi Jews came mostly from Lithuania and Germany, but many more came from Holland with William III. Relations between Britain and Holland were finally friendly. The Ashkenazim, however, weren't comfortable with the Sephardim and so they decided to set up another of their own congregations. There is a reference to this in the Mahamad records of 1693, but it must have started before 1692 because some of the supplementary laws of the community dated from that year. Therefore, the original laws were set down earlier. The likely year is 1690 but there were Ashkenazi groups praying together before that. The Reverend Robert Kirk referred to three synagogues in 1689 so at least one had to be Ashkenazi. References to Ashkenazi rabbis and synagogues appear in many contemporary records, though they ebbed and flowed with the years. There's even one mentioned by an informer in 1660 in Great St Helens which wasn't the Sephardi one in Creechurch Lane. In a book written in 1699 by Josephus ben Gorin, *The Wonderful History of the Jews*, the author refers to the community: 'where there are swarms at present in this city'.[4]

The new Ashkenazi congregation was to be called the Great Synagogue. The moving spirit behind it was another Benjamin Levy. This Levy arrived in London in 1669 with his brother, Solomon and his uncle, Michael, who became the Sephardim's solicitor. Benjamin joined the Sephardim as well. He was the son of a well-to-do Hamburg merchant and came with a fair amount of capital. This he parlayed into a great fortune. When the local parish needed some funds, it happened occasionally that Jews were deliberately appointed to various jobs in the area in order to collect the fines applicable when the Jews didn't want to serve the Church. In 1693 Levy was appointed Overseer of the Poor and paid the maximum fine of £12 to get out of it. He was endenizened in 1688 which cost far more. In 1697 he was admitted as a broker on the Exchange. He was one of only two Ashkenazis in this position, the other being a close friend, Abraham Franks, who would also be a tower of strength to the community.

Levy was the only Jew on the original list of subscribers for the flotation of the Bank of England and he got a new charter for the East India Company in 1698. He was a major stockholder in the concern and the governors had bought £1,000 of his stock in 1693 at 95 per cent. He dealt in large sums; in 1698 the Treasurer of the Navy paid him over £6,000 as discount on a draft for £85,885 and his name crops up in all kinds of official records.

Levy had been married by Haham Abendana in 1684, but unfortunately lost his wife quite early on in their marriage. When Levy married again, it was Ayllon who performed the ceremony. Hitchele Heilbot, his second wife, was given a dowry by her father of no less than £500. She would also suffer bereavement when Levy died in 1704.

Levy recognized that the Ashkenazim would never achieve more than basic toleration among the Sephardim and he started to hold services for his Ashkenazi brethren in a room near the synagogue. The Sephardim didn't object to this and there was nothing they could have done about it anyway. Levy arranged for one of his family, Rabbi Judah ben Ephraim Cohen, to officiate, though this would be temporary. His seat on the Exchange eventually went to one nephew, Moses Hart, and another nephew, Aaron Hart, became the congregation's rabbi. It was very much a family affair.

In 1692 the Sephardim became concerned at the space needed for the Ashkenazi dead in their cemetery. They gave the Ashkenazi community six months to find their own burial ground. In fact, they put up with the Ashkenazim doing nothing until 1697 when Levy bought them land in Alderney Road in the East End, receiving a 999-year lease for £190. He remained a good friend of the Sephardim, however, and gave the largest sum for the building of the new Bevis Marks synagogue when subscriptions began – £35.

The Mahamad were not too concerned about the Ashkenazi declaring independence and they were prepared to be patient about the cemetery, but they objected very strongly when Sephardi members joined the new congregation. The Mahamad, needing every member, threatened excommunication if any Sephardi joined the Ashkenazi community. Members were also excommunicated if they knew someone who had done so and failed to pass on the information to the authorities. The threat of excommunication was countered by the retort that the defectors did not want to belong to a synagogue which gave honours to people who didn't keep the Sabbath and who married non-Jews. This attitude could be considered bigoted, self-serving – some of the offenders gave a lot to charity – or a dignified defence of the need to keep up proper standards. Whatever the viewpoint, some did leave the community.

Ayllon might castigate the backsliders in the pulpit but he didn't try to bring things to a head as Sasportas had. He wasn't really in a position to go out on a limb. He had hardly got his feet under the table when, in 1690, Jacob and Abraham Fidanque, members of the congregation, attacked him as a Sabbateian. Jacob, the father, was the one who had financed Abendana's production of Melek's Bible in Amsterdam, so he would have been well-known as a member of that community before coming to London.

Both Fidanques had known of Ayllon's activities before he came to England. Indeed, Ayllon and Fidanque had first quarrelled when the young rabbi came to London in 1676 on a passing visit.[5] The hatchet seemed to have been buried when Ayllon took up his post and for a while the two got on well. They consulted on legal matters and Jacob even told Ayllon of scurrilous accusations his son, Abraham, was making against the Haham. Ayllon took a letter he got from the son to the Mahamad. It referred to: 'the deeds which you did in Salonika, when you married a gentile woman from beginning to end.'

Abraham had to apologize publicly for what he said he accepted were baseless accusations but Ayllon's marital arrangements had come back to haunt him. Certainly, in some of his sermons there appears to be a hint of a defence against marital irregularities and Ayllon was involved in some questionable divorces during his time in London.[6] But then it is also possible that he was converted to Islam in 1683 while he was in Salonika.[7] The mud slung at Ayllon was worthy of tabloid newspapers and some stuck to him for the rest of his life.

Both Fidanque *père et fils* were taking a risk. Even to make an accusation against the Haham was a clear breach of the *ascamot*. The Fidanques still felt they had to speak up on what they considered was a lot more than rumour, and so they blew the whistle. Jacob Fidanque was a rabbi himself, originally from Hamburg, and it is possible he might have been jealous of the young Ayllon. Perhaps he considered that if the newcomer hadn't been chosen, he might have been in with a chance himself; the overseas signing had won over a more home-grown product. Certainly, Fidanque was very learned; Sasportas called him a scholar, which was praise enough.

An unholy row broke out in the community. The Mahamad stood on its dignity and refused to hear any criticism of its new, young and handsome Haham. They announced that, if you didn't want to be fined £2 or even excommunicated, it was forbidden: 'to any one except the appointed Haham to lay down the law or to render any legal decision'.[8]

Father and son continued to speak out against Ayllon, so a larger committee of the community convened and exonerated the Haham again, and still the vendetta continued. Both Fidanques were again severely admonished by the Mahamad. The contretemps led to more defections to the new Ashkenazi synagogue. It was a short walk from Creechurch Place to Dukes Place a few roads away. The defectors were again threatened with excommunication if they transferred their allegiance, but they countered with criticism of some of the Mahamad's practices. The arguments and counter-arguments dragged on for years.

When Ayllon first took up his post, it was not an easy time for the Mahamad. There was a new King, William III, and the legitimacy of the Jewish position in England had to be fought for all over again. The attempt by James II to achieve toleration for all faiths by the Declaration of Indulgence had been a cover for the legitimization of the Catholic position in the country. This had, however, been one of the causes of the Glorious Revolution as most of the country wanted to remain Protestant, regardless of James' personal views. It had also been established that the 1687 Declaration didn't apply to the Jews and wouldn't, in fact, do so until 1846, so the Jews remained in legal limbo.

It's true William III was from Holland and that country had now built a good relationship with its Jews. Nevertheless, in London, the community members enjoyed both religious and commercial trading benefits which had been provided by Charles II and James II and which could, therefore, be renounced by a new monarch.

There wasn't much likelihood of serious trouble. It costs a lot of money to mount an invasion and William wanted an army of 35,000 men before he tried it. The Jewish merchant, Lopez Suasso – described as the richest merchant, Jew or Gentile, in Amsterdam – came to William III's rescue. He gave William 2 million guilders to finance the project. William asked him if he wasn't concerned for the security of the loan. Suasso shrugged: 'If you are fortunate, I know you will pay me back. If you are unlucky, I agree to lose them.'

As William won, Parliament voted a grant of £600,000 in 1688 to repay the Dutch Republic for the costs of the expedition and, presumably, part of that money finished up with Suasso. The merchant continued to be highly regarded and was even given a barony by King Charles II of Spain in later years for his help to the Spanish economy. How that can be reconciled with the burning of Marrano heretics is truly difficult to understand.

Another Jewish merchant, Isaac Pereira, became William's commissary general, handling shipping and supplies for the king's army. That was worth £95,000 between September 1690 and August 1691. Backing kings might be risky but it was potentially very rewarding. William didn't know whether he could rely on the English Jews as he had on those in Holland. Nevertheless, he recognized the importance of the Jewish contribution to international trade from whatever source. The West Indies was a prime centre for desirable imports and when he was asked by the settlers in Jamaica to deport the Jews and confiscate their property, he very rapidly stamped on that idea.

In 1697, however, the Exchange membership was overhauled. Because the Jews had been allowed in without being Freemen, the precedent was extended to the admission of a number of less ethical applicants. It was, therefore, decided that in future there would be a maximum number of 124 brokers, of which 100 would be English, 12 would be foreigners and 12 would be Jews. The tiny Jewish community got 10 per cent of the membership, which indicates just how important they had become. It looked even more impressive when all the nationals of other countries trading in London had, in total, only another 10 per cent and they weren't pleased about it.

Jewish merchants were also in charge of quarter-mastering for the troops in Montreal and America. William, however, still had to overcome the support the Irish gave the Catholic James nearer home. This is where, in Northern Ireland to this day, we get the famous Battle of the Boyne memorial marches in celebration of William's victory. It wasn't all good news. Pereira would supply the army, but to finance the campaign, the suggestion was made that the Jews, as a community, should contribute £100,000. The House of Commons gave instructions that a bill to that effect should be prepared. William, however, was put on the spot when the Jews petitioned him, saying: 'they would rather leave the country at once than be ruined'.

The government backtracked after four months. The lobbying had cost the Sephardim £193. Instead, the City decided to create a war chest for the new monarch. This time the Jews were asked to contribute £12,000 and when there was a poor response from the community, the king decided in 1690 to withdraw the exemption from alien duties which had been granted to Jewish merchants.

Evading duty had always been at the root of all smuggling and was a popular pastime throughout the country. There were methods other than dealing with government officials, such as sailing with Dutch goods from Amsterdam to a remote port like Falmouth in Cornwall, and then going on to the West Indies as a British cargo. In 1685, a diligent former customs officer, Samuel Hayne, tried to get two of the perpetrators of this particular fiddle, Messrs Gomasero and Losado, convicted, but the jury acquitted them. Hayne was told:

> The Jews are a very Rich sort of people, their trade is very great, they employ many ships, etc., and should that be cut off, abundance of people, both here and in the Plantations, would feel the want of them. Moreover, the King would be much lessened in the Customs by the breaking off of their trade.[9]

Bending rules to further trade was often acceptable to the authorities, particularly where Cornwall was concerned. In Elizabethan days Cornish pirates had taken a Spanish vessel just at the time Elizabeth was trying to negotiate a treaty with Philip of Spain. The jury trying the subsequent court case found the pirates not guilty, even though the queen had sent express instructions that they were to be convicted and punished. So Elizabeth put the jury in prison and insisted on a second trial. That jury found the brigands not guilty as well. Elizabeth gave up.

The battle between the merchants and the Customs in William's time was full of incident. 'His Majesty... vowed that he would not abate the Jews of three pence of what was due to himself.' In the event, some money was paid and some was not. What was collected between 1689 and 1691 was a special universal poll tax. There were higher rates for the rich than the poor and, in spite of their protests, the Jews were lumped in with the wealthier people in the country – Dukes had to pay £50, Barons and Bishops £20 and Jewish Merchants £20. By contrast, for the rest of the citizenry, if you were over 16 you had to pay 50p. Ordinary Jews were taxed at twice the level of any other foreigner. In 1691, however, there was a new poll tax law and the Jews weren't singled out for discriminatory taxation again.

The Mahamad for its part, did its best to help the government's objectives. Ayllon found himself in 1696 jointly declaring with the Mahamad a prohibition on importing gold or exporting silver, except for trading with Spain and Portugal. The problem was that the currency market was a mess and speculating in it was only going to make matters worse. The penalty for disobeying the *ascamot* was a stiff £20 and exclusion from the community for an indeterminate period of time. The Mahamad were also careful to distinguish between commercial and political interests. From 1688–1819 there was an *ascama* in force threatening excommunication for any member who voted in a political election.

Paying unfair levels of tax might be opposed, but Ayllon made sure the calls for charitable donations did not go unheeded. The Sedaca of Terra Santa charity was founded in his time to provide money for the poor in the Holy Land – the objective of his coming to London in the first place. In 1689 no less than £110 was collected for the Jewish congregation in Belgrade, to ransom the captives taken after the sack of the town. Many of those who had survived the horrors emigrated to London. In 1698 the community did even better, providing £144 for the foreign poor.

The money was raised in many ways. One was from the *shnodering* of members 'called up' to say prayers on the *bima* – the platform used for the reading of each portion of the law on the Sabbath. When the Haham was called up for such an *aliyah*, the community paid his offering.

Ayllon was less concerned with unfair taxes than he was with marriages, for which he would be paid. He signed his first *ketubah*, marriage certificate, in 1690. During his time in office 41 *conversos* got married in the synagogue; four men and 37 women. Some were of Jewish origin and were returning to the faith. Some could have been children of mixed marriages. Some had, as before, been married in church in Portugal and wanted to be married again in synagogue. Ayllon was kept busy writing *ketubot* and conducting the marriage ceremonies. There were seven in 1690, 12 in 1697 and there would be 22 in 1724 as the community expanded.

The government had a look at marriages as well. They were, as always, interested in indirect taxation and in 1695, to help pay for the war against France, an act was passed to tax marriages and bachelors. In law, as we have seen, Jews couldn't get married anyway without a Christian clergyman being present. When that didn't happen – which was invariably – the marriage wasn't strictly legal. Nevertheless, the Jews were made to pay the tax on their 'illegal' marriages. It was held

> 'that nothing contained in it [the Act] should be construed to make good or effectual in law any such marriages of Jews or pretended marriages, but they shall be of the same force and virtue as they would have been if the Act had never been passed'.

Again, when it came to the crunch, the courts did hold that Jewish marriages were legal because they were held to be consensual marriages; if you agree to be married, you are married.

The theological struggle continued within the Sephardi community. There was a generation gap too. The students had their own ideas. Ayllon reported to Sasportas that they 'call good bad and bad good'. Their views might be legally untenable but when they were out of his sight, they voiced their opinions with enthusiasm. Sasportas could only respond that he had the same problems with students in Amsterdam.

Ayllon did not have the intellectual nous to deal with his older detractors. He had a Beth Din in Rabbi Ibn Danon and yet another Benjamin Levy, but they couldn't help much. Little by little his reputation was undermined until all the really learned members of the congregation refused to accept his authority. He did have Sabbatean tendencies and the congregation recognized the fact, even if he kept his library strictly Orthodox. As a later Haham wrote: 'Ayllon represented the party favourable to the claims of the false Messiah.'[10]

One row was over the question of whether the congregation should stand up for a particular prayer or not. Not to stand was part of Kabbalist thinking and, therefore, potentially linked to Sabbatean practices. One of the Dayans, Ibn Danon, didn't stand, so Jacob Fidanque attacked him for not doing so. Everybody knew that Ayllon took the same view.

The Mahamad had to support its Haham. In 1699 it forbade the congregation to stand for the Mourner's prayer called *Yitgadal* – now Kaddish, the prayer for the dead. They further announced:

> We have examined the calumnies that have from time to time accumulated upon H.H. S. Ayllon, they have been found to be without any foundation; being conscious of the evident risk of our preservation, tranquillity, and precious peace, we, satisfied entirely of the exemplary virtue of H.H. promise to obey and cause to be maintained the order and regulations of the Mahamad and Elders.[11]

The Elders were a body of senior members from whom the Mahamad were invariably drawn.

The Mahamad and the community disliked changing the liturgy to satisfy Kabbalistic practices, but there were hidden agendas because not everybody was of a like mind. Four of the supporters of a petition supporting Ayllon would join the opposition to any future Haham who was against Sabbatean practices.

For the Jewish community, 1698 saw another potentially disastrous piece of legislation being debated in the House of Commons on an old topic. This time it was a bill to inflict severe penalties on anybody who denied the Trinity and the bill was passed by the House of Lords. There was certainly no way for the Jews to dodge that accusation but the House of Commons defeated the proposal by 140 votes to 78.

As the Sephardi community grew, the Creechurch Lane synagogue became too small to hold them. So it was decided to build a new synagogue in a street called Bevis Marks. The money was raised from the members and Ayllon laid the foundation stone. While the work was being carried out, the synagogue became so crowded that the ladies were excluded from the Ladies Gallery to make more room for the men. This was not just a typical seventeenth-century dismissal of the equal rights of women. The rule in Judaism is that the men should attend the synagogue and take part in the services three times a day; morning, afternoon and evening. That would occupy at least an hour a day altogether. The women, however, do not have the same tasks to perform. It is recognized that they have family responsibilities and these might need to take precedence over going to the synagogue; a sick child, for example. So the men should be in synagogue but the women are excused. Hence the greater need for there to be enough room for the men.

Where would the women pray then? A synagogue is not a law court, the only specified building for a purpose. It has three distinct roles. It is a house of prayer, a meeting place and a place of study. If the synagogue was closed, both men and women could still pray anywhere.

Ayllon, naturally, found his experiences in London very painful. In 1696 he wrote to Sasportas complaining bitterly about the impossible relations between him and the congregation. The Mahamad continued to guard his position, introducing a £5 fine for criticising the Haham and another £5 fine if you heard someone else do it and didn't report them. Ayllon finally lost his sounding board when Sasportas died in Hamburg in 1698, and heartfelt prayers were said in his memory in the London synagogue.

Pressure continued to mount on the Haham to resign and when he was offered the job of associate rabbi in Amsterdam in 1700, Ayllon decided that enough was enough and accepted it. To maximize the effect, he dramatically announced his departure in the course of a sermon in the synagogue. The Mahamad tried unsuccessfully to talk him out of it. It was a rare occasion when the membership prevailed over the oligarchy. Of course, the Amsterdam community also thought Ayllon had given up Sabbateianism. The suspicion that he had not, however, must at least have been a possibility to them after the rows in London on the subject – the grapevine was very efficient.

Losing a major argument was not a situation to which the Mahamad were accustomed. There was little more they could do, however. So they banned Fidanque from holding any future post in the congregation or from carrying out any rabbinical function. They also dismissed the shochet and bodek, gave Ayllon a year's salary – 50 guineas (£52.50) – and they fumed.

Ayllon was not to be forgotten. His collection of Hebrew books had been bought in 1691 by the Mahamad as the basis for its library of hebraica.

In Amsterdam their former Haham found himself getting out of the frying pan but into the fire. Almost as soon as he arrived, he pronounced a highly heretical work quite harmless. The Amsterdam Mahamad weren't so sure, got a few second opinions, and on the advice received, publicly burned the book, an act which amounted to definitive humiliation.

Ayllon's former links with Sabbatean thought also continued to plague him. His years in Holland were marred by disputes with the traditionally Orthodox and he was outshone as a scholar by the new spiritual head of the Ashkenazi community, Zevi Ashkenazi. Ayllon sank to some pretty low tricks to survive, but at least had the honesty to admit that he had wronged Zevi after the latter's death.

Ayllon's period of office in London achieved very little. He left a divided community and he had sown the seeds of future battles between his supporters and the more Orthodox. The Mahamad recognized that his successor would have to be of a very different calibre.

NOTES

1   Gerard Nahon, *Dutch Jews as Perceived by Others*, Brill, 2001, p. 69.
2   *American Jewish Historical Society Proceedings*, Vol. 20, 1911, p. 50.
3   Moses Gaster, *Jewish Chronicle*, May 1901.
4   Cecil Roth, *History of the Great Synagogue*, Edward Goldston, 1950.
5   Lionel D. Barnett, *Bevis Marks Records*, Oxford University Press, 1940.

6   Matt Goldrich, *Journal of Jewish Studies*, Vol. 45, No. 2, Autumn 1994.
7   Ibid.
8   Louis Ginzburg, *Jewish Encyclopaedia*, USA, 1901.
9   Bernard Susser, *The Jews of South West England*, University of Exeter Press, 1993.
10 Moses Gaster, *History of the Ancient Synagogue*, London, 1901.
11 Goldrich, *Journal of Jewish Studies*. Vol. 45, No. 2, Autumn 1994.

7 David Nietto 1702–28

If there was a contest to decide who was the greatest Haham the Sephardim in England ever had, there's no doubt that David Nietto would be in the medals. He is acknowledged to be: 'One of the most original minds of 18th century Jewry'.[1]

Haham Moses Gaster, who would also be in the frame, said of Nietto:

> He represents in his manifold activity, in his wide aspirations, in his deep learning, in his unbounded energy, in his fearlessness and in his own great scholarship, as well as in his artistic inclinations and poetical proclivities, combined with his great medical and astronomical erudition and mastery of many languages, one of the finest types that Judaism has produced. His personality had an invigorating and strengthening effect on the community.[2]

A respected modern judge said of him, 'Since Maimonides no master of such many-sided wisdom has guided the spiritual life of Israel.'[3]

These flattering comments were well justified. Nietto was a good-to-excellent astronomer, doctor, historian, logician, poet and theologian, besides speaking Hebrew, French, Greek, Italian, Latin, Portuguese, Spanish and, eventually, English. He was also a fair artist and calligrapher, skills which served him well in writing books and creating frontispieces. He was human, however; he never got on terribly well with the smaller Ashkenazi script letters, as opposed to the type to be found in prayer books.

Nietto means grandson or descendant and David was the son of Rabbi Phineas Nietto, born in 1654 in Venice. His father was a member of the Venice Mahamad but his main occupation from 1665 was to become a manufacturer of silk stockings. A lot of rabbis also had a trade, for example Akiba, one of the greatest, was a herdsman and Manasseh ben Israel was, as we've seen, a printer. When David was 15 he was living with the family in Rome near the new factory.

When they arrived in 1669 the city must have been buzzing with the visit of Nathan of Gaza the previous year. The Sabbatean movement was still at its height and the lad couldn't fail to be aware of the arguments raging over the claims by its supporters and critics. Even at this early age he became a staunch opponent of the charismatic but false messiah.

Nietto wanted to study both rabbinics and medicine. Rome wouldn't have been a good choice because of: 'the repressive policy of the Popes and the unremitting war upon Talmudic literature'.[4]

The only Italian University which would take him was Padua, near Venice. In that city he could also study for his *semicha*, his rabbinical diploma. It was a long haul academically and he was 33 when he graduated in Medicine and Philosophy in 1687. He got his *semicha* from the eminent local rabbis.

Although he graduated in Padua, he actually went back to live in Leghorn in 1684, to practice medicine. As he became a teacher in the subject, he probably needed some practical experience before he graduated as someone who could educate students. His talmudic ability was recognized by the community in Leghorn who made him a Dayan. He gave responsa to legal questions which involved both religious and commercial activities. He also directed the religious academy, Reshit Hokhma (Beginnings of Wisdom). Both jobs illustrate his standing in one of the most theologically informed communities in Europe.

Support for the religious institutions in Leghorn came from many members deeply involved as merchants in the local trades and seaport. Some of them also managed to sail pretty close to the wind; one of the more lucrative activities involved the destination of cargoes hijacked by pirates in the Mediterranean. The people on board may have often been ransomed, but what about the haul? The pirates' custom was to avoid any Customs by unloading the stash in North African ports and fencing a lot of the goods through the local Jewish merchants. They, in their turn, passed the laundered swag onto the Leghorn brethren, who could get a better price for it in Italy. In modern terms, the prices, which were still low, might have been explained as things falling off the back of a galleon.

In 1693 a strange occurrence sparked off what would become Nietto's life-long interest in calendars. Usually the festival of Passover precedes Easter, but in 1693 it didn't, and Nietto wanted to find out why. Basically, the answer was that the Church was working the dates out wrongly. One of the worst examples of the effects of this error was in England where they used the Julian calendar which, in fact, put

England on short time – the year wasn't long enough. When eventually the country fell further and further behind the true date, Lord Chesterfield had to pass an Act in 1751 to correct the situation. It was quite simple. In 1752 after 1 September would come, not 2 September, but 14 September. The country would then move onto the Gregorian calendar which has kept us straight ever since. There were riots in the streets and cries of 'Give us back our eleven days', but it had to be done. Otherwise, by now, the January Sales would have started weeks before Christmas – even in good times.

Because of the restrictions which apply to everyday life on the Sabbath and festivals, it is essential that Jews know the precise dates and times involved on these occasions. Everything goes from nightfall to nightfall but when exactly does night fall? In the Holy Land the dates themselves were determined by the appearance of the new moon. This would be monitored in Jerusalem and when it appeared, a bonfire would be lit. Seen miles away, other bonfires would be started across the country and the news would travel quickly. To avoid getting it wrong far across the world, Jewish communities outside the Holy Land would celebrate two days for festivals. Incidentally, the system of messages by communicating bonfires was also in force in England in Napoleonic times to warn the country that it had been invaded, and an attempt to change the calendar again in the 1920s would make Chief Rabbi Hertz an international figure.

In 1701, after Ayllon's departure, the Mahamad in London issued a unanimous invitation to Nietto to replace him. There were Leghorn members of the London community who knew all about the brilliant young Dayan and they lobbied for him enthusiastically. The Mahamad recognized that they were signing up a rabbinic star and they were prepared to to pay over the previous odds. They knew that: 'He could be relied upon to do whatever was possible to counteract the pernicious influence of his predecessor.'[5]

Consequently, they offered him twice Abendana's salary – £100 a year instead of £50 – plus free coal and a guaranteed gift of £10 every Purim. The signing-on fee also included £60 to cover the cost of relocation and a free home in the old synagogue building in Creechurch Lane which, with the building of the new synagogue, was now surplus to requirements. They gave him £20.65 to furnish it and £21.50 for other expenses, plus over £40 towards the cost of bedding, mattresses and cushions. After a while his salary went up to £150 a year.

Nietto would also be highly likely to get gifts when he officiated at weddings, barmitzvahs and circumcisions while he would be paid for divorces. The annual number of weddings in the lovely new synagogue went up to over 20 a year. In 1706, they included what the Sephardim would consider a mixed marriage; a Sephardi man and an Ashkenazi woman. The Sephardim were always concerned to maintain the Sephardi rite and avoid the danger of having so many Ashkenazim in the future that this might change. Weddings with the Ashkenazim were discouraged and the more that took place as the years went by, the greater the discouragement. In the records of the synagogue there were occasions when they wouldn't even enter the name of the Ashkenazi woman; the entry simply read 'Tedesca': 'as recently as the year 1944 . . . it was laid down that marriages were not normally to be celebrated unless the bridegroom was a yahid or at least a congregant'.[6]

Nietto had been offered a handsome package and, in return, he agreed to give up practising medicine and concentrate on the new job. As his fame grew in England, however, he did look after a few patients and some of his medical notes have survived.

Nietto arrived with his wife, Sarah, and his three sons, Moses, Phineas and Isaac and, as a future Haham, Moses Gaster, made clear, he: 'took into his own hands the spiritual rule and guidance of the community'.[7]

The specific mention of 'rule' is a sideswipe by the future Haham at those lay leaders who forget who is in charge spiritually. Nietto found a community that had been safely settled in their new city for 40 years. In that time over 100 of them had bought English citizenship from the king and, only a year before, Sir Solomon de Medina had become the first Jew to receive a knighthood – he was also the last for well over 100 years. As a major supplier to the army in the War of the Spanish Succession against Louis XIV of France, de Medina would pay Marlborough, the English GOC, £6,000 a year from 1707 to 1711 for the privilege. The rules of the game often included bribery and corruption. But if an army marches on its stomach, de Medina made very sure it was full. England had little experience of the logistics of keeping an army in the field on the continent, so de Medina's ability was essential.

De Medina's appointment, of course, was another quite illegal decision. The law stated that no Jew could hold an office under the Crown but, typically, nobody at the top paid any attention. Indeed, so highly regarded was de Medina at court that William III had actually gone to the de Medina ménage for dinner. The other side of the coin was that the family of another contractor, Joseph Cortissos, were still trying to get paid by the government over 100 years later in the nineteenth century, for the work they had done during the War of the Spanish Succession.

Nietto arrived in London at the age of 48 in time for the opening of the new synagogue in Bevis Marks. It had cost £2,750 and still stands quietly in the City 300 years later, a lovely building. Admittedly, when you compare the average synagogue with a York Minster or a King's College Chapel, the synagogue is an also-ran. It's no different with Bevis Marks, but it is very homely and has its own majesty. It is still lit by candles and the Ark bears witness to the Jewish participation in the seventeenth-century South American wood trade. One can imagine the Mahamad asking members to bring back a load of the finest cedar wood when they next went to Brazil. Bevis Marks was put up by a Quaker builder called Avis, who refused to make a profit out of the job. In so many ways, the building was a blessing and has remained so.

Everybody flocked to see it. So much so that the City magistrates complained about the number of people gathering in the streets after the services. The Mahamad sternly told the congregation to go home quickly. The City Fathers tended to equate large gatherings with the possibility of riots and were keen to avoid them.

One of Nietto's first tasks was to compose and publish a prayer to ask the Almighty to help William III in his deliberations:

> A fervid and humble prayer addressed to the Great and Omnipotent God of Israel by the Congregation of Jews in London, in which they implore the assistance and help of Heaven at the Deliberations of His Majesty, the Invincible King William III, their Sovereign, of his Supreme Council, and of both chambers of his August Parliament.[8]

Formulating prayers was an easier task than the one which faced the hazan – reading a passage from the Pentateuch every week on the Sabbath. There are no vowels in the scroll but the hazan can recognize the words from their meaning in the sentence. The congregation, on the other hand, have books with vowels. Every Sabbath the reading has to be done absolutely faultlessly, as it is the word of God. So if a mistake is made, the congregation call out the right word and the error is corrected by the hazan. At Bevis Marks the unfortunate hazan was also made to pay a fine of 25p for every mistake he made! On a bad day in 1701 he was fined 75p for three mistakes – in today's money, perhaps about 1.5 per cent of his annual salary. If today he earned £40,000 p.a. he would be forfeiting a thumping £600!

Nietto preached every other week. He was never overawed by the ranks of wealthy merchants in front of him. There was no timidity, no soft-spoken words. He was straight and clear, upright and fearless. He brought up his children to be the same. Moses and Isaac were soon on their feet, giving the congregation a learned *drosha* (religious discourse), probably with a little help from Dad on the content.

The outside world intruded with a vengeance in 1702. The Protection for Converted Children Act laid down that a Jewish father should support his child, even if the child converted to Christianity. A case of this kind came up that year and, although Bevis Marks helped the father fight the case, they lost. It was worse though for the Catholics. They had to divide their estates among their children when they died unless one of the progeny converted to the Church of England. In which case he – or she – got the lot.

In 1702 Nietto published the book on calendars in London which he had started in Leghorn. It was called *Pascalogia* and it illustrated Nietto's friendly relations with the Church, in that it was dedicated to Cardinal Francisco Maria de Medina back in Italy. It was a handsome production, 'exquisitely bound in red Morocco leather with gauffered edges and David Nietto in gold letters'.

The book explained why the Christian and Jewish calendars differed and it is significant that Nietto pretended on the cover that it had been printed in Cologne; he was worried that the English authorities might object to any suggestion from the Jews that the Christians had made a mistake. He needn't have been concerned. In the event: 'London became the centre where books of a polemical [controversial] character could be published'.[9]

Like the Abendanas, Nietto had many Christian clerical correspondents and they began to journey to London to talk to the talmudist. The Mahamad sensibly overlooked the *ascamot* against talking religion with Christians, no doubt basking in the reflected glory of its new minister. 'A far greater number of men of science and of letters gathered round the synagogue or within the walls of the synagogue than ever before or at any time afterwards.'[10]

Great names such as Daniel Israel Lopes Laguna, who turned the book of Psalms into poetry, and Jacob de Castro Sarmento, FRS. It was ironic that professing Jews could be Fellows of the Royal Society but couldn't become undergraduates at Oxford or Cambridge. But then they could be knights but not MPs.

One cleric who arrived was Johan Schult, who would later become court preacher to Charles XII of Sweden. Jews weren't allowed to live in Sweden at that time. An offer to Nietto to settle in the country later in the century could well have been influenced by Schult, after his friendly talks with the Haham on everything from Rashi to divorce law and the importance of tradition. Not that Schult was impressed by all he saw. When he attended the service in Bevis Marks, he reported that: 'A leader was chanting, followed by the whole congregation with a horrid noise.'

In London, over the course of his 27-year ministry, Nietto took on no less than seven major opponents to Orthodox Judaism: the Classicists, the Modernists, Philosophers, Deists, Sabbateians, Karaites and the Catholic Church. Each of the seven set out to prove that Orthodox Judaism wasn't the answer.

The Classicists said that Greek and Roman thought were far superior to the Talmud. They pooh-poohed allegorical stories in the Bible, such as Balaam's ass, which, on occasions, told Balaam what to do. Nietto gave as good as he got. He said that most Classical poetry: 'is exclusively concerned with the love-life and the harlotries of the gods'. He also suggested that there was nothing wrong in speaking in allegorical riddles; hadn't Pythagoras said 'Do not eat beans' and what was that supposed to mean?

The Modernists pointed to the fact that Jewish practice hadn't changed a great deal in hundreds of years. They accused the rabbis of being stuck in the Middle Ages, long after the Renaissance had undermined so many mediaeval structures of thought. They said Jewish thought was restricted by the enclosed attitudes of those who lived in a ghetto, although they ignored the fact that these same Jewish theologians were living in the ghetto because the Church and state had put them there. For the Orthodox, these accusations of being out-of-date were boringly familiar. They had often been voiced in the centuries before and they would still be current, if not choice, in the twenty-first century.

Nietto, of course, didn't fit the alleged pattern at all. He was a graduate of one of the finest universities in Italy where he had studied medicine; he was fully up-to-date, and in each of his literary works he was able to prove that Judaism was either on-message, had created the message in the first place, or was able to find common ground with genuine improvements to knowledge. This was particularly the case with the new interest in philosophic subjects – medicine, astronomy, physics, engineering, etc., subjects which are now classed as sciences. Nietto was also intensely curious about the geographical world and knew of the Jews in Ethiopia (the Falashas), in Babylon, the Balearics and Iraq.

There were Jewish communities dotted around many continents

and everybody had an avuncular feeling about everybody else. There were Jews in Russia in the Crimea as early as the first century AD. They had arrived in Cranganore in India in the sixth century and in China at Kai Feng Fu by the eleventh century. The communities might have a few individual customs but, basically, they carried the full panoply of Orthodox Judaism with them. Where they were in touch, they tried to help each other.

Nietto's period of office in London coincided with Sir Isaac Newton's height of influence as president of the Royal Society. That learned body was created by Charles II, somewhat as a counterpoise to the overwhelming importance of religion in the Reformation world. This was now the age of Newton and Boyle. The importance of science was beginning to be recognized and fashionable. Perhaps, many scientists thought, it was possible to explain the whole world in terms of science, rather than faith and miracles. Reason instead of religion was touted as the new deity.

Rationalism was a stunning new concept. How to avoid it undermining Christianity was immediately tackled by the theologians of the Church of England. Nietto decided he needed to work out the same thing for Judaism. It was a vital task, although marrying science and Orthodox Judaism would hardly create a precedent as there were already plenty of rabbinic teachings in surgery, engineering and astronomy. Like former rabbis, he knew that if he couldn't convince his congregation that Judaism was still entirely relevant to his own world, he would lose a lot of them. The challenge lay in:

> The ability of a Jewish thinker to absorb the dominant theologi-cal position of his Christian contemporaries and to reformulate them as Jewish theology before a recently constituted congregation of assimilated, secularized, highly ambitious but politically and culturally insecure, Jewish merchants.[11]

In 1700 the London Sephardim were indeed still a congregation with limited Jewish knowledge. Most of them still mirrored those earlier Marranos who had hung on to their faith with grim determination but, inevitably, with little study.

Throughout Nietto's ministry he waged this battle, to prove there was no intrinsic barrier between science and Judaism, and he carried the Mahamad with him. It had the right to stop him publishing but, certainly on the scientific issues, it was way out of its depth.

The problem was where to put science in relation to God. What part had Nature played? Which takes us back to the intellectual arguments of the Spinozists. Nietto's answer was clear and delivered in a sermon he gave in the synagogue in 1703, two years after his arrival, when the honeymoon period with the congregation was over. The occasion was to celebrate his appointment as Rosh Yeshivah (head of the talmudic school) and the founding of the first Jewish Orphan Asylum; 'asylum' in the sense of 'refuge' and not 'insanity'.

Nietto's theme that day was that God *was* Nature. That there was, in fact, no such thing as Nature, only God. Factually, the concept of Nature was only formulated about 1000 CE. A typical proof Nietto provided of the longevity of the Jewish position was that King David had written in Psalm 147: 'who covereth the heaven with clouds, who prepareth rain for the earth, who maketh the grass to grow upon the mountain'.

God had done that, not Nature. The sermon was quite unambiguous but it caused the most enormous rumpus. The trouble was that, within the community, there were still a considerable number of Sabbateians. They had lost a major battle when Solomon Ayllon had been forced out and here was Nietto, occupying his position and attacking Sabbateians, to the manner born; eulogizing the elder Fidanque when he died, as Haham Rabbi Jacob Fidanque. Honouring him even though he had attacked Ayllon. How could this newcomer be sabotaged? The Sabbateians saw the sermon as a hammer with which to hit Nietto over the head. They denounced it as Spinozist, calling him a believer in Pantheism, the idea that God is everything and everything is God, which is hardly monotheism, the belief in one God.

The Haham, of all people, was accused of being a heretic. He was temporarily suspended on suspicion of Spinozism. One of the community's barrack-room lawyers, Joshua Sarfatti, who had already been fined for attacking him, ostentatiously refused to go into a house where Nietto was conducting a wedding. He made his reasons clear why and offered to pay £100 if he was wrong. The Mahamad didn't take the bet. It told Sarfatti to sort it out with Nietto and, when he wouldn't, it barred him from the synagogue in defence of the Haham, at which point Sarfatti circulated a pamphlet saying he had been wronged.

The uproar continued when 13 Yehidim asked for a ruling by the Amsterdam Beth Din. Many of the members had been Ayllon's pupils and four of them had supported the petition in Ayllon's favour in 1698. The 13 were also thrown out of the synagogue, but they wrote to Amsterdam anyway and the Dutch Mahamad ordered that a committee of five be set up as a Beth Din to consider the matter. This Dutch Beth Din refused to act because it said it could only respond to a community and not to individuals on a case like this.

The London Mahamad went along with the idea of consulting Amsterdam: 'submitting the point to the greatest Beth Din in Europe.' Which wasn't exactly true and, anyway, Amsterdam could recognize a hot potato as well as the next law court. The Dutch stalled and asked for an agreed statement by both parties on what exactly had been said. Back in London the dispute in Bevis Marks was getting very ugly. It was found necessary to dismiss one of the teachers, Joseph Ibn Danon, who was on the complainant's side, and one of the excommunicated died and couldn't be buried in the Sephardi cemetery because of his expulsion. He now lies in the Ashkenazi cemetery nearby.

The position in Amsterdam was complicated by the fact that Ayllon was a member of their Beth Din and really the only one who understood the arguments. He may have been a closet Sabbateian but he knew a great deal now about rabbinical subjects. Consequently, the Amsterdam Mahamad were far from sure that Nietto would get a fair hearing – it had its own theological arguments raging on the same subjects as in London – and the Amsterdam Beth Din passed the parcel; no, it didn't feel like coming to a conclusion.

The Mahamad in London was furious because the Nietto affair was dragging on and splitting the community, not only into those who were Spinozists and those who were Orthodox, but also into those who were for the Haham and those who were for Ayllon and the Sabbateians, and between those who accepted the authority of the Mahamad and those who resented it. It was also possible to belong to more than one party. The Mahamad decided that:

> The Beth Din were more influenced by personal motives and personal conditions than a hope of a desire of restoring peace and harmony in the Jewish community, they decided never to appeal any more in any question whatsoever to the Beth Din of Amsterdam or have any further communication with them.[12]

At this point Rabbi Aberle from the Ashkenazi community offered to help. He knew Rabbi Zevi Ashkenazi, who was immensely respected across Europe. How about asking him? The Mahamad liked that idea very much. The Amsterdam Sephardim had wanted Zevi Ashkenazi to become Haham at the time. They had offered him a princely £500 a year, which must have annoyed Ayllon considerably, but Ashkenazi turned the job down. He was Ashkenazi and wanted to serve his own community.

No problem was too esoteric for Rabbi Ashkenazi to consider. He had once to come to a conclusion on whether a man created by a miracle worker – an early working of the Frankenstein story and known as a Golem – could make up a *minyan*. (Be one of the 10 men needed for a full service.) If the question seems ridiculous today, so at that time might have been one about heart transplants. Who would bet, though, with what we already know about cloning, that it couldn't happen in the future? Anyway, rabbis deal with the problems they're asked about; they're not supposed to be clairvoyants or write *What the Stars Foretell* columns in the tabloids.

So Ashkenazi considered the evidence about the sermon, talked to a few colleagues and they all agreed that Nietto was right and should be congratulated on speaking out. Sarfatti and the others were declared in error and they had already been expelled from the community. Defeated, they asked to come back and Nietto pleaded on their behalf. All was forgiven and peace reigned again in Bevis Marks. In fact, the row with Amsterdam was very much a family quarrel and, after the death of Ayllon, relations returned to normal in the 1730s.

While all this was going on, Nietto had been continuing with his efforts to link science and Judaism, producing a book called *Della Divina Providencia* in 1704 which set out his case in full.

Although the God is Nature sermon was one of the worst examples of internal conflict within the community, it was by no means unique. The members were rowdy on occasions, even violent towards each other, and many cases came before the Mahamad where fines and temporary exclusion from the community were imposed. Of course, if the Mahamad was all-powerful, the members could always secede. A number did, for example in 1705, dissatisfied when they were told that it was forbidden to hold services even in your own house. Services could only be held in the synagogue; that was the import of *ascama* 1.

The Mahamad wondered if it actually had the power to issue *herems* and, in 1705, asked the advice of the Attorney General, Sir Edward Northey. He was of the opinion that it hadn't: 'I am doubtful that the pronouncing excommunication, being an act of ecclesiastical Jurisdiction, the Synagogue of the Jewes are not allowable by the Lawes of England to exercise the pronouncing of same, and for assuming the exercise of ye power in England.'

'Sir Edward thought that it was probably alright to refuse them burial in the congregation's cemetery but that was about it. After his advice, the Mahamad didn't refer to *herem* in the 1705 version of the *ascamot*: 'they were neither rebuked nor impeded by the Portuguese *kahal* because of certain reasons'.[13] Though they were prepared to fine anybody.

As the spiritual authority of the community there was plenty for Nietto to do; charitable, educational, legal and religious work, besides his writings. For example, he established a Talmud Torah – a religious school to teach the children more advanced theology than had previously been possible. The rabbis knew about the importance of 'education, education and education' long before the politicians.

The annual income at Bevis Marks increased during Nietto's time from £3,400 in 1702 to £6,700 in 1726, partly due to the Portuguese signing the Methuen Treaty in 1703. This improved trade between the nations and Jewish Marrano merchants were in a particularly good position to take advantage of this. So more overseas offices were opened and the community grew to over 1,000 in 1720. The rich were happily flourishing commercially, but Nietto was also concerned with the far larger number of his poor and disadvantaged members, so 25 per cent of the synagogue's annual income was devoted to helping to support them.

There was, in addition, the need to take care of asylum seekers, still coming in from Spain and Portugal. That cost £245 in 1728. One of the advantages of the community to the state was, indeed, that the Jews were seldom a financial burden. It was the Jewish policy to look after their own and, 200 years later, it would be on that understanding that the government would allow 50,000 refugee Jews into Britain from Germany after 1933. Under the heading of 'Pastoral Care' would also come Nietto's new translation of the New Year and Yom Kippur prayers into Spanish for non-Hebrew speaking members.

With war raging again in Europe, many other Jews came to England. They were mostly destitute and trying to maintain them all was a colossal burden for the small existing community. In 1710: 'New and more stringent orders were passed against "Italianos and Verberiscos" who should only be supplied with food for three days and to whom no more than 10 shillings (50p) were to be given to go away.'[14]

The War of the Spanish Succession against the French dragged on and would do so for another four years. The battle honours of Blenheim, Ramillies and Oudenarde were won at great cost in dead and wounded. In a world where, in many places, it was an achievement just to stay alive, the heat engendered by the row over God and Nature might be seen as no more than a reflection of the thoughts of a sheltered group of divines, clerics separated by their study walls from the harsh realities of life. But rabbis didn't live in monasteries. They knew all about harsh realities. For example, Rabbi Ashkenazi's wife and daughter had been murdered by the Prussians besieging Budapest in 1686 and his parents were taken into captivity.

The community had always got on well with the current ruler, Queen Anne. She had visited Bevis Marks and had given a beam to the building fund. Well, large beams cost a lot of money and a beam is as good as a donation. In 1714, when it was known that the queen was dying, the question arose of whom the community should support as her successor; James II's Catholic son, whom the Tories favoured, or the King of Hanover, whom the Whigs wanted.

This was no casual Gallup Poll or potential Referendum. This was now deadly serious. The community couldn't stay neutral and it would be disastrous if they backed the wrong side. In London, pro-Jacobite feeling was very strong and the prospects of James, the Old Pretender, were good, as he was known to have powerful French backing. He had been approached by both the Whig and Tory leaders. Moreover, James III – as he would have been – had already tried to invade the country in 1708. He'd been driven away then but everybody knew he was certain to make another attempt when Anne died.

In 1714 the Whig government fired a warning shot and passed the Schism Bill to close all Dissenter Academies. The objective was less religious than an effort to embarrass the Tory Leader, the Earl of Oxford, who had a Dissenter's background. Nevertheless, the Jews were always counted as Dissenters, even if their tiny Talmud Torah wasn't under immediate threat from the massed forces of the state.

In discussion on whom to back, Nietto would have emphasized the Din; there's a third-century ruling – *dina de-malchuta dina* – that the legitimate ruler in the land in which you live is the one who should be obeyed. The government had invited George to ascend the throne and the Mahamad voted by 19–2 to support him, even if the king, himself, was living in Hanover at the time.

There were also, as is usually the case, tremendous financial implications in backing the wrong side. The Jews had become pillars of the City of London over the years and one, Anthony da Costa, had even become a Director of the Bank of England. By 1715: 'they had engrossed the Portugal and Barbary [North African] trade to themselves...that they were running a close race for that of Spain...that they had got into their hands Barbados and Jamaica; and that by their foreign relations they regulated the course of the Exchanges'.[15]

The Menassah Lopez family was just one among a number in Bevis Marks who helped maintain the stability of the London market. Not that there was no opposition; in 1715 one Jew's application to become a broker was strongly opposed, but the attempt to block him failed. The Jewish merchants now included what had become, effectively, early Merchant Bankers, importing gold to improve the country's bullion reserves and buying gilt-edged stock when it was under pressure. Now Jew Brokers helped steady the pound when the invasion scare threatened panic.

James actually landed in Scotland in 1715 but it was all over in a couple of months and he went back to Paris. The rebellion proved hopelessly unsuccessful, but that was 20:20 hindsight.

By supporting the Hanoverians, the security of the Jews in England was signed, sealed and delivered for the next 100 years. George I had only one claim to the throne; he was a Lutheran. There were, according to Linda Colley, 50 relatives of Queen Anne who had precedence over George – but they were all Catholics.[16] Throughout the eighteenth century and well into the nineteenth, the importance of Protestantism was what cemented the three disparate nations of England, Scotland and Wales. From 1689 to 1815 the British would actually be at war with Catholic France for a total of over 50 years. It was Catholicism which was seen as the ever-present and powerful enemy. In the battles to maintain Britain's Protestant independence in the world, the British Jews had proved in 1715 that they could be trusted to help.

Not that this made the community feel that much more secure. Centuries of persecution – often coming out of the blue – made it difficult to believe that the worst was over. 'Wait till tomorrow, you'll see', was always a popular, if depressing, refrain.

The Sabbateian movement rumbled on. It got a new lease of life in Amsterdam with the arrival of a powerful preacher called Nehemiah Hayyun. Just one of Hayyun's beliefs which he seriously wished to have adopted, was that you could overcome your sins, 'by the satisfaction of all desires, even the most depraved'.

Seldom had the principles of morality been so turned on their heads. Zevi Ashkenazi, the rabbi who had decided in Nietto's favour in the 'God is Nature' case, attacked Hayyun vigorously and there was a head-to-head between Ayllon, still a Dayan in the Amsterdam Beth Din, and the old man. The problem for Ayllon was that Hayyun 'was well acquainted with Ayllon's antecedents and it would have been dangerous to make an enemy of him'.[17]

To take on Ashkenazi talmudically was for Ayllon to have delusions of grandeur. He was taken apart theologically and he fought back desperately by introducing a particularly malodorous red herring. He played the chauvinist card and said that the Dutch didn't need any advice from the German, Ashkenazi.

This Siren appeal to chauvinism worked, as it so often does, and the atmosphere soured more than somewhat. In August 1713 it was officially announced that Hayyun was innocent and that he had been unrighteously persecuted. Which was awkward because, in July, Ashkenazi had, quite rightly, excommunicated him. Now it was Ashkenazi who was summoned by the Amsterdam Mahamad but he refused to be judged by a Sephardi body. So the Mahamad excommunicated him in absentia. Ashkenazi went into voluntary exile in London in 1714, was welcomed as a hero, but he died in 1718.

Ayllon didn't come out of the battle unscathed:

> Ayllon made a sorry figure ... Not alone did Ayllon permit his protégé, Hayyun, to assail the foremost man in Israel with foulest insults, but he supplied him with personal papers containing attacks upon his opponent ... the unfounded nature of which he himself had formally admitted and testified to.[18]

Rabbi Moses Hagiz, a colleague of Ashkenazi in Amsterdam, went hammer and tongs for Ayllon for rulings he had given which certainly appeared outrageous. In one the defendant had promised to repay a debt to the plaintiff. When he didn't and was hauled before the Amsterdam Beth Din, he said he had never intended to honour his promise. Ayllon found in his favour and it was well known that Sabbateians did break oaths and didn't consider this a culpable action. Nietto also joined the fight on Ashkenazi's side, criticizing Hayyun's views as spiritually harmful and likely to foment discord into the bargain. In 1714 he produced a slim volume called *Esh Dat* which showed up all the fallacies in the Sabbateian's thinking. 'His second axiom is that any sin, however heinous, may be committed if the intent is not idolatrous ... will not non-Jews be incited to antipathy against us, just as they were by the exorbitant interest which we exacted from them in Spain.'[19]

Nietto was against sin, even if his own community were committing it. As he pointed out: 'What is to become of us if these teachings reach the ears of the rulers and peoples among whom we dwell.'[20]

In his spare time Nietto turned his attention to the Karaites. The main argument of that sect was that they considered the Written Law acceptable but the Oral Law beyond the pale because it was not divinely inspired. Nietto set out to defend the Oral Law and to settle the Judaism/science argument in what would be his magnum opus, *Matteh Dan*, which was finished in 1715.

The *Matteh Dan* is a commentary on a book called *The Kuzari* in which an eleventh-century poet, Judah ha-Levi, defended the Written Law. In Nietto's hands it also became: 'An eminently readable presentation of the case for Rabbinic Judaism.'[21]

Nietto dealt effectively with one particularly thorny problem – the contradictory opinions you can find in the Talmud. He made the case that they involved minor points rather than essentials. There has been further praise in modern times for: 'Nietto's extreme use of science to bolster the authority of the Rabbis, and to present effectively the virtues of the Jewish faith.'[22] Indeed, one part of the book is devoted to discussing in some detail the relatively new theory of Copernicus that the earth spins on its axis and goes round the sun.

Nietto didn't just display his knowledge in his books. He realized the difficulty of tackling the great tomes and involved arguments of legions of talmudic scholars before him. He tried to make *Matteh Dan* much more simple: 'I implore all who teach the Torah...that they shall teach their pupils the first three dialogues of the book and explain them well. It is for this reason that I have written them in a clear and easy language.'

The City settled down after the collapse of the Jacobite uprising but was then convulsed by the South Sea Bubble disaster. This was a Stock Exchange scam, promoting the shares of the East India Company, which promised a fortune for investors from its trade with Asia. The number of punters who eventually lost their money when the bubble burst was so huge that it brought down the government and led to legislation to stop any company in the future having more than a few shareholders, a situation which continued until 1862. If the *Jewish Chronicle* had existed in the early eighteenth century, its front-page headline might have read 'South Sea Bubble collapses. Hardly any Jews involved.' Of 2,000 voting shareholder groups, only 32 were Jewish and only four of those had more than £10,000 worth of stock. The Bevis Marks Jews believed fervently that on the Exchange there was no such thing as a free lunch, no matter how kosher the promoters made it out to be.

Which still left the Catholic church killing Marranos. In 1705 when it was burning heretics in Lisbon, the former Archbishop of Cranganore in India had addressed the condemned before he had them executed:

> Miserable wretches of Judaism! Unhappy fragments of the synagogue! Scandal of the Catholics and detestable objects of scorn even to the Jews themselves...you are the detestable objects of scorn to the Jews, for you are so ignorant that you cannot even observe the very law under which you live.[23]

All this, when His Grace knew full well that the Portuguese Jews had been forcibly converted in 1497 and forbidden to practice their religion in Portugal for over 200 years. It was only too understandable that, during the Yom Kippur services, a prayer was offered at Bevis Marks for 'our brethren who are imprisoned in the dungeons of the Inquisition'.

London became the headquarters for those who opposed the Inquisition and in 1709 Nietto attacked the views of the Archbishop. In 1722 he went on to write the *Recondite Notice of the Inquisition of Spain and Portugal*, in which his arguments against the Inquisition were powerful. Nietto wrote what he thought of the Archbishop's text. Where the Archbishop had said that the Jews had altered parts of the Bible, Nietto quoted St Augustine who said they hadn't. He mocked the Inquisition for banning books which went contrary to the teachings of Catholicism. Why not follow the Jewish practice of allowing anything to be published and then pointing out the fallacies to their communities? The archbishop took a lot of stick but it couldn't save the martyrs. What it did do was help make the case for the abolition of the Inquisition in Portugal, which the Jesuit, Antonio Vieira, used successfully later in the century. Even so, Nietto only had the *Recondite Notice* published after his death in 1728; he probably feared the long arm of the Inquisition, if not on him personally, then on his family or friends.

Nietto's writings were influential as were his discussions outside the Jewish community. For example, Nietto's interest in calendars led him to a close friendship with John Covel, the master of Christ's College, Cambridge. They wrote to each other in Italian. Covel had been very supportive when Nietto had written to him about the Deist controversy:

> I do not know what plastic virtue leads the particular Nature of everything. How I laugh about these foolish things. From God

alone proceeds every good thing, to his most gracious conduct and government I recommend you, most affectionately, your most humble and devoted servant, John Covel.

Nietto wanted to provide new information on the subject, though he modestly rejected one document because reprinting it would be '*crambem recoquere*' – 're-cooking cabbage'. Covel pointed out the effect on sales of producing a book in any language other than English. Nietto had to admit: 'I am obliged to write in Latin because I do not know English... for a foreign Jew who has no knowledge and no friends, everything fails.'

The project had to be abandoned for this reason initially but, in 1717, he did produce a calendar in his work *Binah LeIttim*. It gave the dates for the new moon and the festivals for the next 83 years. There was also a calendar of past events from the Flood in 3822 BCE up to the opening of Bevis Marks in 1701, and the times for the beginning and end of the Sabbath. Nietto was, in fact, the first authority to fix the correct time for the Sabbath for the latitude of England and for all the daily morning and evening services. It became a family tradition and the last occasion was when Reverend Abraham Nietto in New York produced a 100 year calendar in 1902. He dedicated it to his forebears.

In 1723 Nietto's calendar was adopted by the Ashkenazi community in London. Every Friday before the Sabbath, the Bevis Marks beadle would go to the Great Synagogue and tell them the exact times for the Sabbath the following week. That became a tradition which lasted for the next couple of centuries.

Many of the foremost Christian scholars of the time accepted Nietto as an equal, but he was careful not to offend Protestant Christian sensibilities. Any pills of correction had a thick sugar coating. Addressing one of the most eminent scholars, he began his letter: 'Greatest of Sages, Chief among Preachers, Ornament of Saints, My Master, Distinguished one and Friend, the Great Sage who is adorned with all manner of wisdom and prudence, the exalted, honoured and distinguished Christian, Theophilus Unger'. 24 It would have been hard to take offence after that introduction.

Nietto was always busy. His literary output was phenomenal. He even completed four volumes of a rabbinical encyclopaedia. His last years, however, were dogged by illness and in 1724 he was so poorly he had to hand over responsibility for the Yom Kippur sermon to a friend. He lived to see the Sephardi girl's school, the Villa Real, established in 1726 but he died in 1728 at the age of 74. His wife,

Sarah, received a handsome pension of £35 a year and died at the age of 88 in 1741.

Undoubtedly, Nietto was superior to many of the other Hahamim who served Bevis Marks. It is noticeable how few arguments arose in his time between him and the Mahamad; if the spiritual leader is able enough, you don't get much interference. He didn't live to see many of the results of his efforts come to fruition. Hayyun died in 1730, long-forgotten; the Inquisition wouldn't finally be abolished in Spain until 1834 and the last Auto da Fé took place in Mexico in 1850. The Sabbateians effectively disappeared, as did the Karaites and the Deists, and the Jews went on to produce many eminent and Orthodox scientists. The Oral Law would be attacked again and again in the future, but it was still in place when Nietto died, and that was the most that could be asked of any Haham. If the Bevis Marks community ever started to decline, they could look back on the David Nietto era as a golden age.

NOTES

1   David B. Ruderman, *American Academy for Jewish Research*, Vol. 18, 1992.
2   Moses Gaster, *History of the Ancient Synagogue*, London, 1901.
3   Lionel Barnett, *Bevis Marks Records*, Oxford University Press, 1940.
4   Cecil Roth, *Essays and Portraits in Anglo-Jewish History*, Jewish Publication Society of America, 1962.
5   Cecil Roth, Appendix to new edition of *Matteh Dan*, Jerusalem, 1958.
6   Albert Hyamson, *The Sephardim of England*, London, 1951.
7   Gaster, *History of the Ancient Synagogue*.
8   Israel Solomon, *Jewish Historical Society of England*, 1915.
9   Gaster, *History of the Ancient Synagogue*.
10 Ibid.
11 Ruderman, *American Academy for Jewish Research*.
12 Gaster, *History of the Ancient Synagogue*.
13 Rabbi Zevi Ashkenazi, *Responsa*.
14 Gaster, *History of the Ancient Synagogue*.
15 *Jewish Chronicle*, 10 October 1873.
16 Linda Colley, *Britons*, Vintage, 1992.
17 *Jewish Encyclopaedia*, USA, 1901.
18 Ibid.

19 David Nietto, *Esh Dat*, 1714.
20 Israel Solomon, *Jewish Historical Society of England*, 1915.
21 Rabbi Jakob Petuchowski, *The Theology of* Haham *David Nietto*, Ktav Publishing, 1954.
22 Ruderman, *American Academy for Jewish Research*.
23 Roth, *Essays and Portraits in Anglo-Jewish History*.
24 Moses Margoliouth, *History of the Jews in Great Britain*, London, 1851.

8   Aaron Hart 1705–56

At the end of the seventeenth century the Ashkenazim were the second-class citizens in English Jewry. They had very few connections with the crown or the government and they consisted primarily of refugees from central Europe. Breslau in Poland was reasonably typical of their home towns and when, in 1697, the city council made one of its periodic orders to expel its Jews, Moses Hart was among those who saw his business disappear overnight. He decided that London would give him the best chance to start afresh. His Uncle, Benjamin Levy, had done extremely well there as a merchant and if the restricted life of the ghetto, potential expulsion and penal taxation made life in Germany difficult, then London with its religious tolerance was a highly desirable alternative. Hart got it absolutely right and he made a very considerable fortune as a fashionable jeweller; he was joined a little later by his brother, Uri Phoebus, who became known in London as Aaron Hart.

If the Ashkenazim had initially had to play third and fourth fiddle to the Sephardi synagogue, this was always unlikely to go on for very long. Because Jews had to rely on themselves to survive, many of them didn't make good team players, and what is more, most preferred to be big fish in small ponds. It was a combination which led to the likelihood of a substantial breakaway and the increasing number of Ashkenazi immigrants made a proper, separate synagogue a viable possibility. The Sephardim didn't object in the slightest, so long as none of their own members defected.

Those Ashkenazim who wanted to set up on their own formed a tiny congregation started by Benjamin Levy in 1690. Their lay leadership developed under Abraham Aberle, known as Reb (Rabbi) Aberle, who clashed frequently with their rabbi, Judah Loeb ben Ephraim Cohen. For example, sometime around 1700, it is very likely that Aberle's Dirty Tricks department cut the fringes on Loeb's *tallith* before a synagogue service, rendering him improperly dressed to lead the congregation in prayer. When the problem was pointed out, it was a humiliation for the rabbi. Who had cut the fringes was never discovered, though the shammes in the synagogue was suspected.

Loeb considered himself fortunate that a vacancy occurred soon afterwards for a rabbi in Rotterdam and he gratefully accepted the office. Rabbi Aaron Moses from Poland, via the small congregation in Dublin, then officiated temporarily. He augmented his living by acting as a *shadchan* (a marriage-broker) and was often employed as a scribe, but he was no great intellectual leader, except by provincial English standards. In the Commemoration Book of the Chatham synagogue he was described as 'The Holy' and the Portsmouth community described him as one: 'who fixed times for study and devoted his soul and spirit to the service of his Creator, and whose soul went forth in purity and holiness'.

The community was strongly influenced now by Benjamin Levy's nephew, Moses Hart, who had eventually taken over his Jew Broker's seat on the Exchange. There was a general feeling that a fresh spiritual start was needed, which left the door open for Hart's older brother. Aaron Hart was born in 1670 and had been a not very successful merchant in Breslau before the expulsion. He had, however, been head of the yeshiva and was the son-in-law of Rabbi Samuel Phoebus, the famous Rabbi of Furth.

The ethos of the Ashkenazi community was different in some ways from the Sephardi congregation. The Ashkenazi in London knew the ways of the ghetto on the continent where their life had been far more spiritually intense than the Sephardi experience. The internal quarrels, however, they had in common.

Ideally, the head of the community needed to be both successful in business and a considerable scholar. Aberle was the warden (senior honorary officer) of the synagogue, a rabbi and an acknowledged tyrant. Because of the claustrophobic internal politics in a ghetto community and the traditional rows between the rabbi and the lay leaders, it wasn't always a bad thing to have a tyrant to keep order. The only problem was identified by Lord Acton, when he said, 'Power tends to corrupt and absolute power corrupts absolutely.'

Aberle ordered Aaron Hart around when the future Chief Rabbi was a young man. He persuaded Hart to take over from Loeb although Hart had expressly promised the old rabbi that he wouldn't do so when negotiating Loeb's departure. Hart went back on an oath to that effect, though he applied a fig leaf of compliance by acting as a *locum tenens* for a couple of years before accepting the spiritual mantle in 1705. He subsequently stayed in the job for the longest period of any English Chief Rabbi – more than 50 years.

Officially, his authority only stemmed from the senior lay members of the synagogue – the Vestry. Without their agreement Hart couldn't officiate at marriages or grant a divorce. He couldn't excommunicate and he couldn't deal with private quarrels. That didn't, however, mean that the lay leaders would argue with him on spiritual matters, particularly when they didn't have the talmudic knowledge of an Aberle. After all, he was Moses Hart's brother.

When the Vestry drew up the regulations for their new Great Synagogue there were 92 separate rules. If the congregation thought that was overkill, they were fortunate not to be part of the 1791 community when the number had reached 211.

Seniority in the synagogue depended, primarily, on your purse. In 1722 when the new synagogue building opened, £3.15 was enough to become a full member – Heskath ha Kehillah. By 1740 that had gone up to £10.50. These Privileged Members continued to have benefits, including the automatic right to vote, until 1870. Then there were also the *toshabim* who rented seats in the synagogue but didn't have a vote.

In 1722 the synagogue's annual revenue was £382.70. The main items were seat rental which produced £135, donations for honours in the synagogue services £190, and £50 was given for charity. The main expenditure was £150–£200 for salaries and there wasn't much money to spare for good causes. In 1708 the community in Lubin in Poland were in trouble and Bevis Marks sent them £277. The Ashkenazim managed £7.37.

Sometimes there were windfalls, though. In 1718 Jacob Mazahad, a member of Bevis Marks, died a man disgruntled with his community. In his will he left the Ashkenazim £5,000 on condition that he was buried in the Alderney Road cemetery with their people, rather than at Mile End. At a pinch they could bury him in Amsterdam on the same conditions, but for £5,000 that should have proved unnecessary.

Money also had to be found for the old ladies who fumigated the synagogue to get rid of the evil eye. Notwithstanding all the modern parallels, one difference between the eighteenth and the twenty-first centuries was the belief in superstitions. One eccentric within the community, Rabbi Samuel de Falk, was lucky to get out of Germany without being burnt as a wizard. The evil eye is the sort of curse which can be pronounced by the Wicked Witch of the West in *The Wizard of Oz*. Of course, such nonsense doesn't occur today and there are any number of people who spill salt and don't throw it over their left shoulder, or who walk under ladders. Modern Jews are equally unfazed by such eventualities and if you ask them how they are, you'll only hear 'Fine, kene hora' from a comparatively small proportion of them; maybe 25 per cent! 'Kene hora' means 'may the evil eye not fall upon me'.

An irritating item of expenditure cropped up occasionally when the local churchwardens had their own problems balancing their budgets. That £5 fine if a Jew didn't want to act as a parish officer. Just like the Sephardim. For instance, in 1707 the local churchwardens appointed Aaron Hart to the somewhat menial post of Scavenger for the district. The synagogue quickly paid the fine. The system continued for years and the parish honours weren't always refused. There are a few graves in the Willesden Jewish cemetery, dating from the nineteenth century, where the tombstones faithfully record that the interred was formerly the churchwarden of some famous city church.

The Ashkenazim in London, though small in number, typically had five paid teachers and two scribes. One of them went to the homes of members to teach the daughters of the house, for which a fee would be paid. The most eminent of the talmudists was Jochanan Holleschau, the son of Rabbi Isaac ben Hillel. The international roster of the remainder included Joseph ben Menachem Menke from Leipnik, Simcha Bunem from Pintschau, Moses ben Judah from Posen and Judah ben Mordechai Cohen from Amsterdam. All scholars whose families had survived the mediaeval pogroms and who still devoted their lives to studying and teaching the Torah. Even with all that input, Holleschau commented that the community could just about say their Hebrew prayers, while to know the Pentateuch was really exceptional and talmudic studies were nonexistent.

Whatever else might be said of Aaron Hart, he certainly looked the part. Because of the brilliance of the twelfth-century Moses Maimonides, he was compared to his biblical namesake: 'From Moses to Moses, there was no-one like Moses.' Physically, Aaron Hart was so impressive that he could have been linked with Moses' brother; from Aaron to Aaron there was no-one like Aaron. Hart was also a natural focal point for non-Jews who wanted to see what a real Jew was like: 'His picturesqueness and uniqueness gained him the interest and even the respect of the Gentile world.'[1]

He would have been anxious for the services to be conducted in a proper manner. Among other regulations, which were soon agreed at the Great, was one that ladies would not be allowed to wear crinolines in synagogue because they took up too much room, and another that you could be fined 17¹/₂p if you chewed tobacco during the services.

Soon after Hart took over from Loeb, a typical example of ghetto politics occurred and it illustrated how vitriolic such incidents could become. A member of the congregation, Ascher Ensel Cohen, wanted to make a swift getaway to the West Indies to avoid his creditors. He didn't want to take his wife and, in fairness to the lady, wanted to divorce her before he left. Obviously this had to be done in secret in case the creditors found out. Hart granted the divorce and got the documents drawn up by the Sephardi scribe, so that there was less chance of a leak than if the Ashkenazi scribes had been involved.

Another member, Mordechai Hamburger, a gem merchant and one of Aberle's competitors, denounced the paperwork when the facts became known. He pointed out that, where the details of such documents often had to be redrafted many times as compromises were reached between the parties, the Sephardi scribe had managed to get it totally acceptable first time round. It looked like a put-up job which, of course, it was. The excuse given was that the Ashkenazi scribe, Rabbi Aaron, hadn't been asked to do the work because his son-in-law had been ruined by Cohen playing cards.

To denounce a divorce granted by a properly authorized rabbi was a very serious matter indeed. There was precedent in a case before the Expulsion in mediaeval times. The punishment then had been excommunication without any chance of the ban being lifted. Hamburger, however, was one of the most respected members of the community, so it was a tricky situation. It was decided to summon him to see Hart and David Nietto, the Haham, but he didn't show up and so there was little alternative but to issue the *herem*. There are always jealous people who want to bring an important man down, and often there are VIPs who come to believe that the law doesn't apply to them. Whatever the reasons for Hamburger's downfall, the *herem* was a disaster for the merchant. His Jewish clients wouldn't deal with him, the community would have nothing to do with him and both his business and his social life were completely ruined. No ban was overlooked. At the festival of Sukkot you need access to a large lemon called an *ethrog* for an important prayer. Deliveries were bad that year and the synagogue only had one *ethrog* which Hamburger wasn't allowed to use. His new-born daughter wasn't allowed to be named in the synagogue. Hamburger was designated a non-person, even though he had been one of the most senior members of the congregation.

In isolation, this may seem far-fetched, but the point is that the Vestry had few weapons with which to keep order in the community, so those they had they used to maximum effect.

Hamburger eventually decided to fight back by starting his own synagogue in his home. This would have got him excommunicated on its own, because Aberle had appealed to the Beth Din to issue a *herem* on any group which seceded from the congregation. It was the same ruling as Bevis Marks, but Hamburger was now beyond caring what the Great congregation might do. Holleschau agreed to become the rabbi.

The Great responded by trying to get the City Fathers to decree that there had only been permission given for one Ashkenazi synagogue. This the court confirmed, but Hamburger ignored that ruling as well. What's more he appealed to Rabbi Zevi Ashkenazi to rule on the validity of the *herem* over the divorce. Ashkenazi was a friend of Aberle and related to Aaron Hart. He had already given a ruling in favour of David Nietto in the 'God is Nature' row, so the chances were that he'd come down on the side of the authorities again. Not a bit of it. Ashkenazi decided that the *herem* had been unduly harsh. In this ruling, he quoted support from rabbinic leaders in Altona, Amsterdam and Rotterdam. This time it was Aberle who refused to back down and he also persuaded the synagogue authorities to decree that Hamburger couldn't be buried in their cemetery – when he decided to die. In spite of all this the breakaway synagogue continued to operate, even after Hamburger departed to distant parts of the Empire to try to restore his fortunes.

The City authorities took no action and, after some years, Hamburger returned, once again a rich man. He saw the breakaway community develop and eventually build a substantial synagogue called the Hambro, which opened in 1721. It wasn't named after Hamburger himself, but because the ritual in the synagogue followed the Hamburg format. By 1721 the congregation had already been excommunicated for 15 years, as Aberle had arranged for Hart to declare another *herem* on Hamburger's supporters in 1705, when the idea first came up. It wasn't to be the last occasion when a breakaway synagogue was treated in a similar manner.

Nobody came out of the Cohen divorce smelling of roses, except Zevi Ashkenazi. Only the sage sought peace in the community and was totally incorruptible. Indeed when he moved to Poland, the rabbi sold his silver plate to pay for the journey rather than accept a gift from his many admirers. When you consider that he could have accepted an offer of a vast £500 a year to become a Sephardi Haham, but turned it down because he wanted to stay with his Ashkenazi brethren, the sage was a remarkable man and six of his descendants became Chief Rabbis of Britain. In 2004 a ruling he gave 250 years before – on not needing to celebrate the second day of festivals if you were in the Holy Land – was the precedent for Dayan Lopian giving the same responsa for his congregation in North London.

The new Great Synagogue was only opened in 1722 with Moses Hart, Aaron Franks and Lazarus Simon as the three senior honorary officers. They would figure large in the early years of the synagogue. Hart had spent £2,000 on the building, which was put up on the old site. In 1718 it had been the opinion of the attorney general that the Jews could own land, which removed another disability, though it wasn't tested in court. Franks was a jeweller who had come from Hanover and was a good friend of the future George II. Indeed he lent him some particularly fine jewels to improve the appearance of the crown used for the king's coronation. Simon married Hart's sister, Margoshes, making him the Chief Rabbi's brother-in-law – it was a tightly knit family group. Simon took over Hart's seat as a Jew Broker in later years and, when Simon died in 1764, he was able to leave a vast £3,500 to the poor in his will.

Aberle was eventually ruined when he lost a court case, even though Ashkenazi this time acted for him. Aberle also recovered, like Hamburger, but he was finally bankrupted by his son, who blew the family fortune on a trip to Paris.

With Aberle's fall from grace, the effective lay leadership of the Great community moved without opposition to the wardens. Moses Hart added to his wealth by winning a £20,000 lottery in 1719 with Frank's son, Isaac Franks. When his gambling partner married his daughter, Hart's half became her dowry. Some Jews continued to flourish in the Indian diamond trade and between 1717 and 1766 there were only four years when Christian merchants imported more than Jewish ones. The diamonds were normally paid for in silver. When there was a shortage of specie the Jews switched to paying in coral, which they got from Leghorn, where their co-religionists conveniently controlled the market.

Over the half century of his ministry Hart's position grew in importance until he was accepted as Chief Rabbi of the Ashkenazi community throughout the country. In some ways his path to such eminence was easier than it would have been on the continent. To begin with, he had no local competition. In European countries where there were many Jewish communities, the most eminent rabbis might live in almost any town. A talmudist in Hamburg might find just as great a scholar in the Hanover community. In Italy the sage in Leghorn might be contradicted by the expert in Venice. In Britain there was one major, recognized Ashkenazi rabbi and he was at the Great Synagogue in London.

On the Continent it was very unlikely that the greatest rabbi would be found in the capital city because the Jews were often barred from living there at all. Jews couldn't officially live in Paris until 1750, in Vienna until 1753 and in Brussels until 1794. They were expelled from Prague from 1745–48 and from Moscow in 1791 and again in 1798, and they weren't allowed, of course, in any part of Spain and Portugal.[2]

In Europe the Jews, perforce, established communities in smaller towns and, in particular, in those major ports; Leghorn, Hamburg and Antwerp. In England, Aaron Hart and his successors had a clear run in London. The Chief Rabbinate 'has wielded authority of a type and extent that is rarely, if ever, to be found elsewhere, at least since the close of the Gaonic period'.[3]

Which is saying a lot because the Gaonic period covered the sixth to the eleventh centuries in Babylon. There were two great Jewish academies (yeshivas) and if you got to the very top – you were the Gaon – your rulings were likely to be accepted throughout the Jewish world. It is certain that, purely in terms of academic ability, very few British Chief Rabbis would have been candidates for that role in Babylon. There were, however, never any yeshivas of note in England until the twentieth century.

Of course, it also made it easier to make mistakes when there were no authoritative views available on your rulings. For example, Aaron Hart could have kept the peace in the Hamburger case. On another occasion in the early days there was a dispute between a teacher and the father of the pupil. The question was whether the teacher had done his job properly. Hart told the teacher to declare on oath that he had. The community's parents thought this was a splendid idea. Now they all wanted their own teachers to swear a similar oath. Holleschau said it was against the Din, which it was, and that idea had to be allowed to die quietly.

Another advantage for an English Chief Rabbi, compared to Europe, was that the spiritual leader wasn't in competition with the court Jew. 'Anglo-Jewry rambled along, with the Law Courts and the City of London more stable protectors than Princes' favourites.'[4]

The influx of Jews into Britain during Hart's ministry quadrupled the Jewish population. A considerable number came from Germany as soon as George I was crowned. The immigrants were mostly poor and mostly young. In the Portsmouth congregation, for example, 90 per cent were under 40. They had come because there was a chance to make a decent living. They were in no danger of being held back by the rules of the state, as they would have been at home. If they were paupers, the London Jewish community wanted both to help them and get rid of them. So they were often given some seed-corn money to get started as a pedlar. With their tiny stock of goods, they became a regular sight on the provincial roads and among the villages and hamlets of Britain. By the end of the century it was estimated there were 1,500 of them and they created a number of new communities in the provinces.[5]

They led a perilous existence, both financially and in their occupations. In Penzance, for example, the community could only afford to pay £1 a year to the official who acted as hazan, shochet and Hebrew teacher. When travelling the district, the pedlars were easy game for highwaymen and muggers, as they carried their stock, and the money they earned from it, along lonely roads. Many were killed in the course of the robberies.

Poor, impoverished immigrants traditionally got a bad press. It is usually suggested that they are poor because they are idle, and likely to become thieves and fraudsters to improve their standard of living. On occasions this was obviously true, as any other scenario would probably be as well. The synagogue itself was robbed of £300 in valuables by a Jew in 1748. In 1755 a pair of silver bells disappeared. Condemned as grossly negligent, the two unfortunate beadles, who should have taken better care, were severely punished; one was suspended for six months and the other was fined £10.50 which was more than a year's salary.

The fact remains, however, that economic migrants, seeking a better life, are often the cream of the home crop. Rather than bemoan their fate and sink into apathy and despair, they choose one of Hamlet's options and take arms against a sea of troubles and, by opposing, often end them. Certainly, Britain has benefited from successive waves of migrants over the centuries; from Flemish weavers to Italian restaurateurs. Many Jews at the ports were able to do better than trade as pedlars. In 1747 in King's Lynn, 25 per cent of the community acted as ship agents, providing stores for the ships and handling some or all of their cargo.

When the immigrants formed congregations outside the capital, they still looked to London for spiritual advice, as they had looked to it for financial help when they first arrived. The rabbi of the Great Synagogue was the one who would settle any remotely complex questions in Jewish law, because there would be nobody in their own community who could do so.

Some questions had more than one answer; was turbot kosher, for instance? To be acceptable, the fish had to have fins and scales. A visiting group of Italian rabbis said it was certainly considered alright in Venice. Some varieties of turbot are more doubtful. The Ashkenazi London Beth Din was still intermittently reviewing the position well into the twentieth century.

Hart was contracted to deal with all responsa and to give two sermons a year; before Passover and Yom Kippur. Of course, he often gave more. He also had agreed to say the special prayers for rain and dew at the appropriate times of the year and the concluding service at the end of Yom Kippur. Orthodox Jews pray for rain throughout the winter, and there isn't much likelihood of their prayers going unheeded in northern Europe. They were not, however, praying for English farmers, they were praying for rain in the Holy Land – it was in ways such as this that the umbilical cord between their home and Jerusalem remained intact.

The Jews were particularly adept at surviving in foreign countries, because they had had so much practice. They knew the rules of the game and they tried very hard to make a go of it. The integration always involved adopting some of the practices of the host community and among the first stirrings of Anglicization was the adoption of canonicals by the synagogue hazans by the time Hart died. Canonicals were originally academic dress and a portrait of Manasseh ben Israel shows him wearing them. The fuss about the reintroduction of the habit in the nineteenth-century era of the Adlers linked canonicals with imitating the Christian Church. When, however, Chief Rabbi Jakobovits was asked in the twentieth century whether one of his congregations should be opposed in its wish for its rabbi to wear canonicals, he told them: 'They're not worth a fight.'[6]

The Great and the Hambro communities could now find money for the poor to get started as pedlars and they were generous to those who couldn't help themselves. Between them in 1739 they distributed £1,000 to charity. The two synagogues eventually agreed that no more than 20 per cent of their annual income should be distributed in this way. Outspending the other community was an expensive way of keeping up with the Cohens. On occasions, members of the congregation also remembered the poor in their wills. When Isaac Franks died in 1736 he left £2,500 for coals, clothing and food, to be given at the New Year and Purim to: 'poor German Jews and their families in England'. He also left Hart £100 to pray for his soul.

Small congregations were also founded in London. They were in the tradition of the continental *shtiebl*, where a small group of very Orthodox Jews would gather together for study and prayer. While the Great would take considerable offence at the creation of major new communities like the Hambro, these smaller congregations were tolerated. There was one, for example, in what was Rosemary Lane near the Tower of London, in the centre of the old clothes trade, which was founded in 1748.

On occasions an attempt was made to form a united front with the Sephardim. Attempts to produce a single *kashrut* body in 1745 came to nothing, but then both communities still have their separate Kashrus Commissions in 2006. At least in 1751 there was full agreement about the dangers of proselytization. All the synagogues announced simultaneously that anybody who converted a Christian would be expelled from the community and barred from all the cemeteries.

Hart would also grant certificates to shochetim and issue the appropriate marriage licences. That was how he became the first Chief Rabbi of all the British Ashkenazi communities. However, he was less involved in deciding civil points of law than he might have been at home in Poland. One traditional responsibility of a rabbi is to give decisions in cases of civil litigation. In Europe the Jewish community relied on the disinterested judgement of a rabbi, more than the potentially prejudiced civil courts. In England this was not the case; the law was equally disinterested in who was the plaintiff and who was the defendant. As Holleschau said in admiration: 'If a man give them a houseful of gold and silver they would do no injustice or wrongdoing but act only as is written in their lawbooks.'[7]

In 1749 Chief Justice Willes said in court when it was once again questioned whether a Jew could sue a Christian: 'we are commanded by our Saviour to do good unto all men and not only unto those who are of the household of the faith.'

In the same year the question came up of whether Jews could be trustworthy witnesses if they couldn't swear as a Christian. Lord Hardwicke, the Lord Chancellor, held: 'that all persons who believe in a supreme being, who will punish them if they swear falsely, are competent witnesses, and should take the oath in the form binding on them according to the tenets of their religion'.

There was no such thing as the *More Judaico* which was to be found in some European countries. These were laws that could force a Jew in court to take the oath standing on a pigskin. Before the

Jew's evidence started, he had to call down on himself the most appalling curses to be found in Leviticus if he didn't tell the truth. This went on in France until 1846, in Prussia until 1869 and into the twentieth century in Rumania. The hatred was such that you could almost see the Holocaust gas ovens on the horizon.

So the English Chief Rabbis had little to do with civil law disputes. Mind you, the Mahamad and the Vestry might encourage the congregation to settle their disputes without disturbing the non-Jewish bench, but they couldn't enforce it. If they tried the threat of herem there was the chance that the sinner would tell all to the civil court and then the fat would really be in the fire; trying to pervert the course of justice. There were also times when the Beth Din couldn't settle the argument to the satisfaction of both parties and then the Vestry or Mahamad would reluctantly give permission for the litigants to try the civil court. So, if an English Rabbi forgot some of the 4th Tractate in the Shulchan Aruch, which deals with Civil Law, he wasn't the final appeal court anyway after the Resettlement.

Every Chief Rabbi would like to see a flourishing yeshiva within his authority but yeshivas are very expensive to run. The scholars and students have to live, and supporting them to a reasonable level is a substantial drain on the charitable funds of any community. After about 30 years Hart did manage to found a Talmud Torah which was ultimately incorporated into the Jews Free School in the nineteenth century, but it only had 15 pupils and was a long way from being a continental yeshiva, though all the teaching was in Yiddish.

There is a Jewish saying about the vagaries of good fortune that 'every day isn't Yomtov (a festival)' but it must have seemed that a good day had dawned when Elias de Pass died in 1743 and left £1,200 in his will to build and maintain a proper yeshivah. Unfortunately the legality of the bequest was tested in the courts. Lord Hardwicke, the Lord Chancellor, this time ruled against the community, holding that the legacy was illegal: 'This is a bequest for the propagation of the Jewish religion: and though it is said that this is part of our religion, yet the intent of that bequest must be taken to be in contradiction of the Christian religion, which is a part of the law of the land.'

In addition, it was held that to create a yeshiva was to encourage superstition, which was also against the law. Hardwicke said James II's Toleration Act didn't cover the Jews. So the £1,200 was seized and given to a Christian orphanage to support the salary of a chaplain to preach Christianity. We can only imagine what a blow this must have been to the ageing Chief Rabbi, but this was a rare occasion when it was decided to carry out a discriminatory law against the Jews. Religious laws of the land were normally ignored in their favour. What tended to happen after the de Pass case was that money was left to relatives with instructions on which charities the deceased wished to benefit from the legacy.

The pinpricks of minor discrimination were aggravating but usually little more. One problem was with burials. Aaron Hart was obviously called upon to officiate at many funerals and Jews are always buried in the simplest of coffins with the simplest of shrouds. In death the rich and the poor are treated identically. A seventeenth-century English law, created to encourage the textile industry, laid down that anybody who died had to be buried in a woollen shroud or pay a fine to the parish in which they were interred. The Jewish view was that when you're being buried is no time to disobey the Talmud and so every burial in the Mile End cemetery incurred a fine. The income from the fines was large enough for discussions to take place on whether just one parish should get all the benefit. An order was made to impose: 'fines on Jews for not burying in wool in Mile End hamlet to be divided among all hamlets in Stepney Parish'.[8]

By this time the cemetery bought for the community by Benjamin Levy was getting full anyway. To avoid the need to buy more land, a thick layer of earth was put over the south-west corner of the grounds, sufficient to enable another layer of graves to be constructed. To mark the presence of two bodies, the tombstones were put back to back. Even going to these extremes, more land eventually had to be found and a new cemetery was opened in 1749. Nathan Nathan was the cemetery-keeper for the next 50 years. It was no sinecure – in 1758 he drew his sword to arrest a burglar. The graves needed guarding against vandals and robbers, but then in the eighteenth century, at night, a gentleman needed an armed guard to go from Hyde Park Corner in London just down the road to Knightsbridge. There was one splendidly sensitive regulation for funerals. All the family mourners were provided with identical black mourner's cloaks. In this way it was impossible to tell whether the family were rich or poor – a lovely touch.

By the end of the reign of George II in 1760 the Jewish community in Britain was among the richest in the world however, that didn't mean there was no poverty in the community. There was a very great deal indeed, which affected the vast majority of the Jews, but the rich were very rich, something which was true even earlier in the century. When Joseph Levy died from the after-effects of an operation for a stone – an operation which Pepys had survived years before – the British Gazeteer recalled that he had: 'supplied Prince Eugene with £30,000 when he was here in the late Queen Anne's time'.

In today's money, that was somewhere between £5–6 million. The status of the Chief Rabbi as a reliable witness is further evidenced by the fact that Levy decided to make a noncupative will just before the operation. That's a will made by telling such witnesses what you want done in the event of your death. Even today a noncupative will does not have to be written down.

There is only one record of Hart in his old age and that was when he was visited by an evangelist who wanted to convert him to Christianity. As we've seen, other rabbis had voluntarily converted in the past and would do so again. It would certainly have been a considerable feather in Edward Goulding's cap had he succeeded. As he reported: 'Mr. Aaron Hart, an eminent and very aged High Priest who, as they said, his life and conversation were unblemishable.'⁹ Hart politely declined apostasy, pointing out that Judaism had been good enough for his father and grandfather and he saw no reason for changing.

Moses Hart died in 1756, full of years and honour. Among his other bequests was £1,000 to provide kosher food for patients at the London Hospital, an institution which was always to be closely associated with the Jewish community.

Aaron Hart finally passed away at the age of 86, a few months before his brother. He had been hard at work until the end. A few years earlier, in 1750, he had abrogated the 1706 *herem* on the Hambro synagogue. Keeping up with the times, he had also made sure that there was a regulation forbidding you to bring your sedan chair within the portals of the synagogue. Like travelling to *shul* by car in the twenty-first century, it was highly indelicate to leave the forbidden vehicle in clear sight of the congregation. Agreed, a sedan chair didn't have an engine, but it did have two men carrying it. If they brought a passenger in it to the synagogue on the Sabbath they were working – and that was against the Din.

For a man who was a British rabbinic leader for 50 years, Hart left nothing like as much behind him as David Nietto managed in half the time. The influence of first Aberle and then his brother, Moses, seems to have left him with little of the limelight, but Aaron Hart laid a lot of the groundwork for the future Ashkenazi community in Britain.

To start with, there is no doubt that it was in Hart's time that the concept of a Chief Rabbi was accepted by Jewish Ashkenazi communities throughout Britain. When the Penzance community offered up a prayer for past Chief Rabbis, Aaron Hart was the first on the list. If there was never any competition for a unique institution, that says a great deal for the respect and affection Hart must have built in his ministry. In addition, in Hart's period in office the size of the Great grew substantially and many provincial congregations were successfully created and developed. It is also to his credit that the administration of the community had, in his later years, none of the unseemly arguments which marred the ministries of Isaac Nietto. At the end he 'had authority and eminence'.[10]

Politically, the relationship between the Jewish community and the government remained very cordial and even the opposition to the Jew Bill was soon forgotten once the legislation had been rescinded. Because Hart didn't often make the headlines, his achievements have been credited to the lay leaders, but in spiritual matters his would have been the voice which carried the most weight.

NOTES

1   Norman Cohen, *Non-Religious Factors in the Emergence of the Chief Rabbinate*, Jewish Historical Society of England, 1962–67.
2   Ibid.
3   Ibid.
4   Ibid.
5   Communities officially founded or refounded in Aaron Hart's time included Exeter, 1728, Birmingham, 1730, Hull, 1730, Plymouth and Falmouth, 1740, Portsmouth, 1747, and Liverpool and Chatham, 1750.
6   Lady Jakobovits in conversation with the author.
7   Cecil Roth, *History of the Great Synagogue*, Edward Goldston, 1950.
8   Ibid.
9   Ibid.
10 Charles Duschinsky, *Jacob Kimchi and Shalom Buzaglo*, Jewish Historical Society of England, 1913.

9 Isaac Nietto 1733–41 and Moses Gomez de Mesquita 1744–51

Isaac Nietto was born in Leghorn in 1687 to the Jewish purple. He was the son of David Nietto, the distinguished Leghorn Dayan, the famous doctor, the man who had proved that the Christian calendar was inferior to the Jewish, a man quite capable of giving responsa on civil as well as religious matters. As a child, all the notables in the community knew who Isaac was and smiled on him as his father's son. As an adolescent in London, he would be pointed out as one of the Haham's family. He was the son of an icon.

There are indeed many advantages to being the offspring of a great man. One of the problems you face eventually, however, is how to be known for yourself. To get out from under the shadow of the Dad who made it easier for you to get on at the start.

When his father took up his new position as Haham to the London community in 1702, Isaac was 15. A year later an orphanage was started for poor, fatherless boys – the Saare Orah Veabi Yetomim (Gates of Light and Father of the Orphans). One of the orphan boys gave an address to the congregation and this was followed by further *droshas* by the Haham's two sons, Moses and Isaac. It was an opportunity to give the stage to members of the Haham's family and it emphasized their learning. It seems unlikely they would have been chosen, however, had they been the children of just any Yehidim.

In his privileged position, it was Isaac who was marked down for a rabbinic career and he would have had fine tutors. Nevertheless, it takes many years of hard study to acquire sufficient knowledge to obtain *semicha* and Isaac achieved this, much to his father's pleasure. As a favourite in the community, a later Haham, Moses Gaster, commented: 'He seems to have been a man of amiable disposition rather than commanding intellect.'[1]

Gaster, however, set very high standards and his own translation of the Sephardi prayer book did acknowledge its debt to Nietto's own excellent work on the material. As Isaac's father grew older – there were 33 years between father and son – Isaac would have been able to take some of the day-to-day burden off his shoulders. He was always a scholar and there were 12 talmudic pupils to be taught in the new Beth Hamedresh. He married late, at 41, after his father died in 1728. His wife was Rebecca Carion de Taiba and he had at least two children – Phineas and Esther.

In David Nietto's last years, he was not a well man and more of the work of the Haham was delegated to Isaac. When the Haham passed away, Isaac spoke movingly at the funeral and then took on most of the responsibilities of spiritual leadership of the Sephardi community for the next four years. In 1733 he was finally appointed Haham and accepted the office as the logical successor. His salary was set at £85 a year plus £20 extra every Purim. It was less than his father had received and the fact that it had taken five years to appoint a man in his forties, who was properly qualified and had a distinguished lineage, suggests that at least some of the senior members of the community had doubts about him. Had the apple, perhaps, fallen some distance from the bough on this occasion? It was true, however, that he was succeeding a most eminent rabbi and probably the congregation looked around for a while to see if there was anybody else, equally eminent, who might have been available. It is also often the case that, when you've known someone since they were a child, it's easy for them to seem inadequate for high office.

The previous year had seen a further bright illustration of the enormous difference between England and the Continent of Europe, when it came to religious tolerance for the Jewish community.

In the case of Rex *vs.* Osborne in 1732 the publishers of a newspaper had decided to print a tabloid-type story exhuming the infamous blood libel. This time both a woman and her child were supposed to have been murdered by the Jews who were said to need their blood for religious purposes. Where this had so often before led to riots and pogroms, and would again overseas, this time it did not, although there may have been ugly rumblings among the yobbos in the streets – after all, this was Hogarth's London; the artist of Gin Alley captured for all time the drunken condition of the mob. It was, however, the anti-Semitic publishers who were arrested and tried before the King's Bench for seditious libel. The finding, as there wasn't a scintilla of proof to support the vicious rumour, was guilty as charged. The court held that their accusation was likely: 'to raise tumult and disorder among the people and influence them with a spirit of universal barbarity against a whole body of men, as if guilty of crimes scarcely practicable and totally incredible'.

The judges went on to find that: 'the publication was an

inflammatory libel upon the Jewish community as such, and ordered it to be withdrawn from circulation. This was the sum total of the more violent manifestations of anti-Semitism in England in the century after the Resettlement.'[2]

It's worth remembering this when we come later in Isaac Nietto's ministry to the storm over the Jew Bill in 1753. Then there was anger, but not vicious hatred and successive governments resisted extremism. As Professor Rubinstein points out: 'Remarkably, group defamation against Jews was held to be illegal in English law.'[3] This was a totally incredible degree of tolerance almost anywhere in Europe at that time. The court even went on to give the Jews legal protection against: 'generic libels which might threaten life'.

Mind you, whatever the courts said, the community remained paranoid about the true nature of the society among which they lived. 'Something like the Inquisition could happen here', 'You could easily get another Chmielnicki', 'They all hate us really' would have always been there in the back of countless Jewish minds. The lessons of hundreds of years are not so easily forgotten. The fear was fuelled by these occasional, reasonably minor events but the truth was – and would remain – that it *couldn't* happen in England. The English ruling classes and the Church of England simply didn't do religious fanaticism, although they came close to it with the Catholics. It was easier to know that in retrospect, however, than at the time.

The British were still extremely anti-Catholic – and superstitious. In 1727 a witch was executed in Scotland. It was the last execution of a witch in Britain but Bevis Marks members couldn't be expected to see into the future. The community looked to its security, typically paying £2 in 1736, £4 in 1737 and £3.15p in 1738 to the city marshal and the constables 'for keeping the rabble quiet'.

The rabble wasn't the problem in 1738. The problem was a major fire in the immediate vicinity of Bevis Marks which threatened the building. It happened on a Friday night and with the help of firemen, soldiers and watchmen it was put out, but it was a close-run thing. The roof was badly damaged and, although the synagogue was insured for £1,000, it cost £1,700 to repair and the work wasn't completed until 1749. Nearly £2,500 was donated by the generous members to help those who had lost their possessions in the blaze. There was another serious conflagration in 1741, in which the synagogue was fortunately spared again, but in 1744 it wasn't possible to save the valuable synagogue silver from a burglar. In spite of offering a large reward, it was never recovered. It took £1,700 to replace and eight years to pay for.

There would be occasions which Nietto would enjoy during his ministry. Like the service to celebrate the recovery of Queen Caroline from a serious illness in 1737. Overall, however, Nietto found himself under a lot of pressure:

> Who knows what may have contributed to embitter his life, what internal dissension in the community may have caused him to accept the post reluctantly, and to make him throw it up after he had served the community, as they themselves said, for 16 years with signal devotion to duty without a blemish or fault?[4]

One logical explanation was that: 'Both father and son suffered from attacks from critical, dissatisfied or jealous congregants.'[5]

Dissension in the Sephardi community also arose from the rows that erupted between the Mahamad and individual Yehidim. Even if you left the congregation altogether, it could still cost you money! In 1730 it had been agreed with the Yehidim that anybody who went over to the Ashkenazi Great Synagogue could be fined and Nietto signed the resolution.

In 1737 a Yahid defected to the Great. As a result, he was denounced in the synagogue on the Sabbath and then a special meeting of the Yehidim was called for the following Sunday morning. The Mahamad asked and received from the meeting:

> you would be pleased to give power to the Mahamad, at the same time for them to afflict on the delinquent, or delinquents, at a general meeting of the said Elders, pecuniary and other penalties enabling them to enforce the same, under conditions that the said Elders should never consent to there being any other synagogue than the present one.[6]

On that point they would remain rigid for more than another 100 years. The Mahamad members were only elected for a year at a time and, of course, could be fined if they refused to accept office. The candidates were nominated by the existing members and, therefore, could constitute a self-perpetuating group. The Elders were also available in any kind of crisis and they were composed of ex-members of the Mahamad. There were still disagreements in plenty. Of the 71 members elected during the period, there were 21 refusals to serve. One, Moses Lamego, refused three times. Nobody was elected more than four times during the 10 years; Benjamin Moses da Costa did the four stints and it was he who bought the rest of the Bevis Marks leasehold in 1747. He paid nearly £4,000 – 28½ years purchase at the rent of £135 a year. The freehold was bought much later. He wasn't in office when the cemetery freehold was bought from the lord of the manor in 1737. The community had to pay £200 for that, a large sum, but the owner said the property had been improved over the years by the landscaping the community had carried out! Whether that was anti-Semitism, sharp practice or striking a hard bargain, depends on your attitude. It certainly contrasted unfavourably with Mr Avis, the Quaker builder of Bevis Marks who wouldn't take a penny profit for the work.

Only five members were elected on three occasions, but the picture that emerges is of a small group of men who were often connected by marriage or were members of the same families; there were six different Mendes da Costas and five Fernandes on the Mahamad during the period. In all, 44 members of the synagogue held office during the decade and 21 of them were only elected once.

Those who didn't play the game from within their own ranks horrified the Mahamad even more. In 1745 Jacob Israel Bernal, who was the presiding officer at the time, resigned his position and applied for permission to marry an Ashkenazi Jewess. Even considering his eminence – he had held the same post in 1732 and was on the Mahamad in 1736 and 1740 – the conditions on which he was eventually allowed to do so were draconian. The members of the Beth Din and the hazan were forbidden to go to the wedding. Bernal wasn't to be called up, no *shnodering* was allowed in his name and no celebrations could take place at Bevis Marks. Bernal's name disappears for ever from the conclave of the Mahamad, and this was a man who could afford to settle £1,500 on his wife when they married.

Soon after David Nietto's death, the daily, Sabbath and new moon services were privately translated into English in 1729. It's difficult to know who did the work and for whom, because only one copy of the manuscript exists. There are a number of inaccuracies but the translations, overall, were in the future to be given the approval of no less an authority than Simeon Singer, and Singer's prayer book is still in use in a large number of British Orthodox congregations. However, the errors certainly wouldn't have passed Isaac Nietto's eagle eye and the prayers were probably translated for private use. Abraham Mears had also produced a translation in 1736 but the Mahamad refused to sanction it and, for Orthodox community prayers, there has to be common approval of the text.

In 1738 there had been the first public attempt to translate the prayers into English. The bashful author's nom de plume was

Gamaliel ben Pedauzur and his work included not only lots of mistakes, but also some questionably theatrical instructions, such as, 'The Reader goes on with a loud voice.' Future translators would tackle the obscurer elements of the material with more success than Pedauzur who was, not the least embarrassed to explain to his readers that: 'This paragraph of Rabbi Yeshmoel is just the same incoherence in the Hebrew as it is here in the English.'

Moses Nietto, the Haham's brother also asked for permission to translate the prayers into English and this was also refused. The Mahamad were motivated by a strong belief that once the process of change was started, there was no way of knowing where it would stop. Step into the unknown and unforced errors are going to lose you points with other communities around the world. The way to keep everyone singing from the same hymn book is not to change the hymn book. Moses Nietto tried to ignore the Mahamad and continue the printing, but he was fined and threatened with being thrown out of the community. He soon caved in.

Another attempt was made to produce a new translation and it was 'thundered forth from the tebah [pulpit] that all Yehidim were strictly enjoined not to have so dangerous a book in their possession.'[7] If you were found to have the book, you could be fined £5.

Nietto achieved much more. During his period of office he honed his skills as a linguist and in 1740 he produced a much better translation of the New Year and Yom Kippur prayers into Spanish than had been seen before: 'The English translation by Pinto (years later) is based on Isaac Nietto's Spanish one. Alexander and de Sola [later translators] speak well of it.'[8]

Nietto's opinion on the previous attempts to translate the prayers into Spanish didn't beat about the bush. He said of the Spanish idiom used that it was in: 'Un Castillano-Hebraico que no es ni Hebraico ni Castillano. [A kind of Spanish-Hebrew which is neither Hebrew nor Spanish.]'[9] In fact, translators of Sephardi prayers in England do seem to like taking pot-shots at the competition. The first complete translator, David Levi, would follow suit in 1789 by saying of his predecessors' efforts that: 'they had been executed in a manner so faulty, defective and erroneous, as tended rather to bring disgrace on the service, than to recommend and explain it'.

De Sola in the 1837 edition would then say of Levi's poetical prayer translations: 'he is very unsuccessful in transfusing the spirit of the original which completely disappears among the mass of unnecessary Hebraisms and pleonasms [longer phrases than needed] that obscure the sense of his version'. Only de Sola's edition escaped any criticism by Haham Moses Gaster when a new version appeared in 1901.

In the meantime a number of members of the mid-eighteenth-century synagogue were prospering. The state of the economy made good profits possible from many types of activity: 'Profits from servicing the war machine; profits as more and more colonies were won; profits from new markets forced open by naval power and treaties; profits from cheaper raw materials and exotic commodities.'[10]

The impost on the turnover in business of members could bring in as much as £2,000 a year, with a single yahid contributing £100 or £200. The Great's annual income was nothing like this. The favourable conditions enabled the successful Sephardi members to be generous in their charity. In 1730 the Villa Real School for Girls was endowed and this enabled an initial intake of 16 poor Sephardi girls to benefit from the tuition. This was remarkably in advance of its time. The education of girls just wasn't a consideration in the general community until well into the nineteenth century, and even then it hardly applied to poor girls. In addition, both schools in 1736 started to teach English, where before they had only taught Hebrew. This was as a result of a reorganization of the Beth Hamedresh in 1733, but it would be necessary to have another in 1758 and a third in 1759. Neither good intentions nor financial support were lacking.

The problem which perpetually plagued the community over the years was the quality of the teaching. Obviously, there were good and dedicated teachers, but there were far more who weren't up to the job. Villa Real would be in existence for 190 years and the Ashkenazi community couldn't compete, managing only a Beth Hamedresh in the eighteenth century. In *A Peep into the Synagogue*, an unpleasant piece of mid-eighteenth-century scuttlebutt, the apostate author took the proffered hammer and clobbered the educators: 'these teachers are in general masters of much hypocrisy, cunning and deceit. Thus it is, they get a little money to begin the world with'.

Had the teachers been better, the congregation would have been much strengthened but the importance of children's education was always easier proclaimed than done. Being better than the Ashkenazim, however, was a game of one-upmanship that the Mahamad took seriously. The Ashkenazim fumed at the superiority of the Sephardi congregation but it was difficult to deny. For example, the Sephardim could travel to Paris without a passport, but the Ashkenazim had to go through stringent customs regulations before they were allowed in.

More generosity – this time from Benjamin Mendes da Costa – enabled a yeshivah – Mahane Rephael – to be founded in 1735. Da Costa provided £1,900 in South Sea Company shares and they were converted into long-term annuities. In spite of the scandal of the South Sea Bubble, the company actually survived until 1853. The yeshiva increased Nietto's income, as he was offered £12.60 a year to preside over it and to take a personal interest in its work. The Haham was delighted to accept.

There was, however, another side to the prosperity coin. Additional wealth made it possible for some of the more prominent members to buy estates for themselves in the country and they would go off at the weekends to enjoy an English gentleman's way of life. In England at the time the landed gentry took a keen interest in commerce and there was little of the snobbery against people in 'trade' which would emerge in the nineteenth century. Obviously, it was easier to be welcomed into such society if you were Protestant and a number of the most prominent Sephardim left the community to become just that, or to convert their children to Christianity. It was a continuous process and if the Sephardi community had not been reinforced by new waves of immigration from overseas, it would have shrivelled. For example, that same Moses Lamego, who had turned down office three times, gave £5,000 to the synagogue in 1757 in memory of his son who had died; £4,000 went to the Orphan Society and £1,000 to pay for an English master at the school. By the nineteenth century, however, the Lamegos were no longer members of the community.

The congregations overseas were frequently in a less comfortable financial condition. In 1737 the Venetian synagogue, the grand-mother of the London community, was in such trouble that Bevis Marks raised nearly £5,000 for it. Officially, the money was a loan – it would have been less embarrassing for the proud Venetians – and a nominal 2 per cent interest was agreed. The Venetians would pay the capital back in 10 half-yearly instalments when things improved. Only they never did; the 2 per cent was paid until 1802 when the Venetians said they could no longer afford it and the capital repayment remains outstanding.

Other cries for help came from communities as far distant as the Holy Land, Rhode Island, Persia, Bohemia and Moravia. Bevis Marks did its best to help and, in the traditional manner, considered it their duty to do so. In 1729 they had made a donation to the building of the Sephardi synagogue in New York, and Jacob Mendes da Costa also gave the American congregation money for a school. In their turn, the Americans responded to requests for help from

Europe when they could. Contributions came for both Safed and Lisbon during the period. Closer to home the Ashkenazi Dublin community asked the Great for financial help to build a wall round their cemetery. The Vestry refused, so Dublin asked Bevis Marks, who sent a donation.

Charity wasn't the only need, however. During the 1730s the colonial government put a tax on merchants dealing with the West Indies. This would have severely affected the Jews in Jamaica and they wrote to Bevis Marks for help in 1736. As a result, a delegation of 39 Sephardim called on George II and asked for the tax to be remitted, which the king graciously arranged.

London's influence continued to grow in the New World: 'By 1748 the influence of Bevis Marks synagogue in London became dominant in the organizational structure of Shearith Israel [New York]. This manifested itself in the creation of a body of Elders, on the pattern of Bevis Marks.'[11]

Poor Jews continued to come to London in considerable numbers. There were a lot of immigrants from Italy and the eastern Mediterranean who could replace the defections from the English ranks. The need to support the indigent stretched the community's resources, however, and the Mahamad set out to get them to move on to other countries. During Nietto's ministry they managed to obtain grants of land in Georgia for paupers who fancied emigrating to that part of the American colonies. Few took them up on it, though, any more than they fancied South Carolina a few years later. A short-lived community did start in Liverpool from which the boats left for America, but there wasn't much call for that either.

In 1749 the Mahamad would try again, this time trumpeting the attractions of Nova Scotia in Canada, with a similar lack of success. The prospective migrants could well have heard stories of the very overambitious efforts of the Scots to develop a colony in South America on which they had spent much of the national wealth earlier in the century. It was a disastrous flop and resulted in the Act of Union with England in 1707, when the Westminster Parliament, as part of the deal, promised to give the Scottish investors back the money they'd lost. Economically the Scots might have seen this as recovery, but so many of the prospective settlers had died of various diseases that migration into the unknown became a far less attractive prospect to the man in the street.

In one instance the offer of help to a congregation received no reply. Word had reached London of the Jewish community in China and Nietto wrote asking them to say if they needed anything and requesting more information about the community. In fact, the oldest Jewish community in China was a lot more ancient than the Sephardim in London. They probably came from Persia and nearly 1,000 years later they were welcoming Jewish refugees from Nazi Germany. No reply to Nietto's letter was ever received.

One of David Nietto's interests was pursued by his son. In 1740 Isaac published a calendar for the next 22 years. In 1762 he would publish another for 13 years and in 1791 his own son, Phineas, would publish one for the next 47 years.

By 1740 Nietto had had enough. He offered his resignation and it was reluctantly accepted. What triggered the move is not known. It could have been the way the Mahamad used its power. On one occasion an offender was punished by not being allowed to shave for six weeks. It was childish and OTT at the same time. It could have been that Nietto was just bored with the routine; he'd been involved in synagogue administration for the best part of 20 years and might have wanted to do something else.

When he resigned, Nietto went back to where he was born in Leghorn. It was in Leghorn that he would find rabbis held in high esteem, the study of the Talmud in full spate, and a lot of work being done in Spanish. In 1753, after he'd left again, the Spanish translation of a prayer book was published in the city and the publisher attributed the authorship to Nietto.

The condition of the Jews in Leghorn was similar to London, in that it was the only major city in Italy where there was no ghetto. The grand dukes of Tuscany, who had invited the Marranos to settle in the city back in the sixteenth century, had kept their word and treated them well. The Mahamad waited a respectable four years and then appointed Moses Gomez de Mesquita to replace Nietto.

'Respectable but hardly distinguished', was the somewhat damning opinion of Haham Moses Gaster on de Mesquita when writing his history of Bevis Marks some 150 years after de Mesquita's death. On what basis Gaster came to this verdict is a mystery, because practically nothing is known of de Mesquita. He certainly looked the part and could be described as handsome and distinguished. What is more, his talmudic education had been gained at the Etz Haim seminary in Amsterdam which was a fine grounding.

When Nietto resigned there were three candidates to replace him. As well as de Mesquita, there was a local London teacher who didn't have the Amsterdam quality label and there was Samuel da Solla, also from Amsterdam but not a Dayan like his compatriot. It was really a shoo-in for de Mesquita under such circumstances.

The new Haham was born in 1688, just a year after Isaac Nietto, and was 56 when he took up his post in 1744. He found a shrinking community. Marriages in Bevis Marks were beginning to drop. Between 1740 and 1800 they fell by over 40 per cent. This was, of course, partly due to members leaving Judaism or marrying Christian partners. The situation might have led to more marriages between Bevis Marks members and the Ashkenazim had these not upset the Mahamad so much.

The Mahamad also tried to achieve the impossible by prohibiting gambling. This was like King Canute trying to instruct the tide not to come in. The Jews were not only fully prepared to gamble on such popular sports as horse-racing, boxing and cockfighting. In addition: 'They simply wagered on the day of arrival of the Dutch Mail, an incident which seems to have happened with sufficient irregularity to warrant its causing some excitement.'[12]

There were soon to be bigger problems. Just a year after de Mesquita's arrival, a less welcome visitor to Britain was the Stuart invader, Bonnie Prince Charlie. In 1715, David Nietto and the Mahamad had decided that the community should support the ruling king, according to the Talmudic law, but the Old Pretender had not eventually posed much of a threat.

Bonnie Prince Charlie was different. He landed in Scotland to considerable acclaim and captured Edinburgh in September. He then gave a terrible hiding to Sir John Cope's army and early in November crossed the border and headed south. Back in London, with the news all bad, government stock fell like a stone as everybody waited to see who would win, the King or Charlie. The people cautiously decided to put their gold under the bed and, as a consequence, the supply of money started to run out. It was expected that very soon the Bank of England would have to stop paying interest on gilt-edge stock. Although de Mesquita composed services in the early stages of the rebellion, a little self-help was needed as well.

At the eleventh hour, a white knight by the name of Gideon arrived. The Gideon brothers – Rehuel and Samson – were from a Portuguese family, via Europe and the West Indies. Both were Bevis Marks members and Rehuel held all the senior lay offices at one time or another. Samson started off his business life in London as a lottery ticket salesman but soon became one of the 12 brokers on the Stock Exchange. In 1745, whether the Mahamad had forbidden gambling or not: 'he advanced every guinea he possessed, he staked his credit and he held as much stock as all the remaining speculators together.'[13]

Gideon believed the government were odds-on favourites to beat a Scottish army whose supply lines were being stretched ever further as they marched south. He did more though; as bank notes started to be sold at a discount for gold, he agreed, with 11 other brokers, to buy them all at par from anyone who wanted to sell. He arranged for gold to be imported. He raised £1.7 million for the government. When they raised a loan on the receipts from future land taxes, the Jewish brokers as a whole bought 25 per cent of it, even though the terms weren't very good. Gilts stabilized. At the end of the day, when the Battle of Culloden sealed Bonnie Prince Charlie's fate and things returned to normal, Gideon had doubled his fortune. De Mesquita composed two more services to mark the defeat of the Young Pretender. All the Hanoverian prayers had been answered.

Gideon's actions when so many were panicking was in the tradition of the support other Jews had given Charles II and William III. One investor who was less confident of the Hanoverian dynasty was a Mr Snow who wanted his £20,000 investment in gilts returned. Gideon got 20 £1,000 notes from the Bank of England on his own surety and sent them round to Snow wrapped round a bottle of smelling salts.[14]

Gideon was knighted and became the most famous Jew in the country. At which point he left the community and had his children baptised, the reason being that he wanted to be made a peer and that couldn't be achieved as a Jew. It also couldn't be done for a Jewish convert, but they made his son a peer instead. When Gideon died, however, he pointed out in his will that he had never stopped paying his dues to Bevis Marks and he'd leave them £1,000: 'in case I shall be buried in the Jew's burying-place at Mile End in the carreira [a regular row of graves] and an *escaba* [prayer for the dead] said every Kippur [on the great fast day]'. Which it still is to this day.

De Mesquita had his own Jewish concerns as well in 1745. Maria Theresa, the empress of Austria, decided to expel all the Jews from Bohemia. The continental Jews appealed to Aaron Hart and this time the community worked together. An Ashkenazi delegation asked for the king's help. George II told the British ambassador to do his best to get the order rescinded. A British delegation, including the 70-year-old Moses Hart, travelled to Vienna to plead the cause. Eventually the pressure succeeded. De Mesquita played his part and: 'A touching prayer on behalf of the unhappy Jews of Prague is contained in a little manuscript volume of devotional writings... which was... discovered in Dutch Guiana.'[15] Which, unfortunately disappeared again. All the English synagogues contributed to the relief fund for the Bohemian Jews which raised £900.

So de Mesquita couldn't say that his first couple of years in office lacked incident. He found the position of Jews in England very much better than in continental Europe. For example, they could go where they wanted, unlike Europe where they had to pay the Leibzoll, a tax on travelling, which also applied to cattle. The impost wasn't rescinded until the end of the century.

After the uprising, the problem of the diminishing community could be addressed again. One of de Mesquita's more harrowing responsibilities was to conduct funeral services for dead children, and infant mortality was appalling. From 1728–34 no less than 625 small children were buried in the Sephardi cemetery. In 1749 the Mahamad created another charity, the Sephardi Lying-in Hospital.

Now it was possible for women having babies to get better attention and the children would have a greater chance of surviving. The Jewish hygiene laws might well have also avoided a mortal danger to the mothers when they gave birth in hospital – puerperal fever. Nearly 100 years later, in the Vienna General Hospital, one-third of the women in childbirth were dying of this disease. It was only then that a Hungarian doctor named Ignaz Semmelweis worked out that the cause might be the doctors touching dead bodies in the morgue and then examining the mothers immediately afterwards without washing their hands. He was right but, because he was both a Hungarian and a Jew, the Austrian doctors wouldn't listen to him; either origin would have damned him, but both! Semmelweis had no chance.

It was a situation which wouldn't have arisen in the Sephardi hospital simply because, in Jewish law, there is nothing more impure than a dead body and you absolutely must wash your hands after being anywhere near one, even if you've only been to a funeral and had no contact at all with the corpse. The Jewish doctors, as they washed-up after examining a dead child, wouldn't have known why the law had been promulgated. They simply carried out the *mitzvah* because it was a *mitzvah*. Just another instance of civilization eventually catching up with the Talmud. After 1768 Bevis Marks actually started a register of births; it cost you 5p to register the arrival and the Great followed suit in 1791.

On a happier note, de Mesquita had the pleasure of marrying his daughter to Moses Cohen d'Azevedo, a future Haham, in 1749. He died in May 1751 at the age of 65 and Isaac Nietto spoke at the funeral. There was another address at the graveside: 'by Rabbi Aaron Hart of the Ashkenazi Great Synagogue – somewhat surprisingly in view of the growing jealousy between the two communities.'[16] They had, however, worked together only a few years earlier for the

Bohemian Jews, so perhaps they'd kept their sense of proportion. Certainly, it suggests that the intermittent pettiness of the Mahamad and the Vestry on occasions did not have to affect the clergy. In trying to keep their communities on the straight and narrow, they had more in common than causes for disputes. In fact, at the very end, they were working together on the problem of proselytization: 'which is contrary to the express conditions annexed to our first establishment here'.

The problem was that a Rabbi Perez, unattached to either Bevis Marks or the Great, was carrying out conversions. De Mesquita asked Hart to punish any of his members who helped someone convert. It was agreed and *herem* was threatened, which would cover both the offending officiant and his wife and children as well. Little changed.

Meanwhile Nietto had been pining for London. He was pleased to hear that Bevis Marks had escaped the second fire in 1741, and after a few years he came back: 'This learned rabbi came to London in the year 1747, probably from a residence in Leghorn...and he was much esteemed for his urbanity and scholarship.'[17]

Nietto decided to become a notary. Now, notaries were important because they were experts at drafting papers and they provided authentication for many documents which were accepted by the courts. It was an ideal civil occupation for a man steeped in the formulation of Jewish religious law and one of the earliest professions which produced no religious problems in setting up in practice. Nietto had lost his wife, Rebecca, and soon after his return, he married again. The lady was a widow, Leah Supino, whom he would have known in the past. The Supinos were prominent in the community and Haim Supino had been the senior warden in 1739. The then new Haham, Moses Cohen de Mesquita, officiated at the ceremony in 1747.

On his return Nietto found that the first non-synagogal organization had been formed in 1745. This was the Initiation Society and it is still responsible for the training and supervision of mohelim – the experts who perform circumcisions on male babies at the age of eight days. The operation is conducted without anaesthetic but the overwhelming majority of the tots are no worse for the experience within 24 hours. In addition to epitomizing the Jews' age-old covenant with the Almighty, the hygienic effect of circumcision is acknowledged to be beneficial. As the Jews have been performing it for 5,000 years, they are accepted as experts and many of Europe's current royal males have had the operation carried out on them as babies by Jewish mohelim.

When de Mesquita died in 1751, Nietto was asked to take on the spiritual leadership of the community again, but he chose the role of Ab Beth Din (the Chairman of the Beth Din) as he didn't want to give up his practice as a notary. It caused him no aggravation and at the age of 64 he would have recognized that if his resumption of office at Bevis Marks didn't work out again, he would need some other way of supporting himself.

If de Mesquita didn't make a substantial mark on the history of the community, it seems only fair to point out that it is difficult to become very distinguished if you only have six years in which to achieve that status.

By this point the Bevis Marks membership were going through a crisis: 'Towards the middle of the 18th century and for some years afterwards, Bevis Marks lost much of its best blood by conversion or simply abandoning the faith.'[18]

A solution to the problem was when they were replaced by the Jewish Sephardi immigrants, who continued to come from the Levant (the eastern part of the Mediterranean), North Africa and Portugal. The Inquisition was still at work and when the Portuguese Marranos fled, they continued to be remarried in the synagogue, with the entry reading 'Vindos de Portugal' – refugees from Portugal. The last Auto da Fé in that country was in 1765. One new member was Moses Vita Montefiore, who came to London in search of trade and married Rachel Lumbrozo de Mattos. From that union came a famous son; Moses Montefiore.

Nietto was very much against increasing the membership by allowing more proselytes. The Mahamad proclaimed that Bevis Marks didn't approve of them, that Manasseh ben Israel had promised not to accept converts and if any member attempted a conversion, they'd be thrown out of the community. After consultation, the same wording was used by the Great and the Hambro and that meant that neither Sephardi nor Ashkenazi cemeteries would bury a defaulter. This was a serious disincentive but the practice didn't cease.

The question of an agreement with Cromwell was repeated over the centuries. The only Haham to have gone deeply into the subject appears to be Moses Gaster, who in 1901 was writing in the *Jewish Chronicle* about the attempt of two Norwegians to become converted in 1752. The Mahamad refused permission, saying that it would be, 'contrary to the express conditions of our first establishment. ' Gaster commented that: 'not a trace of any such "express conditions" is found in all our old deeds and documents.'[19] It hadn't affected the Abendana marriage three quarters of a century earlier.

In 1753 the government, now headed by the Duke of Newcastle, decided that one Jewish disability might be ameliorated. A small gesture of thanks for the '45 would not be out of place. So they introduced the Jewish Naturalization Bill, known as the Jew Bill, to make it slightly easier for some of the richer Jews to become British citizens.

For those who were useful to the state, it had always been possible to cut corners. In Charles II's time, anyone involved in making tapestries or in hemp or flax dressing could be endenizened after three years. An act passed in 1740 by George II ensured that if you had served two years in the navy or on a merchant ship in time of war, you could become a citizen.

All the new bill did was allow foreign-born Jews to apply to Parliament for naturalization after they had been in the country for three years. They also wouldn't have to swear on the sacrament. The Sephardim – who had more rich members interested in the legislation than the Ashkenazim – left the negotiations to one of their 1751 elders, Joseph Jessurun Rodrigues. As, however, three eighteenth-century measures to do as much for non-C of E had foundered on opposition from the Church and the City, the omens weren't particularly good. Nevertheless, the bill sailed through the Lords and struggled through the Commons. The second and third readings were marked by protests in the City, led by the Lord Mayor, and the Common Council denounced the measure as: 'tending greatly to the dishonour of the Christian religion'.[20]

The bill received the royal assent in the summer, at which point the opposition to Newcastle in Parliament had been presented with a convenient stick which which to hit the government over the head. For six months the opposition switched its activities from Parliament to the streets. The opposition newspapers went to town and demonstrations against the bill soon followed. To make the appeal even wider, the slogan 'No Jews, No Wooden Shoes' was adopted. The wooden shoes referred to the Dutch Huguenots who also constituted a substantial immigrant community. Verbally, the Jews had everything thrown at them from the Blood Libel to the suggestion that if the Jews weren't stopped at this point, eventually it would become an offence to import pork. A great deal of anti-Semitism emerged although, as usual with anti-Jewish feeling, there was a plethora of petitions and little actual violence. Rodrigues was booed in the theatre and had to leave.

As the bill had been supported by some of the bishops in the House of Lords: 'The spiritual peers who had supported the bill were roundly accused of delivering the Keys of the Church to those who had murdered their Saviour and were hooted when they appeared in public.'[21]

By the end of the year the government, with a general election coming up, decided to bow to public opinion and rescinded the bill on 20 December. The successful demonstrators went back to work and the bill had few after-effects on the general relations between Jews and Christians in the country. An attempt to withdraw the right for Jews to be naturalized in the colonies, first established in 1740, was defeated in the Commons by 108–88. Parliament simply wasn't interested in persecuting the Jews. It would be another 27 years before there was a really serious religious disturbance and then it would be over the Catholics.

There was a lot of dissension in the community during Nietto's second spell. The standard of the shochetim, the lack of deference shown by his rabbinic colleagues to an old man, and the standard of Jewish education in the community were just three nerve ends which got vigorously rubbed. The outside world intruded in the reaction to the Jew Bill, which must have led to different views on how the agitation should best be tackled. After all, the bill only benefited a few rich Jews and it was the whole community which was suffering from the reaction to it. As the unusually high levels of expressions of anti-Semitism mounted, the question of who was to blame must have been the topic of conversation on everybody's lips; in times of trouble, there is always a wish to find someone else responsible for its creation.

The poorer members of the community would have blamed the richer for lobbying for the legislation, even though it had been impossible to foresee its outcome. Even when it was all over, the shock of the vehemence of the resistance would inevitably leave the community on guard for years; those popularly held to blame would remain unpopular, though Rodrigues, the appointed negotiator, retained his own support. He was elected to the Mahamad again in 1755. Overall, it was a very unhappy time.

From Nietto's point of view, to make matters worse, he found the standard of the Sephardi schools had now become totally unacceptable. Commenting that: 'the boys are steeped in crass ignorance' Nietto attacked truancy and the fact that the masters often didn't turn up and exerted no discipline. The schools were reorganized in 1758 and 1759.

Some questions required considerable thought rather than urgent action. For instance, Nietto was asked, in a London more dangerous than today, whether you could carry a sword on the Sabbath. You might need it to protect yourself but what was the Din? Nietto decided that it was alright – but the sword would have to have a wooden blade. It was an interesting responsa. There is no question about it – it is forbidden to carry anything on the Sabbath and a sword is no exception. What would make it permissible if it had a wooden blade would be that, although it was not a useful weapon, it could be considered part of the normal dress of an English gentleman at the time. Anything which is part of normal dress is permissible. But what's the point of carrying a useless sword? Well, if you were a mugger, would you take the risk that your proposed victim's sword only had a wooden blade?

Another problem was again the standard of *shechita*. In 1755 the Mahamad elected Haim Albahaly to control the supply of kosher meat to the community. The new official decided that many of the existing shochetim were incompetent and dismissed them. A new Beth Din was appointed. They reinstated the shochetim and fired Albahaly. Nietto got involved and asked for the shochetim not to be reinstated.

The Mahamad wanted to know what was wrong with the shochetim. Nietto said their prices were too high for the poor. Beef was 1p–2p for 500 grams, mutton was 2p–3p. This he considered the poor couldn't afford. The Haham provided a long explanation in English of his reasoning and the Mahamad bridled at being criticized. Admittedly, the Beth Din said that they agreed that Nietto was the senior spiritual adviser and should always be consulted. They even apologized for not having done so, but nothing much changed and the dispute dragged on.

Other congregations overseas had much worse trouble. The Seven Years War had broken out; England and Prussia *vs.* France, Austria and Russia. That meant more refugees. There had also been a catastrophic earthquake in Lisbon in 1755. The congregation had many relatives in all the areas of turbulence. The British armed forces were having their worst season for many years (armies normally went home for the winter), and George II ordered a Fast to be observed. Nietto had addressed the congregation: 'to implore God's blessing on our fleet and armies, and for humbling in view of this late visitation by earthquake, more particularly in neighbouring countries in alliance and friendship with us'.

Well, that was fair enough and by now Portugal had been a friend of Britain for a number of years, but that hadn't saved a lot of Jews from dying at the hands of the Portuguese Inquisition; the Mahamad approved the prayer.

Nietto's own *annus horribilis* turned out to be 1757. He was very upset when the Mahamad wanted to appoint one of his pupils, Moses Cohen Dazevedo, as the new Haham. At the same time his daughter, Esther, fell ill and died. It all got too much for the old-timer. In March 1757 Nietto was 70 years old and resigned once more: 'He preferred the retirement of private life to the turmoil of certain disagreeable public affairs.'[22]

The Mahamad didn't ask him to reconsider. Out of office, Yesterday's Man, he was never to know power again. With the vast majority of VIPs, from prime ministers to CEOs, it does tend to end in tears. Elections are finally lost, successors are appointed, the eulogies at retirement parties are soon forgotten. There are two ways of dealing with such situations. You can either console yourself that you had a good innings and it was fun whilst it lasted, or you can become an embittered old man. Nietto took it hard. In the year before he died he received a kind letter from a distinguished rabbi, Haham Isaac Lurie, to which he replied:

> Even if all the heavens were pages, all the reeds pens and all the seas ink, it would not be possible to write what joy it has afforded me to see your love and esteem for me . . . for your love is better than all the chief spices . . . and it came to pass when this [was the] dirge of Isaac and his eyes were dim from seeing the faults of the circle of friends . . . whose gates of answer have been closed . . . and they turned their eyes away from the precept laid down by the rabbis in Berakhoth [the first tractate of the Mishnah] to enquire after the welfare of one's friend.[23]

He also lamented the neglect of Rabbi Isaac Belisario, who had been asked to preach a sermon at Bevis Marks on the occasion of the death of George II in 1760; another old war-horse put out to grass.

Embittered though he might have been, life had also toughened him. He produced his 14 year calendar in 1762 and, at over 80, he decided on just one more hurrah, one last effort to show the congregation that he was still a force to be reckoned with. It was to be the effort which has kept his memory alive ever since in Sephardi circles; he translated all the the daily prayers and the minor festivals into Spanish so perfectly that every amendment since has been based on his text. *Orden de las Oraciones Cotidianas, Rose Hodes Hanuca y Purim* was finished in 1771 when Nietto was 83: 'It has uplifted and comforted them through its contents, and through the form in which it was conveyed to them.'[24]

Nietto lived to be 86, an extraordinary age at the time. The day before he died nobody wanted to know him. When he died, all those who had 'turned their eyes away' came along for the enormous funeral. It was said that he was sincerely lamented. The *Gentleman's Magazine* produced an obituary: 'January 26th 1773. Isaac Netto, Notary Public and once archsinagogus of the Jew's synagogue.'

At the end of the day, if he wasn't in the same league as his father, who was?

NOTES

1   Moses Gaster, *History of the Ancient Synagogue*, London, 1901.
2   Cecil Roth, *A History of the Jews in England*, John Trotter, 1964.
3   W.D. Rubinstein, *A History of the Jews in the English-Speaking World*, Macmillan, 1996.
4   Gaster, *History of the Ancient Synagogue*.
5   Albert Hyamson, *The Sephardim of England*, London, 1951.
6   Gaster, *History of the Ancient Synagogue*.
7   *Jewish Chronicle*, January 1874.
8   Gaster, *History of the Ancient Synagogue*.
9   Reverend D.A. de Sola's edition of the Sephardi prayer book, 1837.
10 Linda Colley, *Britons*, Yale University Press, 1992.
11 Solomon Gaon, Anglo-American Jewish Historical Conference, 1970.
12 *Jewish Chronicle*, October 1873.
13 Ibid.
14 Beth Zion Abrahams, *Jews in England*, Robert Anscombe, 1946.
15 Lionel Barnett, *Bevis Marks Records*, Oxford University Press, 1940.
16 Hyamson, *The Sephardim of England*.
17 *Jewish Chronicle*, 1874.
18 Barnett, *Bevis Marks Records*.
19 Moses Gaster, *Jewish Chronicle*, August 1901.
20 Roth, *A History of the Jews in England*.
21 Ibid.
22 *Jewish Chronicle*, 1874.
23 D.S. Sassoon, *Jewish Chronicle*, May 1935.
24 Gaster, *History of the Ancient Synagogue*.

10   Hart Lyon 1756–63

He had had grave doubts from the beginning, even though being England's Chief Rabbi was certainly a first-class career move. Rabbi Zevi Hirschell, to be known in London as Hart Lyon, was 35 years old in 1756 and had been trained for a top job, like England's Chief Rabbi, ever since he was a small boy. He was born in Reisha in Poland and came from a long line of eminent Rabbis. His father, who had recently died while serving as rabbi in Amsterdam, was Aryeh Loeb Loewenstamm. Lyon described him as one of the most humble of men with a quiet disposition, a saintly life and a man to whom worldly goods meant nothing. The apple didn't fall far from the bough.

Lyon's grandfathers strengthened his rabbinic lineage even further. They were Saul Loewenstamm and the great Zevi Ashkenazi, while his great-grandfather was Heschele Cracow, and he was also descended from Rabbi Meir of Padua, and Rabbi Weil of Regensberg. He was born to be a Talmud Hakham – a disciple of the wise – as surely as generations of Rothschilds finished up in banking. It was his mother, Miriam, who had died in 1753, who was the daughter of Ashkenazi, so it was no surprise that, from the age of 5, he studied Hebrew from morning to night until, by the age of 16, he had already won fame as a fine talmudic scholar.

He continued to steep himself in the Torah study he loved, and always fought the good fight. When he was only 30 he 'wrote in 1751 with much vigour against Rabbi Jonathan Eybeschutz who was regarded as an adherent of . . . Sabbatai Tzevi'.

Yet when he was approached by representatives of the Great Synagogue in 1756, he was far from sure he wanted the job they were offering. It is fortunate that a number of manuscripts survive which contain his actual comments and sermons, so we know his feelings on many subjects.[1] In 1757 his brother, Rabbi Saul of Amsterdam, was asked to help persuade him:

> Had he not pushed us away with both hands last year he would, by now, be peacefully settled here and would have saved me

also a lot of trouble during this year. We are now awaiting your answer so as to send the Rabbinical letter [the contract] and hasten his coming here.

The problem, as Lyon saw it, was illustrated by the standard of shechita in London. The Sephardim had been arguing internally about the problems for some years. Many now preferred to buy from Ashkenazi sources. Lyon was concerned that when the Mahamad and its critics finally made peace on the subject, it would be held to be binding on his own future community. He made his position clear: 'If the Ashkenazi Shochetim slaughter also for the use of the Sephardim they must observe the laws and customs of Shechita of both sides, whichever are the strictest.'

The fundamental question for Zevi Hirschell was whether he was going to be in charge of spiritual matters, or was only supposed to preside over agreements formulated by lay officials. The Great Synagogue were keen to reach an accord with him. When he was satisfied that he would have total spiritual authority, he signed, knowing how badly they wanted him. For example, his terms of employment included the promise that every Saturday he would be one of the seven congregants invited to say prayers before and after a portion of the Pentateuch was read to the congregation. This honour was much prized and, with a large congregation, was usually only possible once or twice a year for each member.

So London and the Great Synagogue might be exciting prospects. He had never actually had a community before and his authority would be recognized by the Hambro and by the New Synagogue when it opened in 1761, as well as by many smaller Jewish communities in Britain. Naturally he was keen to make his mark, but unfortunately, it didn't quite work out that way. As he said in 1760:

> When I first came here I was anxious to do something great, something that would benefit the whole congregation…You brought me from a far-off land…incurring great expense thereby, and I said to myself 'This surely is the work of God'… Now, after having been with you for four years, and never having refrained from pointing out your failings, I see that nobody has hearkened to me and that things have not improved in any way.

What had gone wrong? He had certainly found a well-paid position, £250 a year – including £100 from the Hambro – £80 more than Aaron Hart, his predecessor. In those days an English village parson was 'passing rich on £40 a year'. He would get a house as well and the community were bound to give him presents on many occasions, as inevitably happened. For instance, in November 1760 he was given £25 when his daughter got married. There were, admittedly, six children to look after, three boys and three girls, but Golda would remain by his side as a good wife for another 40 years. She was at home with synagogue politics, her father being a lay leader in Golgau.

Lyon's mother, the daughter of the ultimate judge in the Nietto 'God is nature' dispute, would have known how well Rabbi Zevi was looked after when he came to London. Wasn't England the most tolerant country in Europe? No ghettos and no persecutions. England's superiority was clearer still when you looked at taxation. In Germany, during the Seven Years' War, Jews not only had to pay extra war taxes, but also had to give up all their gold and silver boxes, watches and rings. If the tax wasn't paid, the state would have no hesitation in taking hostages from the community until it was. In England, by contrast, although the price of foodstuffs had risen because of the war, and while the economic situation was unsatisfactory, taxation levels didn't depend on your religion.

In 1700 there had probably been not more than 1,000 Ashkenazi Jews in England. By 1760 there were around 6,000 and most of the increase had come from German immigrants. The Sephardim were now only about 25 per cent of the whole. The appeal of a land of toleration and opportunity was very great. Look how well the Hambro was doing. It was a small but wealthy body – as it remained to the end. A controlling group of gem merchants managed its destinies, and their influence was even visible in the quality of the decor and the appurtenances of their synagogue.

For Lyon, however, the root of the problem lay in the community. What were the shortcomings? It was difficult to know where to start:

> I warn you against the small sins you have fallen victim to. The shaving of the beard, a non-Jewish custom, strictly and repeatedly forbidden in our Torah; immorality among young people ... the desecration of the Sabbath ... you regard them as minor matters, not realizing they are the pillars on which Judaism stands. You direct a non-Jewish servant to light the fire, to make fresh tea or coffee on Sabbath ... People carry things on the day of rest even outside the city boundaries.

The rule is, indeed, that Orthodox Jews can't work on the

Sabbath, which includes carrying anything in the street. Odd, therefore, that remark about 'outside the city boundaries'. When Lyon specifies 'outside', the only logical explanation must be that it was acceptable to carry things *inside* the city boundaries. There is a way of making this possible. You can carry things on Saturday within your own home and garden and the limits of your property are often marked out with walls or fences. So the rabbis decided that these limits could be widened by, in effect, enclosing a larger area, such as a section of the town. Then you could carry things within that area.

The resulting fence is called an *eruv* – which means mixing – and the walls of the City of London, enclosing the city, must have been accepted by the congregations as an *eruv*, 'its boundaries being closed by the City bars'.[2] Not working on the Sabbath also applies to your servants, unthinkable in any civilization up to – and well beyond – this time. The fourth of the ten Commandments, however, is quite clear on the subject.

The point about shaving your beard illustrated another divergence of custom between the Ashkenazim and the Sephardim. When the Sephardim appointed their next Haham, a decision on his beard would not be in line with Hart Lyon's comments.

The congregation in the Great Synagogue were seldom in any doubt about the Chief Rabbi's views. Somewhat ungratefully, in view of his substantial salary and perquisites, he said:

> I... had no fear of anybody, have done nothing with the object of finding favour in the eyes of anybody, or in order to gain pecuniary advantage... I... have never made gold my idol. Thanks to the Almighty, I possess enough gold and silver, but do not think I acquired it here. God knows, one cannot become rich from a Rabbinate.'

Lyon was the kind of rabbi who fervently believed it was his job to castigate the community for any backsliding. For example, as already illustrated, on the autumn festival of Sukkot, the rule was that you ate and slept outside your house in a *sukkah*. This was a flimsy shelter, open to the elements, to remind you that your normal creature comforts were the gift of the Almighty. When he saw that most of the congregation remained comfortably indoors, Lyon went on the offensive, even if the congregation found it offensive:

> There I lived during the whole seven days of the festival... The bulk of the people go into the Sukkah, say the blessing but do

not eat even a morsel of bread there, and go home to have their meal outside the Sukkah. Such blasphemy! . . . By doing things which even the Gentiles do not do on Sundays, I ask you 'Why do you come to the house of God?'

He complained that they cooked on the Sabbath and he remonstrated that they didn't examine the *ethrog* for imperfections closely enough before using it on Sukkot. In 1758 a disaster hit the Portsmouth community when 11 members of the congregation were drowned in an accident. Lyon was afraid that this was the hand of the Almighty punishing the community for disregarding the laws of purity; Orthodox Jews look to their own faults for the explanation of tragedies, rather than blame others. For 200 years thereafter the names of the lost were recited four times a year by the congregation.

Lyon knew very well the enclosed world of the small, oppressed continental Jewish community, surrounded by Christians who showed in many ways how much they disliked them. In England there was none of this. Unrepresentative elements might occasionally bully individual Jews a little but, in general, the Jews were welcome to mix with the rest of the population, who were basically decent neighbours, and the Jews were delighted to do so. Hart could see dangers in this. 'All our efforts are to associate with the Gentiles and be like them. See, the women wear wigs and the young ones go even further and wear décolleté dresses open two spans low in front and back.'

Of course, the fashionable ladies at court in Charles II's day went topless when they dressed up, so décolleté was actually a step up the modesty ladder. There is a commemorative plate for William III's wife, Mary, in which she is regally dressed but topless.

> We dress on non-Jewish holidays better than on our own festivals; the Christmas pudding which the Christians prepare in memory of the Apostles is more favoured than the Matzo. Even the children call the non-Jewish feasts 'Holy' days . . . soon they will come to regard the 'Habdalah' service [when the Sabbath ends] as a sign for the beginning of the Sabbath!

Hart was also concerned about losing members of the community through intermarriage with Christians:

> The children of a non-Jewish wife are sure to become Christians, and, although the non-Jews of our days cannot be regarded as heathens, still they are . . . outside the Covenant of Abraham and have not taken upon themselves the observation of the Torah and its precepts. To marry a non-Jewish woman is,

therefore, tantamount to abandoning the faith, even if she should become a Jewess.

Many of those who married out of the religion wanted to continue to be given the honour of opening the Ark or being called to the reading of the law. They were not welcome to these honours if Hart was involved.

Lyon felt acutely aware of the fact that he was now deprived of a group of like-minded scholars, anxious to get even more information out of the bottomless well of the Talmud. The Chief Rabbi would come to consider his time in England as a talmudic study winter. However, as he also needed friends who would pray with him on a regular basis, he set up his own Beth Hamedresh in his home – a study and prayer group, which must have given him a degree of comfort. His absence from synagogue services, however, when he preferred to pray with his friends, led to grumbling in the community that his place was in the synagogue. Hart stated his reasons:

> I know full well that many criticize me for not coming to Synagogue...do not judge me, you who sit in the evenings in beer-houses and music halls...my conscience is quite clear...I pray to God in my Bet-Hamidrash...I do not sleep [the service starts early] but pray with a congregation of ten [the minimum number you need to say certain important prayers]. I would neverthe-less, go to Synagogue out of respect for the congregation but for my weak state of health...the physical impossibility of standing.

This does sound a little like special pleading. After all, the rabbi was 37 on his appointment in 1758 and lived to be 79. If you stand in synagogue for certain prayers, you stand equally for them in your home. Is it possible that Hart Lyon was a little like Florence Nightingale, who was dying, according to her own account, from a very early age and still managed to struggle on till she was 90! It was likely that the chance to continue enjoying the pleasure of worshipping with equally committed co-religionists was worth the telling of a small white lie.

Lyon disliked gossip behind his back anyway. It's a real curse for anybody in authority. With a community of varying attitudes, you're bound to upset someone, no matter what you do, and then the tittle-tattle – often malicious – starts to spread: 'Within the synagogue all seem to be friends and have confidential news to tell one another, but outside disunion reigns among the members.'

The Chief Rabbi had also expected a famous community like the English Ashkenazim to have had the features a religious Jew would associate with such an organization. He was very unhappy that they didn't.

> The former times were better than these. See how many hospitals and houses for the poor were built and maintained, and here, with us, not one institution is to be found. If anyone does support a poor man or a poor official, they would like him to behave as if he were their slave... [The Vestry wouldn't have liked that.] Try and imitate the Gentiles in this! See how many houses for the poor they have built and surrounded with beautiful gardens. They have houses for learning, called Academies... but we do not possess even one single Bet-Hamidrash. Look at our brethren, the Sephardim, they have a Bet-Hamidrash and support several scholars...especially laudable are they as many Ba'ale Batim [members] also take part in the Shiur [a learned lecture followed by a discussion].³

The new Hart Lyon remembered the German communities of Zevi Hirschell. 'Are they [the German congregations] larger than yours or richer than yours? And yet how many Synagogues and Bate Midrashim have they founded.'

The Chief Rabbi did try to create a yeshiva. It wasn't very successful: 'The Yeshibot are going from bad to worse... and the children are, first of all taught by their parents the English language and customs and when they grow older they do not want to learn Hebrew... all this is the result of our mixing among the Gentiles and of the desire to be like them.' Again,

> Our sages say... Raise up many disciples... I was not able to follow this rule in your congregation. I have no pupils, not even a colleague with whom I could pursue my studies.
>
> I established a Yeshibah but have not succeeded with it... They waste their time in coffee-houses and clubs playing cards, instead of... studying the Torah. It were better if you would read at least secular books instead of playing cards.

Why Hart Lyon couldn't find anybody to study with is hard to explain. One of his members, Wolf Liepman, had gone to live in the West End of London and started a small synagogue called the Westminster Congregation (later the Western Synagogue). In 1768 the community hired a teacher for adult education on the Sabbath afternoon at a salary of £3 a year. Each member gave a farthing a week to pay for him and agreed to be there for the tuition. So there were Jews keen on studying if they were approached properly. There was also Rabbi Eliezer Speyer in London, who had a good reputation, and other rabbonim as well, like Rabbi David Solomon, who died in 1786 aged 100. Lyon still maintained that his only pupil was his son.

Unfortunately, there was a lot of discord among the sages. We have a first-hand account of the London talmudic world from a visitor in 1755 called H.J.D. Azulai. He speaks warmly of Rabbi Isaac del Vali and Rabbi Jacob Kimchi. He also, however, talks of the atmosphere in London:

> And also among the Hahamim [learned men in this instance] of the town I saw disunion, they speak with abuse of one another, scorch one another with the heat of their words, and the one would like to swallow the other alive. It is a great shame [that this should be so] in the eyes of the congregants, and woe to eyes that have to look at such disgrace of the Torah and learned men.[4]

There was no Haham at the time to keep the peace and Lyon hadn't yet arrived. Keeping academics in line is often a task for a very strong leader, which only emphasized the need for both the Sephardim and the Ashkenazim to appoint one. In academic circles tempers can get very heated and perhaps Hart Lyon didn't just have academic prowess as a yardstick for collaboration.

Certainly there was room for improvement in the Beth Din's mastery of English law. Commenting on a case involving the inheritance of a daughter in 1759, soon after Lyon's arrival, Lord Keeper Henley had to deal with the original marriage settlement, and said: 'I do think, notwithstanding the boasted learning of the Rabbis, who were said to have prepared it, that there is not an Attorney from London to the Lands End, who would have drawn so senseless and inconsistent a statement.'

One argument Lyon certainly knew very well was the 'modern times' rationale which suggested that the biblical rules were old-fashioned and didn't matter so much in the up-to-date sophisticated world of the eighteenth century. He knew the hidden agenda which so often lay behind this approach: 'What they really have achieved is that they believe in themselves, in the great power of their own mind. We Jews have to believe in the Torah.'

For all his powerful criticism of the community in the pulpit, outside it Hart Lyon, like his father, was considered a man of calm and even temperament. He disliked quarrelling, but he did get worn down by his own lack of success. As he complained in 1762: 'God Almighty only knows how weary I am of my life here. I cannot bear any longer to behold all that you do in public and in your private life.'

What also increased his frustration was that the congregation didn't just ignore his strictures. The honorary officers produced a loophole in their original promise, in order to stop Lyon getting involved in the spiritual matters of other communities. The *shechita* problem was still rumbling on. The critics were led by a Bevis Marks member who sold slippers near the Royal Exchange. Like many others, he might be a pedlar on the street, but in the synagogue he was respected for his Orthodoxy and knowledge. He was one of the early examples of those families who would keep the Orthodox light shining as more illustrious names disappeared into the assimilation gloom. It was the same Jacob Kimchi whom Azulai had commended, and when Hart Lyon arrived, he called on him, explained his concerns and asked him to look into the matter. Kimchi wrote: 'As soon as he arrived I put the matter before him, and he asked me to bring the whole case before him in writing. He promised that if he saw we were right, and should there be any doubt between us and him, he would ask other authorities, and thus would try to restore peace in the community.'[5]

The Vestry stopped their new rabbi becoming involved. He was not allowed to reply to Kimchi's letter, and he had to allow the criticised shochetim to carry on with their work. Kimchi attacked him thereafter, appealing to Eybeshutz in Hamburg, who was hardly friendly to Lyon and got his support. Inevitably, if Eybeshutz said 'yes', the other German sage, Jacob Emden, who had family in London, would try very hard to find a reason to say 'no' and agree with Lyon.

So Lyon said he would attempt to umpire and his parnassim said no, he wouldn't. They didn't want to interfere in what was a Sephardi dispute and upset the Mahamad. Lyon felt that a joint approach with the Sephardim was always desirable, but found he had to do what he was told. When Kimchi published critical pamphlets on the subject, he homed in on the perceived refusal of Lyon to give a judgement, which annoyed the Chief Rabbi even more.

In fairness to the parnassim at the Great, the responsibilities of the Chief Rabbi had been clearly set out where they concerned the Ashkenazi community. Where the Sephardim were concerned, the Great not only wished to act politely to the 'Other Nation', they were also determined not to give Bevis Marks a stick with which to beat them. It was bad enough that the Sephardim considered themselves superior to the Ashkenazim because they had been organized in England for a mere 40 years before the Ashkenazim really got going.

The officers of the Great were not going to make the Sephardim's sometimes patronising attitude more justified by acting discourteously. They decided that subjects such as Sephardi *shechita* were not their concern. Equally, however, if the position was reversed, they were not going to let the Sephardim steal a march on them – both groups attempted unsuccessfully to get the Jew Bill revived in the 1760s.

If Lyon was to make all the decisions on ritual questions for the Ashkenazi community, the number of queries brought to him were limited. Indeed, when he was asked at the end of his stay why he was going, he replied that this was the first question he had been asked since he arrived! By then he must have conveniently forgotten Kimchi. He was also committed to preach twice a year before the major festivals, conduct weddings, deal with divorces and be a witness to the correct performance of *halitzah*. What's *halitzah*? A woman becomes a widow and doesn't have children. If her husband has a brother, the brother is supposed to marry the widow to look after her. If he doesn't want to, he has to say so publicly – the *halitzah*.

Two sermons a year may seem like short measure for the community. It compares with the 50 that Sasportas gave 100 years earlier. That was the agreement, however. They took place on the Sabbath afternoon before Passover and the one before Yom Kippur. The custom of sermons on those afternoons is still followed. When they occurred they were occasions to remember. They normally started with a talmudical discourse – which went on for an hour and a half – and then there was an equally long haggadic lecture. So you could look forward to three or four hours of concentrated wisdom. (The haggadic system uses a story to illustrate a point of law in the Talmud.) Hart Lyon chose to preach more frequently and when he didn't give a sermon, there were often travelling preachers (maggidim) who would carry out this important function. Their visits were much appreciated.

Both sides knew that the Chief Rabbi's main duty was to study the Talmud and spread the knowledge it contained. His reputation would eventually depend on whether he was regarded as a great scholar and how he was esteemed in the Jewish world. It would not be based on what he did for his community. This focus would have a shelf-life which only expired with Nathan Marcus Adler, nearly 100 years later.

There was a lighter side to Hart Lyon as well. Where the Mahamad had forbidden the traditional noisy eruptions when the Book of Esther is read in the Purim service, the Chief Rabbi's emphasis was more on the appropriate joy of the occasion, when Jews remember one of their few victories in the later years of the Biblical Holy Land.

He reminded his flock of the talmudical saying: 'Everybody must drink wine on Purim until he does not know the difference between "cursed be Haman" and "blessed be Mordecai".'[6] (The villain and the hero.)

When Lyon arrived in London the Seven Years' War was not going well for the English side. In 1756 they were defeated by the French in Minorca and part of the English fleet was destroyed in battle in America. The King decided to ask for the help of the Almighty. Lyon was impressed. As he said from the pulpit in 1757: 'The fact that the King has commanded a special service is proof that he does not rely on his own strength alone, but prays for the help of God.' On behalf of the community, the Chief Rabbi said they would play their part: 'We Jews can help the King as much with our prayers as by joining the army.'

If this seems somewhat half-hearted support, we ignore the belief in the power of prayer in the minds of religious people. Furthermore, war is not always justified in the first place, as history will eventually decide. Lyon quoted Aristotle in justification of his position:

> Often apparently trifling events cause war, so that it is difficult to understand how sane people should risk life and honour and fortune for such issues. Only the monarchs and the leaders of the peoples know the real reasons that cause wars – invariably it is the hope to enhance the renown of their countries; it is the prestige for which they are all fighting.

Lyon offered the congregation an alternative game-plan: 'Men and nations must fight for self-respect and wage war against every-thing that threatens to reduce them to a lower level of morality.'

Four more intercession services were held throughout the country in 1759 and 1760. In 1760 George II died. The Sephardim, according to custom, instructed their nominated *deputados*, their representatives, to go to to see the prime minister, the Duke of Newcastle. They were to ask him to give their congratulations to George III on his accession and to promise their continued loyalty. This time the Ashkenazim were furious not to have been invited to go along with the *deputados*. They issued a formal complaint to the Mahamad. The *deputados* obligingly called a meeting to discuss the complaint and invited Aaron Franks to represent the Great Synagogue and Levy Salomons (the great grandfather of Sir David Salomons, the first Jewish Lord Mayor of London in the nineteenth century) to join them from the Hambro Synagogue.

The Sephardim said that, with due deference, they had only gone to offer good wishes on behalf of their own community. They meant no offence and in order to try to make it up to the Other Nation, if they wanted to join them in a loyal address to the new King's mother and the royal family, they would be very welcome to do so. The Ashkenazim were mollified, but suggested that in future, they should talk together about official deputations before doing anything. The Sephardim said they would be delighted, but talk to whom? The Ashkenazim didn't have a representative body. The Other Nation swiftly formed a committee to represent them all, at which point Aaron Franks for the Ashkenazim joined with Joseph Jessurun Rodrigues for the Sephardim to kiss hands with the royals.

This was the beginning of a body which has now stood the Jews in good stead for over 200 years – the Board of Deputies of British Jews. On the Sephardi side: 'Leave was granted them to expend from time to time such sums as might be needed. They were desired to keep records of their proceedings which . . . they were not bound to show.'[7]

The secrecy might be necessary. In their past dealings with authority, gifts of silver, large amounts of chocolate and bottles of wine had been publicly sent to those who might be helpful. Some campaigns against unfair legislation had been very expensive for the community to fight. Bribery of public officials is now a criminal offence but in the eighteenth century 'such sums as might be needed' might be discreetly provided 'which they were not bound to show'. As so often happened, the Jews were forced to play the parliamentary legislative game with the rules stacked against them, so they needed some way of evening up the odds. In fact, however, the deputies in the next 100 years would only meet about once a decade and when the disabilities were finally abrogated, the Jewish Chronicle commented in the nineteenth century: 'We fail to perceive that the efforts of the Deputies contributed to any great extent to the removal of Jewish disabilities.'[8]

In so far as the creation of the deputies brought the two nations closer together, the Chief Rabbi was all in favour. After all, he had more in common with Haham Dazevedo that he had with most of his congregation.

In 1761 another breakaway from the Great came with the creation of the New Synagogue by disaffected members. The Vestry were not best pleased:

> We do hereby charge our Priest now and hereafter that he does not directly or indirectly, or other in his name or with his knowledge and permission, officiate either Publick or private in the services of Marriage, Burials, Circumcisions or any other act of priesthood for any person whatsoever belonging to the said society.[9]

This was the Vestry fighting for its authority, but to stop a rabbi circumcising a Jewish child was to stop him performing a *mitzvah*. Lyon was, as with the question of the Sephardi *shechita*, presented with a fait accompli on a serious spiritual matter. His patience was not inexhaustible.

There is no question that the Chief Rabbi was perfectly sincere in all the views he put forward. Without the opportunity to study Torah in congenial surroundings, and with the Vestry involving themselves in spiritual matters, he was an unhappy man. So when in 1763 the Halberstadt community offered him the position of rabbi at a salary of £150 a year, instead of the £250 he was getting already, he still jumped at the chance. Halberstadt was a town with a very chequered Jewish history, the Halberstadt Jewish community having been expelled from the city in 1493 and 1594. They had built a synagogue which was destroyed during the Thirty Years' War in 1621. They built another and the mob, helped by the local militia destroyed that in 1669. Their safety and security left a great deal to be desired as did that of so many German congregations. It wasn't an unusual situation. In 1762 when the congregation in Jungbunzlau in Bohemia had their synagogue burnt down, they appealed for help from the Great and a collection was taken up.

In addition to the potential dangers, the Jewish community in Halberstadt had to pay exorbitant taxes, once again far more than their Christian neighbours. To make matters worse, in 1760, during the war, the French had captured the town and demanded money. They had taken hostages, including two Jews, in order to get the loot paid over. But – and it was the only 'but' that mattered to Hart Lyon – the small community had a great tradition of being strictly Orthodox. In 1763, when they asked him to be their Chief Rabbi, they made him an offer he couldn't refuse. They promised to help him establish a yeshiva and they guaranteed that they would pay the living costs of maintaining 12 scholars: 'They had heard that... he was anxious to exchange his present office for one in a really observant congregation on the Continent.'

Frustrated by the refusal of the Great's congregation to change their non-Orthodox ways and angered by the ban on his dealing with all spiritual questions, Hart Lyon walked away.

The Vestry at the Great had overplayed their hand. After the malleable Aaron Hart, they imagined they could dictate to any Chief Rabbi and he would do what he was told, even in religious matters. After all they would have thought they were paying him enough. They had picked the wrong man. Hart Lyon was not in it for the money. As far as Hart Lyon was concerned, rabbis gave responsa if they were asked by any community to do so.

The Vestry must have squirmed. The prospect of an eminent rabbi telling all and sundry across Europe of the way the London laymen had tried to teach him the Torah, was a disgrace they could well do without. They tried to persuade him to stay but he was adamant and he became the second and last English Chief Rabbi not to die in office, until compulsory retirement was introduced with Israel Brodie in the twentieth century.

The lesson Hart Lyon taught the Vestry by his resignation must have been remembered for a very long time. Many future Chief Rabbis were to aggravate the honorary officers but, at the end of the day, the ones who stuck to their guns almost always won. No matter how eminent the lay leaders, they didn't know as much about the law as the Chief Rabbi. When members of the community had tried to take on a David Nietto on spiritual grounds, they had looked stupid when he was vindicated. When the Vestry took on Hart Lyon, he walked. A strong Chief Rabbi could always get his own way in spiritual matters if he was determined to do so. The weapons of the lay leaders were restricted to cajolery, argument, bribery, invective, pleading and withholding financial support. The more highly regarded the Chief Rabbi, the greater the power of the office. The Mahamad were to avoid the problem this posed for their hegemony by going for long periods without appointing a Haham at all. After Haham Dazevedo died in 1784, the office was vacant for more than half the next 220 years.

Rabbi Zevi Hirschell was to end his days as the Chief Rabbi of Berlin. He summed up his career when he said: 'In London I had money but no Torah, in Mannheim Torah but no money, and in Berlin neither the one nor the other.'

NOTES

1   Adler Manuscript collection, now at the Jewish Theological Seminary in America.
2   Charles Duschinsky, *The Rabbinate of the Great Synagogue, London*, Oxford University Press, 1921.
3   Ibid.
4   Ibid.
5   Charles Duschinsky, *Jacob Kimchi and Shalom Buzaglo*, Jewish Historical Society of England, Vol. 7, 1913.
6   *Talmud Bavli Megillah 7b.*
7   *Jewish Chronicle*, 9 January 1874.
8   *Jewish Chronicle*, 5 December 1873.
9   Elkan Nathan Adler, *History of the Jews in London*, Jewish Publication Society of America, 1930.

11   Moses Cohen Dazevedo 1761–84

It would be fair to say that Moses Cohen Dazevedo was not without his critics. Even the rabbi who gave him *semicha*, Isaac Nietto, condemned his appointment as Haham as: 'irrespective of his want of merits or qualifications for the post'. During his term of office it was said that: 'mediocrity, to use the mildest term, reigned supreme'.[1]

Yet Dazevedo came from still another great Amsterdam rabbinic family. He was the son of Haham Daniel Dazevedo but perhaps, like Isaac Nietto, he found his father a hard act to follow. He was born around 1720 and when he was little more than an adolescent, he decided to emigrate to London where the competition was still a lot less stiff than at home, and where he could get a job on the Bevis Marks staff. Even after 100 years of being able to train their own, the community was still looking to Amsterdam for candidates to fill many of their junior posts.

Dazevedo fell in love with a daughter of the new Haham, Moses Gomez de Mesquita and they were married in 1749. Isaac Nietto, now a notary, did the paperwork. De Mesquita died two years later and the Mahamad decided not to replace him for the time being. From this point on, 'the time being' for the Mahamad could be for anything up to 40 years; on this occasion it meant ten.

Dazevedo worked hard as a teacher in the community but Nietto said he'd only given him *semicha* on the understanding that, if he had a problem, he'd come to Nietto to sort it out. The Mahamad, on the other hand, thought highly of him and in March 1757 they appointed him a Dayan and put him on the Beth Din. This annoyed the normally placid Nietto intensely. He didn't think Dazevedo was up to it. He thought that a man under 40 didn't have the necessary experience and he suggested that Dazevedo had gone backwards in the level of his knowledge since he'd given him the rabbinical diploma. He also felt a pupil should defer to the views of his master. In the event he was so annoyed with the Mahamad for interfering that he resigned from the court within 24 hours of

Dazevedo's appointment; for the second time in his life, Nietto had had enough.

The Mahamad wasted no more time on what they saw as temperamental behaviour. They welcomed his departure and in July they forbade the former Haham to lay down the law in any circumstances, which was not unreasonable as, of his own volition, he was no longer a member of the Beth Din. Nietto was reduced to complaining that, as he'd taught the members of the Beth Din, they should always consult him when a decision was needed. By 'consult' he meant they should still do what he told them. The Dayanim wrote him a letter of apology and said they'd do so in the future, but they didn't; the decisions of a Beth Din should be made according to the Din and not to the seniority of one or other member.

To make matters worse for Nietto, the Mahamad wanted to appoint Dazevedo as de Mesquita's successor. This infuriated Nietto even more and he complained bitterly about it officially. As the London Beth Din couldn't settle the argument because one of their members was involved, it was decided to appeal to the Beth Din in Amsterdam. The threat never to darken the doors of the Amsterdam law court after they had refused to umpire the David Nietto 'God and Nature' sermon had been forgotten. It was somewhat like a father and son relationship, with family quarrels reconciled after flare-ups, and anyway, the Amsterdam Beth Din had already been urging the London Beth Din to sort themselves out. In 1755 there had been a case before the London court about the legitimacy of a child and they had asked Amsterdam for help. Amsterdam sent the case straight back to them, with the injunction: 'You represent the hand of religion in your community', and they were left to get on with it. Another row erupted when they just asked the Amsterdam Mahamad for help in finding a Haham. This time: 'The London request was rejected so curtly that the letter was entered twice in the records and the Elders resolved the letter be remembered each time the community wrote to Amsterdam.'[2]

Both the Mahamad and Nietto agreed, however, that whether Dazevedo should be Haham obviously needed an unbiased decision. The Amsterdam Beth Din considered the facts carefully and then decided in Dazevedo's favour. There was nothing to stop him becoming Haham and Dazevedo certainly had a good training for it: two years with his father, five with Nietto and 17 on his own. Amsterdam said that even if Nietto had only given him *semicha* conditionally, it didn't matter. A *semicha* could not be revoked. A rabbi could only lose the distinction if he committed a crime. The same question would arise a century later in Haham Gaster's time. Nietto remained a very angry old man: 'From his retirement he poured out a stream of criticisms of the decisions of his successors and he went so far as to declare that the meat provided under their control was improper to be eaten by Jews.'[3]

Since 1732 the old system of subcontracting the *shechita* work to a member of the congregation had been changed. Now there was a free market in kosher meat, so long as the shochet held the Beth Din's certificate of competence. Nietto's objection was that many of the animals had been killed according to Ashkenazi practice, which he considered inferior to the Sephardi. He even went so far as to threaten to set up his own butcher's shop in competition, but was persuaded within a week that this would be unwise – it's a strenuous life for a senior citizen. Nietto tried to involve his Ashkenazi colleague, Hart Lyon, but, as we've seen, the Great's Vestry warned him off, aggravating Lyon who wanted the best standards available, whichever community supervised. Eventually, Nietto contented himself with writing a book on the subject, exposing all the gory details, and this was published in Salonika in Greece in 1761. The row over *shechita* was a long-running saga.

Many writers have suggested that the latter half of the eighteenth century was something of an intellectual wilderness around Bevis Marks. Eminent Christian Hebraists at the time, such as Anselm Bayley, would not have agreed. Bayley produced *A Plain and Complete Grammar of the Hebrew Language With and Without Points* and was greatly impressed by the fact that, for learned Jews, Hebrew was still a living language: 'This is a fact affirmed by every Jew of knowledge that I have conversed with and whom I have experienced to be men of understanding, candour and integrity, particularly the following, who bear the title of hakhamim, which answers to our Doctor: Moses Choen D'Azevedo, Isaac Netto...'[4]

There was very considerable intellectual argument between the best rabbinic brains on the Jewish side and the Christian Hebraists. The battleground was on the correct translation of the Hebrew Old Testament into English and then its interpretation. To give an example, there is a Hebrew word *karan*. The common meaning is an ox's horns but it has another meaning which is a spiritual glow on a face, as in 'his face lit up'. Michelangelo, when he produced his magnificent sculpture of Moses, made the head with horns rather than with an inspired expression. Not the most flattering image of a great Jewish leader.

The Hebraists set out to prove that the Old Testament anticipated the events in the New Testament, and the rabbis set out to prove that it certainly didn't. In an open-minded English society, the language of the scholars was often heated, but the rabbis gave as good as they got. Outside England the Jewish side would never have been granted this degree of tolerance.

The Bevis Marks Mahamad would still have wanted their own clergy to keep their heads down, but they couldn't influence the Ashkenazi experts, such as David Levi, who was both an impecunious hat-maker and the first English-born, recognized talmudic scholar. The wish to defend the Jewish version of the Old Testament against its traducers has to be seen in the light of the concern in the community after the demonstrations over the Jew Bill of 1753. The Mahamad would have been even more determined that the congregation keep away from controversy and the potentially dangerous results of upsetting the Church. If Dazevedo had gone public with his views by publishing a defence of the Old Testament wording, his official position as Haham would have made this a good news story. If his views were transmitted through others, however, there was little danger of this. In a small community where everybody knew everybody else, Dazevedo would have had discussions with David Levi, Raphael Baruh and other Jewish scholars working in the field. Christian Hebraists, too, probably discounting the community's intense sensitivity, naturally looked for an input from the Jewish side. It was: 'quite reasonable to assume that such contacts ... in the field of Hebrew studies were commonplace in 18th century England'.[5]

There is also the question of how Dazevedo's scholarship would measure up to that of contemporary Christian academics. While scholarship is universal, the Jewish rabbis did have some advantages over their Christian counterparts. In addition to being fluent in Hebrew, they had been studying the material, uninterrupted, since it was written. For Christian academics, there had been the centuries-long, intellectual wilderness of the Dark Ages; the Abbot of Cluny in France was just one of those who had to get Christian scholarship back on track in the tenth century. The churchmen also had limited access to the work of eminent rabbis; their ideas of mediaeval collaboration had often been to publicly debate the issues with Jewish clergy in the shadow of the rabbi's forthcoming and rapid execution if he didn't convert at the end of the meeting. The Church's position was, naturally, always upheld and many eminent rabbis died rather than apostatize.

Very often, the eighteenth-century Christian clergy in England had less rigorous standards of scholarship than the great talmudic schools in Leghorn or Hamburg. For example, the major Christian protagonist for the reassessment of the wording of the Old Testament was Bishop Benjamin Kennicott. He wanted to collect all the various versions of the Bible from all over the world and then produce the perfect English translation. To this end he asked for, and was readily given, permission to study the Bevis Marks manuscripts. He then produced his immense work and, with the greatest courtesy, David Levi, whose family was originally from Leghorn, academically chopped him up for firewood. He had little difficulty in casting serious doubt upon Kennicott's thinking when trying to deal with inconsistencies in the various books he had collected. So, when Dazevedo is criticized for his lack of talmudic ability, it might be by Formula One standards when the competition was taking part in less high-powered contests.

Dazevedo took office in 1761, having served over three years as a Dayan and after the Mahamad had carefully debated a cosmetic point they considered came within their orbit; should the newly appointed Haham retain his beard for the installation or not? After some debate it was decided that he should not.

There is a sound case for believing that such a decision was a spiritual matter and, therefore, not up to them. Dazevedo could have pointed out that the Bible explicitly forbids the cutting of the corners of the beard (Lev. 19:27), but he did as he was told. At almost the same time, Hart Lyon was criticizing his community for the barbering – it was one of those minor differences between the Ashkenazim and the Sephardim.

The community's finances were erratic. On the one hand the custom of giving the spare money to their broker, Abraham Ricardo, showed much sense. He loaned it out on their behalf to people who had property, an early form of a Building Society. The returns delighted the congregation and every year there was a vote of thanks to Ricardo, which the Yehidim enthusiastically supported. It enabled them, for instance, to send £80 to Leghorn to help pay the ransom for 14 prisoners who had been captured by Mediterranean pirates and were uncomfortably incarcerated in Malta.

The collapse of the Dutch East India Company produced a deficit in the accounts as those who were affected reduced their contributions. The Mahamad had to recommend cutting back on charitable donations and on the money provided to help the poor. It was agreed that there would be no charity given to newly arrived Jews unless they had a good reason for emigrating to London. In 1775 the

Mahamad turned down a plea for help from the poor Jews in Smyrna and they also couldn't support the building fund of the Jews in Charleston, South Carolina. The community built the synagogue anyway and it is still a lovely building, one of the oldest in the United States, but it is no longer Sephardi.

In 1780 things were so bad that the Mahamad were even forced to the extreme of ending a tradition – the Lord Mayor of London didn't get his annual piece of silver plate and about 40lb (18kg) of chocolate. He asked why not and was told the money was needed for the poor. Not everybody was poor, though. When Moses de Castro decided to present a new Sefer Torah to the synagogue, the scroll cost him 16 guineas (£16.80). To that, however, had to be added £50 for the silver bells that adorned it, £16.50 for the lace cover and another £53.25 for the party when it was handed over; the confectioner's bill alone came to £3.15. So the whole bill was about £120. In today's money there would be no change out of £10,000.

Just as Jewish communities abroad would, on occasions, ask for financial help, so they might have spiritual needs as well. For example, in 1757, the elders of the New York synagogue, Shearith Israel, had written to the Mahamad for recommendations for a hazan. The Mahamad recommended their cantor, Isaac Pinto, who got the job and served for many years.

The traditional source of new Bevis Marks members – expatriate Portuguese – was just beginning to dry up by this time. The Inquisition was in decline and the remaining Portuguese Marranos were less in danger of persecution. A large number had married Christians and, indeed, many had married into noble Portuguese families. In the 1750s King Joseph I told his minister to issue an order that anyone with Jewish ancestry would have to wear a yellow hat. The minister left the king and came back soon after with two yellow hats; he told the king that one was for Joseph and the other for himself; many had married into very noble Portuguese families.

There were, however, still plenty of Jews, from many parts of the world, arriving destitute in England. When they came to Bevis Marks they had to convince the Mahamad that they could support themselves before they were even permitted to pray in the synagogue. A practice which is certainly indefensible on religious grounds. If they wanted money, they were now only given it on the strict condition that they left the country within five days of receiving it. None of this worked because too many of the immigrants had overcome every kind of obstacle to reach England and weren't about to leave again. Bevis Marks might not see them any more, but more Jewish pedlars were likely to appear in the English countryside.

Some of those who stayed and didn't fancy working, became criminals. There were Fagins in those days, as in the time of Charles Dickens. Jewish fences and pickpockets made for bad publicity and the newspapers were as attracted to salacious criminal cases as many tabloids in the twenty-first century. The Jews suffered from the same poor image that the black community is unfairly labelled with today, a small proportion of those trying to live decent lives letting down the rest.

By contrast, many of the richer members were becoming ever more deeply embedded in English society. Judaism was becoming more fashionable and both synagogues and cemeteries became tourist attractions for Christians. There were articles in the popular press on the merits and shortcomings of Judaism. When Horace Walpole, the former prime minister's son, was entertaining in 1763, he noted that he had invited two bishops, five countesses and 14 Jews. Members of Bevis Marks were also on the list of families for Haydn and Mozart to call upon when they visited England. Mozart visited no less than five Jewish families. Many spread their generosity widely; Solomon da Costa Athias gave the British Museum his collection of Hebrew books which had originally belonged to Charles II. Both Reynolds and Romney were retained to paint portraits of leaders of the Jewish community. Just a few were astonishingly rich; when Abraham Franco passed away in 1777 at the grand old age of 96, he was 'said to have died worth £900,000'. Even baptised Jews, however, still couldn't become Freemen of the City of London and have a shop there.

Was there still a necessity for the community to concentrate on 'holier-than-thou' image-building with the general public? Well, the latent antagonism towards non-Church of England sects was to show up in sharp relief in the events of 1780. The background was that the government needed more soldiers for its war in America. It had difficulty in recruiting Catholics because they had to take an Attestation Oath that they were Protestants. The government, therefore, passed the Catholic Relief Act in 1778, making the oath unnecessary and giving the Catholic community some minor relief from its very considerable disabilities. The Catholics were discriminated against much more than the Jews. For example, as we've seen, if a Catholic father had several children, but one converted to the Church of England, that child became the sole beneficiary of his estate on his death.

Lord George Gordon, the son of a Scottish duke, was anti-Catholic and accepted the presidency of the Protestant Associations formed to get the Catholic Relief Act repealed. A large petition was organized and, in June 1780, the 28-year-old Gordon, who had been elected an MP, went to the House of Commons to try to get the act annulled. Only six members voted for his motion but the Protestant Associations had backed up the petition with a march on the Houses of Parliament. When the crowd outside the House of Commons learned that the measure was not to be repealed, scuffles broke out. Then bands of yobbos, who had been waiting for their chance, joined in and full-scale rioting started. From the Friday when the House considered the proposal, until the following Thursday, the mob pillaged considerable parts of the City.

All the major prisons were stormed, the prisoners were released and there was burning and looting. There was no policing of any consequence and the military refused to be involved unless the Riot Act had been read first by a Justice of the Peace. As the one justice who had the courage to do so, had his house burnt down, the others decided that discretion was the better part of valour. The military, therefore, couldn't act and the yobs rampaged through the Metropolis.

The prime minister, Lord North, had been warned in advance of possible trouble and admitted later that he had forgotten to do anything about the advice. No wonder his government lost the American colonies. The Lord Mayor had also taken no action to prevent the riots which, of course, were originally aimed at Catholic victims. When the mob was burning Catholic chapels and the chapels of the ambassadors of Catholic nations, the outbreak could be explained as anti-Catholic violence. When the rabble went on to storm breweries and attempted to break into the Bank of England, it became obvious that simple looting had become the real objective.

Gangs of armed men accosted householders and people in the street demanding financial support for the protest. When facing a man armed with a crowbar who said in front of a gang, 'God bless this gentleman. He is always generous'[11] few were likely to decline to contribute. It was anarchy, and London was in the hands of the mob for nearly a week. To escape the rioters many Jews and Catholics placarded their houses with signs which read 'No Popery' and 'This house is True Protestant'. As, however, all the Jewish houses would have had a *mezuzah* (a scroll containing the important Shema prayer) on their doorposts (as instructed in the Book of Deuteronomy), it was fortunate that the rabble didn't appreciate its significance or they would have known for certain that it was light years removed from a Protestant house.

Not until George III personally got the attorney general to agree that the military could act without being instructed – legally, very questionable – did the mob face any real resistance. The army then poured into London from many parts of the country and fired on the crowds. Then it became a massacre as many hundreds of people died. A considerable number of the demonstrators were also quickly hanged once order had been restored.

Lord George Gordon was tried in 1781 for treason but was found not guilty because he had never envisaged his protest leading to such violence. He was, however, a marked man. The Ashkenazi Chief Rabbi, David Tevele Schiff, who had seen the ravages of the riots, was not best pleased when, in 1786, Gordon decided he would now convert to Judaism. Schiff, sensibly, wouldn't even see him, at which point Gordon accused him of having been bribed by his congregation – Gordon was definitely not good news. Even so, the Hambro Synagogue had no such qualms. They not only accepted him, but he was circumcised and attended the *mikveh* for the necessary ritual submersion. Gordon grew his beard, covered his head and when called up, he *shnodered* £100. He ended his days as a Jew imprisoned in Newgate for very publicly insulting the French monarchy, dying of gaol fever in 1793.

The importance of the Gordon Riots to the Jews was that the chaos had shaken the government and threatened both the monarchy and parliament. MPs and members of the House of Lords had been roughed up when trying to reach their chambers, their coaches destroyed and the homes of senior parliamentarians were burnt to the ground. It was the worst week of rioting the capital had ever endured and it started because of a bill to slightly diminish Catholic disabilities. The tumult was far, far worse than the demonstrations and petitions which had resulted from the passing of the Jew Bill in 1753. In times of trouble – and they would come again in the years of the Chartists in the early days of Victoria's reign – the events of 1780 would not be forgotten by the aristocracy who ruled the House of Lords and, effectively, the government.

The country went back to being generally tolerant. In 1791 there was even a play written entitled *The Jew* in which that worthy was the hero; a curmudgeonly character with a heart of gold and played by 'Handsome Jack Bannister'. Unfortunately, the writing wasn't as good as *The Merchant of Venice* and nothing much has been heard of the play for the last 200 years.

Nor, on occasion did the Mahamad's own attitude help. When Asser del Banco wanted to marry an Ashkenazi Jewess, they refused him permission without giving any reason. Disaffected members started to leave the community in greater numbers. Many a Jewish city magnate disappeared for weekends in the country. It could be a very good life, but the more they were accepted, the more acceptance they craved. Many also considered they had better things to do than bother to get involved in synagogue politics: 'The best minds of the congregation refused to take any further interest in its welfare or in its prosperity.'[6]

Moses da Costa was elected Parnass in 1769 without even being asked if he wanted to serve. He objected but was fined anyway for refusing the honour: 'Defections became the order of the day; the ranks grew thin; few names of prominence in literature or in art can be mentioned during the last half of the 18th century.'[7]

The political aim of the Mahamad remained to stay as close to the court as possible, consistent with not getting involved in politics. In 1763, for example, the Sephardi *deputados* decided not to send George III congratulations on the peace achieved with the American colonies: 'Peace or war being political concerns, addressing would be taking a part in matters we ought to avoid.'

Patriotism was alright though. On the eve of a major naval campaign against the French in Canada, the then Reverend Dazevedo produced a prayer, ringing with loyalty:

> To thee, O gracious Lord, are all praises due, for the great progress the arms of our sovereign made in the course of this year; and as it is notorious that our pious monarch does not make war but for the just defence of his dominions, may that be, O righteous Judge, a motive that you may be pleased to continue your auspicious protection to his royal person; May his arms again obtain glorious victories by sea and land; assist his honourable ministers and counsellors with thy grace... preserve and prolong, O Eternal Father, the precious life of our sovereign lord, King George II, for many and happy years.[8]

It was a wise precaution to ask for protection for George II, as he was to be the last English king to lead his troops into battle. It was to little avail, however, as he died suddenly only 18 months later.

The sermon itself had to be translated from the Spanish and in 1766 another effort to introduce some part of the English language into the services was rejected. This time it was a translation of the prayers which had been published in New York by Bevis Marks' old hazan, Isaac Pinto, but the Mahamad insisted it wasn't to be used in England. It was so popular, though, that a second version had to be published in 1776. The Mahamad would only license a new Spanish translation: 'The Jews of New York, however, in their beginnings showed a not unnatural regard and almost feudal loyalty to the Sephardi community in London.'[9] Even though the Mahamad had recommended Isaac Pinto in the first place, they still wouldn't use his prayer-book.

In 1770 there came yet another attempt to translate the normal service prayers into English, this time by two gentlemen called Myers and Alexander. The translations were quite dreadful and the Mahamad wouldn't give the authors permission to publish them either. At this time, with a not very effective Haham, the Mahamad felt they had to be increasingly firm. The new *ascamot* were, thought Moses Gaster, a future Haham: 'narrow, tyrannical and much given to restricting details with the wide conceptions, the high understanding of duties incumbent upon the congregation characteristic of the First *Ascamot*'.[10]

Whether Gaster thought much had improved by the time he was settled in office, 125 years later, is doubtful.

So the prayer-book problem, for an increasingly English-born congregation, remained for some years. As one critic wrote: 'The version in use was full of unsuitable, barbarous, uncouth and obsolete expressions. Were we to venerate mistakes because they were old or to venerate what is unbecoming because it is ancient?'[11]

Bevis Marks, however, continued to have many powerful and successful members, and to be on the receiving end of an irate, powerful man in full spate is seldom a happy experience. Only the toughest Hahams were likely to give as good as they got. So when Sarah Ximenes eloped to Paris in 1772, her infuriated father came storming to the Haham demanding action. Dazevedo decided that he certainly wasn't about to fight City Hall in these circumstances and promptly excommunicated the less than happy pair. Unfortunately for Dazevedo, the bridegroom's family were also not without clout and they pointed out in no uncertain terms that the marriage in Paris had been 100 per cent kosher. On what grounds then were the lovers being excommunicated? The Haham retreated. The Mahamad insisted on a court of enquiry which could find nothing wrong with the wedding; the Mahamad retreated; everybody in London had egg on their faces. It was not a pretty sight.

If all this wasn't bad enough, there was to be a new cause of dissension within the community. It emerged from an influx of

Sephardim from North Africa and Gibraltar, after the civilians were evacuated during the third Spanish siege of the Rock in 1782. England had gained Gibraltar after the War of the Spanish Succession and by 1776 a third of the 3,000 inhabitants were Jews, but the Spaniards wanted it back. The newcomers to England had different traditions from the Sephardi Portuguese founders and it was all too easy to argue over religious minutiae. Sometimes these had, temporarily, to be overlooked. For example, when Isaac Aboab died at the age of 90 in 1786, his two non-divorced and surviving wives mourned him.

The community certainly gained new members from the influx but they were looked down upon, as all former *tedescos* had been. The newcomers were known as *berberiscos*. You would have thought that Jews who had been treated as inferiors in the wider community would have been sensitive about committing the same offence within their own. After all, the Jewish dislike of drunkenness – if not overeating – reflects the ease with which that condition can lead to violence in non-Jewish circles. A mob is bad but a drunken mob is worse. As far as creating classes is concerned, however, the snobbery displayed by the richer Bevis Marks members at the time seems very much like a way of bolstering their own self-esteem.

To hear Dazevedo at work in the pulpit, we can turn to the sermon he gave in 1776, which was both translated and published. George III had proclaimed a solemn Fast Day because of the somewhat disastrous progress, from the British point of view, of what we now call the American War of Independence. Dazevedo told the congregation:

> This solemn day, on which we are assembled here, by command of His Majesty, our Gracious King, to humble ourselves with abstinence and fasting in the presence of Almighty God, to implore his Divine Assistance on behalf of His Majesty's Arms, that he may obtain victory and success over those American provinces, that have withdrawn their Allegiance and raised a Rebellion against the lawful Prince and the Constitution of this Kingdom, and also that he may... incline the mind of those deluded fellow-subjects, that they may return to the obedience of their offended Monarch, that these Kingdoms may again enjoy the return of peace, quietness and tranquillity.[12]

There was to be no favourable outcome for the Brits but the success of the colonists didn't affect the relationship between American Jewish communities and Bevis Marks. New York still looked to London for support and guidance and to the Haham for rulings in difficult religious matters. They would still need officials who could, hopefully, speak English as well as Hebrew, and they still needed money if they were building new synagogues or had other financial problems. Responsa from the Haham continued. There hadn't even been much need to change the Prayer for the Royal Family, and the American version now implored, 'May he who giveth salvation unto kings and dominion unto princes, bless the President of the United States, George Washington'; today's prayer differs very little.

Isaac Nietto had died in 1773 but his poor opinion of Dazevedo certainly seems to be justified when you consider the state of the education provided in the synagogue classes. These had been reorganized in 1758 when Dazevedo was one of those in charge. Now, in 1779, over 20 years later, there were 64 pupils and it was identified that, after seven or eight years of religious instruction, only about 15 per cent of them could read Hebrew. This only underlined the gravity of the situation, for practically none of them knew their daily prayers either, and this in spite of the fact that the school cost the community £600 a year to run: 'The school, like the slaughterhouse, was constantly being reconstituted, to remain as faulty as before.'[13]

It wasn't due to any shortage of teachers. When one vacancy occurred, there were 16 candidates to fill it. The real problem now was that the teaching was still in Spanish and the children had usually been born and brought up in England; they were being taught in one foreign language how to read another foreign language. Boredom and indiscipline were almost inevitable and the children didn't always get a good example from their elders.

For example, the festival of Purim in 1783 necessitated the calling in of the police. As the villain, Haman, is mentioned more frequently as the telling of the story progresses in the Book of Esther, hazans with poorer concentration can get severely distracted by the ensuing noise. In 1783 when the Haham was an old man, the police had to be called to restore order. The racket had become deafening because one enthusiast and his friends had arrived with something rather more powerful than a rattle – a kettle drum! The Constable duly removed the offenders. It was really the Mahamad being very stuffy, because the Purim service is great fun and the children love making a noise, normally with official consent for once.

Relations with the 'Other Nation' were still conducted somewhat at arm's length. Although the Board of Deputies had gone with Ashkenazi representatives to deliver a loyal address in 1760, the

Ashkenazi synagogues were not automatically invited to attend future meetings, for it was, primarily, a Sephardi initiative. The Board met infrequently anyway; the next occasion was 1778 when the most important decision was that the minutes should be in English rather than Portuguese. After that it only met seven times in the next 20 years. The subjects under discussion ranged from congratulating George III on not getting assassinated, to making sure that individual government legislation didn't affect Jewish Brokers, Jews as dissenters, or Jews in trouble in such remote outposts of the empire as Gibraltar and Port Mahon in the West Indies. In 1779 the community in Port Mahon asked the elders what the congregation should do if the country was invaded. The elders said it should join up for active military service, which many subsequently did, when war was declared on France after the revolution.

In one way the Mahamad became more tolerant. In the year of Dazevedo's death they finally altered *ascama* 7 to allow Ashkenazi Jews to be given honours in the synagogue service if they were relatives or friends of Yehidim celebrating marriages, births or barmitzvahs. It was a step in the right direction but the combination of a tyrannical Mahamad, an uninspiring Haham and a more welcoming society outside the synagogue was a sure-fire recipe for decline.

Even so, Dazevedo must have been a good family rabbi, doing his, perhaps inadequate, best to keep the community together, but comforting the mourners, visiting the sick, dealing with responsa and the myriad other tasks of spiritual leadership. While all the time trying to set a high moral standard in an increasingly materialist world. There is a letter in which he handles a quarrel between two of the members and another where he denounces the birth of a bastard child. There would have been many more dealing with the everyday problems of his congregation, but 20 years' hard work left only the faintest of imprints on the sands of time.

Dazevedo died in the autumn of 1784, but the family tradition of service to the Bevis Marks community continued. His son, Daniel, had been appointed the hazan two years before his father's death and served until 1812. Another son, Benjamin, was also a minister and was recommended by the Mahamad to the congregation in Charleston, South Carolina. Benjamin travelled hopefully to America but this was another instance of travelling hopefully being better than arriving. The Charleston community did not take to the new arrival and sent him home again. The Mahamad were, not surprisingly, very annoyed.

It was to be another 21 years before Bevis Marks appointed a new Haham. In the meantime, when the New York synagogue wrote to the Haham for advice about their cemetery, the Mahamad replied that: 'they supply the place of the Haham'. That was always their privilege.

NOTES

1   Moses Gaster, *History of the Ancient Synagogue*.
2   Evelyne Oliel-Grausz, *Dutch Jews as Perceived by Themselves and by Others*, Brill, 2001.
3   Albert Hyamson, *The Sephardim of England*, London, 1951.
4   David B. Ruderman, *Jewish Enlightenment in an English Key*, Princeton University Press, 2000.
5   Ibid.
6   Gaster, *History of the Ancient Synagogue*, London, 1901.
7   Ibid.
8   Ruderman, *Jewish Enlightenment in an English Key*.
9   Elkan Nathan Adler, *The Jews of London*, Jewish Publication Society of America, 1930.
10   Gaster, *History of the Ancient Synagogue*.
11   Ibid.
12   Dr I. Abrahams, Jewish Historical Society of England 1918–1920, p. 120.
13   *Jewish Chronicle*, 1874.

12   David Tevele Schiff 1765–91

It is often difficult to get a rounded picture of the earlier Chief Rabbis because they seldom left much of themselves behind. We are luckier with David Tevele Schiff because some of his correspondence with his brother has survived. As a result, while there is no reason to doubt Schiff's faith in the sanctity of his calling, the picture which emerges is of a first-class, professional executive in the rabbinical business. He was a role model for a London Business School case study: intellectually brilliant, properly trained, cool under pressure, resilient, diplomatic and tough. The face in the portrait is of a firm chief executive officer. It isn't surprising that Jacob Schiff, the great American banker, was a descendent.

Schiff was born into a family of rabbis in Frankfurt in about 1720. They lived in a house called 'Zumschiff' – for ships. Hence the family name. He was the son of Rabbi Solomon Schiff and Rabbi Aberle's daughter, Roesche. The same Aberle who had ruled the roost in London's Ashkenazi circles in the early days of the community. He was trained by two excellent talmudists, Jacob Poper and Jacob Joshua Falk and his marriage to Breinle Sinzheim had the bonus of getting his career off to a good start. One of his wife's uncles was Leb Sinzheim who had founded the Beth Hamedresh in Worms, about 50 miles from Schiff's home. By 1743 Schiff was the head of the institution and went on to Vienna as a preacher and then back to Frankfurt as a Dayan. One of the leaders of the Ultra-Orthodox Jews in the twentieth century, whose standards were far higher than average even in that community, said he was: 'possessed of great Talmudic erudition and had an international reputation to that effect'.[1]

In 1764 when Hart Lyon left London, Aaron Goldsmith, a power in the Great Synagogue land, was recommended to appoint Schiff, who was his cousin, by the rabbi of Hanover, who was his uncle. The original idea within the community had been for Lyon's successor to be in charge of both the Great and the Hambro, as before. There had even been an agreement between the Great and the Hambro to that effect: the Great would pay £150 of the salary and the Hambro make up the other £100. There were other candidates, however, and one of them came from equally impeccable rabbinic stock; his cousin, Rabbi Meshullam Zalman, the son of Rabbi Jacob Emden. The infighting for the job became ferocious, as Emden recalled:

> My son... was elected as Rabbi... of the Hamburger congregation in London... after I nearly gave up every hope for it. For he had many opponents on the part of the Synagogue in Dukes Place... It was, however, from God, and so all the plotting and obstacles... could not frustrate his election. Even after he had been duly elected they conspired against him, and people wrote me letters threatening that, if he came to London, they would attack and abuse him.[2]

Zalman's supporters at the Hambro did all they could for him but the Great wanted their own favoured candidate. Eventually, the two communities went their own ways; the Great appointed Schiff and the Hambro and the New appointed Zalman. For the next 15 years there were two ministers claiming to be the English Chief Rabbi.

It was a delicate situation for Schiff. Agreed, the Great was the largest and most powerful London synagogue, but Zalman was supported by both the Hambro and the New. There were also the provincial communities to be considered. Portsmouth, one of the most important, split in two; a small number of eminent old-timers chose Schiff and the majority of the Young Turks went for Zalman and left the congregation to set up on their own. The original community sent their honorary officers to London to have meaningful talks with the Vestry at the Great. They then made a courtesy call on Schiff in his home and solemnly agreed their future relationship. Offerings during their services would be in honour of the Chief Rabbi, who would settle any differences which the Portsmouth authorities found too difficult: 'if it should be a hard matter, however, then they should bring it before Rabbi Tevele HaCohen.'

In addition, each year the Portsmouth community would send 2½ kilos of wax to the Great to be made into candles to light the synagogue on Yom Kippur. Above all else, scandal was to be avoided: 'They must not dare to go to the non-Jewish tribunal, but it is to be settled by our congregation.' In fact, the youngsters' breakaway community only lasted for about 20 years and they then rejoined the original congregation, definitely older and probably wiser.

The Jewish population in England had spread during Aaron

Hart's time. Wherever there was a major port in the southern half of the country, there was likely to be a Jewish presence; Plymouth, Bristol, King's Lynn, London and Portsmouth. As the attraction of England to Jewish immigrants was the opportunity to get on without the state legislating to hold you back, it was mostly the young people who decided to try their luck on the other side of the Channel. In Plymouth, for example, at the end of the century, 43 out of the 56 members of the community had come from Germany, which effectively meant from a ghetto. Thirty of them were aged between 20 and 26, and the rest were either between 16 and 19 or between 27 and 30. A group of ambitious youngsters who were determined to 'take arms against a sea of troubles and, by opposing, end them'.[3]

The immigrants were not all impoverished, intellectually or materially. Admittedly Levi Nathan was only a pedlar at the time, but he was also: 'the founder, inspiration and leader of a society for Talmudic study'.[4]

A richer immigrant, who arrived in 1770 from Amsterdam, was a 30-year-old merchant called Levi Barent Cohen. Cohen had six sons and six daughters, some of whom eventually married into the Rothschild, Montefiore and Samuel families. From the interlocking marital alliances and subsequent marriages into clans like the Sassoons, the Montagus, the Goldsmids and the Cassels emerged the dynasties which became known as the Cousinhood. It was from their ranks that the majority of the lay leaders of Anglo-Jewry would come for the next 200 years.

The original patriarchs of the Cousinhood were mostly Ashkenazi, and Orthodox to a man. Men like Cohen, himself, Nathan Mayer Rothschild, Moses Samuel and Aaron Goldsmid. For generations the families would sire brilliant academics, artists, bankers, doctors, industrialists, lawyers, politicians and soldiers. They would make fortunes, create great companies and serve their country well at the highest levels.

Eventually, however, a very large percentage of the Cousinhood offspring succumbed to the attractions of the prospect of full acceptance into the British Establishment, and the opportunity to divorce themselves from any connection with their poorer co-religionists and their foreign origins. Often to their parents' sorrow they finally became Christians or agnostics. One was even to become a bishop.

It would often take a long time and there were exceptions, but by the twenty-first century, Ashkenazi Orthodox communities would usually only see the Cousinhood represented in plaques on old synagogue buildings, their names inscribed on the synagogue silver or long-forgotten in dusty archives. Even so, on the road to assimilation, their future members were going to be the lay leadership with whom the Chief Rabbis would often have to contend if they wanted to uphold the Orthodox rules.

Already the quarrel with the Hambro had cost Schiff £50 a year of the original proposed salary; the Great, now on its own, decided that £200 a year was the right figure. They restored it to £250 again in 1768, only for it to go back to £200 in 1771. It didn't exactly reassure Schiff about the financial stability of the post.

Moses Hart's original synagogue had been amply large enough at the time it was built, but by 1760 it was bursting at the seams. In 1764 it had been decided to enlarge it and 15 members subscribed £2,000 between them for the building fund. The rest of the money was raised in traditional and non-traditional ways. Benjamin Alexander, for instance, gave £200 to the synagogue in return for an annuity of £25 a year for his wife for life – a substantial 12.5 per cent and in marked contrast to today's somewhat lower pension rates.

A considerable sum still came from shnodering. The system was somewhat of a surprise to a Christian visitor who left this report of how the money was provided:

> In the synagogue there was a Clerk, called a Shamos, who mounts the pulpit, as an auctioneer does his rostrum, and then explains aloud 'One penny for opening the door of the Ark'... Another bids more, a third more still, and sometimes the contention is so strong... that six, seven or eight guineas is given for the superstitious privilege... indeed it has sometimes happened in London, when two or three obstinate, rich Jews, stimulated by pride, ignorance or folly to oppose each other; but one of these mitzvous, or good deeds... has cost the buyer no less than 20 guineas.[5]

Well, it was an honour to take part in the service and all the money was bound for good causes. Having said all that, there are still less ostentatious ways of donating to charities.

One of the definite disadvantages of the practice of *shnodering* was that it could extend the length of the service interminably. The members called up to the reading of the law could ask the hazan to say a *misheberech* (a blessing) for his relatives. If the blessing took a minute, then asking for six blessings for six relatives took six minutes. As this could apply to around 10 members each week, the *misheberechs* could add another hour to the service. The Vestry agreed that the maximum number of blessings per member should be five and that the minimum amount that could be given was 2½p. As the income was important, if the hazan made the blessing without receiving the promise of the gift, then that unfortunate official would be fined 12½p.

It took 18 months to persuade the neighbours to sell their adjoining plot of land for a larger synagogue, but the contract was finally signed in March 1765. Schiff took the synagogue silver home for safe keeping and nearly lost the lot. As a local newspaper reported: 'Yesterday three men were carried before the Right Hon. the Lord Mayor on suspicion of breaking into a house near the Jews' synagogue, belonging to the High Priest, with an intent, as is supposed, to steal the plate belonging to the Synagogue deposited there while that building is repairing. They were sent to the Wood-street Compter.'

The dedication of the new, enlarged synagogue took place in August 1766. The order of service was printed in Hebrew and English and the proceedings were conducted 'with the greatest pomp and solemnity'.[6] Moses Cohen Dazevedo came along from Bevis Marks with a number of other rabbis and Handel's Coronation Anthem was performed 'by a numerous band of most eminent musicians'.[7] Schiff consecrated the new synagogue, read the prayer for the Royal Family in English, and then delivered himself of a sermon in Yiddish which was widely distributed not only in England, but in Europe as well. Everywhere there were congratulations. A considerable number of non-Jews also attended the dedication service and they were very impressed.

Relations between the Great and the New were patched up. The relative ease with which this had been achieved now led to another breakaway. This time it helped with the problem of the increasing number of Ashkenazi Jews who were moving to the West End and had nowhere close by to worship. Thus, in 1768, Wolf Liepman started one of the most famous independent British synagogues, the Western.

The prime objective for Schiff in his early days in London was to win a popularity contest against Zalman, and that was what he set out to do. Zalman would not eventually prove very difficult competition.

Schiff's relations with his honorary officers at the Great were always warm and cordial. There were none of the rows that had marked Hart Lyon's period of office. At the very beginning they had eliminated one cause of conflict, when Schiff readily agreed not to hold services in his own house but always to come to the synagogue.

On the other hand, Schiff, like Hart before him, was concerned about the congregation's inability to understand the prayers. As the Mahamad refused permission for Pinto's English prayer book to be published in London, in 1772 Schiff welcomed a new prayer book, which was in Yiddish.

That year was, however, a personal disaster for Schiff, as his wife Breinle died at a very early age. The Schiffs only had one child, Moses, and, now a widower, the Chief Rabbi turned to his niece, Middel, and asked her to act as his housekeeper. Eventually Moses and Middel married, but Schiff remained single for the last 20 years of his life. This was surprising because rabbis were supposed to be married. Where the Catholic clergy were not, the Jewish position was that, if you were going to be involved in family matters, you'd better have first-hand knowledge of what it was like. There is no evidence that any pressure was ever put on Schiff to remarry but, if there were, he didn't give in to it.

Schiff steered a steady course over the years among the many rocks of community politics. Like all experts he had the advantage of knowing his subject backwards. Early in his ministry a butcher was selling *trefa* (non-kosher) meat as kosher. The Beth Din withdrew his licence and Schiff told the congregation of this from the pulpit. The butcher immediately sued for slander, but Lord Chief Justice Loughborough agreed that Schiff had the right to make a judgement and had acted correctly. As cousin Aaron wrote to Meir Schiff, while the new Chief Rabbi might only have been a Dayan in the past: 'and yet, thank God, we know how famous he is'.

Schiff was soon accepted as the head of a first-class European Beth Din by his peers on the continent. As London was still a small community, this was no mean achievement. The correspondence between the various cities was continuous, with Schiff consulting rabbis such as Steinhart of Furth, the great Isaiah Pick of Berlin, Landau of Prague and Mass of Frankfurt. He was consulted in return by congregations on the continent and as far away as America and India. He gave decisions on many knotty problems. There was a woman whose husband left her and went to Jamaica, but he died at sea. The question was were there sufficiently reliable witnesses to this to enable her to get a proper divorce document? Or the Cohen (a member of the priestly tribe of the Jews) who had married an Indian lady. Where did he stand? In halachic trouble was the probable answer.

One example of the problems which landed on Schiff's desk illustrates the growing affluence of some of the Great's members.

They bought themselves country estates and many planted orchards. The question they asked Schiff was when could they eat the fruit? The Chief Rabbi consulted his nephew, Mordecai Adler, the Rabbi of Hanover. What was under discussion was the precept of Orlah (Leviticus 19:23–5). There it was clearly laid down that you can't use the fruit for the first four years. In the fourth year you can use it for decoration but you can only eat it in the fifth year. Schiff ruled accordingly.

As Schiff's reputation constantly increased, so that of Meshullam Zalman declined. To begin with, he was quarrelsome and where you might get away with this if you were always right, Zalman wasn't in that happy position. In 1774 he privately approved a divorce brought from Amsterdam in 1768. He then invalidated it in public and received, 'a torrent of uncomplimentary criticism from a Sephardi scholar, Shalom Buzaglio'.

Schiff was asked his own view. He asked the Haham, Moses Cohen Dazevedo, what he thought. It was considered that: 'The few lines of Haham Dazevedo are very carefully worded and he does not commit himself to an opinion one way or another.' In a strictly Ashkenazi quarrel the Haham came down squarely on the fence. The Vestry restraining Hart Lyon on the question of the Sephardi shochetim had been reciprocated in kind.

Then Zalman checked on the acceptability of a carcass as kosher. He made another mistake with a lung adhesion, which also became public knowledge. His father, the eminent Rabbi Emden, would have gone ballistic with anybody other than his son for making such an elementary error. In 1777 he managed to improve his image some- what with the publication of a sermon he had given in December 1776 when there was a General Fast for the success of British arms in America. This was the first Ashkenazi sermon to be printed for the general public in England and Zalman 'attracted by the smoothness of his tongue'.

In 1778 it all went pear-shaped again. This time he fell out with his wife very publicly and the papers had a field day, to the considerable embarrassment of the community. Stories along the lines of 'The Jew Priest' of the Hambro synagogue being divorced from his 'Priestess' did not go down well in the Vestry at the synagogue.

Eventually the Hambro congregation decided they'd had enough. As the American War of Independence ground on, the British econ- omy fell on hard times and taxes had to be increased. The Hambro found its income dropping and its rabbi becoming an expensive luxury. In 1780 they forced him out. Schiff wrote to brother Meir in Amsterdam: 'From hour to hour he begged the community to allow him to remain.'[8]

It was no good. The Hambro gave Zalman a pension of £50 a year and he left, heartbroken, for Russia. The Great lost an official at the same time, though, on this occasion, it was hardly their decision. The hazan, Isaac Polak, was imprisoned for debt and only after much negotiation was he released to sing at the High Holydays services. In the hazan's defence, he had guaranteed the bill of a friend who had not waited around to face the music.

Schiff took Zalman's place and was now the undisputed Chief Rabbi, though at no higher a salary. He agreed with Meir: 'Your astonishment still holds good why I should have to do everything without being paid for it, apart from the presents at Purim and Rosh Hashonah.'[9]

He reckoned the Great would be lucky to get £50 a year from the Hambro towards his salary and he wouldn't see any of it. He didn't even mention that in 1780 a new community was established in Manchester for the first time, which added to his work load. Unfortunately for Schiff, although Hambro members had got rid of Zalman, that didn't mean they were enamoured of his replacement. In 1775 Schiff had been complaining that the Hambro members didn't ask him to perform weddings. The Hambro Vestry laid down that the congregants could choose between the rabbi and the hazan and the latter had an effective but unfair marketing ploy, 'As the hazan – wrongly – flatters the congregation.'[10]

Schiff only did one Hambro wedding in 1775. There would be other causes of dissension in the future. In fact, there would always be disputes and warring factions. As he told Meir: 'You imagine London is a Kehilla. Far from it.'

One extraordinary group owed its allegiance to Chayim Samuel Jacob Falk, who was known as the Baal-Shem. Falk was a mystic and a Kabbalist and he lived in London for about 40 years before dying in 1782. He ran his own synagogue and his main claim to fame was as a miracle worker; the stories of his amazing feats lost nothing in the telling. When there was a blaze at the Great, Falk was said to have written four letters in Hebrew on the wall of the synagogue and the fire went out. He lit his Sabbath light and the one day's oil was said to have burned for three weeks; the festival of Hanukkah commemorates, in part, the miracle of one day's oil lasting for eight days, thanks to the intervention of the Almighty. Falk was suggesting he could achieve three times as much.

Then again, his silver plate was seized for the non-payment of a debt and the items were said to have removed themselves from the custody of the pawnbroker and returned to Falk's home of their own volition. Falk and Schiff got on well together, partially because the Emden/Zalman party were anti-Kabbalist. With Sabbateianism dying out, Kabbalism had become an option again for the Orthodox. When Falk eventually died he left Schiff £10 a year in his will.

England now had an undisputed Chief Rabbi to whom congregations in the empire could also turn for decisions. It was a unique situation, not created by government decree, but emerging because it suited the community. As the years passed it would become a tradition and, in England, there is seldom any enthusiasm at all for abandoning traditions. 'If it ain't broke, don't mend it', is an Americanism with which the British would heartily agree.

In 1770, Charles Wesley came to the Great – the very elderly composer of 'Hark, the herald angels sing' was there for the music. His brother, John, might equally have benefited by comparing notes with Schiff, because the Chief Rabbi was a preacher of considerable power.

Charles Wesley wrote afterwards: 'I was desirous to hear Mr. Leoni sing at the Jewish synagogue...I never before saw a Jewish congregation behave so decently. Indeed the place itself is so solemn, that it might strike an awe upon those who have any thought of God.'

Myer Leoni was, indeed, an opera singer, but came to the Great to harmonize with the hazan, alongside a *meshorrer* (a tenor), as a two-man choir. Excellent singer that he was, it was eventually felt necessary to make a change when Leoni took part in a performance of Handel's *Messiah*, a somewhat infelicitous choice of roles for a synagogue official, even if only part-time. The *bassista* (bass) eventually went off to Jamaica as well, to the disappointment of many in the congregation but to the relief of the Vestry. It saved them 40p a week into the bargain.

Money was a constant worry for Schiff. He bought tickets for the lottery. He bolstered his income with fees as a marriage broker and by acting as an agent for Jews who wanted debts paid in London from overseas. It wasn't that his income was inadequate but, as he told Meir: 'The salary of £200 I have from the congregation is insecure and at every meeting of the Kehal they speak about reducing the salary of the Rav.'

The problem was that the members had overspent on the new synagogue and all the salaries had to be, temporarily, reduced. In the end, the problem was solved by mortgaging the synagogue for £1,700. The Vestry never did come to the crunch and cut Schiff's salary permanently, but it was always a possibility hanging over him. Meir was also finding it difficult to make ends meet and appealed to his brother for help. Eventually Schiff became exasperated:

> Leave off with this! It is impossible for me to help you. I have enough to do to keep myself... were it not for the little I receive in interest from Government Loan I could not exist, as the expenses increase on account of the war, the taxes are great and heavy, and for other causes. My salary of £200 is not being paid to me punctually.

Not that Schiff was overanxious to pay the taxes. When he wrote to Meir asking him to buy some things for him in Amsterdam: 'With regard to the white caps, these and the handkerchiefs must be washed there on account of the duty payable here.' If they were washed, they couldn't be new and, therefore, couldn't be imports subject to tax! The handkerchiefs were to be yellow – Schiff loved his snuff, and it would have been a pity to discolour the handkerchiefs.

The 1770s were a very difficult decade for the government. Events abroad led to the loss of the American colonies and at home there was an ongoing battle over the freedom of the press. John Wilkes, the foremost protagonist, was regarded as a hero by the citizenry and there was much popular unrest. Such events, as the Jewish community well knew, might easily have turned on the continent into anti-Semitic manifestations, as whipping-boys were needed, but this would happen only once in Britain – in 1911. It did illustrate, however, that the community still felt it couldn't afford to put a foot wrong. It was significant that when naturalization was made easier through the Irish Naturalization Act of 1783, the Jews were specifically excluded from its provisions, even though both communities tried to influence the legislation. Nobody wanted another 1753.

Where the Jews always needed some good PR was in the area of criminal activities. Poverty makes the rewards of crime more attractive, and most Jews suffered the miseries of grinding poverty. A number of unpleasant cases came up, which involved Jews trading in stolen goods, and this worried the city authorities. The local magistrate, Sir John Fielding, cofounder of the famous, but very limited, police force, the Bow Street Runners, asked the synagogue for help in reducing the number of Jewish criminals. The Great responded energetically. It immediately placed an advertisement in the papers:

> It is with the deepest concern and the strongest indignation we have lately observed the many daring and atrocious crimes committed by a set of foreign miscreants, who stain our religion by calling themselves Jews. Anxious to put a stop to this growing evil... we think it our duty to give every assistance to the Civil Magistrates... for which reason we most solemnly exhort and entreat every honest member of our community to aid and uplift us in this pious cause... and in order, if possible, to strike terror in the wicked hearts of these abandoned offenders, we hereby declare our determined resolution to grant them no burials... that they may be for ever excommunicated from our community, as well as to deter every Jew from receiving stolen goods or concealing such, or harbouring any persons guilty of any theft.

In one case the synagogue offered a £20 reward to anybody finding the killers of a servant in a Jewish household. The newspapers were soon able to respond: 'The Jewish synagogue has much Credit with the Public for its Activity in apprehending the miscreants lately executed, having expended no less than £1,500 to promote the Ends of public justice.'

When the three Jews were eventually hanged for the murder, Schiff excommunicated them on the Sabbath after they had been publicly hanged at Tyburn, at the crossroads between Edgware and Bayswater Roads, adjoining Hyde Park. The crowds, who had flocked to Tyburn since 1300, were to enjoy similar spectacles for another dozen years. The expenditure of £1,500 was a vast investment in public relations but, if it was in a good cause, it was also money well spent.

The reputation of the community was always given a high priority and it was now enhanced by the favourable publicity. It wasn't always a question of money, though. A young Jew had some friends who were highwaymen. They were caught and the Jew was implicated, although it was more guilt by association than anything else. He was condemned to death, like his mates, but Schiff worked tirelessly to get him a reprieve and was probably successful in the end.

After the Gordon Riots it was, perhaps, no coincidence that Schiff applied for other rabbinic positions. As he wrote to Meir: 'You know my nature; I like to be peaceful and keep my head clear.' In 1781 he wanted to be the rabbi in Rotterdam where the Emdens were well installed. He didn't get it: 'Who can stand up against the people?'

So in 1782 he tried for Wurzburg, only to have his application lost on board a ship sunk by enemy action. Undoubtedly, Schiff missed the emphasis on talmudic scholarship which permeated the ghettos in Germany where he had been brought up. Like Hart Lyon, he lamented to Meir in 1780 that: 'I have no colleagues nor pupils to study with.'

Since, however, he had eminent colleagues on the Beth Din in Rabbi Speyer, Simon ben Meshullam of Prague, Abraham Hamburger of Nancy and Jacob ben Eliezer, there has to be a suspicion that he was exaggerating more than somewhat at the time he wrote this. What is more, he certainly: 'expounded the words of the Torah in the Beth Hamedresh' because it says he did on his tombstone. It would have been worth listening to as well because: 'He knew the six orders of the Mishnah by heart.'

Schiff's expertise must have been valuable to Christian Hebraists such as Bishop Kennicott. He did know him and, indeed, gave Kennicott a letter of recommendation to the European rabbis so that they would help him with his researches. Although books on eighteenth-century Hebraists do not mention Schiff, he was hardly likely to have just been asked for a letter. If the results of discussions with Kennicott were private, rather than widely publicized, as in the disputes with David Levi, this was appropriate between a bishop and a Chief Rabbi.

The economy remained in poor shape after the American War of Independence. Confidence, that powerhouse of progress, was also at a low ebb; the British usually won wars in the eighteenth century. Losing one badly shook their self-esteem. Money remained tight and there was an enormous amount of poverty throughout both the Ashkenazi and Sephardi communities. A collection for the poor in 1767 only raised £196 and that had to be distributed among 300 Jews in monthly allowances which, if you could get one, were the equivalent of between 12p and 34p today. Things became so bad that in 1770 the synagogue, like the Sephardim, decreed that any foreigner who was given help would have to leave the country within five days and that they couldn't come to synagogue in the meantime. Even then, though, it was added that the Zedaka (the poor fund) should help them all it could. Money was tight for the Church as well. There was an attempt to impose a tax called Church Greats on the synagogue in 1771, but this was taken to court and ruled to be inapplicable.

How were the poor immigrants to avoid living on charity and still keep a roof over their heads? What did they know? What could they do? They had not been taught handcrafts and so a large number had no occupation available except to sell old clothes. One other answer was that they could try to teach Hebrew to the children of better-off families. As they had no training, couldn't speak English and often weren't interested in what they were doing, it was a perfect recipe for turning the children right off the religion. Critics often exaggerate, but the anonymous author of the contemporary book *A Peep into the Synagogue* voices objections to the teachers which were to be repeated over the centuries:

> Some of them, who can jabber a little fluently the mixed jargon [Yiddish] . . . will perhaps worm themselves into some creditable ignorant family . . . to teach the children the Hebrew Alphabet and Bible with their German gibberish mode of translating it, by which they are made most miraculous scholars, in a language not recognized by any Nation under the Sun.[12]

What else were the poor scholars supposed to do to survive? The parents they served were at least doing more than those families who totally neglected the children's education. It was too little, though, and it often came too late.

Even a number of the rich Jews suffered financially, as Ashkenazim were also shareholders in the Dutch East India Company when the company ran into serious difficulties. The merchants continued to import diamonds from India and pay for them in coral. From 1750–74 licences to export coral totalled £1.6 million. Of this very large total, £1.2 million was granted to Jews.

There was, as always, a great difference between the few rich Jews, with their estates in the home counties and their lavish life-style, and the majority of the community who were in the direst need. The Ashkenazim endeavoured, nevertheless, to try to keep their poverty-stricken brethren from being a burden on the state. Among other charitable initiatives, in 1779 the Society for the Relief of the Aged Needy of the Jewish Faith was established and did good work for many years.

It wasn't all gloom, however. The community still always managed to enjoy Purim. In Goulston Street, just off Whitechapel High Street in the East End of London, the annual Purim Fair was held. The festivities started with a Fancy Dress Party in the street outside the Great Synagogue and in 1788 a gallows was constructed on which to hang, in effigy, the villain of the biblical piece, the wicked Haman. At the fair there would be clowns and puppet shows and you could see genuine wild animals as well; part fair, part circus. As Purim comes towards the end of the winter, everybody was ready for a party by then.

Poverty-stricken or not, the community as a whole also remained great gamblers. In 1788 when Daniel Mendoza, the Jewish boxer, fought Richard Humphries, no less than £20,000 changed hands. Mendoza and the Jews lost heavily. In 1789, though, there was a return match, and this time Mendoza won, to become the 16th English Heavyweight Champion. So those who backed him again, could have recovered their losses.

Moses Schiff was growing up and if he wasn't to remain a burden on his father, some useful occupation would have to be found for him. Schiff wrote to his brother in Frankfurt when Moses was thinking of becoming a business agent in exports:

> I spoke of it to Rabbi Jacob Rotterdam who does a lot of commission business to your place...and we came to the conclusion that it would be worth while to be an agent for East Indian goods but not for woollen merchandise...it does not pay, because most of the goods which the merchants from there [Frankfurt] buy, they order direct by letter from the manufacturers in this country. What a commissionnaire sometimes sends there, he must have credit for [here] because all the goods are sold on terms of credit for six months or more...what you write about understanding [the business] is folly...someone has told you there a foolish thing that sometimes one might buy from a swindler! That might happen once in 70 years.'

Jewish merchants around the world anchored their businesses firmly on dealing with unimpeachable integrity. It had enabled them to survive and prosper in international commerce for centuries. What Moses would need was to understand the territory and then have the ability to finance his cash flow. He'd also have to choose his area of expertise in trading very carefully. The most serious problem was that the Indian diamond market was diminishing in importance and the Ashkenazi merchants found their livelihoods vanishing as a consequence. In addition, a considerable number of the Jewish rich decided to convert themselves or convert their children. The wealth would have to be replaced if the community was to remain self-sufficient. A new generation of Jewish entrepreneurs would be necessary in the future.

Although Schiff had now been in England for some 15 years, he still didn't speak good English. He looked for help, among others, to David Levi.

Levi translated both the Sephardi and the Ashkenazi liturgy into English, as well as the Pentateuch. Although he was always desperately poor, scraping a living as a cobbler and then as a hatter, his work on the Hebrew material was outstanding. He was far better than Alexander Alexander whose 1773 text had many errors. In addition, for those who didn't speak English well enough, Moses Hyams, for his part, had produced three volumes of the liturgy in Yiddish.

Levi also wrote pamphlets and polemics and the Christian Hebraists found in him a Jewish one-man anti-defamation committee. In 1783 the *London Chronicle* gave his *A Succinct Account of the Rites and Governance of the Jews* a full-page review, and his major work was a a monumental, three-volume *Lingua Sacra* which was both a major Hebrew grammar and a comprehensive dictionary. Unfortunately, scholars are often badly underpaid and although the Goldsmids at the Great managed to provide Levi with a regular pittance of 90p a week, his work was the epitomization of a labour of love.

Schiff was glad of the help and, indeed, one of his more endearing traits was his modesty. His responsa, novellae and sermons were much admired and he was encouraged to publish the work he had written. It was a temptation few would have resisted but Schiff – always concerned about money – still made the excuse that he had doubts about his own learning and that he would never have his material published until after his death. The truth was he didn't feel it proper to write for the sake of receiving plaudits. He worked for the cause, not for the glory. So it was only in 1822 that Moses put the responsa, sermons and expositions together, and had Offenbach publish *Leshon Zahab (The Golden Tongue)* in Europe.

There were limits to Schiff's influence. When in 1788 a new Orphan and Charity School was opened, it was significant that, at last, English and arithmetic were to be taught. Doubly significant was that one of the rules of the school stipulated that there should be no interference in its running by the ecclesiastical authorities. Too many of those who provided the money from now on would be, primarily, concerned to turn out Jewish children who would be able to take their place in English society. Religious education was, increasingly, going to be put on the back burner. The school was created for boy orphans, between the ages of 6 and 10 when they started. They had to be able to read the prayer book in Hebrew and they came to school wearing uniform: 'of mulberry colour, lin'd with shallon [with] brass buttons'. They also couldn't stay at the school for more than six months after their Barmitzvah at 13.

In 1790 the growing size of the community finally decided the Great's Vestry to knock down their venerable synagogue and build a new one. There was no preservation order at the time on the first Ashkenazi synagogue to be built in England since the Restoration. Moses Hart's synagogue was replaced and his daughter, Judith Levy, made the largest contribution – £4,000 – towards the new one. It was a massive donation, but when the new synagogue still needed additional spending on it, Judith Levy proclaimed herself upset that they hadn't asked her for more. But then Mrs Levy was the rich exception that proved the rule. Her income was a vast £6,000 a year and it was reported that she played quadrille for high stakes with the Countess of Yarmouth and Lord Stormont.

Typical of the far more prevalent poverty was the occasion in 1790 when the dead body of a poor Ashkenazi Jew was left in Dukes Place because no synagogue was prepared to go to the expense of burying it. The Sephardi Mahamad met at 9 o'clock at night to consider this disgraceful and demeaning situation, and decided that the Leadenhall Street synagogue should take the responsibility. They ordered the wardens of the shul to come round, ignoring the hour, and the honorary officers reluctantly agreed to do so, even though it was really no business of the Sephardim. On occasions, the Mahamad even fixed the fees that smaller Ashkenazi synagogues would pay the Great for dealing with the burials of the impoverished. In 1794 the three Ashkenazi synagogues sank their original differences and combined their funds to help the poor.

The financial state of most of the Ashkenazi community then was lamentable. There was an appalling degree of misery, to the extent that a considerable proportion of the Jews were totally demoralized. Unable to work in manufacturing industries because they lacked the training, they tried to scratch a living by selling such articles as cane strings, barley sugar and sweet cakes. A few of them went into domestic service, a standby for large numbers of the impecunious. As late as Edwardian times, one-third of the women in employment were servants, but it was difficult to maintain religious standards of observance in such a position, and so the jobs were unattractive to the Orthodox. The synagogue authorities took the view that, as a general principle, it was much better to teach the unemployed how to earn money rather than just give it to them, which they feared would simply lead to idleness. That was why they gave start-up money to so many pedlars. This approach would be reiterated by Chief Rabbi Jakobovits in the 1980s as the best way forward. It would be warmly welcomed by the prime minister of the day, Margaret Thatcher.

An additional problem for the pedlars – and there were at least 1,000 of them – was that the anti-alien legislation in 1792 applied restrictions to the movement of foreigners, as Britain went to war with France and contemplated the possibility of invasion. The navy's control of the English Channel had been eroded by the growth and success of the French and Spanish fleets and it seemed unlikely that the Royal Navy could resist a determined foe. It would have been easy for spies to masquerade as pedlars, so the government stopped them travelling. This was particularly disastrous for the Jewish community as so many additional refugees had fled the continent to escape the war. The pedlars who managed to move around also found that local landlords were turning tenant farmers into working labourers by taking over what had previously been common land. That pauperized much of the countryside and there was less to spend on the pedlars' wares. The 'increase of foreign poor...at the end of the last [eighteenth] century was increasing at an alarming rate...The Ashkenazi Jews...found it no easy task to cope with an evil that was assuming yearly more gigantic proportions.'[13]

By 1791 the community's size had reached 12,000, of whom 11,000 were in London. An additional cause for the increase had been further pogroms in eastern Europe. More synagogues were needed and these took many forms. The Great gave permission for a small Polish synagogue to be built near Hounsditch in Gun Yard in 1792, and a new synagogue in the Strand opened in 1797.

As was normally the case in times of war, the Jewish congregation heard from the pulpit of their duty to the king and constitution, but there was an additional need to emphasize this after the French Revolution broke out. One of the results of 1789 was the full emancipation of French Jews and it was considered possible that this might get the French some support among the British community. The Americans were popular for abolishing all the religious rules for serving the state and there was initially a lot of support in England for the French manifesto of liberty, equality and fraternity; it was in 1791 that Tom Paine published *The Rights of Man*. In the end the support of British Jews for the French Revolution was negligible. Even with all their financial problems, Britain's side of the Channel still seemed the better political bet.

In 1790 Schiff celebrated his Silver Jubilee as Chief Rabbi and if no records have survived of the event, it must still have given both the man and the community a great deal of pleasure. As it said, among a lot of other things, on his tombstone:

> he bore the burden of Rabbinical office for 27 years with outstanding grace. He planned the future to lead the ignorant in the ways of uprightness and rebuked them with bruises of love. For those near and far he was an advisor... true Torah was in his mouth with a sweet golden tongue... they testified about him as to his pleasant deeds.

None of our stilted twenty-first century 'In loving memory...'. Schiff died at the end of December 1791 and a vast crowd came to the burial service. No less than 110 coaches were needed and both the Jewish and Christian shops in the neighbourhood shut for the day. The *Morning Post* recorded that: 'He was accounted the most learned Jew of the age', but still took the opportunity to emphasize the plight of the majority of the Jewish community: 'we have not as yet been able to ascertain if he made any provision for his poor, who are at present in a starving situation.'

After Schiff died, there was no replacement for 10 years; Rabbi Moses Myers from the New Synagogue acted as Chief Rabbi. Responsa, where necessary, were obtained from abroad. In 1793, for example, a surgeon wanted to dissect the corpse of a Jew who had died of gallstones. Was that permissible? Jews have to be buried within 24 hours of their death and the bodies are sacrosanct. The Chief Rabbi of Prague said that, in the cause of medical research, it was just about acceptable. One wonders what was happening to the body while the Chief Rabbi made up his mind.

The Great's problem was that, like the extension to the synagogue in 1766, it had overspent its budget on the new building. To make matters even worse, the war with the French brought inflation and shortages. They were temporarily embarrassed and couldn't afford the expense of the Chief Rabbi's office.

In 1794 it was agreed that the contract for Sephardi and Ashkenazi grain for Passover matzos should be given to one miller, but even that economy wasn't sufficient, with the price of flour rising sharply to between £3.25 and £3.50 a sack. Charity was still given to the poor on the festival, but only two-thirds could be in matzos and the other third came in potatoes. It was also agreed that paupers should get 5p a week, of which the Great would provide $2^1/_2$p and the Hambro and New $1^1/_4$p each. There was even an attempt to form a Joint Shechita Board with the Sephardim, but this came to nothing at the time. The Sephardim's Secretary wrote somewhat unctuously to the Vestry: 'We shall be happy to cultivate that harmony and good understanding that subsists between our congregations and which are so essential to our welfare.' In effect, thanks but no thanks.

When high standards are set for a long time, it often takes years for the organization to decline, even without its charismatic leader. This was the case with Schiff's Beth Din, which continued to have the respect not only of the community but of the British courts as well. In the case of Lindo *vs.* Belisarius in 1795, expert evidence on the authenticity of a Jewish marriage was given by a Dayan from the Beth Din, which the Consistory Court described as: 'courts of great authority and on matters of Jewish law entitled to the greatest respect.'

Schiff did a first class job. It's still a pity we don't know exactly when he was born.

NOTES

1   Bernard Homa, *Footprints on the Sands of Time*, 1990.
2   Charles Duschinsky, *The Rabbinate of the Great Synagogue*, London, 1921.
3   William Shakespeare, *Hamlet*.
4   Cecil Roth, *History of the Great Synagogue*, Edward Goldston, 1950.
5   Ibid.
6   *Annual Register* 1766.
7   Ibid.
8   Duschinsky, *The Rabbinate of the Great Synagogue*.
9   Ibid.
10   Ibid.
11   Christopher Hibbert, *King's Mob*, Longmans Green, 1959.
12   Mordecai M. Kaplan, *Educational Abuses and Reforms in Hanoverian England, Jubilee Volume*, Jewish Theological Seminary of America, 1953.
13   *Jewish Chronicle*, 1874.

13 Solomon Hirschell 1802–42

If you were walking through the City of London on a weekday afternoon in early Autumn, around 1810, the streets would be thronged with carriages and drays, carts and horses. Without a congestion charge the pace of the traffic would be slow, but everybody would get to their destinations eventually. Unless it was the day when everything ground to a halt. Which wasn't even because of an unseasonable snow shower. Along the street that afternoon came an enormous procession, headed by a six-foot tall, charismatic figure in a long white robe, followed by thousands of his faithful. More would join the parade at every street corner, all heading for Custom House Quay on the river. This was Chief Rabbi Solomon Hirschell, on the first day of the Jewish New Year, going to the Thames to perform the ceremony of Tashlich. To throw bread into the water, and chant from the book of Micah, 'thou wilt cast their sins into the sea'. Because on Yom Kippur, the great fast, in 10 days' time, the Almighty would make a judgement on what would happen to you next year, on the basis of how bad those sins had been this year. This was unlike casting bread (Ecclesiastes 11:1), where you hoped to get something back – on this occasion the hope was that the sins would disappear for good.

What the Christian City financiers made of it is not recorded. It showed the confidence of the Chief Rabbi, however, that this did not worry him. Over the last 100 years the community had dug its roots deep into the hospitable London clay.

Solomon Hirschell was the second-longest serving Chief Rabbi after Aaron Hart. His father was Hart Lyon, Chief Rabbi from 1756–63 and his great-grandfather was Zevi Ashkenazi. Hirschell was Lyon's youngest son, born in Cock and Hoop Yard in Hounsditch, in the East End of London, in 1761. He was brought up in Halberstadt, Mannheim and Berlin where his father was, successively, the rabbi. In 1778 he had married Rebecca Koenigsberg and they had eight children whom, in retrospect, they may or may not have considered a blessing. By 1794 Hirschell was also a rabbi serving the community in Prenzlaw near his father in Berlin. There is a tendency to dismiss Hirschell as an old-fashioned, pre-Enlightenment Chief Rabbi, so different from the cultivated Nathan Marcus Adler who would succeed him. What is easily overlooked is that Hirschell was brought up in Berlin by his father, Hart Lyon, who was one of the finest talmudists of his day. The apple didn't fall far from the bough.

The Great had played with the idea of replacing David Tevele Schiff in 1794. Hirschell had applied for the job, but the community couldn't afford the cost. It wasn't until March 1802 that the economic prospects looked brighter as the Treaty of Amiens briefly halted the Napoleonic Wars. The congregation started looking again and, by June, Hirschell easily won the vote.

The *Gentleman's Magazine* commented:

> The Congregation of German Jews in London have elected, after a vacancy of 10 years, a new High Priest for their great nation. The choice has fallen on Rev. S. Hart. The new High Priest was born within the City of London and the great Jewish nation here in London must surely profit by his return.[1]

Hirschell's ministry was in an age of intellectual turmoil. The old pillars of society were being uprooted one by one. Napoleon had destroyed the idea that the kings of Europe and their institutions were irreplaceable. The Industrial Revolution was beginning to transform the processes of manufacturing, and the rights of the individual were being trumpeted as never before. The supporters of change at all levels of society grew in influence and effectiveness. In Britain, as long as the country was fighting Napoleon, the ideas of the French Revolution could officially be rejected; they were the ideas of the enemy and defeating Napoleon's armies and navy was by far the more important objective. What was more, Napoleon was anticlerical and maintaining Christianity was part of Britain's case for opposing the French.

When that had been achieved in 1815, the position changed and the new French philosophy could be considered on its merits. The Revolution's secularism did, long-term, weaken the hitherto all-important influence of religion and the Church in society. The concept of greater equality had also been seen to work quite well. The machinery of advocating equal rights for all was going to slowly mesh into gear, but not everywhere – Russia firmly put the clocks back. Many states in Germany reintroduced the ghetto. But in western Europe the concept of freedom from all discrimination was no longer going to be thinking the unthinkable. At the same time, in such an atmosphere, Orthodox Judaism would come under pressure as well and Hirschell was there to ride out the storm, although he would have to do without some of the great families who had supported his father. Moses Hart and Benjamin Levy had no male descendants and the Franks youngsters had left the religion.

Hirschell was faced with challenges which would have stretched many of his predecessors. Although Napoleon was eventually defeated, many of his enormous changes had a lasting effect on the countries he had invaded. Though minor revolutionary innovations like new names for the months – Thermidor, Brumaire – might be abandoned, nothing was now so sacred that it couldn't be questioned to see if it could be improved.

Just as David Nietto had had to deal with the growing influence of science, now the Chief Rabbi had to deal with the effects of this new movement for freedom and equal rights. Was it to include the freedom to change Judaism? Was it going to upset the former overall control of the Mahamad and the Vestry? What was going to be the effect on English Jews of moving still further out into the wider community? If more opportunities were to be made available for Jews, did the Jews in return have to try to become more like the majority of the population?

Fundamentally, England was a Christian country. It was a Christian government and members were only accepted on the oath of the true faith of a Christian. The king had to be Protestant and the bishops sat in the House of Lords. Now, on the horizon, the influence of the Church was under threat from secularism, not from another sect, but from the idea of no sect.

It was a battle that would go on for at least 100 years. Slowly but surely the Church of England retreated. The future Chief Rabbis would give way a fraction, but it would be a tactical retreat to secure fully justified equality. As the pendulum slowly swung away from the strict standards of observant Orthodoxy over those years, it would be necessary to hope for a few 'white knights' to arrive to ensure this latest battle wasn't lost. Just in time they did, though they looked more like black knights. We'll meet them later.

Hirschell was in his prime at the time of his election. With his 'commanding personality and force of character, regarding which many stories were still current down to the beginning of the present [twentieth] century'.[2] He was highly regarded outside the community as well. The *Morning Post* told its readers of Hirschell conducting a wedding with 'great and interesting solemnity'. He was a witty man as well: 'I can reduce a wealthy man to poverty very quickly. It is enough for me to ask for £20 for a needy family – he can never afford it.'[2]

He certainly needed a sense of humour as he inherited a full-time office which had been understaffed for a decade:

> Throughout the 19th century, the duties devolving upon the Chief Rabbi were onerous and variegated. As chief of the Beth Din he had to decide, either alone or in that court, all religious points that might be submitted to him by a synagogue, its ministers or a private individual. He had to settle all questions of ritual and compose prayers and draw up forms of service for special occasions, such as days appointed for National Thanksgiving or Humiliation or the Dedication of a synagogue or a communal institution. He was principal and chief teacher of the Yeshiva, he had to authorize the appointment of synagogue officials, shochetim, mohelim and shomerim. Matters relating to Jewish marriage and divorce were subject to his jurisdiction and, in addition, he was a sort of Consul General for Jews all over the world.[3]

Hirschell's bailiwick did indeed cover all the communities in Britain and he was consulted by many overseas congregations as well; Philadelphia, New York and Charleston, Melbourne and Tasmania, among many others. As he wrote in 1833 after there had been a great deal of emigration, due to the slump after the end of the Napoleonic Wars: 'In our generation America, Asia and Africa have become like the environs of London.'

To have the approval of the Chief Rabbi in London meant a lot in the United States and, sometimes, for the oddest of concepts. In 1818 a crank called M.M. Noah decided the time had come to build a new city called Ararat on Grand Island near Niagara Falls. He wrote to both the Chief Rabbi and the Haham, inviting them to be commissioners. Both hastily declined but Noah put them on the letterhead anyway. The project was not a success.[4]

There was a wide variety of more Orthodox topics. Some he won and some he lost. In 1803 he appealed for more of the time of the small roll of children in the orphan and charity school to be devoted to studying the Talmud. The governors said they couldn't afford the teachers, but the truth was that the pupils were being taught secular subjects to keep them off the poor rate when they grew up. In fairness, a knowledge of the Talmud wouldn't be as likely to prevent them becoming paupers, and the unwavering policy of the British

Jews was still never to allow their co-religionists to become a burden on the rates of the local population. In 1830 the Poor Law Amendment Act condemned paupers to the workhouse. If they were Jews they were not forgotten. Appeals were made in 1834 and 1842 for the Jews in such establishments to have access to kosher food and to be excused work on the Sabbath.

In 1804 a tiny, very Orthodox seed was planted when the Chevra Shass synagogue was founded for Polish immigrants. It was small, it was insignificant, but it was a tiny, right-wing shoot.

In 1804 discussion began again on combining some of the activities of the three main Ashkenazi synagogues. For four years there was an annual meeting at Nathan Mayer Rothschild's house to try to reach agreement. Eventually in 1808 they were successful. Burial, *shechita* and the charities would henceforth be organized centrally. From now on, among other improvements, there would be free burial for Jewish paupers. No more would the Vestry have to be called to the Mahamad in the dead of night to discuss unburied bodies lying in the street.

The influence of the Rothschild family had grown steadily during the Napoleonic Wars. In particular their brief to invest £600,000 on behalf of the ruler of Hesse Cassel in Germany, looking for a safe haven for his wealth, bolstered their image of having almost unlimited funds at their disposal. With Nathan Mayer Rothschild a warden at the Great synagogue, a lot of Hirschell's needs for charity were satisfied.

The questions flowed in from the provincial communities onto Hirschell's desk. What were the honorary officers in Exeter to do in 1823 if there was too much noise in the synagogue during Purim, when Haman's name was mentioned:

> Call a constable and treat him or them as the Act directs, being protected by the Bishop's licence...no person above barmitzvah is to make any noise in the synagogue neither with hammers not in any other way whatever under fine of Five Shillings [25p].[5]

Schiff's kettledrum would not have gone down well in Exeter.

Hirschell found officers for the communities as well. He recommended a shochet to Penzance in 1811 and suggested, good-humouredly, to the congregation that they: 'would behave to him properly, for you may rest assured those articles are very scarce in the market'.[6]

The Penzance community still had rows with the shochet.

Hirschell also had to be consulted about conversions. It was necessary to confirm to him, for example, that the female convert had been to a *mikveh*. Conversion was still a sensitive subject and it was still illegal in England. The rabbis have never been keen on conversions anyway, except in especially difficult circumstances. In the book of Ruth, Naomi tried to discourage her daughter-in-law from converting. The motivation had to be a love of the Almighty and not a love of Naomi.

An analysis of the weddings which took place at the Great over a 50-year period, shows that about 2 per cent of over 3,000 weddings involved a proselyte; the clue being the entry of the wife as being the daughter of 'Abraham, our father', a synonym for a convert. 7 What usually happened was that the lady received instruction in Judaism under the supervision of the Beth Din. When they decided that she was sufficiently knowledgeable to become a Jewess, she would be sent to Amsterdam where she would be converted by the Dutch rabbinate, there being no objection to the practice in Holland.

There was at least one exception, though, which is very difficult to explain. In 1816 a rich Bath merchant had a non-Jewish partner and a child by her. He wrote to Hirschell asking if the lady and his daughter could be converted to regularize their relationship. As we've seen, this was not a good enough reason for conversion; only a sincere belief in the Almighty as the one and only God is acceptable. In King David's time the economy in the Holy Land was flourishing and lots of people wanted to convert to enjoy the benefits. No converts were allowed on that basis either. Yet 150 years after the initial letter from Bath, a *ketubah* for the couple was found at the Western synagogue, confirming a religious wedding between them some five months later. Perhaps the merchant ran a strictly Orthodox household, which would have reduced the time needed for conversion, but hardly to a few months. How the conversion could have been carried out that quickly is only one difficulty. That it was at the Western is another. The wedding would have had to be authorized by Hirschell but the congregation at the Western was independent and the ceremony would normally have been at the Great: 'No normal conversion could have been effected within so short a period.'8

The high point of 1809 for the community was 14 April when the Dukes of Cambridge and Cumberland visited the synagogue for a service on the Friday evening. The dukes told Abraham Goldsmid of their intention rather than the synagogue authorities. Goldsmid and his brother, Benjamin, had been instrumental in raising very large loans for the government to finance the Napoleonic Wars. They had flourished through their efforts but their selection as brokers depended on the attitude of the political party in power and when Pitt died in 1806, the instructions ceased. Benjamin Goldsmid became deeply depressed at their misfortune and committed suicide in 1808. Hirschell had been close to him. Indeed, on the Goldsmid estate in Roehampton a section of the grounds had been set aside to grow wheat which was reserved for the Chief Rabbi's matzo at Passover.

The visit was partly to thank Abraham Goldsmid and the excitement was, naturally, intense. Mrs Rothschild did the flowers and Nathan Mayer, who was one the wardens, provided new hangings and trimmings for the inside of the synagogue. Rothschild had only moved to London permanently the year before and was still in business as a textile importer from Manchester. So the hangings probably came from stock. Goldsmid had a robe of white satin made for Hirschell and the path to the front door of the synagogue was strewn with flowers. Two years later Goldsmid raised £14 million for the government but then he, too, fell prey to depression and in 1811, like his brother, took his own life.

Hirschell became very friendly with another member of the royal family, the Duke of Sussex. His Grace was a keen Hebraist and he asked Hirschell to teach him the subject. They spent a lot of time together. Hirschell's ability to make the Jewish case led Sussex, until his death, to often speak in support of bills in the House of Lords to end Jewish disabilities.

A less salubrious spotlight on the congregation in 1809 was occasioned by the raising of the price of theatre tickets in Drury Lane. There were demonstrations against the increases and some of the Jewish theatregoers were condemned as the ringleaders. The theatre management decided to hire Jewish boxers to keep order and Hirschell was asked to intervene to restore order. This he did by removing 100 Jews from the charity list at the synagogue and threatening *herem* on anybody who brought the community into disrepute. Fortunately for their reputation, if not for playgoers, the theatre burnt down in 1810 which solved the problem.

George III's jubilee was also celebrated in 1809. This was a biblical reckoning, as the King had been on the throne for 49 years and the ancient Jubilee was, indeed, 7 × 7 years. In biblical times debtors had been let off the money they owed in the momentous year and, to mark the occasion, the community set out to raise funds to pay off at least the smaller debts of congregants. Many were released from prison as a result of this generosity.

To many of his tasks Hirschell brought particular skills. As David Nietto had been able to marry Judaism and contemporary science, so Hirschell set out to prove that Hebrew was a modern language and not just the tongue of the ancient Bible. While Hebrew had always been considered *loshen kodesh*, the Ashkenazim's lingua franca was Yiddish and the Sephardim used Spanish and Portuguese. The rabbis might be fluent in Hebrew but it wasn't in current use. It had developed little over the centuries. To that extent it was a dead language.

The Haskalah was the movement which brought Hebrew literature up to speed in the modern world, and Moses Mendelssohn in Germany was the engine room of the effort to achieve this. In Berlin, Hirschell's father, Hart Lyon: 'was intimate there with, and greatly respected by, Moses Mendelssohn and his circle' and was influenced by them in his intellectual, though not in his theological outlook.[9]

Lyon passed on the objective to his son. The idea was to remodel Hebrew and have it used by scholars as a modern and colloquial idiom. Hirschell learned to use the language in that way. He preferred to use Hebrew rather than Yiddish when he wrote to the wardens of the synagogues which acknowledged his authority. Whether they, for their part, were happy with this is questionable, as they might well have had difficulty in translating the Chief Rabbi's messages. What Hirschell was saying was that there was a need to study Hebrew more, and to make it an up-to-date method of communication. Hirschell wrote verses in Hebrew, notably to salute the agreement for the City synagogues to work more closely together in 1805. If you got a *kiddush* cup from the Chief Rabbi – his favourite present – it would always have Hebrew verses inscribed on it. When the State of Israel was able to use Hebrew again as its common tongue after nearly 2,000 years, it was because of the efforts of old-time scholars like Hirschell to keep it alive. The near-contemporary *Voice of Jacob* was full of praise for his efforts: 'the correctness and purity of his style in Hebrew composition and the fluency with which he wrote that tongue showed evidence of his superiority over other rabbis of his age, among whom grammatical study was much neglected'.

Judgements on Hirschell have to take into account that he was 41 when he was appointed and 80 when he died. The energy and the attitudes of an old man are often dissimilar from those of early middle age. The *Jewish Chronicle*, soon after his death, commented: 'He presided for 40 years over the numerous Congregations of Britain; but he left no works of learning, no charitable foundation, no public institution to perpetuate his name.'[10]

Certainly the Anglo-Jewish publications of the time said that he had no influence on the shaping of the community, but then journalism was never a perfect science. For one thing, it is very difficult to look into the future and know which ideas will die and which will develop.

If the press weren't happy with Hirschell, he wasn't all that enamoured with his occupation. He wrote to his son that it was: 'well nigh intolerable by reason of its servitude and aggravating no less than the bitterness I experience in the dissensions and shamelessness of our times'. It could be that he was in the wrong job. In 1827 he wrote: 'I had never the intention of becoming a rabbi. I wanted to be a wine merchant.' He also said he would have preferred to be: 'a grower of grapes for wine and a teacher in my spare time'.

No period of 40 years, however, is going to be all gloom and doom. Not all the initiatives can be judged by the events of the next few years. The reinvigoration of Hebrew was a case in point. Equally, Hirschell's support for the new Jews' Free School was to help a great educational establishment survive its teething troubles. From that small acorn grew a great tree of knowledge, although it owed its birth to the work of Christian missionaries.

The reaction of many fervent Christians to the questioning of the former foundation of society was to go onto the attack. Preachers such as John Wesley brought enormous enthusiasm to their efforts to maintain the gospels at the heart of society. As always though, inspiring their own adherents wasn't their sole ambition. The Jews remained a target for the evangelists, to be converted to the road the Christians followed.

The London Society for Promoting Christianity among the Jews was founded in 1809. Looked at from one angle, the Church Missionary Societies were just spreading the gospel, endeavouring to help the poor and needy and saving souls. From a Jewish point of view they were a nineteenth-century variation of Little Red Riding Hood. What is indisputable is that the LSPC – and the London Missionary Society – created three schools in the East End of London in the early 1800s, which welcomed poverty-stricken Jewish children, fed them during the day, clothed them and attempted to persuade them to embrace Christianity.

Not perhaps surprisingly, Solomon Hirschell objected strongly. As he said in the Great Synagogue in 1807:

> I had occasion...to forewarn every one...not to send any of
> their Children to the newly established Free School until we had
> ...determined if it be completely free from any possible harm

to the welfare of our religion...Now having since been fully convinced...that the whole purpose of this seemingly kind exertion, is...a decoying experiment to undermine the props of our religion; and the sole intent of this Institution is...only to entice innocent Jewish Children, during their early years... from the religion of their fathers and forefathers.[11]

The message was pretty stark: don't send the children or be thrown out of the community for putting them in the way of temptation. For a devoted parent with a hungry child dressed in rags, that was a terrible choice. Many continued to obtain the material benefits for their kids at these schools, but the success rate of conversion as a quid pro quo was very limited indeed. The missionary societies claimed after 10 years that they had converted 300 Jewish children but it is suggested, even in non-Jewish circles, that this number is probably exaggerated.[12]

The solution, of course, was to start Jewish schools which would offer their pupils the same benefits. There was also a serious need to teach the poor children how to earn a living. As Patrick Colquoun, a liberal-minded magistrate, wrote about the Jewish children in 1796:

very seldom trained in any trade or occupation by which they can earn their livelihood by manual labour; their youths excluded from becoming apprentices, and their females from hiring themselves generally as servants, on account of their superstitious adherence to their ceremonial traditions.

This was a classic example of contemporary Christian views: I follow the true faith, you have superstitious adherences, they are savages. The simple fact was that a poor Jewish lad couldn't get an apprenticeship with a Christian master if he insisted on keeping the Sabbath and festivals.

The Talmud Torah at the Great had been established in 1732 but it was always very small. Now Joshua van Oven, the honorary physician to the Great and a governor of the Talmud Torah, managed to raise £20,000 towards the creation of a Jewish school which would train far more pupils. The money was eventually used to build the Jews' Hospital which opened in 1806. It was an old-age home for ten senior citizens and a school for ten boys and eight girls. From such tiny beginnings came the Jews' Free School. By 1817 it was hived off, purely a school, with its own building and 220 pupils. By the end of the century it would be the largest school in the country with over

4,000. There was another one formed in 1853 by the independent Western synagogue, eventually called the Westminster Jews' Free School and both concentrated on the secular rather than purely religious education. Even so, the top class for the JFS was the Great synagogue's Talmud Torah. The governors of the schools always resisted the Chief Rabbi having ultimate authority over their operation, but the relationship between them was warm and friendly and the schools in the future remained Orthodox institutions. As did the Jewish Infants School which was founded in 1839.

The end of the Napoleonic Wars was cause for celebration on a massive national scale. Hirschell was staying in Brighton at the end of the war and made his own contribution by displaying: 'a large tree with four branches representing Austria, Prussia, Russia and France, united together at the root by England and surrounded by scriptural quotations'.[13]

There were aggravations for Hirschell as there must inevitably be for any leader. His learning and published prayers were attacked by Solomon Bennett and Levy Alexander. He was annoyed and sometimes upset, but he could well afford to give them little of his time. His own position with the community was rock solid and he was much-loved. His opponents were comparative pygmies when it came to stature in the wider world.

As the years went by, Hirschell retired more to his study, as befitted a senior citizen. A rabbi was, anyway, a 'scholar in residence', supposed to devote himself to learning. Unfortunately, Hirschell took his faith so literally that he weakened his metabolism with continual fasting, until he was subject to constant fainting fits. This in spite of the fact that the Din frowns on any action which undermines your health. Hirschell became an onlooker at many of the alterations which affected the community. In 1830 a Jewish Emancipation Bill was introduced into Parliament. It was to be the first of many which failed to get sufficient support to become law. It wasn't that prime ministers, like Wellington, Grey and Melbourne were anti-Semitic. Wellington – and Grey in particular – were massively more interested in the progress of the proposed Reform Bill. This would make the nation's constituencies somewhat more representative of where people actually lived when it was finally passed in 1832. To pass or block a Reform Bill would involve the votes of the bishops and their supporters in the House of Lords. Every vote was going to be vital and the bishops were not in favour of abolishing Jewish disabilities. Prime ministers were always tempted to curry favour with them by blocking pro-Jewish legislation.

Where the Houses of Parliament weren't involved, there could be progress. In 1830 there was finally a change in the oath to become a Freeman of the City of London and Jews were at last able to own shops in the city. In the same year Parliament did agree that a Jewish marriage could become as valid as a Christian one, even if there wasn't a vicar present. On the other hand, in 1835 David Salomans was elected an alderman of the City of London and the election result was annulled. In 1841 a bill to enable Jews to hold municipal office was passed in the Commons but killed in the Lords. It was hard going. Some of the old Jewish traditions remained in effect as well. Lewis Eleazar Pyke was the beadle of the Great Synagogue for many years and he would still approach the massive doors every day before the morning service and ceremoniously strike them three times. This was meant to ensure that the congregation did not arrive to find still in residence the spirits who were believed to occupy the synagogue during the night.

The idea that Hirschell became something of a hermit, however, is unfair.[14] There was plenty of communal work to keep him busy. Between 1822 and his death in 1842 he licensed 150 shochetim for the various communities which acknowledged his authority. He also dealt with about 15 divorce cases a year and many of these involved the consort's transportation to Australia. It was always questionable whether the husband would live to complete his sentence and it would often be difficult for the wife to prove his death. It therefore became the practice to grant conditional divorces (a Get) before the convict ship sailed, which ensured that the wife wouldn't remarry during the period the husband was away, but could remarry if he didn't come back.

In Europe the affairs of the Jewish communities were often subject to state interference. Hirschell was consulted by governments, like Russia, Poland and Austria when they needed a recommendation for a good rabbi. His base in Britain gave him great prestige in their councils. He was the community's representative at official functions and: 'on several such occasions, the *Gentleman's Magazine* made mention of his sartorial elegance when attending Mansion House functions'.[15]

If he didn't actually visit his provincial communities, he certainly kept in touch with them, and encouraged each one to start a Jewish school. He was prepared to help them on any religious topic, no matter how far away they might be. In 1830 he sent one of his Dayanim, Aaron Levy, to Australia to deliver a Get and to see if there was anything he could do for the Jewish congregations there.

One of his last acts was to grant Abraham Hart the right to establish a congregation in Wellington, New Zealand, when he emigrated to that country.

The year 1840 was a particularly difficult one for the 79-year-old Chief. According to the *Zohar*, the chief Spanish Kabbalist text, it was the year in which the Messiah would arrive. The Messianic fever was led by Joseph Crool, who taught Hebrew at Cambridge and had filled ministerial posts in Exeter and Nottingham. Hirschell didn't hesitate to condemn his activities and, because of the Chief Rabbi's standing, the Messianic movement made little headway in Britain.

In the spring of 1840 things got worse. A popular Italian Catholic priest in Smyrna in the Turkish province of Syria disappeared. A mob accused the Jews of murdering him. Many were arrested and confessed under torture. The claim was the old canard that his blood had been needed to make matzo for Passover. The European diplomats in the city were equally adamant that the Jews were guilty and several prisoners died from the effects of the barbaric treatment inflicted upon them. In Greece a 10-year-old boy disappeared on the island of Rhodes and, again, the local Jews were accused of the crime on no evidence whatsoever, other than the suspicion of ritual murder.

The aged Solomon Hirschell made it clear there was no religious foundation to the accusations. Never mind matzo – if there is *any* blood left in a slaughtered animal then the meat isn't kosher. Precisely because ancient pagan worship often involved human sacrifice, dishes containing blood had been specifically forbidden to the Jews in biblical times. Sir Moses Montefiore, the lay leader of the community, discussed the position with his French counterpart, because France supported the Syrians against their overlords, the Turks. The French Jews declined to act and the French consul in Damascus led the attack on the Jews, his anti-Semitic views being very well known. Moral support came from London where the Lord Mayor denounced the accusations. In addition the British foreign secretary was Viscount Palmerston, who was very helpful. As the French instructed their embassies to help Roman Catholics, so Palmerston told the Foreign Office to do what it could for the Jews in their areas.

Money was raised by many European Jewish communities to help the persecuted victims of the arrests and Montefiore sailed for the Middle East to fight for justice in both cases. In this he was successful and obtained the release of the prisoners who had survived. It was a typical expedition for Montefiore, a Sephardi who was president of the Board of Deputies, and it further enhanced his tremendous reputation – even Queen Victoria came to admire him. To tackle these outbreaks of anti-Semitism the French Jews created a new defence organization called the Alliance Israélite Universelle, and from that came the British Anglo-Jewish Association.

Towards the end of Hirschell's life Judaism was coming increasingly under the microscope, particularly in the German heartland. Those who wanted radical change became known, collectively, as the Reform Movement. In England those who became known as the Reformers owed little loyalty to the German movement. Some of the changes they wanted in the Sephardi community in 1836 were not to prove contentious in the long run; sermons in English, somewhat shorter services and the introduction of a choir were granted within both Orthodox communities during the nineteenth century. Some later changes were more radical; the use of an organ, no repetition of the *Amidah* (a key prayer in the Sabbath service), group barmitzvahs and the abolition of the second day of festivals. However, it was only when the Reformers had totally broken away a century later that the floodgates were opened. The changes became more fundamental as time went by. A hundred years later we find that: 'Reform Judaism nonetheless declares anachronistic such differentiatory [from Christianity] practices as covering the head at worship, the dietary laws, the use of the phylacteries, etc.'[16]

The breakaway group proclaimed their intention of forming a separate organization in the West End and, after much unsuccessful pleading and agonizing over the effects on the community of a split, Hirschell excluded every dissenter from the Orthodox body, an action which was extremely painful for him. One of his pupils was the Reform Minister, David Woolf Marks, and when Hirschell's wife went blind, Marks came by every Sunday for years to discuss the Midrash with her.

The elders of the Sephardi community wrote to the reformers:

> Painful indeed will be such proceedings...for it cannot lose sight of the fact that the members...have always been zealous supporters of our Ancient Congregation...and that their rank and station in the Community entitled them to every consideration; a severance, therefore, from such valued and respected friends...some who may trace their descent from the original founders of our Establishment, must be considered a deep sacrifice of personal feeling to a sense of religious duty.

The affection held for the seceders – they could even be relatives

– had to take second place to the ultimate responsibility to maintain the faith. If the split seemed to come over unimportant details, Hirschell, David Meldola, the Sephardi Ab Beth Din and the Mahamad considered extreme care in dealing with change to be fully justified. Once the process had begun, there was no saying what would be left of the religion at the end. The new prayer book devised by David Woolf Marks was the crunch point. It was the crossing of the Rubicon. You can create new prayers for deaths, battle victories, etc., but not otherwise. Prayers are fixed by halacha – and there is a continuing argument even today about whether new prayers are allowed. Rabbi Soloveitchik, one of the giants of twentieth-century Orthodox Judaism, was very wary on the subject.

The core problem for the Jews in England was that Solomon Hirschell in 1840 wasn't Nietto in 1701. Hirschell was a very old man – he would have been a good candidate for compulsory retirement at 70. Raphael Meldola was younger, but he died in 1828 and wasn't replaced in time. So the burden fell mostly on Hirschell and he was very much influenced by Moses Montefiore, whose interests were, primarily, those of the Sephardi community. The Ashkenazim didn't like branch synagogues near the Great any more than did Bevis Marks, but they hadn't tried to excommunicate the Western synagogue members, and the aggravation with the New synagogue hadn't lasted long. If the Sephardim were in thrall to their *ascama* 1, that wasn't the case with the Ashkenazim. If Hirschell had been prepared to compromise on this point, however, Montefiore was stubborn and would not. He had also become the president of the Board of Deputies in 1835 and would remain in that powerful communal office for the next 30 years.

After waiting five months in the hope that the rebels would change their minds, Hirschell for the Ashkenazim and Meldola for the Sephardim took the step they had been dreading; they issued a Caution, effectively cutting off the dissenters from the community. The strain undoubtedly hastened Hirschell's death.

Hirschell's last great effort in 1841 was to try to turn the Ashkenazi Beth Hamedresh into a full-scale yeshiva; a school, a Beth Hamedresh and a theological seminary. He managed to raise £1,500 for the project but his death came too soon for the concept to be put into practice. Even so, the image of an old man who never ventured out of his study doesn't marry with a spiritual leader still active as a major fund-raiser.

There was one oddity about Hirschell's private life for which there is no explanation – money. The Hirschell's eight children caused them an immense amount of trouble. Concerned that they might go astray if they stayed in the somewhat less than strictly Orthodox London community, the Chief Rabbi sent them abroad to find careers, husbands and wives. This was not a good move. Two of them, David and Ephraim, became 'Remittance Men' – dependent on their father for a monthly handout. Saul died at 33 and Hirsch became a dishonest wine dealer. Goldah and her husband in Poland were given the responsibility of distributing money raised in Britain for poor Jews and took far too large a cut for the work. Rosa was always asking for financial help and Fanny's husband went mad. It cost Hirschell a lot of money to get her a divorce. Nothing is known about Jeanette.

Not surprisingly, much of Hirschell's surviving correspondence has to do with finance, with the Chief Rabbi pleading poverty to his children as a necessary defence mechanism against ever-increasing demands. It would not have been surprising had the Chief Rabbi died penniless. In fact he left £14,000 – which today would be about £700,000. He certainly hadn't been rich when he came to London and, unlike Aaron Hart, he had no rich relatives. He nevertheless managed to save 50 per cent more than his entire basic salary for the 40 years of his ministry. His will speaks of the disposition of his bank and foreign bonds, his fine quality stores of cigars, wines and snuff. His personal effects, including his collection of walking sticks, some with gold tops, sold for £1,400. He had railway bonds as well and he was an ardent collector of Hebrew prayer books, silverware and rare snuff boxes.

The source of his wealth might well have been that he had congregants, like Nathan Mayer Rothschild, who could have given him tips on the Stock Exchange. Certainly, it has been very unusual for a Chief Rabbi to die rich.

Rebecca died before the Chief Rabbi and when Hirschell passed away, there was a great funeral. As tradition demanded, his body was removed from the coffin, buried in its shroud and the coffin was broken over it, as is the biblical practice. Alternatively, the coffin is made of the flimsiest wood and has holes in it to assist the decomposition of the body. The coffin used today would have originated as a government regulation. Hirschell's sons were not there. Saul and Ephraim had predeceased him. Neither David nor Hirsch could come from the Holy Land where they lived, and the prayer for the dead Chief Rabbi was said by one of his grandsons.

So much of what Hirschell achieved would only come to fruition after his death: the burgeoning of the Jews' Free School, the creation of Jews' College, the reintroduction of Hebrew as a modern working language and the successful resistance to the Missionary schools. He played his part in the efforts to eliminate Jewish disabilities and his friends at court were a great help in this. What is more, he was always an excellent figurehead for the community. The *Jewish Chronicle* may have been right that his name was not perpetuated in his achievements, but he could be well satisfied with the progress of the initiatives he had been influential in getting off the ground.

NOTES

1   Cecil Roth in Leo Jung (ed.), *Jewish Leaders*, Bloch Publishing, 1953.
2   Cecil Roth, *History of the Great Synagogue*, Edward Goldston, 1950.
3   Elkan Adler, *History of Jews in London*, Jewish Publication Society of America, 1930.
4   American Jewish Historical Society, vol 2, 1893.
5   Bernard Susser, *The Jews of South West England*, University of Exeter Press, 1993.
6   Ibid.
7   Angela Shire, *Great Synagogue Marriage Registers, 1791–1850*, Frank J. Gent, 2001.
8   Hyman A. Simons, *Forty Years a Chief Rabbi*, Robson Books, 1980.
9   Cecil Roth, 'The Haskalah in England', in *Essays Presented to Chief Rabbi, Israel Brodie*, Soncino, 1967.
10   *Jewish Chronicle*, October 1844.
11   Gerry Black, *JFS*, Tymsder Publishing, 1998.
12   Cyril P. Hershon, *To Make them English*, Palavas Press, 1983.
13   Roth, *History of the Great Synagogue*.
14   Simons, *Forty Years a Chief Rabbi*.
15   Ibid.
16   Cecil Roth, *The Standard Jewish Encyclopaedia*, W.H. Allen, 1966.

14   Raphael Meldola 1805–28

At the beginning of the nineteenth century Moses Cohen Dazevedo had been dead for nearly 20 years and the Bevis Marks congregation were in dire straits. In 1795, out of 2,000 recognized Sephardim in England, 1,000 were so poor they needed help to survive but the number of rich members who could help them was dropping. By this time society was wide open to any Jew who could afford to be part of it and the Jews had become accepted in ever-wider social circles. Genuine acceptance was still, however, more likely if you joined the Church of England.

Consequently the Bevis Marks congregation suffered from a considerable number of conversions at the end of the eighteenth and the beginning of the nineteenth centuries. Moreover, there were a lot of members whose ambitions for themselves and their families were thwarted by the disabilities which still applied to the Jews. As the *Jewish Chronicle* reflected later in the century:

> The wealthy Jew was unable to serve his country, for the senate was to him a dreamland altogether beyond his reach; the magistracy would not be contaminated by his presence; all political, civil and municipal offices were strictly closed against him, and even society looked at him askance...Then what could he do with his sons? A university education was as unattainable as if they had been Hottentots; the army would disclaim to admit Israelites within its ranks; the Bar carefully excluded them.[1]

It wasn't, of course, that the Jews couldn't have done the jobs. One of the Goldsmid clan even managed to become a major general in Wellington's army, but he had had to hide his Judaism to get a commission in the first place. With a name like Goldsmid it was probably fortunate that Napoleon's opponents came from very varied backgrounds.

As a consequence of the disabilities, many of the great seventeenth-century names in the community vanished through the apostasy door and many of those who remained were too busy socially to want to take synagogue office. Indeed, morale was so poor that in 1794 a number of members felt that the Mahamad needed a vote of confidence and publicly undertook not to refuse office if they were appointed or, alternatively, they offered to pay a vast £100 penalty. Not all felt that way. One who didn't was Isaac d'Israeli, who fell out with the Mahamad on just this point of involuntary election, left Bevis Marks and had his son baptised. A comparatively trifling disagreement which led to Britain getting a Jewish convert as prime minister when Isaac's son, Benjamin Disraeli, finally reached the top of the greasy pole.

Synagogue income was also dropping as a result of the defections. Money was tight. Worse, the French were doing all they could to blockade England, they controlled much of European agriculture, and prices rose as shortages grew. In 1794 the four London synagogues had at last agreed to co-operate in order to get a wholesale price for their matzo flour-buying during Passover.

An extra burden was the question of alien Jews in a nation at war. Although Dayan Almosino had preached a sermon assuring the king of the community's continuing loyalty, in Spanish, the Aliens Bill in 1792 was still promulgated to control the movement of foreigners. It was rigorously enforced and, rather than face the need to support their own poor aliens on a day-to-day basis, the Mahamad set out to find the money to try to bribe the foreign Jews to leave the country. They felt the old ways of solving the problem were still the best.

Unfortunately, financial problems were not the only difficulties faced by the Mahamad. On the spiritual front attendances were dropping at the synagogue services. The reason wasn't hard to find if you took the faith even mildly seriously: 'The Service was conducted in a slovenly, unimpressive manner; decorum was little regarded; choral music was not known and a general indifference seemed to reign in the community.'[2]

Another effect of the French Revolution was to undermine traditional thinking and authority to a drastic extent:

> The revolution in France, the Napoleonic Wars, the Peace of Frankfurt, the emancipation of the Jews on the continent, the new spirit manifested therein, the desire to identify the political emancipation with religious changes, had created a state of unrest and dissatisfaction in the ranks of Jewry, and had brought about great troubles in the religious life.[3]

Nothing was considered automatically sacred, not even the

bodies in the cemetery. Doctors, anxious to improve their knowledge of anatomy, were in need of more corpses to dissect. There were plenty of people willing to provide these for an appropriate fee, and bodysnatching became one of the Enlightenment-age crimes. The Mahamad responded as best they could. A Christian lady, visiting the Sephardi graveyard at the time, observed:

> Besides the keeper of the place, who lives in a house adjoining, two men constantly sit up every night in a movable watch-box, which wheels over the last grave; this has been done for four or five years, in consequence of the ground being robbed by resurrectionists.

In one instance, a Jew Broker called Moses Lumbrozo de Mattos left 200 guineas (£210) to Bevis Marks to have his grave watched for a year. Members, in rotation groups of three, guarded the cemetery with blunderbusses.

Faced with so many problems, the Mahamad copied the traditional tactic of a government in trouble; they set up a commission in 1802 and bought themselves some time. The committee reported in 1803 that they needed a Haham to teach the children, regulate the Beth Hamedresh better and to establish a school or a yeshiva. Isaac Mocatta told a meeting of the Elders that education had been sadly neglected. 'He insists in formidable language on the thorough change in their mode of education and on the substitution of English for the then still prevailing system of translating only into Spanish.'⁴

The trouble was that there was little in the way of a consensus. The original members wanted change but the newcomers from Gibraltar and North Africa didn't. 'The one was best strict and the other very strict in the obedience to the law.'⁵

It was to be another 40 years before a sermon was delivered in English at Bevis Marks. The congregation couldn't just continue to drift, however. If they did, as one of the ever-present Mocatta family told the elders: 'the study of the law will be entirely lost, and the Kahal [community] will become an object of contempt and ridicule'.

Even after 140 years, and although there were estimated to be 4,000 Sephardim in England in all, the *kahal* only had 242 members. It was still – albeit reluctantly – recognized by the Ashkenazim as the more powerful community. It was, for example, up to the *deputados* at Bevis Marks to decide when national affairs demanded a Jewish response and a meeting of the Board of Deputies. In the 1790s it met only once, in 1795. This was to discuss an unclear clause in the

Sedition Bill of that year. It was decided that they would approach the government and the offending clause was duly dropped.

The Mahamad recognized that they needed a particularly able Haham at this low point in their history. As there was, as usual, no suitable candidate available in England, and with the community in Amsterdam in decline, they turned to that trusty standby, the Council of Rabbis at Leghorn, still a powerhouse of talmudic learning, in the hope that they would come up with another David Nietto. The council, in fact, recommended one of their most distinguished Dayanim, Raphael Meldola.

Meldola was the grandson of the Haham of Pisa and the son of Haham Moses Meldola who held the chair of Oriental Languages at the University of Paris for some years. His uncle was a rabbi as well, in Amsterdam. The family: 'had given many a scholar and many a rabbi to Jewish communities for at least two centuries'.[6]

What is more, the Haham of Toledo in Spain in the fourteenth century had been Isaiah Meldola and London's first Haham, Jacob Sasportas, knew the clan well. Originally, the family came from Toledo, whose Jewish community went back to Roman times. This was the scion of a particularly noble breed.

Raphael Meldola had been something of an infant prodigy in Leghorn, being enrolled in the yeshiva at the age of 15 in 1769. He continued his studies until he received his *semicha* in 1796 at the age of 42, but was appointed a Dayan in 1803. It may seem late to get *semicha* but you didn't need the title if you were staying in your own city where everybody knew your worth. The senior Leghorn rabbis were famed talmudic scholars throughout Europe and they were expected to publish learned works. Meldola had, himself, written a book on the duties of the biblical high priest in 1791 and another in 1797 called *The Bridegroom's Canopy* for those about to get married. He carried on writing all his life and one book, *Faith Strengthened*, was even published after his death.

Meldola had everything going for him. Married with a family of four sons and four daughters, he was recognized in Leghorn as wise, pious and learned. The Mahamad could hardly ask for more and they nominated Meldola in 1804 at a very generous salary of £250 a year. In the view of Alexander da Sola, admittedly a child of the community's hazan, in future the community would be: 'Under the spiritual direction of a Chief Rabbi whose fame as author, theologian and scholar was world-wide.' 'No more zealous friend and promoter of religious education could be found.'[7] If this amounted to special pleading, it was still the view of a man with the technical ability to recognize religious talent when he saw it, and of one who was much closer to the times than our modern commentators.

If you were looking for a snag – and the Mahamad weren't – Leghorn was not like London. The Council of Rabbis in Leghorn not only decided spiritual questions; they were equally knowledgeable on Jewish civil law. As with David Nietto, in his years in Italy, the Dayanim dealt with legal cases and the community did not trouble the Italian courts if they could avoid it. Meldola was used to wielding authority and he was 52 years old when he came to take up his office in London in 1805. Wherever he'd officiate, Meldola would expect to run his congregation. In 1809 when he'd only been Haham for four years: 'He explained that if the Mahamad thought that he would spend his life merely sitting in his Medrash they were mistaken.'[8]

Study was all very well but he soon made it clear that he was there to act and not merely to speak. Early on in his ministry, in the d'Israeli case, he made his disagreement clear to the Mahamad. He was quite prepared to agree that the Mahamad had the authority in secular matters and he only in spiritual ones, but his definition of what was spiritual was considerably wider than that of the lay leaders of the congregation. Never afraid to speak his mind, this was to lead to many clashes in the future. In fairness, though, Meldola had been brought in by the Mahamad to clear out an Augean stable and it was regrettable that, when he tried to do so, an irresistible force met an immovable object. As one of the early Jewish historians, James Picciotta, insensitively wrote of him in later Victorian times: 'He fulfilled his function with zeal, if not always with the tact and discretion desirable in a man occupying his responsible post.'[9] Well, tact and discretion were not attributes for which the Mahamad were famed either.

It all started with sweetness and light, though. Meldola arrived on the eve of the Jewish New Year in 1805. It had been a circuitous journey, via Innsbruck, relatives in Hamburg and a voyage by ship to London – the Napoleonic Wars having stopped traffic between France and England. Meldola was one of a trickle of Jewish newcomers during the wars. He arrived with his cousin, Raphael, who would translate, as Meldola couldn't write English and he only spoke it with difficulty. Normally he spoke German or Spanish. The conversation in Leghorn would obviously have been in Italian but, for the most part, if you can speak Italian, you can manage in Spanish. When Raphael David Meldola went home after the war, Meldola's son, David stepped in to assist.

Where neither could help was in the pulpit and when Meldola

preached in Spanish, it was often to near-empty benches: 'The strange German speech and the very questionable Spanish in which Haham Meldola gave his religious instruction to his congregants, were necessarily only understood by a small minority of them.'[10]

Except, of course, for special services to mark the battles of Trafalgar and Waterloo, George III's Jubilee, and in 1814, a thanks-giving service for a good harvest. Not in fairness, that there were a large number of Sephardi farmers but all the churches were saying 'thank you' and it would have been discourteous not to follow suit. Meldola's shortcomings in the pulpit matched those of Solomon Hirschell, though Hirschell mastered English quite soon after his appointment.

There was a very warm welcome for the new Haham with the Rosh Hashonah New Year candles lit and a meal ready. He was seated next to Hirschell, who was delighted to have such a distinguished colleague arrive in London. Hirschell had only been in office a couple of years, at 43 he was the younger man, and after dinner the new Haham was led to his home with songs. The next day Hirschell invited Meldola to join him for Tashlich. The two rabbis then went back to the Great Synagogue for the afternoon service and agreed that they would look forward to studying together.

Meldola valued Hirschell's friendship very highly:

> My great friend, the Gaon, Rabbi Solomon Hirschell, was to me like a friend and brother, and from time to time we discussed in confidence every difficult problem that arose within the communities of all English towns and attempted to probe the real problems honestly, so that the Din should emerge in full truth, in love and brotherhood.[11]

Meldola's reputation almost immediately improved the status of Bevis Marks in the wider community:

> His scholarship attracted around him a circle in which there were many of the most distinguished men of his day...He maintained a literary correspondence with many of the most prominent Christian clergymen and scholars of his time; and his acquaintance with the Archbishop of Canterbury and the Canon of Windsor led to his being received by King George III.[12]

Relations between Bevis Marks and the Great over the years had continued to be somewhat frigid, though no less than five wardens and four Dayanim had represented the Sephardim at David Tevele Schiff's funeral. Now there was this very favourable new beginning and both rabbis agreed that there was no reason why the two communities shouldn't settle their differences amicably. They soon made a joint declaration that their congregations should keep to the Sabbath rules more strictly and, in 1805, at Meldola's instigation, the long discussions about a joint board of *shechita* were started again and this time brought to a successful conclusion.

If the profits were welcome – each of the four synagogues shared £400 in the first year – the need to work as a committee and to find ways to compromise over different views, created difficulties. Years later the Mahamad criticized Meldola for not attending a meeting of the Board of Shechita. The Haham tartly replied that he wouldn't attend meetings called to overturn the Din. The differing laws of *shechita* between the Ashkenazim and the Sephardim remained a sensitive area.

In the new climate the Mahamad felt it only courteous to write again to the Great to ask them to nominate new members for the Board of Deputies. It was only a gesture, though. Provided with the information, they still failed to call a meeting until 1812.

If there was one single event which did more to bring the communities together than anything else, it was the wedding in 1812 between Moses Montefiore and Judith Barent Cohen. Montefiore was from one of the most distinguished Bevis Marks families and Ms Cohen was the daughter of Levi Barent Cohen, one of the stalwarts of the Great. The Mahamad smiled on the union and 'mixed' marriages in the future were subject to far less hassle. The marriage cemented the relationship of the Sephardi and Ashkenazi Cousinhoods. The families would in future intermarry with each other, work in business together and visit socially all the time. Their religious beliefs and commitment might differ on occasions but they would remain family. Moses Montefiore was reasonably typical; the banking Goldsmids were his cousins, David Salomons, who would spearhead the fight to eliminate Jewish disabilities, was his brother-in-law and Lionel de Rothschild, who would succeed him as president of the Board of Deputies, was his nephew.

All the early nineteenth-century religious leaders had much to talk about. Napoleon was pulling up roots all over the place; abolishing ghettos, undermining the power of the papacy, replacing a ramshackle Paris with broad Boulevards and knocking rulers off their thrones with regularity. Religion lost its rock-solid place in the Establishment in many European countries. What had gone almost unquestioned during the eighteenth century was now under attack. If there were elements who wanted change at Bevis Marks, they were

matched in the Church of England; the clerics found they had
common ground in opposing that, at least: 'Possessed of a
remarkably virile mind, [Meldola] was a dominant factor in the
British Jewry of his generation.'[13]

Nevertheless, in those illustrious interdenominational circles
Meldola was 'humble and unpretending'. In contrast, within his own
community, although he was kind-hearted, he had a temper – an
'active temperament' as Picciotto put it – which he didn't always
bother to control. He had packed something of the Italian outlook
with him when he came to London.

Meldola settled in and then went to work. In 1807 he denounced
the Jewish shopkeepers who opened on the Sabbath. In fact, if you
have a non-Jewish partner, according to the Din, you can open the
shop but all the profit from the Saturday trade has to go to your
partner.

Both the Mahamad and Meldola were, naturally, anxious to look
after their own officials. When Benjamin Dazevedo had been thrown
out soon after he arrived to take up a post with the Charleston
community in America, he returned to London to much sympathy,
and was appointed a teacher at one of the schools. Meldola was
severe on errant colleagues – in the same year he complained that the
hazan wasn't completely covering his head with his *tallith*. In 1809
he criticized him for not being more attentive during the service, for
drinking non-kosher wine and singing frivolous songs. The
Mahamad weighed in alongside the Haham with a £1 fine every time
the hazan failed to read out the name of a benefactor at the
appropriate time of the service. Being hazan remained no sinecure.

Meldola was also critical of the fact that the Sefer Torahs hadn't
been examined for years. For example if, through long use a letter
had faded away, according to the Din, the scroll couldn't be used. As
Benjamin Franklin had said some years before: 'Perfection is made
up of little things, but perfection is not a little thing.'

Perhaps the most extreme example of Meldola's insistence on the
letter of the law was his complaint about the way in which the hazan
was pronouncing a single word. The arguments about this raged
over many years. It got so bad that when a barmitzvah boy, at 13,
was saying his *haftorah* and the offending word came up, there were
corrections from one part of the congregation, countered by shouts
of approval from other parts. The boy was so upset that he couldn't
continue.

It would appear to be getting things entirely out of proportion,
but there is a logical explanation. Meldola's position was not unlike

that of a regimental sergeant major who trains the officer cadets at Sandhurst – when roused, his volume and tone of voice could match that of an RSM too. For example, in 1812 he attacked the decorum and standards of the synagogue. When attempts at mediation were made: 'He roared in arbitration and denounced one party as a "ferocious savage" and "Algerine dog" with whom he would have no intercourse.'[14]

Meldola's job was to drum into a failing congregation such a sense of discipline that, under fire and in the most desperate situation – Enlightenment, the German Reform movement, etc – they would automatically follow Orthodox King of King's regulations. No breach of either the Written or Oral Law could be tolerated, because survival would depend on perfection. In that environment the tiniest detail becomes important. Meldola had been appointed to restore discipline and he adopted the regimental sergeant major's dictum. By aiming for perfection, a higher standard of religious observance than otherwise would become attainable. Wellington was fighting the French. Meldola had to resist the philosophy of the Enlightenment.

If, however, you didn't believe in the principle – and a number of the older members of the congregation didn't – then the rumblings of discontent were going to grow. The Mahamad were certainly less concerned with strictures about internal discipline than they were about relations with the outside world. In 1807 Meldola got the Mahamad's permission to denounce in the synagogue one of the schools set up by Christian missionary societies. The Mahamad could see the danger of the children of poorer Sephardim being tempted to attend them. When, however, in 1809, Meldola also sent letters to six other missionary societies complaining of their activities, the elders told him that he had no right to do so without their express permission.

With a de Mesquita or a Dazevedo that would have been enough. Meldola, however, wrote them ten foolscap sheets of paper justifying his actions. The Mahamad confirmed the instructions of the elders. Meldola told them to mind their own business. It was indeed difficult to argue that the activities of the missionaries did not come under the heading of spiritual matters. Meldola maintained that what he had written was uncontroversial and conformed with the *ascamot* – an equally difficult position to maintain.

That both Meldola and the Mahamad were dictatorial cannot be denied and sometimes Meldola was simply out of order. In October 1805 he went to Nelson's funeral and preached a eulogy in the synagogue, which was fine, and the community would have been entirely on his side. In 1806, however, his mentor back home, Rabbi Hayyim (HYDA – Hayyim, Yousef, David, Azulay) Azulay died. He had been a great teacher in Leghorn and it was very understandable that Meldola should sincerely mourn his passing. But to instruct all the Jewish shops around Bevis Marks to close while he gave a funeral oration! Where was that in the Din?

The constant effort to get the congregation to live up to his own high standards was, inevitably, frustrating. The equivalent of the guardhouse for the sergeant major was fines for the Yehidim, and the Mahamad had *herems* as well as fines; both of which were indeed handed out with great liberality. Another alternative for Meldola was that explosion of temper at the miscreant, and he certainly didn't mellow with age, if anything, just the opposite.

Amidst the uproar, the Mahamad tried to keep the peace and balance the books. They found themselves dealing, increasingly, with two congregations in one; the Gibraltar and North African influx at the end of the century had settled down and found their feet. Their rules on ritual were not identical with those observed by the original members and where they were Yehidim, they could vote for their own candidates at elections to the Mahamad. So power could be obtained if they could get enough votes. In the meantime they influenced the atmosphere at synagogue services, not always to the liking of the other side: 'it was not a place of devotion, and prayers could be better said in a closet'.

That was the comment of one member who wrote to warn the Mahamad of a possible schism in the future. At least, in 1809, the Mahamad grasped the financial problems of the community by the horns. A special meeting was called. It was so solemn that the doors were locked at 11 o'clock and latecomers were excluded. Psalms were chanted and prayers said. Then the meeting agreed to raise the compulsory membership income from £900 to £1,400 a year. The community finally took the difficulties seriously. The Yehidim debts to the community disappeared. No longer could you find a list of them pinned to the synagogue door, as before. The finances also improved when Sam Bensaken breathed his last in Philadelphia and bequeathed £1,200 to the synagogue. Furthermore, nobody could now hold a religious service if the building was up to six miles from Bevis Marks, rather than the previous four.

In 1811 Meldola's home was destroyed by fire. The congregation immediately had a collection and raised £100 to help him restore whatever wasn't covered by insurance. Meldola spent £30 of it on religious artefacts and books, and then arranged to have his new house insured by the Sun Fire Office for £800. The comparison between a £250 a year salary and a house worth £800 suggests that property values in the City have beaten the level of inflation by quite a lot since that time.

When peace came, some continental pre-war disabilities disappeared. For example, in Portugal the Jews were finally allowed to admit to their faith in 1816. They were also allowed to buy land for a cemetery where previously their dead had been buried in the English cemetery.

When the war first ended in 1814, Meldola wrote a thanksgiving prayer, which seemed innocuous enough. Nevertheless, another war started, this time with the most punctilious devotee in the country of the correct translation and interpretation of the Bible and the prayers – Henry Bennett. It would go on for years. The problem was that the absolutely correct translation of the Bible will still have scholars arguing until the end of time. The difficulty is a mixture of ancient languages, political correctness, special pleading, hidden agendas and a wide choice of esoteric meanings. All developed by thousands of scholars over 4,000 years. It is an industry where there need be no fear of unemployment among the workers.

Bennett's main attack was on the flyleaf of his pamphlet which had a devastating sting in the tail:

> Critique on the Hebrew Thanksgiving Prayers...Portuguese Synagogue...Thursday, the 7th of July...General thanksgiving for the happy restoration of peace. In which the stupidity of the Rev. Raphael Meldola...will be clearly shown.

Incidentally, for those who have an image of the quiet groves of Academia flowing serenely on, it should be pointed out that academic disputes can take on the savagery of any contested multinational corporation take-over bid, and frequently do.

Bennett was ridiculing Meldola all over the city and Hirschell was suffering even more than Meldola. The virulent criticism was over textual points in original Hebrew documents. Bennett was a literalist. Commenting on a book on Hebrew for children, Bennett said that the author didn't care whether his lessons were in line with the text of the Pentateuch. That he didn't care if the precepts were in accordance with the Hebrew forms. The implication was that the author was addicted to sloppy work. It was a variant on the dangers of change, but 99 per cent of the English Jews wouldn't have known what Bennett was talking about.

What they would have understood, however, was the comment about stupidity, although that could be seen as a typical problem of high office; you're there to be shot at. Hirschell wanted Meldola to issue a *herem* against Bennett in 1815, but the honeymoon period when Meldola and Hirschell worked so well together at the time of Trafalgar was now but a distant memory. At this point Meldola took the view that there was more involved than their personal reputations. He wrote to Hirschell:

> What have you ever done by way of literary production? Did you ever take pen in hand to defend Judaism against its enemies, the Missionaries? Bennett has an established reputation for learning in this metropolis, and it would be unpardonable to disgrace such a man who is held in public respect. It is for you to vindicate yourself and not lightly to thunder papal excommunication.[15]

As Hirschell had struggled valiantly for better Jewish education, this was hardly fair. He had certainly denounced the missionary societies from the pulpit and encouraged Hebrew as a living language. Then in 1818 there was an error in a slaughterhouse, leading to the question of whether the shochet's licence should be withdrawn? Meldola announced that a final decision should await Hirschell's opinion. Hirschell responded: 'It appears to me a mystery that the Haham declines giving his opinion and, therefore, I answer that they be prohibited until Haham Meldola gives his answer.' Both rabbis were worried that if they withdrew the licence, the shochet might take them to court for an unfair loss of profits.

Bennett continued to lambast the Chief Rabbi and the Haham. Eventually Meldola did appeal to the Mahamad for protection and their support was readily granted. Ten years on, in 1825, Meldola and Hirschell had the opportunity to attack Bennett in return. They patched up their own disagreements and excluded him from the community when he took it upon himself to perform a marriage, which was against the Din. This was because it wed a Cohen with a convert, which was entirely against the rules. The fact remained that, if Bennett was pretty well ostracized by the Jewish authorities as early as 1815, he still remained very popular with Christian Hebraists. The latter were, naturally, far more concerned with an accurate translation of biblical sources than on whether the Haham was being denigrated.

After the war the national mood changed. Where before there had been a united effort to beat Napoleon, now minds shifted to other considerations. One was the possibility of an attempt to overthrow established government in Britain, just like the French Revolution. The portents were there if you were looking for revolutions under the bed: the Luddites, breaking up new machinery, the attempt to form early trade unions, Peterloo, where the military in Manchester charged a protesting crowd, causing many deaths, and the Cato Street conspiracy when there was a plot to assassinate the Cabinet. All in the first few years after Waterloo. The plot failed but the pressure on the British leaders remained severe. In 1817 a young Jewish pedlar sold a cheap penknife to the Foreign Secretary and Castlereagh used it to commit suicide. If violent change was in the air, the Mahamad stood their ground. They were only prepared to make concessions of an extremely limited nature. In 1819 it was agreed that, after 160 years, the records of their proceedings should be kept in English. For the most part, however, the revision of the *ascamot* in 1819 left the rules very much in place.

Authority was under attack and – not to be outdone – there were members of the congregation at Bevis Marks who felt the Mahamad should also be flouted. On occasions, the attacks even came from Meldola himself. In 1818 there was a vacancy for a new hazan and Meldola held that the candidates should be examined by himself and his Beth Din. The Mahamad, relying on the *ascamot*, said they'd do the interviewing but Meldola could give his opinion afterwards. Meldola must have been reasonably happy with the eventual choice, as Hazan David de Sola became his son-in-law within a year when he married Rebecca Meldola.

Two of Meldola's other children, David and Abraham, tended to be as hot-headed as their father. Sometimes all three would be in dispute with individual members of the community. While the Mahamad were constrained by Meldola's position from remonstrating too often with the Haham, they were not inclined to have his children upsetting the members too. Both David and Abraham protested in mitigation that they were only restraining their father, who had been told by his doctors that he was not to over-exert himself. It could well have been true. In a rage, Meldola might well have looked like a heart attack waiting to happen.

Even in the Haham's social life, the Mahamad and Meldola found themselves at loggerheads. They criticized Meldola for going on holiday in 1818 without their permission. One view would be that it was entirely reasonable for a spiritual leader to go on holiday at the age of 65. The other viewpoint was that alternative arrangements would have to be made and the Mahamad should have been kept informed. The bad feeling came from the necessity to get 'permission'. On one occasion they went still further; they wanted to set up a tribunal to establish the facts in another altercation involving the Haham. Meldola refused to appear before it, pointing out that, according to the Din – if not the *ascamot* – any tribunal set up to judge a rabbi has to consist of members of equal status. The Mahamad checked that this was correct and, reluctantly, gave way.

In 1822, another major row erupted, this time with a group of the members from Gibraltar. They attended a baby's *briss* and, as it was just before Shavuot (the spring harvest festival), they held a service to say the appropriate prayers. This, technically, broke the famous first *ascama*. When this was reported to the Mahamad, the Yehidim were stripped of their membership and given fines of £10 and £20. Condemnations were read out in the synagogue and a mountain was made out of a molehill; a reprimand would, surely, have been quite enough.

The Gibraltarians were among the most religious members of the community. They were horrified to be excommunicated. One of them lost a child and the Mahamad wouldn't even allow it to be buried in the cemetery. In the meantime Meldola had been worn out by all the rows, so he went along with the Mahamad's decision. Eventually, the members apologized and were readmitted in 1825, but the rancour aroused among the Gibraltarians had a lasting effect. When those who had punished them wanted, over the next 20 years, to make changes in the ritual, the Gibraltar Yehidim wouldn't give an inch: 'The congregation became split into two contending and opposing factions, which succeeded one another with more or less regularity in wielding the power vested in the Mahamad.'[16]

As a sideline, new technology could also pose a threat to the calm of the community. The Blackwall Railway Bill came before Parliament and, had it been passed, it would have resulted in steam trains passing within a few metres of the synagogue and only a few metres below the ground. Immediate representations were made to see the bill was rejected and, as a result, the trains made tracks in different directions.

Meldola continued to work for a better relationship with the Ashkenazi community. In 1825 it was agreed that if they came to Bevis Marks, there was no reason to deny them an *aliyah*. In 1826 Meldola also attended the consecration of the new Ashkenazi Western Synagogue with which Bevis Marks had very friendly relations.

A couple of years later, the elders were asked to prepare a report on how the synagogue could be better run. Meldola must have been highly amused at the result, though the same was unlikely to have been the reaction of the Mahamad. The recommendations of the elders included the suggestions: 'that the Wardens themselves should attend services as often as possible, that they should abstain from conversation and give a good example to the congregation by not stirring from their seats until the end of the service'.

Proclamations should henceforth be in English and there should be a sermon every Sabbath afternoon in English; the content having been approved by the elders in advance. Gagging Meldola, if necessary, was a prime objective and, of course, the restriction was already in the *ascamot*. They did try the idea of the sermons in 1831 after Meldola's death, but it had to be abandoned as not enough members turned up to listen.

By 1841 membership had dropped to 193, which was smaller than the Ashkenazi Hambro Synagogue on its own. Jewish congregations, however, are well accustomed to hanging on by their fingernails and at least the Sephardim still had Moses Montefiore, the undisputed lay leader of all the English Jews. Montefiore was quite capable – financially, spiritually and administratively – of carrying Bevis Marks on his own broad shoulders, and in the years to come that was, effectively, what happened. What he could only try to alleviate was the shocking amount of poverty in the community which had worsened in the post-war slump.

In his diary in 1829 he estimated that now 1,200, out of the total Sephardi population of 2,500, were getting charity in some form, and the same applied for the Ashkenazim. Montefiore had, himself, given 13 houses for almshouses for the poor in 1823 and there were, on occasions, extremely generous bequests, like Joe Barrow's £2,000 for almshouses in 1809, and Abraham Pereira's £14,000 for the poor. Unfortunately, they were a drop in the ocean of demand.

Meldola had firmly resisted the calls for change and a relaxation of the rules. He had made sure the vast bulk of the small congregation would still support the Orthodox position and he had earned the respect of the wider community. The downside was that he had driven the Mahamad to distraction and, as a consequence, they would not be keen to have a successor for nearly 40 years.

There was a great deal of genuine regret when Meldola died in 1828, at 74. Nobody could ever have doubted his commitment and sincerity. You might not agree with him, but Yehidim knew you were both on the side of the angels. For the funeral, the synagogue was completely hung with black and it was packed. Afterwards, 40 black coaches made their sombre way to the old cemetery:

The remains of the deceased were placed again in the hearse and conveyed, followed by an immense multitude, to the Portuguese Jews' Hospital in Mile End, behind which is an ancient burial ground belonging to a former generation. The funeral oration was delivered by the Rev. Solomon Hirschell in English . . . The ceremony commenced at 10 o'clock in the morning and was not concluded until 7 in the evening.[17]

The shops near Bevis Marks all closed and the Aldgate Church bell tolled respectfully:

the body was taken out of the coffin and laid, in wraps in the winding sheet, in the grave, while the Reader proclaimed the divine titles of the deceased. The coffin was then broken into pieces and thrown over the body and the whole multitude, as a mark of respect alternatively assisted in filling up the grave.[18]

Meldola was buried, as he had asked, next to the grave of David Nietto. They had both been Hahams in difficult times, they were both Italians and if Meldola's ministry had not achieved quite the quality of his illustrious predecessor, they had both fought the good fight.

It is a fact, however, that in the 164 years between the appointment of Jacob Sasportas in 1664 and the death of Meldola in 1828, the Sephardim had a Haham three-quarters of the time. In the subsequent 176 years they only had one for just over half the years. It certainly wasn't entirely the Meldola effect! He would have successors who were equally able to irritate the Mahamad in every respect.

If the community felt that peace would break out after Meldola had gone, they were soon disabused. There were sensible advances. In 1836 the first translation of the liturgy into English was approved and David de Sola, who would be hazan for many years, produced five volumes of a high quality. Unfortunately, there were also to be constant disputes over the next ten years about the services, the decorum and all the old favourites. In 1831, during the cholera epidemic, both the hazan, Aaron de Sola and David Meldola, the Haham's son, were invited to give sermons to ask for the protection of the Almighty for the congregation. They both declined on the grounds that whatever they decided to say could be censored by the Mahamad.

The fact was that the lay leaders had to be careful. It was true that the need to avoid upsetting members of the Church of England had diminished in importance, as the Jews were now accepted as part of the British people. At the same time, the Jews were still burdened with a number of disabilities. A benign public opinion of the Jewish community could well be seen as highly desirable in supporting the efforts being made to get those conditions abolished. Contentious sermons were to be avoided, particularly as the press had sometimes reprinted the words of the Chief Rabbis from the pulpit.

Internally, the rule was even more appropriate. Haham Meldola had, on a number of occasions, written scurrilous letters and pamphlets about members, which had caused a great deal of ill will. The Mahamad had only repeated what was in the original *ascamot*, that they had to approve written material in advance. In order to nip any future disputes in the bud, it made good sense to have a sight of the material first.

What did Meldola achieve? His had been very much a holding action. As the pressure for radical change started to gather pace, particularly in Germany, it made little progress at Bevis Marks in Meldola's time. The community was kept firmly to the straight and narrow and had the necessary commitment to remain strictly within the fold. This was an achievement in itself because the attractions of the new thinking and the ability to play a more equal role in the world, would seduce many away from the familiar demands of the faith.

NOTES

1   *Jewish Chronicle*, 3 April 1874.
2   *Jewish Chronicle*, July 1874.
3   Moses Gaster, *History of the Ancient Synagogue*, London, 1901.
4   Ibid.
5   Ibid.
6   Ibid.
7   Reverend Dr Abraham da Sola, *David Aaron da Sola*, Wm. H. Jones, 1864.
8   Jewish Historical Society of England, Vol. 21.
9   James Picciotto, *Sketches of Anglo-Jewish History*, 1875.
10 *Jewish Chronicle*, August 1873.
11 Jewish Historical Society of England, Vol. 21.
12 *Jewish Encyclopaedia*, USA, 1901.
13 Ibid.
14 Lionel Barnett, *Bevis Marks Records*, Oxford University Press, 1940.
15 Arthur Barnett, *Solomon Bennett*, 1761–1838. Jewish Historical Society of England, Vol. 17.
16 Gaster, *History of the Ancient Synagogue*.
17 *Sunday Herald*, 8 June 1828.
18 Gaster, *History of the Ancient Synagogue*.

15   A Pause for the Reform Movement

The greatest religious threat to the continuity of Orthodox Judaism in Britain since Sabbatai Tzevi came about when Solomon Hirschell was nearly 80 and when the Sephardi community had no Haham. The official name of the new organization was the West London Synagogue of British Jews, but it is commonly known today as part of the Progressive movement, which includes Reform. It was started, primarily, by a few members of Bevis Marks and it is true that their original stance, back in 1836, had been to flirt with some of the Reform principles practised in a few German congregations at the time. The threat of a small factional split on religious grounds had been in the wind for a while. In December 1836 a petition was laid before the elders, asking them to sanction: 'such alterations and modifications as were on the line of the changes introduced in the Reform Synagogue in Hamburg and in other places'.

In addition, the desire for a branch of Bevis Marks had been growing for many years as more and more members left the City and went to live in the West End. On a cold, rainy day the long walk to synagogue took a good deal of devotion. Worse, not to trudge the distance would trigger that eternal guilt complex again. A large number of Yehidim sent a counter-petition to the elders asking them to oppose strongly any changes whatsoever. The potential defectors amended their position when they recognized how much opposition within the community there was to the Reform theology.

Reform was an ideology that had its birth in Germany with Israel Jacobson. It was Jacobson who opened the first Temple – as he decided to call his synagogue – in 1810. The creed of his Reform movement was, however, to have practically no effect on the West London synagogue members during the nineteenth century, although when Kershon and Romain wrote *Tradition and Change* in 1995 as a history of Reform, they said that the movement had 'never lost sight of the founders' original aims and ambitions'. Whatever they considered these were, they had very little to do with early nineteenth-century German Reform theology and Progressive Judaism, as it is now called, has changed enormously in Britain over the last 160 years.

The final theological negotiating position of the Bevis Marks breakaway members was written down on 15 April 1840 at a meeting in the Bedford Hotel in London. The 19 Sephardim and 5 Ashkenazim founders signed the following declaration:

> We, the undersigned, regarding Public Worship as highly conducive to the interests of religion, consider it a matter of deep regret that it is not more frequently attended by members of our Religious Persuasion. We are perfectly sure that this circumstance is not owing to any want of a general conviction of the fundamental Truths of our Religion, but we ascribe it to the distance of the existing Synagogues from the places of our Residence; to the length and imperfections of the order of service, to the inconvenient hours at which it is appointed; to the unimpressive manner in which it is performed and to the absence of religious instruction in our Synagogues.

That was it. They didn't want to walk four miles or more from the West End to the City on the Sabbath and they would settle for a shorter service at more convenient times, more religious instruction and more decorum, in a new synagogue. The Sephardi and Ashkenazi congregations they left adopted many of their suggestions within a few years of their departure. As the *Jewish Chronicle* reported in an article in November 1874: 'It will be remarked that not a word is here said respecting instrumental music in synagogue or the abolition of the second days of Festivals; the two points most objectionable to strict Jews.'[1]

It was a breakaway Orthodox community. As the history of the Reform movement says: 'West London had not been a deliberate breakaway premeditated from the outset but had been pushed into existence by the refusal of the Bevis Marks authorities to countenance a branch congregation.'[2]

Today the website home page of the Union of American Hebrew Congregations tells a different story when it sums up the position of the largest body of Reform Jews a century and a half later: 'One of the guiding principles of Reform Judaism is the autonomy of the individual. A right to decide whether to subscribe to this particular belief or to that particular practice.'

The Reform movement in Britain say that they don't always have the same views as the Americans, which illustrates the difficulty in agreeing a common international approach. In their publication *What is Reform Judaism?* they set out to explain their own creed.

The answer to the question they pose 'What about Kashrut?' brings a typical answer:

> On Kashrut...we try to encourage a deeper and more fully-lived Jewish life through study and experience rather than endeavouring simply to legislate. We recognise that individuals will come to their own decisions but are as insistent as possible that those decisions be based on Jewish thought, knowledge and experience.

By contrast, the Orthodox only recognize the overriding authority of the Written and Oral Law. As one of the Reform London rabbis puts it, their position is that we are now: 'In a modern post-enlightenment world, where individual autonomy has taken the place of divine sanction.'[3]

There has obviously been considerable movement away from solely wanting a synagogue nearer where you live, shorter services at less inconvenient times and more religious instruction. Even if you add sermons in English, the elimination of the second day of the festivals and a choir – all of which became part of the practices of the new community when it started life – you would still be in agreement with Orthodox beliefs on 95 per cent of the rules. It was no wonder that Nathan Adler, the Chief Rabbi, could offer to agree to differ with the defectors in 1854. In the event, Orthodox branch synagogues in London were developed later in the century by both the Ashkenazi and Sephardi communities, the Orthodox services were made slightly shorter by Adler and a choir had already been introduced at Bevis Marks in 1839. It can also be agreed that there is never any argument in ecclesiastical circles about the need for more religious instruction.

Of the breakaway group, 80 per cent were Sephardim and this was, fundamentally, a few of the older Spanish and Portuguese family members splitting off from a community in which the North African element was becoming more dominant. It was significant that a number of the Gibraltarians who had been excommunicated back in 1822 were now members of the Mahamad. If they sought revenge for that deeply upsetting experience nearly 20 years before, here was an ideal opportunity.

The thinking of the Mahamad on the appeal for permission to start a new synagogue was entirely consistent with the history of Bevis Marks. One of the main reasons they didn't want to sanction a breakaway congregation was because of the financial implications. They were already finding it very difficult to finance the multitude of demands made by the synagogue, its permanent officers, its internal costs and its charitable work. The Mahamad felt that the establishment of a new community would diffuse the efforts which could be made to help the poor, to teach the children, to maintain the burial ground and a host of other calls upon their income. Their worries were perfectly genuine and the disappearance of some of their wealthiest members into the dissenting synagogue was something they tried hard to avoid.

As far as sermons were concerned, they were extremely attached – as was their community as a whole – to the Iberian languages they had used from the time of the Resettlement. They had only finally abandoned keeping the synagogue records in Portuguese in 1819.

The Sephardim were equally attached to their prayer book, which dated back to the thirteenth century in Castille in Spain. To allow a youngster without *semicha* like the new congregation's minister, David Woolf Marks, to revise and shorten the prayer book was totally unacceptable. Other than that, the Mahamad had given way on the choir, replacing the two singers who had normally accompanied the hazan for 100 years and more. There was even continental Orthodox Sephardi precedent for using an organ on the Sabbath; it is still to be found in a number of those synagogues today. Looking at the original breakaway members, it would be far too simplistic to home in on the divergence from Orthodoxy in their religious beliefs as a rationale for a new movement.

The Mahamad and the Great Synagogue appealed to the dissidents not to leave the community. It was not impossible to accommodate the 1840 manifesto while retaining the Orthodox position. Only after waiting five months, in the hope that the proposed new synagogue wouldn't take root, did Hirschell for the Ashkenazim and David Meldola, the head of the Sephardi Beth Din, take the step they had tried so hard to avoid; they issued a caution excluding the dissenters from the community, ostensibly for rejecting the Oral Law but, primarily, for setting up a new synagogue, against the ruling in *ascama* 1. It was an action which split families and which forced some of their most distinguished members out of mainstream Jewry.

As another Reform historian has written: 'West London was not a German Reform congregation. Its innovations were sermons in the vernacular, an organ and a shorter service... the slow emergence of the Reform Synagogues of Great Britain evidenced the majestic gradualism and spirit of compromise of the British scene.'[4]

On the evidence, the slow emergence could more likely be put down to the founders trying to observe 95 per cent of Orthodox Judaism. And the organ was not an initial innovation. It came later.

As observant members of Bevis Marks, the 19 defectors accepted the Oral Law, which the Reform movement would eventually decide was outdated. They would have denied trying to create a synagogue whose members could decide for themselves which rules were pertinent and which not. Marks said in his first sermon to the community in 1842: 'let it not be supposed that this house is intended as a synagogue of ease or convenience'.

Obviously, many of the founders strictly observed the Written and Oral Law. Marks wrote of Francis Goldsmid, one of the defectors: 'to him, more than anyone else we owe ... that our congregation was brought ... into being'. But barrister Goldsmid wouldn't appear in court on the Sabbath. Indeed, most Orthodox religious practices weren't reformed by the original British reformers. For example, in 1841–43 when the new prayer books were produced for the congregation, it was decided that the entire service, except the sermon, was to continue to be said in Hebrew. This decision was in effect for nearly 100 years until the 1930s.

It must also be recognized that the vast majority of the Sephardi and Ashkenazi membership in London stood four-square with their ecclesiastical authorities in rejecting the position of the defectors. They didn't follow them out of the community and Reform membership was a minute percentage of the total number of Jews in Britain throughout the rest of the century. If the argument was over traditional practices vs. modernity, then the Orthodox community voted for traditional practices – 75 per cent of the community still do.

The Jewish status of the defectors was to be denigrated by many within Orthodoxy. As Rabbi Friedlander, one of the most distinguished Reform Rabbis said: 'one could list dozens of declarations by Right-wing Orthodox leaders denying Progressive Judaism even the right to consider itself part of Jewish life'.

Then was the caution not to mix religiously with the new community an over-the-top reaction by power-mad, narrow-minded bigots? The reaction of the defectors to their banishment at the time would have been a resounding 'yes'. It is much easier today to see what all the fuss was about – it was about the thin end of the wedge.

World Jewry was not like Britain where the House of Commons could legislate and the results would become the law of the land. If there were to be changes in the laws and practices of Judaism, these would have to be agreed throughout the world by all the Orthodox communities. Otherwise who would know what the law was? Was it the Australian law or the Austrian law or the American law? In Reform Judaism that question would need to be asked even of individual synagogues. What did they practice and what had they decided was out-of-date? In Orthodox Judaism it would only be, was it Sephardi or Ashkenazi, and then the variations would be in minutiae, not in fundamentals.

As mentioned earlier, the classic Orthodox way of ultimately defining the law was to ask the sage who was acknowledged to be the cleverest available, what was the law as laid down in the books? The row over David Nietto's 1703 sermon was a typical example of the accepted process. By contrast, the new synagogue made all its own decisions. Marks was, indeed, a distinguished Hebraist – he was Professor of Hebrew at University College London from 1855–98 – but without even semicha, the idea that Orthodox Jewish communities around the world would accept any changes he recommended would have been laughable.

Of course, there is precedent for world-famous rabbinic sages not having *semicha*. There is no need for the certificate if everybody locally knows what you've been trained to do. Marks in 1840, however, had no qualifications – written or otherwise – to be considered a rabbinic sage. He was only 30 when he rewrote the prayer book. What was more, for all Marks' scholastic eminence:

> The West London Synagogue of British Jews was run by its Council of Founders and their committees, not by the Clergy. The Minister had to refer to the governing laity on nearly all Synagogue matters, taking instructions as to when and where to preach.[5]

Although both the Ashkenazi and Sephardi ecclesiastical authorities had warned their congregations not to join the breakaway members in prayer, there were continuous efforts to get the *ascama* 1 caution lifted. The Sephardi Beth Din, under David Meldola, refused to do so for eight years. Eventually it was agreed that the dissenters would apologize to the Mahamad for starting a synagogue within the prohibited distance. On which terms Meldola found it possible to lift the caution. If it had been impossible to paper over the cracks on the religious differences between the Reform community and Bevis Marks, that couldn't have happened. The Dayanim would have stuck to their guns. The initial differences were just not that great, which continued to be the case.

Reform historians still puzzle over why there were no intellectual arguments about Reform thinking at the time. Was it: 'torpor with regard to the ideological dimension of Reform Judaism in its nascent state'?[6]

According to the contemporary statements of the Upper Berkeley Street wardens – the congregation moved to a new synagogue there in 1870 – it was the fact that the founders all wanted to remain Orthodox. What's more they were very concerned that accusations of not being so should be given any credence. Among the 19 Sephardi seceders were no less than nine members of the Mocatta family and one of them, Moses Mocatta, was the son of Abraham Mocatta, one of the Orthodox leaders of Bevis Marks. Moses became the warden of the West London and his reaction to change must have been acceptable to the Council of Founders when he said, 'For any least deviation, unqualified censure will be heaped upon us and the self-styled Orthodox of our co-religionists will gladly seize on the minutest point to vilify our Minister and cast obloquy on our congregation.'

Avoiding that mattered a great deal to the Victorian defectors, and one very likely deviation was on the question of keeping two days for festivals. While it was perfectly true that with the coming of the telegraph, the accurate date of the first day of a festival could have been provided world-wide easily enough, the Orthodox objection was that it would create a precedent after 2,000 years. The Orthodox don't like setting precedents and, particularly, unnecessary ones.

When the Reform community in Manchester in 1860 voted to abandon the second days, their respected – and, originally, Orthodox – minister, Solomon Mayer Schiller-Szinessy, resigned. Here was a man who felt strongly enough about the Hungarian uprising in 1848 to face death for supporting it. Sentenced to be hanged, he escaped to Manchester, but he couldn't face giving up the second days and fled again. He said he was concerned about drift, defections and apostasy. His was an extreme example of the position of many Reform Jews at the time, but at the consecration service in Manchester in 1858, the most important element of the Orthodox status quo was reiterated by Marks in the pulpit: 'To reaffirm his allegiance to the Mosaic laws which were universal and the Keystone of Judaism.' In 2004 the second day of the festivals are being observed once again at West London and at other Reform synagogues. The original argument of them being out-of-date in the 1840s has been overturned by other considerations.

From the point of view of the Council of Founders, therefore, the prime objective of the Upper Berkeley Street leaders was to remain theologically respectable in the eyes of their friends and family. It was not to make a radical departure from Orthodoxy in partnership with the German Reform movement.

If the Mosaic laws were the keystone, did that mean there would be no further unauthorized abandonment of traditional Orthodox practices? From the Orthodox perspective, the core question was where would the Reform changes eventually stop? If laymen could change one rule, no matter how small, they might go on to change elements of the religion which were far more fundamental. The Orthodox knew that, for them, such innovations could not possibly take effect without an international consensus. If the Orthodox community in Britain agreed unilaterally to changes, they risked being outlawed by every Orthodox community outside the country.

Marks' respect for the Written Law was well illustrated when the Board of Shechita refused to recognize a butcher's licence granted in Rotterdam. The butcher sued in 1868 and Marks was called as part of his pleading in the case. To the plaintiff's discomfiture the Reform minister supported the Orthodox Chief Rabbi, Nathan Marcus Adler. The butcher lost the case.

Marks' much later justification for the changes he made in Orthodox practice was that he was differentiating between two elements of Orthodox rules – the Written Law and the Oral Law – between the biblical word of the Almighty and the laws which rabbis over the generations had decided emerged from it. Marks said that, in the modern world of the nineteenth century, some of those laws should be changed because they were out-of-date. The Oral Law could be questioned. The Written Law remained sacrosanct as far as he was concerned.

Hirschell and Meldola would say that their initial concerns were well-founded. The Reform position on many fundamentals in the Written Law today are not those of the Orthodox. Take an Orthodox fundamental like *kashrut*, which is described in Reform as a way of remembering Jewish values when you're eating. Whether you choose to remember Jewish values in that way is up to you. If you decide that you will remember in some other way, then there is the autonomy of the individual to give you the right to make up your own mind.

By contrast, the survival of Orthodox Judaism – whether you consider that desirable or not – has been entirely based on the premise over the centuries that the Din is divinely laid down. That didn't just involve obeying inconvenient rules. It meant putting up with the curses, the ghettos, the additional taxes, the punishments, the expulsions, the pogroms and the autos-da-fé; all imposed because the Jews would not give up their decision to live by the Din. Admittedly, it was always the simplest thing in the world to avoid these penalties of second-class citizenship or worse. All you had to do was give up – the survival of Orthodox Jewry was the victory of those who wouldn't.

The majority of the increase in the total numbers within the Reform movement would, naturally, come from the Orthodox Jews who decided over the years to join them. Both the Reform and Orthodox communities would lose membership through apostasy in future years. In addition, as both communities became more middle-class, they would have smaller families. Demographically, they would both have difficulty in reproducing their numbers through their birth rates. It would be the ultra-Orthodox who grew to become a far greater percentage of the total number of Jews in Britain than anyone would ever have believed possible. One reason was that, in the twentieth century, they would set out to have far larger families than the increasingly middle-class communities of the middle-of-the-road Orthodox, the Reform and the future Liberal Jews.

Hirschell and Meldola knew what was likely to happen with the breakaway group. They could recognize the thin end of the wedge. Within 25 years of the foundation of the West London Synagogue it was necessary, because of lack of support, to suspend the Sabbath afternoon service and many of the weekday morning and evening services. In 1870 Marks congratulated the community from the pulpit for the: 'improvement in devotion and numbers' over the position in 1840. As so many services had been abandoned because nobody would attend them, the mental convolutions of the preacher must have gone into overdrive. Fortunately 'devotion' could be taken to include decorum, and the level of decorum in Orthodox Jewish services was a constant target for the dissenter's disapproval.

Decorum in synagogue services has, indeed, been a constant problem over the centuries. A rabbi who has no complaints about the level of decorum at major services in the synagogue is a *rara avis* indeed. Sabbath services take about two and a half hours and major festival services take about three. The New Year morning service is five hours long and the Yom Kippur service lasts for up to three hours in the evening and up to ten hours the following day. Most nineteenth-century Orthodox Jews would have arrived late for services, prayed and talked to their neighbours and then prayed and talked some more, as many still do. In 1825, after Hirschell had been Chief Rabbi for more than 20 years, the authorities at the Great Synagogue had said that it was: 'Important that some immediate steps be taken to generally improve the harmony of the devotional services.' By which they meant the decorum. In fairness, although it is no excuse, it is difficult to maintain devotional concentration for hours on end – back to the guilt complex. It is always hoped that the next generation will maintain a higher standard.

One of the tragic results of the creation of the Reform movement was the pain that was caused to the young Jews who were caught in the crossfire. In 1856 the West London Synagogue of British Jews had a bill passed in Parliament to allow them to issue valid marriage certificates. They were then able to decide which marriages to solemnize, involving Christians who wanted to convert in order to marry Jewish partners. It was normally Jewish men marrying Christian women. The Reform movement took a much more lenient view of the necessities for such conversions than the Orthodox. As a consequence, where the wife in such a marriage was not born to an Orthodox Jewish mother, neither the mother nor the children were acceptable to the Orthodox, because in Orthodox Judaism the religion of the child is the religion of the mother.

So the children of those marriages, according to the Orthodox, were not Jewish. When they grew up and wanted to marry Orthodox Jews, those marriages in the Reform synagogue were considered invalid as well. Effectively, if they went through with them, the Orthodox male partner was leaving the British religious mainstream. The anguish that caused to the Orthodox family was immense. Parents disowned children, cut them out of wills and never spoke to them again. The Orthodox families were considered disgraced by large numbers of their family and friends. When the daughter of Lionel Cohen, the president of the Board of Deputies, married a non-Jew, her father resigned his distinguished position, even though, because any children of the marriage would have had a fully fledged Jewish mother, their status as Orthodox Jews would not have been affected. Cohen would have believed he had let the side down, that all those Cohen ancestors who had suffered for their Orthodox faith had suffered in vain. The questioned conversions affected the entire community, poor and rich, Ashkenazi and Sephardi.

The accepted law was crystal clear; unless the mother was Jewish, the children were not and the proselyte mother could only be considered Jewish if she had been properly converted according to the Orthodox rules. It was as hard for those who administered the law as for those involved in the marriages. The Orthodox religious authorities were not ogres; they were carrying out the law. Nobody with any sense was querying the decency, humanity or moral and ethical standards of those who were not officially Orthodox Jewish. The vast majority of those who wanted to marry were in love and simply wanted to spend their lives together. In condemning them to do so outside the Orthodox community, the Chief Rabbis were protecting what they, and their communities, considered the greater good.

Throughout Jewish history there had been converts; sometimes individuals, such as an English Dominican, Robert of Reading, burned at Oxford in 1222; sometimes whole communities like the Khazars in the eighth and ninth centuries. From biblical and Roman times there had been periods when Jews actively proselytized, but the ferocity of mediaeval persecution intensified Jewish reluctance to receive converts, which the Church strictly forbade then anyway. Now it could happen without penalty and it caused untold misery. Could the Orthodox law be changed? Nobody has yet found a way. The gap has grown too wide.

Yet the *Jewish Chronicle* reported in 1874:

> We may state that the members of the new congregation deny altogether the impeachment of having renounced the Oral Law. Professor Marks and Mr. Elkin, in the earlier days of the Reform, strenuously maintained the general fidelity of their congregation to the Jewish tradition... There is probably less discrepancy between the Jews forming what are called Orthodox congregations and Jews who are members of the Reformed Congregation of London than is apparent within the bosom of a single denomination of Christians we will say the Church of England. [The Reformed synagogue] cannot be characterized other than as a secession.[7]

The year before, however, when the Bevis Marks congregation had not increased in size in a century, the *Jewish Chronicle* put this down to defections to the Reform: 'whose religion was their convenience and whose God was Mammon'.[8] This denunciation, however, was far more about the actual behaviour of rich Reform members than it was about their official religious position. Most of the Reform members were well-off.

The involvement of the West London Synagogue with Jews' College illustrates the general accord within the community at the time. There could hardly have been a more Orthodox organization than the theological college which Nathan Marcus Adler had striven so hard to bring into existence. Yet in 1882 Philip Magnus, a noted educationalist but also a minister at the Reform's Upper Berkeley Street Synagogue, was accepted on the Council of Jews' College. The synagogue also sent a donation of £50 in answer to the college's appeal for funds. It made annual grants. Isidore Harris, a Jews'

College graduate, became a Reform minister and was still invited to write the jubilee volume for Jews' College in 1905. None of this would have happened had the Reform members not accepted the vast majority of Orthodox practice.

Where changes were made, they were often locally inspired. If there was a mixed choir in Manchester in 1860, there was a traditional all-male choir at Upper Berkeley Street until 1938. Independence took precedence over uniformity. The early leader of the Manchester community, Tobias Theodoris, had made this clear when he denounced Marks in 1856 as 'our Vatican [Pope]'. But then 29 out of the 44 founders of the Manchester Reform synagogue had been born in Germany, where the Reform philosophy had developed to a much greater extent.

Another reason for this difference in approach was that the Manchester Reform community had appointed, after Schiller-Szinessy, a rabbi who had been trained in Germany in a truly Reform congregation. Rabbi Dr Gustav Gottheil was determined to move far away from the Orthodox standards. During his ministry he took every Orthodox service passage from the Mishnah and the Talmud out of the liturgy, said most of the prayers in English and introduced mixed seating: 'so that husband and wife might not be separated during their worship ... as has hitherto been the case, contrary to the spirit of the century'.[9]

The London community did not follow suit and when Gottheil left to become the rabbi at Temple Emmanuel in New York:

> Fragments of evidence suggest that this drift did not meet with the unanimous approval of the Congregation and that Gottheil's departure was followed by a long struggle between conservatives and radicals in which the former achieved final victory.[10]

Certainly, the new minister, Lawrence Simmons, often officiated at services in the synagogue on the second days of festivals. Each Reform community could obviously do its own thing but, as Nathan Adler said, in defence of the Orthodox prayer book: 'the prayer book of Margaret Street [the original address of the London breakaway synagogue] has not been adopted by any village, not even in America where all kinds of experiment are exercised'.[11]

In 1896 there was a bitter discussion at Upper Berkeley Street about the introduction of some prayers in English. The suggestion was defeated and Reform historians, themselves, recognize the Orthodoxy of the community in those years: 'It can be argued that the conservatism of Berkeleystreetites was a prime force in the creation of Liberal Judaism.'[12]

The Reform honorary officers did not have to compete for authority with a Chief Rabbi. Their elected representatives could run things by themselves. Typical of this control was the formidable presence of Helen Lucas, née Goldsmid, a member of the Cousinhood in excellent standing, a most philanthropic and hard-working leader of the women in the Upper Berkeley Street community. She also: 'supervised much of the women's work at the Board [of Guardians] with a firm hand'.[13]

Movements like the suffragettes did not appeal to respectable ladies such as Mrs Lucas. Enfranchising women in the synagogue was: 'a move that, not surprisingly made Upper Berkeley Street, if anything, even more conservative. Mrs. Lionel Lucas stood prepared to denounce any hint of concession or change.'[14] Indeed, one contemporary said that: 'It is largely due to her influence that the Reform ritual has suffered so little change during 60 years'.[15]

For the likes of Mrs. Lucas: 'the retention of the old service was "a matter of life and death".'[16]

It was the kind of attitude which would make it possible for every principal Orthodox synagogue to be represented at the 50th anniversary service of the opening of the breakaway synagogue in 1892, and for the Sephardim to agree to have a joint cemetery with them at Golders Green in 1895. This is still operated by a Joint Board. In 1878 the Board of Deputies (BoD) had agreed to the creation of a Conjoint Foreign Committee with the Anglo-Jewish Association (AJA). This would represent the community, with 50 per cent of its members being from the BoD and the other delegates from the AJA. Many of the AJA were Reform and, through their membership of the Conjoint, they achieved a position of power their numerical size didn't warrant. In 1886 the Board of Deputies went further and finally agreed to accept Reform members. The Cousinhood were manipulating the processes.

To improve the religious instruction available for the youngsters, the West London Synagogue opened the West London Metropolitan School with 61 pupils in 1845. In 1846 they also opened a girls' school. By 1897, with now only a girls' school still functioning, they gave up. The explanation given was the alternative education available from new schools, like UCS in nearby Hampstead. The Christian Societies' Jewish schools, in which Jewish children would be encouraged to convert to Christianity, had also long vanished. The Reform attempts were unsuccessful, the conversionist schools were closed. The Orthodox Jews' Free School in the East End of London, which had been founded to compete with the Christian conversionist efforts, grew by the end of the nineteenth century to be the largest school in Britain with 4,000 children.

After the Bradford Reform Synagogue opened in 1873, the next new Reform synagogue was the Settlement Synagogue in 1919, nearly half a century later. The vast influx of Jews from the pogroms hardly affected the Reform movement at all. It would be 1933 before another Reform synagogue was started.

Reform in Britain was not only under attack from the Orthodox. One of its prominent members, Claude Montefiore, didn't think it had moved far enough away from the Orthodox position. Montefiore had been turned off early on in life: 'The influence of his early upbringing in the old, narrow, and somewhat rigid school of English Reform Judaism in which Rabbinism was anathema.'[17] He was concerned that the younger generation was being lost, and in addition he believed that there was much to be gained by emphasising the common ground between Christianity and Judaism. He offered: 'persistent pleading for a spiritual rapprochement with Christianity'.[18]

For many of the younger generation of middle-class Jews, Montefiore was a role model and a class act. A great-nephew of Sir Moses, he was an Oxford graduate – and from prestigious Balliol at that. He was wealthy, a warden at Upper Berkeley Street, a popular writer, an excellent communicator, a very generous philanthropist and a distinguished academic. He was able to appeal to Jews who had only a passing interest in their religion. Moreover, Montefiore was able to go about things in a big way. When he decided he didn't know enough about the talmudic background to Judaism, he persuaded one of the most famous European talmudic scholars, Rabbi Solomon Schechter, to move to London as his personal tutor.

Schechter eventually became Reader in Rabbinics at Cambridge and president of the Jewish Theological College in New York. It was Schechter who persuaded the government in 1897 to allow him to remove the contents of the Cairo *genizah* to England. A *genizah* is a room in a synagogue where you keep documents written in Hebrew after they have become unnecessary or unusable. You may not throw them away because they are in *loshen kodesh* – the holy language. The *genizah* in the Cairo synagogue had no door but possessed a shelf some feet above the ground over which the material was tossed – for 1,000 years! Not surprisingly, they're still analysing, collating and sifting it at Cambridge 100 years later. The additional information it provided has been a scholar's dream. So Montefiore had a great Orthodox teacher – who later regretted having to own up to having him as a pupil.

Montefiore's Liberal movement, well to the left of the Reform, began in 1890. Together with others who were seeking a *nouvelle vague*, it started to hold Sabbath afternoon services at the upper-class town hall in Hampstead. It initially attracted an audience from across the Jewish spectrum, including one or two Orthodox ministers, also seeking to reach out to the younger generation. The attendees were, primarily, women who weren't in the background, as they had been at morning services in the synagogues. In 1902 the infant movement became the Jewish Religious Union (JRU) and its leaders were Montefiore and Sir Samuel Montagu's daughter, Lily. Montefiore's thinking had been outlined in a series of lectures he had given in Oxford in 1892, and now he made it clear that: 'he and his supporters in the Union did not accept the literal interpretation of the Bible and even questioned the scriptural account of the giving of the 10 commandments'.[19]

At the first service of the JRU there was little Hebrew, no hazan and no sefer torah. The Orthodox ministers withdrew from the movement in some haste and Solomon Schechter, now in the United States, lamented that: 'what the whole thing means is not Liberal Judaism but Liberal Christianity'.[20] Montefiore became a prime example of the Jew whom Chief Rabbi Hart Lyon had identified during his period of office 150 years before: 'what they have really achieved is that they believe in themselves, in the great power of their own mind'.

Montefiore was intellectually satisfied with his 'modern approach'. but initially it only attracted a very limited number of adherents. Montefiore and Montagu could, however, also offer a heady mixture of novelty, professional hype, high fashion and a coterie of bright young things. He had the support of many of the good and the great among the Cousinhood. He declared inconvenient *mitzvoth* old-fashioned and abolished them. Conversions would be made still easier. The charismatic Montefiore stood for a new English Jewish spirituality against the old, 'foreign' ways and he scorned the alleged fuddy-duddies who couldn't see his light. Such a programme gained him some additional support and a larger number of new Liberal communities emerged in the next 20 years than the Reform managed: North London in 1921, South London in 1927 and Liverpool in 1928.

Montefiore remained a power in the Jewish community for years. He was president of the Anglo-Jewish Association from 1895–1922 and served on the Conjoint. He was an expert on the synoptic gospels and a member of the London Society for the Study of Religions – from which eventually came the Council of Christians and Jews. From a communal and intellectual vantage point, he could attack both the Orthodox and the Reform for being behind his times. As far as the Orthodox were concerned, Montefiore was a menace. His only saving grace, as many of them saw it, was that he was a menace out in the open. Too many communal leaders who were fellow travellers with Montefiore, remained members in good standing of designated Orthodox bodies.

In 1910 attendances in Reform synagogues were dropping. So the service was shortened by half an hour and more prayers were said in English. Seating men and women together was still rejected by the community. The situation did not improve. Helen Lucas was very much against these further moves away from Orthodoxy. She disliked Montefiore's movement very much. As the Liberals didn't have their own synagogue initially, they made enquiries about borrowing Upper Berkeley Street. Mrs Lucas commented: 'If you lend the synagogue to them, you may as well lend it to the church.'[21] Mrs Lucas finally came to the conclusion that: 'The spirit of unrest would never have existed if you had not allowed innovation.'[22]

Many of the Upper Berkeley Street Synagogue members did join Montefiore. His motive of winning back the uncommitted by making the religion more understandable was well meant. Ironically, his old tutor, Schechter, was also keen on innovation. It was Schechter who started the Orthodox Jewish Theological Seminary in New York on the path to conservative Judaism, which would come to have much more in common with the Reform than the Orthodox.

Both the Reform and Liberal movements had common ground with the United Synagogue and the Sephardim, in that they wanted to be considered good and loyal citizens by the government of the day. Which accounts for the fact that both the Reform and Liberal leaders were very anti-Zionist. In his presidential address to the Anglo-Jewish Association in 1898, Montefiore stated: 'For the work of the Association... and for their relationship with the government of various countries, it was of cardinal importance that they should not seem to commit themselves to, or in any way be in relation with, the Zionist movement.' Almost everybody agreed. It wasn't until after the Balfour Declaration that the Reform and Liberal movements slowly started to alter their stance.

It was Montefiore's co-founder, Lily Montagu, speaking at a conference in Berlin in the 1920s who told the women in the audience that they should come down from the ladies' gallery and join their husbands. This was to be one of the major distinguishing marks of the non-Orthodox service in the future. It became the practice in the Reform in 1933.

The Liberal synagogue invited the Reform to join them in 1926 but this didn't happen, as the Reform were still hoping for a rapprochement with the Orthodox. After all, Sir Robert Waley Cohen, the head of the United Synagogue, was much in favour of this and it was hoped that he could win over the Chief Rabbi.

It was the appointment of an American rabbi at Upper Berkeley Street in 1929 which resulted in that possibility finally being abandoned. Rabbi Harold Reinhart was accustomed to the American Reform movement practices and he was a powerful and persuasive advocate of breaking entirely with Orthodox tradition. He felt that the British Reform synagogues were in danger of becoming the junior partner on the left of the community because they were really in line with the American conservative congregations which, at the time, were far closer to the Orthodox positions. Reinhart thought that reconciliation was impossible and he suggested that, instead, the Reform movement should ally itself with the Liberals in a joint organization. In 1930, at the urging of Lily Montagu, it was agreed that the Reform would join, with the Liberals, the World Union of Progressive Judaism.

From that point on, the community split completely. The atmosphere increasingly soured, the niceties were less and less observed. Where Adler had attended the memorial service for David Woolf Marks and Hertz the one for the cremated Morris Joseph, where the Orthodox Hertz and Arthur Barnett from the Western had preached at Upper Berkeley Street, there would now develop two camps, antagonistic to each other's beliefs. When the refugees came from Germany in the latter part of the 1930s, the progressive movement was also much strengthened by co-religionists from that bastion of the left wing.

The total non-acceptance of the Reform and Liberal communities by the Orthodox would continue to pain the progressive members deeply. The large number of families with members in both camps were equally distressed. The sincerity of the progressive movement was in no doubt and their own forms of worship were always performed with dignity and reverence. They felt unfairly rejected. Their view was that if the Catholics and the Protestants could come to a form of accord, why couldn't the Orthodox and the progressives achieve the same? Weren't they just another branch of Judaism? No, said the Orthodox. There weren't any branches to Judaism, just a trunk. The progressives pointed out continually that the Orthodox didn't keep to many of the rules they insisted upon. This, said many progressive critics, made the Orthodox hypocrites. The Orthodox view was that if a lot of people smuggled more than their allowance of goods through customs when they came home from holiday, that didn't mean that customs should be abolished. It meant that a lot of people succumbed to temptation. If they broke the speed limit or parked in an illegal place, that didn't mean they had to reject the rule of law.

The search for equality with the majority Orthodox community remained part of the progressives' agenda as the century advanced. They were readily welcomed on charity committees and in non-spiritual settings. They made some progress. The Board of Deputies had in their constitution a rule that in spiritual matters, the diktat of the Chief Rabbi should always apply. In 1970 this was changed, so that if the subject matter affected the progressives, their spiritual leaders should in future be consulted. The progressives had won a measure of recognition. The result was that, in protest, the right wing walked out of the Board of Deputies and haven't returned. The two sides remain poles apart.

NOTES

1   *Jewish Chronicle*, 13 November 1874.
2   Kershon and Romain, *Tradition and Change*, Vallentine Mitchell, 1995.
3   Rabbi Helen Freeman in a letter to the author.
4   Albert H. Friedlander, *Second Chance*, in J.C.B. Mohr, 1991.
5   Kershon and Romain, Tradition and Change.
6   Ibid.
7   *Jewish Chronicle*, 13 February 1874.
8   *Jewish Chronicle*, 17 November 1874.
9   P.S. Goldberg, *The Manchester Congregation of British Jews, 1857–1957*, Manchester, 1957.
10 Bill Williams, *The Making of Manchester Jewry 1740–1875*, Manchester University Press, 1976.
11 Ibid.
12 Kershon and Romain, *Tradition and Change*.
13 Eugene C. Black, *The Social Politics of Anglo-Jewry 1880–1920*, Basil Blackwell, 1988.
14 Ibid.
15 Ibid.

16 Ibid.,
17 Harvey Meirovich, *A Vindication of Judaism*, Jewish Theological Seminary of New York, 1998.
18 Vivian G. Simmons, Jewish Historical Society of England, 1939.
19 Raymond Apple, *The Hampstead Synagogue*, Vallentine Mitchell, 1967.
20 Ibid.
21 Black, *The Social Politics of Anglo-Jewry 1880–1920*.
22 Ibid.

16   Nathan Marcus Adler 1844–90

Solomon Hirschell had been Chief Rabbi for 40 years. He had done much good and was much loved by the community, but he had probably outstayed his welcome. He died at 81 and it was generally agreed that Hirschell in his dotage wouldn't be a terribly hard act to follow. It was also felt, however, that the next Chief Rabbi should be better educated and reflect the fact that Jews were now far more a part of the general community. If the Jews were about to play their part in local politics, the professions and the academic world, then their leaders felt that their spiritual head should be secularly as well as religiously educated. The Chief Rabbi electors were now looking for a spiritual leader who had the necessary qualifications.

The difficulty was, as usual, that there wasn't a good English candidate. Applications were invited and 15 prospective candidates applied for the post. There was a wealth of choice and the favourite in an early informal discussion was Samson Raphael Hirsch, who would go on to be a massively important Orthodox leader in Germany and the inspiration of the right wing long after he had passed away. When it came to a vote, however, the overwhelm-ing winner was Nathan Marcus Adler, the Grand Rabbi of Hanover. Only five delegates voted against Adler – all from the very independent Western synagogue – not to be confused with the West London, which had no vote.

Adler had many things going for him. First of all, his father had also been the Grand Rabbi in Hanover when it was still ruled by the kings of England. Both Adlers were well known to the viceroy, the Duke of Cambridge. Although George III never visited Hanover and George IV and William IV only once each, George IV's brother was very popular. When the duke, Queen Victoria's uncle, was giving away the prizes at the Western Jewish Girls' Free School in 1850, he said on the platform that he had been instrumental in getting Adler appointed. That wasn't necessarily the good news, for Adler inherited a community cutting many religious corners. For example, Adler would have been diplomatic enough not to wonder out loud in his early days who had been instrumental in getting the Western Synagogue minister appointed. Moss Levy served the community from 1849–73, but he was a bachelor. It would have been unthinkable back in Hanover. Jewish spiritual leaders always have to be married.

Adler's case also benefited from the fact that he was related to David Tevele Schiff as his grandmother was Schiff's sister. He was a genuine talmudic scholar and only 27 when he became Grand Rabbi of Hanover after taking over from his father in 1830. He came from a famous rabbinic family, his brother, Gabriel, was a rabbi and another brother, Baer, a Dayan. This was a time in Germany when the Jews were finally let out of the ghetto and allowed to take part in German social and cultural life. So Adler served in the army and he had also taken advantage of the new liberalism to study philosophy at four universities – Göttingen, Erlangen, Wurzburg and – best of all – Heidelberg. He had both semicha and a doctorate.

At Göttingen one of his friends had been Prince Albert of Saxe Coburg, which certainly wouldn't do him any harm when Albert became Victoria's husband. The prince found it a pleasure to be able to talk again to someone who was equally steeped in the culture he knew best. Albert was a good friend to the godly and it was his intervention, in his position as Chancellor of Cambridge, that persuaded the University to admit its first Jewish undergraduate in 1849. Albert would even recruit Adler to help him with the Great Exhibition in 1851. By 1859 the government would consult him on education. For his part, Adler would fervently thank the Almighty for the failure of the attempt to assassinate Queen Victoria in 1849, and that would be echoed on three subsequent occasions during her reign.

Adler's academic attainments also put him on a par with the educated members of his new British community. Admittedly, at the start he didn't speak English and the agreement reached was that he would learn it within two years – not a problem for Adler. He was fluent in the language in 12 months and thereafter could fairly claim to have created the English-speaking Jewish pulpit.

Adler had always recognized that the effect of releasing the German Jews into society back home would lead to major strains on Orthodoxy. The ghetto was discriminatory, oppressive, restrictive and municipally unsanitary, but it did have one advantage; it kept the Jews together and it made it relatively easy to set high standards of religious observance. Failure to keep to the Din would quickly become common knowledge, because the ghetto was such a confined area. To be respectable, you had to be observant. Furthermore, within the ghetto the Jews ruled themselves, so there was no deviation from the Din. Now all that was gone and already the German Reform movement was creating new forms of Judaism which denied the relevance of parts of the Oral Law. The reformers weren't only motivated by religion. They felt they had to abandon whatever militated against their being fully accepted into German society, a position which they craved. Adler was prepared to consider whether in Britain there was room for compromise between the demands of the upwardly mobile and the traditional practices of Orthodoxy, but from the very beginning he was very careful to only allow changes if they were not against the Din.

The biggest spiritual problem the community had when Adler took up office was, of course, the split which had created the new breakaway synagogue, the West London Synagogue of British Jews, and the caution against its founders. Could Adler be relied on to uphold the Orthodox position? Adler had a track record. In 1844 at the Brunswick conference in Germany to make the case for German Reform, he had protested against the ideas of the movement. It was Samson Raphael Hirsch who had spoken for all the antis:

> The old Jewish religious legislation, which forms the funda-
> mental statute of every Jewish community, has given the
> Israelitish congregation also the fundamental rules for its
> religious guidance, and nothing could nor can obtain validity in
> it which is not in accord with this religious legislation, as it has
> been handed down to us in Torah, Talmud and the rabbinical
> codes of the Shulchan Aruch.

That was where Adler stood and he was elected as a result of this and all his other qualities. He knew the difficulties he faced in England. He had been told before he took office that the community: 'rely very much on your wisdom and high learning that you will treat the enquiry in the calm, dispassionate and learned manner'.

At his installation in 1845, at the age of 41, he spelt out the major problem, as he saw it, with applying the Din. He said that it was:

> extremely difficult to guard it at a time in which one party seeks
> its glory in pulling down existing structures of religious theory
> and practice; the other in preserving everything hallowed by
> age, though opposed to the foundations of the law; in which
> one Minister worships progress and the other adores
> conservatism.

Where the Reform movement in Germany was very attractive to many in the Jewish upper classes, the vast majority of the leaders of English Jewry were not interested in joining the new breakaway synagogue. There were many reasons for this but the most important was their own concern to be fully accepted into Christian society. Germany wasn't the United Kingdom. In Britain, society supported the Church of England which could easily be identified as the Christian equivalent of Orthodox Judaism. They equated the breakaway synagogue with the Christian dissenters, who were seldom members of the establishment. The English culture was also one of evolution rather than revolution. England had escaped the political upheaval wrought by Napoleon throughout the rest of Europe and was proud of the fact. It maintained a gradualist posture, and in 1845 Britain was the greatest nation on earth and the Jews wanted to join the Club as full members. That seemed more likely to happen if they remained Orthodox.

In contrast, the English Protestant case against the Catholics was that they had strayed from the teachings of the Bible because of the rulings of the popes. The Protestants wanted to go back to those biblical origins and, initially, the Jewish breakaway members took a few steps down that road. The Orthodox, on the other hand, were not prepared to give up the teachings of centuries of rabbinic Oral Law.

Adler's first line of defence was to judge the support he would have for resisting change. For example, if a member of the breakaway synagogue wanted to marry a member of an Orthodox community, could that be banned because Adler considered the entire breakaway congregation heretics? The answer which emerged was that, if either party came from a rich and powerful family, Adler would not get the support he needed. So he allowed such marriages, as long as both the bride and groom had mothers born from an Orthodox marriage; that remained a *sine qua non*. Adler knew that all the members of the breakaway had important relatives within the Orthodox ranks, who wanted to remain in spiritual touch with them. As he told Rabbi Solomon Eger, back home in Germany in 1847, he was: 'afraid to fight publicly with the wealthy to publicize such a decision about the reformers'.[1]

Adler also needed all the rich members of the community to support the poor. Sir David Salomons, one of those rich supporters, pointed out that otherwise he was 'running the risk of losing the heads of your schools, the patrons of your benevolent institutions and the supporters of your charities, for many of such honourable positions were held by members of the Margaret Street congregation'.[2] Such as Francis Goldsmid who was the president of the Jewish Infants' School. To some extent, money still talked.

With a relatively free hand, Adler, throughout his ministry, was a first-class administrator. He fashioned a much larger Jewish community infrastructure and by the time he died, he had seen most of the foundations of the institutions of the twenty-first century firmly laid down. His seal of office had an eagle (Adler) on it and he watched over his international flock with the bird's intensity. The first task had been to set down the rules by which all the congregations would abide. As early as 1847 came his *Laws and Regulations for all the Synagogues in the British Empire*. It was a comprehensive list and the spiritual power was totally vested in the Chief Rabbi. It contained *ascamot* such as: 'The duty of superintending the Synagogue, as far as religious observances are concerned, devolves on the Chief Rabbi, when present.'

Even so, a number of the policies of the breakaway synagogue were quietly adopted. There were also changes demanded of which Adler approved anyway. He wanted better decorum in synagogue and in 1845 approved the decision not to allow children under the age of 4 to attend services in the Great. He was happy with the resolution that there should be no talking in the *shul* during services and nobody should leave the synagogue before the end of the service. Legislation was easier than gaining obedience on either count. He welcomed the new concept of choirs at the Great and the New because he'd introduced them in his time in Hanover. In 1849 he approved the setting up of the Central Synagogue in the West End. On minutiae, it was decided that ladies couldn't wear crinolines in *shul* because they took up too much room and if you chewed tobacco, you stood to be fined half a crown (12½p).

Recognizing that there was merit to some complaints, Adler set out to correct them. He shortened some parts of the service which had become extended over the centuries and he cut down the number of *misheberechs* that could be requested when a member was given an honour in the synagogue. In 1852 the Western Synagogue abolished *misheberechs* altogether but they were the only synagogue to do so.

There were also changes that Adler would not approve, but he often had to adopt a subtle tack. On the Sabbath, services started at 8 a.m. because the morning prayers have to be said early. The members at the new Central Synagogue in the West End of London wanted to start later. Adler let them do so, but stopped any other synagogue, on the grounds that their traditions (*minhag*) shouldn't be changed.

Of course, most Jews didn't go to synagogue anyway. In 1855 there were between 20,000 and 25,000 Jews in London and the pews for them in synagogue numbered 3,692. The exception, where the seating was entirely inadequate, was Yom Kippur, when overflow services would be held in many different venues. At the Jews' Free School, High Holy Day attendances of up to 3,000 were common. Normally, however, many synagogues found it necessary to pay poor Jews a regular income to attend synagogue on weekdays in order to make up the ten-man quorum which has to be present if prayers for the dead are to be said. Having a *minyan* is, therefore, very important to a member if it's the anniversary of the death of a near relative. The breakaway synagogue abolished the daily services, so they didn't need *minyan* men, but by 1853 even the Sephardi West End synagogue only held morning services on Mondays and Thursdays.

The exceptions to the drift from observance were the small, very Orthodox congregations, located mostly in the East End. Some of these *hebra* had been in existence since the eighteenth century. These very Orthodox Jews would tolerate no changes, but they were usually poor and lacked influence. Their families didn't disappear from Judaism, though, at anything like the same rate as those who would give up almost anything to gain acceptance in Christian society.

In public, the vast majority of the Jews wanted the rules of the religion to be seen to be maintained, even if they didn't follow the same rules at home. There would be tables with kosher food for his Jewish guests at the inaugural banquet of Sir David Salomons, the first Jewish Lord Mayor of London. It would be eaten, however, off plates which were not kosher because they had been used before for non-kosher dishes. During the Great Exhibition of 1851, visitors had to sign a book when they went in. The Jews got agreement that they didn't have to sign on the Sabbath. All they had to do was produce their tickets. This got over the prohibition on writing, but the prohibition on carrying things on the Sabbath existed as well, and that had to be conveniently ignored.

The standard of observance of most Jews continued on a steady decline, but the vast majority of the community still remained in the Orthodox fold. Adler recognized what was happening all too well, but for any Chief Rabbi, there is always the bright hope of tomorrow: 'He was pre-eminently a realist, interested in safeguarding his personal position and influence in the community.'[3]

It is not surprising that the main accusation against the Orthodox Jews by the breakaway members and the non-observant was that they were hypocrites. If they obeyed one element of the Oral Law, why didn't they obey it all? The Orthodox answer was, because nobody's perfect and their willpower wasn't likely to be strong enough to resist all the temptations. Welcome to the human race. But that didn't mean, for the Orthodox, that giving every individual the right to obey or disregard the laws could make everything alright. Even though keeping to all the rules in Judaism is a great deal more difficult than obeying the country's laws, because the Din covers almost everything you do in life. For the Orthodox it's a case of back to the old guilt complex.

The caution itself was deeply unpopular with many of the most senior lay members of the community but equally supported by many others. *The Voice of Jacob* reported that one meeting to discuss the subject in 1846 was adjourned: 'amidst a sense of confusion which beggars description'. So could Adler find a compromise and also get the Sephardim to approve it? After all, the breakaway group consisted mostly of their members, but they still had no Haham to sort it. They finally agreed that the caution was no longer valid because *ascama* 1 had been abolished, and that you couldn't issue a caution on a whole community. In fact, in David Nietto's time the attorney general had held that the Haham had that authority, if he chose to use it. Whatever the legality of the community's behaviour, the breakaway community leaders were allowed to apologize for breaking the *ascamot* in the first place and the caution was lifted by a 15–3 vote of the elders in 1847. Adler helped to find the compromise.

However, it only papered over the cracks. The new synagogue was not really acceptable to the majority of the Sephardi or Ashkenazi communities. In particular, Bevis Marks was still smarting from the row which had occupied so much time and heartache only those few years ago. The Hambro Synagogue was the most Orthodox of the major Ashkenazi London congregations and would concede the least. On the other hand, the leaders of the Great and the New had many connections with the breakaway community and wanted an end to hostilities.

The lay leadership, as a whole, was also still more concerned about its remaining disabilities than about the internal spiritual differences. The first four parliamentary bills to allow the Jews, if elected, to take their seats in the Commons without swearing 'on the true faith of a Christian' were introduced in the 1830s and all were defeated. By the time Adler became Chief Rabbi the Disabilities Removal Act had been passed and Jews were able to take their places in city councils and on judicial benches; many but not all offices in the public sector were now open to them. In 1846 the ordinance of 1271 which stopped Jews owning land was repealed. The Religious Opinions Relief Bill repealed an act of Queen Elizabeth which laid down that everybody had to go to church. In 1854 Jews were allowed to take degrees at Oxford and in 1856 religious tests were abolished at Cambridge.

When, however, Lionel de Rothschild was elected MP for the City of London in 1847, the wording of the compulsory oath remained unchanged and he was still unable to take his seat. English respectable society then was far more religious than it is today. Prayer, for instance, was an integral and crucial part of daily life. For example, in large hotels today, it is customary for the general manager to have a meeting with the senior staff early in the morning. Throughout the industry, this conference is called 'Morning Prayers' – a throwback to Victorian times, when the staff – and the guests – would assemble in the morning to pray together.

The respect for Christianity was one reason it had been easier to get agreement to eliminate the disabilities of dissenters than it was to offer the same equality to Jews. At least the former were Christians where the latter most certainly were not. There were, however, more practical considerations now as well.

In December 1847 the prime minister himself, Lord John Russell, introduced a bill to change the wording of the Christian oath to solve Rothschild's problem; it was passed in the Commons but killed in the Lords. For the next 11 years there were a succession of emancipation bills being voted down in the House of Lords, even as the City of London continued to re-elect Rothschild in defiance of the ban. It wasn't until 1858 that Rothschild was finally able to take his seat. This has always been recognized as a victory of liberal thinking over aristocratic anti-Semitism.

But the story isn't that simple. Why were the Lords so determined not to pass the bill? The suggestion that it would overthrow that centuries-old tradition of Britain as a Christian country, hardly holds water. Even had Jews had some very minor say in the running of the realm, it was hardly likely that the measure would ever lead to the election of hundreds of Jewish members, enough to form a seriously powerful bloc. What is more, day-to-day political strategy is usually about the art of the mundane possible, rather than about intellectual philosophies.

What is being ignored here is the Chartists and the European uprisings of 1848. The Chartists were a mass movement that wanted, among other things, universal suffrage, paid MPs and the chance to become an MP even if you didn't own property. They started in 1838 and soon were collecting monster petitions to back up their demands. Their pressure tactics turned ugly on occasions. There were riots in Newport in 1839 with a number of deaths resulting. The Chartist leaders involved received prison sentences and some were transported to Australia. Revolution became a serious option under discussion by the Chartist leader, Feargus O'Connor and his senior followers.

The potential danger of a movement like Chartism, as a real threat to the stability of the established system, came home to roost in February 1848. In that month the political status quo in Europe started to implode. The monarchy was overthrown in France and four Italian states were forced to grant constitutions. In March Metternich, the most powerful minister in Austria, was forced to resign, the Hungarians demanded independence from Austria and the King of Prussia was driven to summon a constituent assembly. Uprisings and riots in Europe were skittling governments like ninepins. The Chartists in England then set the date of 10 April for the delivery to Parliament of their new 5,000,000-strong petition. (It was really 2 million and many signatures weren't genuine, for example, Queen Victoria's!) Even so, questions were anxiously asked about whether the rulers in Britain might also be overthrown?

The government panicked – or took sensible precautions, depending on your viewpoint. They decided that the prospects were so dire that the Queen and Prince Albert should be evacuated and would leave London for the more easily defended Isle of Wight. George VI and Queen Elizabeth wouldn't leave London during the Second World War Blitz, but Osborne House had the royal family on 8 April 1848.

The obvious fear was that the presentation of the petition to Parliament would trigger another uprising, as had happened on the continent. There was ample precedent for serious disturbances on such occasions. When the minor Jew Bill had been passed in 1753 to make it easier for a few rich Jews to become naturalized, there had been demonstrations in the country. In 1780, in much worse anti-Catholic riots, London had been in the hands of the mob for days. The assembly in St Peters Fields in Manchester, as recently as 1819, had culminated in the infamous Peterloo massacre. The Lords were concerned that the situation remained calm. After all, who would have suffered alongside the monarchy had a revolution against the existing system succeeded? Parliament would be next and the aristocracy would get it in the neck. Indeed, the guillotine had not been forgotten. The power of the House of Lords was obviously under serious threat.

When the petition was due to be presented, the Whig government did a little more than stop all police leave in London. They got the Duke of Wellington out of retirement and gave him 8,000 regular troops as well as the 4,000 policemen in the capital. They then swore in no less than 85,000 special constables. 4 They were that scared of the potential danger. Under these circumstances the form of the Jewish affirmation was the merest side-show – it was about as important as not striking a match in the middle of a forest fire. As the *Jewish Chronicle* commented in the July of that year: 'The voice of the people, which at the beginning of the session, spoke kindly in our favour, has now been hushed into silence by the thunder of the revolutionary Continent.'[5]

Unsurprisingly, the Chartist leaders decided that discretion was the better part of valour. After careful consideration, they agreed not to take on the best part of a 100,000-strong army. The demonstration stayed at its base camps in London parks and the Chartists then walked away from possible trouble, but they didn't give up. Propaganda continued, the government remained on its guard, and the House of Lords brushed away successive emancipation bills as an irritant while everything quietened down over the next ten years.

It could not be expected that peers would talk at such debates of their fears of revolution if they let the Jews off the Christian oath; the face which would be lost as a result would be totally unacceptable. The Christian foundation argument was safer, credible, more appealing and more noble. It is also true that the bishops and many peers did feel very strongly about the Christian foundation of the nation and understood little about their Jewish fellow-citizens. After all, one bishop said it would be no use talking to the Chief Rabbi on the subject as he, the bishop, didn't speak Hebrew! Nevertheless, the lengths to which the government went to restrain the Chartists was proof of just how seriously they took the possibility of revolution and how badly they wanted to avoid inflaming feelings.

In 1858 a compromise was reached that both houses of Parliament would choose the form of their own oath of allegiance. The Commons were then able to accept Baron Lionel de Rothschild at last, but the Lords didn't change their form of affirmation until 1885 when Rothschild's son, Natty, was raised to the peerage.

Adler had been elected by both the London and provincial congregations, so he was no longer effectively controlled by the honorary officers of the Great Synagogue. His salary was paid by over 20 communities in all, and his spiritual authority was acknowledged in many parts of the British Empire, as well as in substantial parts of the United States. An Orthodox rabbi could easily feel isolated in the colonies and would be very pleased to have support from the big battalions back in London. For example, Adler wrote to the overwrought rabbi in Cape Town in 1860:

> if you wish me to speak of these to the community, I will readily do so, I will support you wholeheartedly and encourage them to pay attention to you and to strengthen what you have established. My advice is that you should not leave your position but carry on with your work.

Adler wasn't really responsible to anybody, as it was highly unlikely that he would do anything so contentious that all the congregations would unite against him. With his appointment, therefore, the position of the Chief Rabbi changed. It was only when the London synagogues combined into the United Synagogue in 1870 that a body emerged which could attempt to control the Ashkenazi Chief Rabbi again, if it felt so inclined. Nevertheless, like politics, spiritual leadership was, on many occasions, the art of the possible.

What Adler was maintaining was the responsibility of the rabbunim to maintain Jewish practice and not laymen. The use of the native language for sermons is not prohibited in the Bible; therefore Adler could adopt the principle. The laws of *kashrut* are set down in Leviticus; therefore Adler wouldn't have dreamed of changing them any more than would his predecessors or successors.

In grasping the reins so firmly, Adler was continuing to fulfil the role that Hirschell had undertaken. No matter how far away the community was from London – Manchester or Melbourne, Chatham or Cape Town – you could invariably get an authoritative answer. It was what the smaller communities, in particular, wanted very badly. As the *Voice of Jacob* commented the year Hirschell died: 'though independent-minded enough sometimes, they have found reference and subordination indispensable in *shechita*, marriages, divorce, etc., etc. and hence, not from design or system, but from inevitable necessity, the late Rabbi was recognized as the spiritual head of most Jews claiming British origin'.

Adler had a wide enough remit, but the invention of the railway helped considerably in carrying it out. He was the first Chief Rabbi to travel regularly around the country on pastoral tours of his congregations. As they didn't have their own rabbis, he was also not short of matters requiring his responsa. The variety of problems brought to Adler's desk in London was wide-ranging. Could a member with doubtful morals have a synagogue honour? If a couple were living together, but not married, did the Din allow them to get married in synagogue? If a child ran away from home, must the parents take it back? If a father died owing money to the synagogue, could the honorary officers refuse to allow his son to put up a tombstone for him unless the debt was paid? Adler dealt with them all. For example, he wrote about the debt: 'Our law demands that the son should not suffer for the father, therefore we are not justified to do such an open insult to an innocent man.'[6]

No matter how abstruse or complicated, Adler could provide the answer. He would also continue the tradition of acting as an employment agency. The communities were often poor and could not afford decent wages. The only possible candidates were refugees and European immigrants, and their cultures might well clash with those of the community they were going to serve. On the other hand, with such difficulty in filling posts, every effort had to be made to keep staff. On one occasion when a shochet accepted a better job, the Falmouth community withheld his salary. Adler had to write to them: 'Mr Herrman is leaving for Sheffield and complains that you object to him leaving. I think you have no right to form an impediment to the man's promotion in life.'[7]

Because the refugees were poor, they were not always treated with the courtesy they deserved. In 1851 after a row in Exeter, Adler wrote: 'I cannot suppress stating that no respectable Reader will go now to Exeter to be exposed to such insults.'

Adler reached out to all his flock. He asked the governor of Dartmoor prison not to insist that the Jewish prisoners worked on the Sabbath. He also sent money for the convicts, particularly to enable them to buy matzos for Passover, and he kept in touch with many of them individually.

War with the breakaway congregation soon broke out again, but in all his spiritual activities, Adler could count on the support of the president of the Board of Deputies, Sir Moses Montefiore, who always referred to Adler as 'our excellent Chief Rabbi'. The editor of Sir Moses' diaries, Louis Loewe, confirmed: 'as President of the Board of Deputies... [when he] had to give his opinion on religious matters, he invariably referred to the Spiritual Head of the community for guidance; he regarded a word from him as decisive, and obeyed its injunctions at whatever cost to himself'.

There had been an effort to increase the membership of the Board of Deputies 15 years earlier, to bring in more of the provincial congregations. At the time there had been little response, as the congregations said they couldn't afford the expense. By 1853 things had changed. The elections to the Board that year produced four successful candidates who declared that they would represent the views of the West London Synagogue of British Jews. There was immediately a tremendous row at the deputies' meeting on whether this could be permitted. The arguments grew so fierce that Montefiore, as president, had to call the police to keep order. Anthony Rothschild stopped the constable entering the Hall, an obvious case of obstructing a police officer in the discharge of his duty, but that was soon forgotten. Montefiore then adjourned the meeting without discussion and hurriedly left the building in a hardly dignified manner. At a later meeting, the two opposing groups were still evenly matched. Out of eight Bevis Marks delegates only one voted for acceptance. The hatchets were still out, rather than buried, in the Sephardi community. Montefiore eventually used his chairman's casting vote to refuse to accept the West London supporters. Jewish newspapers such as the new *Jewish Chronicle* had finally been allowed to report the meetings. They had a field day but Montefiore was immovable.

According to the constitution of the Board of Deputies at the time, Montefiore was abiding by the rules. The first clause of the constitution of the Board of Deputies gave its objective as: 'In order that no infraction upon the religious rites, customs and privileges of the Jewish community' be approved. Montefiore held that the breakaway synagogue members had themselves committed an 'infraction' and, therefore, couldn't be represented. The Board of Deputies was a religious body. He remained immovable all the rest of his life and the reformers were not admitted to the Board of Deputies until his retirement from the board in 1874. But then it wasn't until 1863 that it was even agreed at Bevis Marks to accept charitable donations from the seceders.

Montefiore could keep the deputies in line but there were powerful lay leaders who, on occasions, opposed the wishes of both Montefiore and Adler. When the laws on marriages were revised in 1866, the government initially agreed to exclude the Jews from the regulations. Some marriage relationships – uncle and niece, for example – were permissible in the Din but would be banned by the forthcoming legislation. Influential lay leaders, like Sir David Salomons, persuaded the government to apply the bill to everybody, because they didn't want Jews treated differently from other people, even if the Din couldn't be applied as a consequence. Their view was that, if they wanted total equality and no disabilities, they couldn't also ask to be excluded from legislation they disliked. Montefiore's concern that a dropping of disabilities could be bought too expensively at the cost of outlawing parts of Jewish law, proved perfectly correct.

The dissent at the Board of Deputies in 1853 didn't harm the standing of the Chief Rabbi because Adler kept well out of it. That firm accord with Montefiore meant that he didn't have to voice his views in a no-win situation. If he had become involved, he would have alienated whichever side lost the vote. Montefiore would know Adler's views and act accordingly. So Adler stalled – the Board of Deputies asked his advice and it took him two months to fob them off with a reply which left him as neutral as before.

But Adler didn't completely avoid the flak. The growing Manchester community, for one, was furious with Montefiore and the move for local independence from London gathered strength. The Mancunian Jews decided to give their rabbi, Solomon Schiller-Szenessy, the title of Local Rabbi. They wanted him to take on Adler's responsibilities in many areas. From their point of view Schiller-Szenessy was impeccably Orthodox and had semicha, so he knew the Din.

The move for local autonomy was sternly resisted by Adler because he was afraid that the reformers in Manchester might persuade any local rabbi to their way of thinking. He didn't trust Schiller-Szenessy not to wilt under the pressure. There was a powerful group of Manchester members who had been brought up in Germany close to the more extreme German Reform programme.[8] This group worked hard to gain supporters by making local autonomy and Reform principles a package: give up the Chief Rabbi and, while you're at it, give up Orthodoxy as well.

Adler and Montefiore saw their opportunity. They recognized that the group had gone too far. While there may have been support for local autonomy, there was far less for Reform. They were able to discredit both, and when Schiller-Szenessy accepted the position of rabbi at the new Reform synagogue, they were able to say that their initial concerns about local autonomy had been fully justified. It was widely recognized that Orthodoxy was only safe in the hands of the Chief Rabbi.

It was the Manchester experience which led Adler to try to ensure that there was no rabbinic competition to his pre-eminence in the future. His son, Hermann Adler, adopted the same platform when he succeeded his father. There were to be few ministers with *semicha* among the mainstream Orthodox communities in Britain for many years. However, the resentment against the ultimate authority of

London over Manchester did not evaporate completely. It just simmered and the chance for a rematch came in 1917, to the enormous advantage of the future state of Israel.

While some members of provincial communities resented the pre-eminence of the Chief Rabbi, others were extremely glad that such recognition existed. As more Jews entered the country and as the patterns of manufacturing changed, there was a need for new communities and a shift in the old. Jews headed for newly developing areas, such as the increasingly industrial north-east of England. In 1863, accompanied by his recently qualified son, Adler consecrated the new synagogue in Sunderland. In 1872 he consecrated Hartlepool and in 1874 Middlesborough – and when he left there the mayor came down to the station to wish him bon voyage. Without the Chief Rabbi the new communities were small groups of foreign strangers with eccentric habits. With Adler as their leader, presented by Sir Moses Montefiore at the queen's levée – friend of Prince Albert and protégé of the Duke of Cambridge – they were regarded far more favourably by the local municipal leaders. The local Jews were, however, always encouraged to merge with their neighbours where possible. In 1880 when Adler sent his son to consecrate the new synagogue in Newcastle the, by now, delegate Chief Rabbi told the congregation to get themselves a minister who spoke English.

Adler could go too far and sometimes found it difficult to distinguish between Jewish and non-English. While Solomon Hirschell led his community through the London streets to perform *tashlich* at the New Year, Adler said of the *mitzvah* in 1874: 'Our foreign brethren... must not bring discredit on their generous or freeborn British brethren by their unpleasant vagaries.' *Tashlich* is a richly symbolic, harmless, happy family occasion which the children enjoy particularly. When you start to call it an 'unpleasant vagary' you're beginning to lose the plot.

At least relations between the Sephardim and Ashkenazim, as a whole, had improved. In 1849, Adler was at last invited to preach at Bevis Marks and various hatchets were now discreetly buried. Adler and Benjamin Artom, when he was the Haham, got on very well.

As the whole community settled down again to relatively peaceful co-existence, Adler concentrated on education. Like every other Chief Rabbi he knew its overriding importance and, as he said at his installation: 'I purpose to superintend your establishments for education.' He was, however, way out of step with the majority of his community and almost all his lay leadership. In 1852 he made his views clear on the standards of teaching he had encountered: 'Our pulpits and our schools...are not seldom entrusted to men of ill-furnished minds, untutored, or at least unprepared for the performance of their sacred function.'

In Liverpool in the same year he made the case against neglecting the education of women: 'Those who believed that the destiny of a girl was poverty – that her destiny was an inferior one – might entertain such an erroneous opinion; but those who knew that she was fashioned for a higher life – for a better life – could not doubt that schools for girls were of the greatest moment.' To only educate boys was: 'not in accordance with the spirit of the Torah'. The Torah had been supporting feminists in the educational field for a long time.

The Sephardim had, of course, taken the same position over 100 years earlier and the Jews' Free School in London also took girls. JFS was doing well, but this was because it was designed for poor children and there were always a large number of them. Their parents could not contemplate fee-paying schools and JFS, together with the Western Synagogue's school, were very good, free options. By 1850 JFS had 1,300 pupils and this number had increased to 1,600 in 1855 and 1,800 in 1863. Amazingly, for the age, there was no corporal punishment permitted in a Jewish school.

The success of JFS wasn't even affected by the 1870 Education Act, which saw the government invest an enormous amount of money in new schools. The options available to the poor in the East End were vastly improved and the government had agreed that the new schools would not be allowed to insist on Jewish children receiving instruction in Christianity. The London School Board soon opened a brand-new school just a few hundred yards from JFS for 1,250 children. It was state-of-the-art, but in the first few months it attracted less than 100 children. The Jewish parents in the East End only wanted to entrust their children's education to Jewish teachers they felt would not let them down.

JFS had been run by its own governors since its inception and always resisted outside influence, even if it came from the Chief Rabbi. Adler would have preferred a degree of control over the curriculum because the school still provided a much fuller secular than religious education. Back in 1851 the government's Committee of Council for Education (CCE) had been in discussion with the Board of Deputies about giving grants to Jewish schools. The CCE said they presumed that the Board of Deputies was the single representative body through whom they should negotiate. The Board of Deputies said they were certainly the only Jewish medium of official communication with the government of the country. Which might have been true of matters affecting the entire community but was not true of those schools which ran their own affairs without interference. And, of course, if the Board of Deputies had been given the central role they claimed by the government, they would have been able to supervise the religious curriculum in all the synagogue schools. Schools across the spectrum, from JFS to the WLSBJ objected strongly and the Board of Deputies stood aside. Adler was disappointed. He wanted control but he didn't get it.

Adler also redoubled his efforts to achieve his greatest wish – the creation of a talmudic college for the community. He didn't want a yeshiva where the only subjects covered were religious; he wanted a school and a college whose curriculum would cover both secular and Torah-based topics. Throughout his ministry he put a tremendous amount of effort into the project but the results were to disappoint him. It took him from 1852–55 to raise enough money to start a school and a college, but it was only just enough. The rich members of the community didn't support the concept with any real enthusiasm. It ran counter to their own wishes. The Rothschilds and Salomons didn't even turn up for the fund-raising events and Montefiore damned it with faint praise.

In their efforts to be accepted as 100 per cent English, the lay leaders wanted to cut themselves off completely from the vestiges of a European origin which they perceived to include talmudic colleges: 'The old concept of the Jews, as a people in exile among the Gentiles with little interest in the world outside of their own community, was no longer satisfactory for individuals who wanted very much to enter the secular world and play a part in it.'[9]

The great majority of the well-to-do also wanted their children to go to English public schools, where they could be brought up to become English gentlemen and, hopefully, go on to English universities. As far as the new Jews' College would be concerned: 'The reality was that the school and the college failed to attract significant numbers or adequate material support.'[10]

Adler had wanted to expand the Great's Beth Hamedresh to offer more advanced talmudic training. This idea had to be abandoned as some benefactors specifically insisted that their donations should not be applied for this purpose. Overall, there were no substantial endowments. When Adler finally got the college opened he said at the inauguration: 'Some regarded [it] as unnecessary, nay injurious, to the progress of the community.'

Talmudic college, no, but the lay leadership still wanted a trained

Anglo-Jewish ministry. The question was, trained for what? Before the Enlightenment the Ashkenazi rabbi in Europe was scholar and teacher, judge and legal authority. In those days the pastoral duties of a vicar were not high on his priority list. By contrast, Jews' College did not set out to produce rabbis; the lay leadership felt that the graduates had no need for the extensive rigours of talmudic scholarship. Their job was to be pastoral and their training weighted towards the secular.

The support the community gave Jews' College was always inadequate. At the meetings of the United Synagogue in the future: 'No budget night of the olden days would have been complete without an amendment by Sir Adolph [Tuck – just about the inventor of the non-Jewish Christmas card] to the proposed meagre grant to the college.'[11] In 1881 a Building Fund was started for better premises. It was estimated to cost £3,000. The United Synagogue was only asked to contribute £100. The motion scraped through by a majority of 23–17.

Jews' College went on to produce, primarily, hazans and part-vicars. That, in itself, was progress. In 1857, when the Great needed a second hazan, there wasn't a single English applicant. There were exceptions. The Hambro, which had a rich congregation of devout Jews, always had a rabbi. In 1852 Adler dispatched a properly qualified rabbi to Australia to serve the communities there. There would always be rabbis serving on the Beth Din but they mostly had to be recruited from abroad. The outstanding figure in Jewish bibliography at the time was Moritz Steinschneider. On a visit to England he commented that very few Jews could be found with 'even a tincture of rabbinic learning'.

The community would have preferred the students to come from well-to-do backgrounds but, instead, in 1866, a report said that: 'The students were almost invariably from those classes which cannot afford the expense.' Which wasn't surprising as the ministers were usually poorly paid and poorly treated by the lay leaders.

The poverty of the candidates was considered more important than their scholastic ability. The raw nerves came from the fact that old-established Jewish families had been talked about behind their backs for so long by polite society, as moneylenders, pedlars, foreigners and cultural barbarians. In a nutshell, what terrified the families was the thought of being considered common. One of their major objections to the ultra-Orthodox was that their lingua franca remained Yiddish, rather than English. Lord Rothschild, the president of the United Synagogue for 36 years, found Yiddish – the language of his grandfather – particularly offensive. Of course, the other side of the coin was that the small right wing were not happy with the curriculum at Jews' College because they didn't think it was Orthodox enough, but they were very few in number and without any real influence.

In many public schools there was a quota of Jewish children the governors were prepared to accept as pupils. In many cases the public schools said they had no objection to taking Jewish children, but their entrance exams were on Saturday morning and every pupil was expected to attend Christian prayers every day. Many headmasters felt that they were the acme of tolerance when they permitted Jewish pupils to miss school on either Yom Kippur or Rosh Hashonah, but not both. Similar attitudes would still apply in some public schools at the end of Chief Rabbi Jakobovits' ministry in the 1980s. Yet these were still the schools offering the best education and Jewish parents wanted the best for their children. They wanted them to grow up to be English of the Jewish persuasion.

If the children went to the schools, their natural desire to conform with their classmates often made their Jewish practices a barrier and an embarrassment, *tsitsit* and *tephillin*, for example. The Chief Rabbi well knew the price the parents were paying for the fine secular education; it was all too often the alienation of the child from Judaism. Even Hebrew lessons at home often became a chore for the children. 'To Adler, such an arrangement involved at best [Jewish] educational minimalism and at worst so scanty a Jewish education as to spell danger to the Jewish child in the Christian environment.'[12]

The aims of the societies, against whom Solomon Hirschell fought by supporting the Jews' Free School, were still being promoted, if under a different banner.

There were still some quite good private Jewish schools, but they withered as more scholastic opportunities became available outside the community. University College School and the City of London School were two in the capital which proved attractive alternatives. In 1879 the Jews' College school had to be closed, much to Adler's disappointment. Outside London the only community which offered a good Jewish education was Birmingham. Reverend Raphael was the headmaster and was paid £80 a year in addition to his salary as the congregation's minister. Two other teachers were also paid the £80 and one got £60. It was a substantial investment in the children's religious future.

One thing was certain; if Adler wasn't going to get a proper yeshiva, he definitely wasn't going to imperil his own son's religious education by being satisfied with the Jews' College standard. In 1860 Hermann was sent off to Prague to study and to get a proper *semicha*. When he returned in 1862 he became the temporary principal of Jews' College and was appointed the minister of the Bayswater Synagogue, one of the most fashionable in London. He also helped his 60-year-old father and was obviously being groomed to take over in due course. Everybody recognized that at least the spiritual head of the community had to be talmudically competent, so the snub to Jews' College raised few hackles.

You could say that, at least in England, the children's education in Christian schools was a voluntary decision by the parents. In Bologna in 1858 a 7-year-old child called Edgardo Mortara was kidnapped by papal police because his Catholic nurse had informally baptized him some years before. The Papacy refused to give him back to his family even after Moses Montefiore had paid a personal visit to Rome to plead the family's case. The boy eventually entered the priesthood and the Alliance Israélite Universelle was formed in Paris to oppose such scandals in the future.

A British chapter, the Anglo-Jewish Association, was created soon after, but when the the Prussians occupied Paris after the Franco-Prussian war, the English branch became independent. Although anyone could join the AJA and it had no official standing, its VIP membership made it a force in the community quite quickly. The members were usually well off and it was handsomely endowed by one great Jewish philanthropist, Maurice de Hirsch, with many millions of pounds. It went on to help Jews and Jewish companies get started in the Holy Land, as well as South America, Russia and Canada. In its work in the Holy Land it was a forerunner of the Chovevei Zion movement which had Adler's enthusiastic support.

The Anglo-Jewish Association was one of the routes by which the leaders of the breakaway synagogue returned to some political power in the wider community. Another opened up when it was agreed, after Sir Moses stood down, that the breakaway synagogues could be represented on the Board of Deputies. It was also decided that the Board of Deputies would not be the conduit between the community and the government in foreign affairs. Instead a Conjoint Foreign Committee would be set up with equal numbers of Deputies and AJA members; seven of each. The chair would alternate and that gave the reformers their opening. It was hardly universal suffrage but the Conjoint did a lot of very good work in years when many overseas Jewish communities needed all the help they could get.

Adler had many great achievements to his credit. One was the creation of the United Synagogue. This finally joined together as one body the three main London Ashkenazi synagogues in the East End and the two in the West End, the Central and the Bayswater. Adler broached the idea over breakfast to the guests in his *sukkah* in 1866 and the resulting organization was established by an act of Parliament in 1870. As it was to be a charity, the spiritual authority of the Chief Rabbi could not be included in the United Synagogue Bill, but it was carefully spelt out in the constitution. In 1874 Adler refused to allow the appointment of a minister at the New unless he examined his competence for the post. The New lay leaders refused but the minister agreed. Adler established the precedent for future occasions. The United Synagogue remains to this day the Chief Rabbi's power base.

At the time it was Adler's prestige and encouragement which got it off the ground, and it took a lot of tact to get the synagogues to forget their differences. There had always been arguments about poaching members between the synagogues and this now stopped. A lot of duplication and waste in administration was eliminated as well. Best of all, it was an excellent way of providing new congregations with the expert help they needed to get properly started.

Adler set the tone for the United Synagogue. It was an inclusive organization anxious, within an Orthodox framework, to try to find common ground, rather than insist on extreme levels of observance. It compromised where it could and, over the next 100 years, the vast majority of the community remained Orthodox on a steadily less observant basis. In 1880 the old man came under great pressure at a Ritual Reform Conference for the London synagogues to permit minor modifications in the synagogue services and liturgies, according to the wishes of individual *shuls*. Only the Hambro wanted nothing to do with it. In a very few instances he had to give way, for example, allowing certain poetic prayers to be left out of festival services. For the most part he stood firm and the Great changed nothing. Adler did ensure that there were two permanent Dayanim, one of whom, Rabbi Ya'akov Reinowitz, he paid out of his own pocket. Rabbi Dov Spiers was the other, but neither was allowed to be called up in synagogue by their correct rabbinic title.

In his seventies Adler was still visiting his provincial communities. A reporter for the *Liverpool Daily Post* covered his attendance at the local synagogue and told his readers that the Chief Rabbi was:

a prelate, a venerable and graceful divine, whose utterances on

public occasions are duly chronicled in the London newspapers along with those of the preachers at St. Paul's, Westminster Abbey, etc.... At his present age pathos is his leading or at any rate his most impressive characteristic. He mounts slowly and with an appearance of failing sight to the rostrum... His voice is tremulous although sonorous, and a strong German accent gives his speech a careful and almost anxious deliberation to which the idea of tender pleading attaches... he never fails to implore his flock most plaintively to be true to the model of Judaism which is known as Orthodox... there is in his manner no vehemence, nor even rapid fluency, but there is evidence of deep feeling and genuine meditation.

The journalist emphasized that preaching was a relatively recent innovation in the service, and the effect the Chief Rabbi had on his congregation would have been the more impressive for its comparative novelty. He was also hard at work on his most important intellectual study, a Hebrew commentary on the *Targum Onkelos*, the best Aramaic translation of the Pentateuch, which was published in Vilna in 1875. The time was coming, however, when someone had to take part of the burden off his shoulders and, after considerable debate and controversy, Adler's son, Hermann, was asked to accept the position of delegate Chief Rabbi in 1879.

After Hermann Adler took over from his father, Nathan Adler still made his views strongly known whenever he was moved to do so. He lived in Brighton but his influence continued to be felt all over the country. When he died in 1890 he had been in active office for 45 years: 'He was instrumental in maintaining the nominal loyalty of the overwhelming majority of Anglo-Jewry throughout the Victorian period and was able to serve as the community's unchallenged spiritual leader for over 40 years.'[13]

In fact, it was Adler's strictly Orthodox but flexible management of the community that played such a large part in the failure of the breakaway congregation to make much impact during his ministry. By contrast, the majority of American Jews, lacking the benefit of the Adlers' hard work, would leave Orthodoxy. He was lucky in one way, however; 1858–80 was a Jewish golden age because there was, temporarily, no longer a real rationale for anti-Semitism in Britain. The situation would change markedly for Hermann Adler and his successors.

NOTES

1   Steven Singer, *Orthodox Judaism in Early Victorian London 1840–1858*, UMI, 1987.
2   *Jewish Chronicle*, 1853.
3   Singer, *Orthodox Judaism in Early Victorian London 1840–1858*.
4   J. Saville, *Chartism and the State*, Cambridge University Press, 1987.
5   *Jewish Chronicle*, July 1848.
6   Bernard Susser, *The Jews of South West England*, University of Exeter Press, 1993.
7   Ibid.
8   Bill Williams, *The Making of Manchester Jewry 1740–1875*, Manchester University Press, 1985.
9   Singer, *Orthodox Judaism in Early Victorian London*.
10 Israel Finestein, *Anglo-Jewry in Changing Times*, Vallentine Mitchell, 1999.
11 Israel Finestein, *Scenes and Personalities in Anglo-Jewry 1800–2000*, Vallentine Mitchell, 2002.
12 Sonia and V.D. Lipman, *The Century of Moses Montefiore*, Littman Library, 1985.
13 Singer, *Orthodox Judaism in Early Victorian London*.

17   Benjamin Artom 1866–79

Raphael Meldola died in 1828 and there was then a 38-year long interregnum before another Haham was appointed. Initially, the Mahamad must have been glad of the rest; the battles of the Meldola era had been divisive, time-consuming, aggravating and expensive. If all this arose because there was a spiritual leader, then maybe they could do without one, at least temporarily.

As the years went by, the community came to rely for talmudic guidance on Meldola's son, David, but they considered that a position as the head of the Beth Din was as high as he would go. One problem was that he was every bit as quarrelsome as his father, an excellent reason for not elevating him to a role where he could cause even more *broigas* (an irreplaceable Yiddish word for a rich mixture of aggravation, annoyance, dispute and disruption).

When the arguments over change ended in the secession of the 18 members to form the West London Synagogue of British Jews, it was Meldola and Hirschell who jointly issued the caution. Nevertheless, it was the Mahamad, the Elders and the Yehidim who negotiated unsuccessfully to avoid a breach; at such a difficult time, the Mahamad wanted the reins of power firmly in their own hands.

In the early 1840s David Meldola turned his attention to journalism. He had been asked to write for one of the earliest Jewish newspapers and the Mahamad gave their permission. After only a very short time, however, they withdrew it when an article he produced was not entirely to their liking. Meldola passively resigned from the paper, but even such obedience did nothing for his career prospects.

Bevis Marks had Sir Moses Montefiore in charge anyway, and nobody was really going to argue with the acknowledged head of British Jewry. The experience of Sir Moses stretched back well into the eighteenth century and his views were very much coloured by the ancient history of the Sephardi community. There was a particular need for strong leadership from the time of the death of Meldola until the end of the 1850s, because the war finally to eliminate

Jewish disabilities was fought on a pretty continuous basis. The caveat Sir Moses had about the effort was that he was not at all sure he liked the potential cost of winning the battle.

Admittedly the Jews couldn't be MPs or sit in the House of Lords, but then the Sephardim had promised Cromwell in 1656 not to meddle in politics – it was a tradition. Furthermore, from the point of view of Sir Moses, the Sephardim had always dealt directly with the king when that was necessary, and the system had worked very well. If there were laws against the interests of the community, a word in the royal ear had always ensured that the attorney general was told to make sure the law wasn't applied. These matters were quietly settled out of court by the Court. Might not this new insistence on equality disrupt the status quo? For instance there was the effect of the 1835 Marriage Act. The government had never before paid any interest to Jewish marriages, with the judges maintaining that Jewish marriages were a law unto themselves. Now the 1835 Act prohibited certain marriages which were allowed in Judaism; a widow marrying her late husband's brother, for instance. Did the law apply to the Jews as well? Nobody was quite certain, but Sir Moses recognized the potential implications. As he wrote in his diary in 1837: 'I am most firmly resolved not to give up the smallest part of our religious forms and privileges to obtain civil rights.'

The powerful body of opinion that did want the disabilities abolished found Sir Moses lukewarm on the subject, at best, and Sir Moses was the head of the Board of Deputies as well as of the Elders of the Sephardi community. Moreover, a new Haham would take time to break in and, after 1845, whenever Montefiore scanned the legislative sky for signs of any approaching religious storm affecting Judaism, he could also count on the wisdom of Nathan Adler. If, however, a Haham was appointed, Montefiore would be duty bound to listen to the spiritual head of his own community. Montefiore got on very well with Adler. By the time the new Ashkenazi Chief Rabbi had arrived, Montefiore was an old man and he preferred things to stay the way they were.

So no Haham. David Meldola did the work at the Sephardi Beth Din and became a fixture. The Yehidim didn't really want to lower the status of a respected and loyal friend by having anybody appointed above him, and anyway it helped the synagogue finances to be relieved of the costs of a Haham.

While there was never any danger of Bevis Marks running out of money, the size of the community was still dropping, partly due to assimilation. The names of the great merchants of previous centuries were no longer to be found in the community – Franco, Salvador, Lamego, Osorio, Seixas – they were all gone. In part it was also from the loss of members who had defected to the breakaway congregation, and from infant mortality and diseases such as smallpox, tuberculosis, diphtheria and cholera. In the 1860s 50,000 Londoners died of cholera. In addition, there was no particular influx from a persecuted congregation overseas; the eighteenth-century immigrants from Portugal, North Africa and Gibraltar had dried up.

So the community was declining and synagogue attendances began to thin out. As the 1860s wore on, the Yehidim reluctantly decided that something had to be done. Sir Moses was now approaching his nineties and couldn't go on for ever. Perhaps the last straw was the decision to close the Sephardi yeshiva which they had started in 1842 to produce candidates for the rabbinate. In 23 years they hadn't managed to turn out a single qualified candidate. It was time to find a new Haham and so they voted for one to be appointed. The Mahamad then set out in search of a suitable candidate.

The Victorian age was a reaction to the bawdiness, moral laxity and pleasure-loving world of Regency youth, so well exemplified by extravaganzas like the wonderfully flamboyant Brighton Pavilion. George IV had set the moral tone as a dissipated bigamist who refused to have his allegedly unfaithful wife crowned queen – an enormous pot calling a spitting kettle black. His brothers had many illegitimate children, their squandering of money infuriated Parliament, and the royal family were deeply unpopular. In the twenty-first century it is, perhaps, difficult to realize just how well off we are in this area of public life.

Victoria had set out to change all this, particularly after she married and had, by her side, her high principled husband, Albert, to back her up every inch of the way. They had over 20 years to set a good example, and when she went into deepest mourning after the Prince Consort's untimely death in 1861, the atmosphere in official circles became even more solemn, dignified, respectable and restrained.

The Mahamad wanted a candidate who would lend lustre to the community in the current atmosphere. They had recruited great talmudists like Jacob Sasportas and David Nietto in the past, but now they had the ambition to acquire a Haham who would be full of refined and cultured savoir-faire as well as talmudic expertise.

After all, the Ashkenazim now had the son of Nathan Adler to parade the virtues of an English education and membership of the Cousinhood. Any new Haham must maintain the position of the

Sephardim in the future. Only as long as Montefiore was around was this pretty certain. The old man had, however, provoked a considerable amount of hostility in the leaders of the community, as is inevitable if you preside over any office for 30 years or more; you can't please all of the people all of the time. The choice of a new spiritual leader after nearly 40 years was going to be a crucial one.

At which point there arrived a handsome, 31-year-old, Italian rabbi, with a fine physique, who was full of the joys of spring and one of the most inspiring preachers the Jewish community would ever have. Benjamin Artom was in love with his religion and his calling. He was fully prepared to be the Sephardim's new Nietto, to embrace all his brethren in other communities and to communicate to non-Jews as well. As he would write in his book of sermons: 'our real doctrines are still imperfectly known to the followers of other creeds'.[1]

He was a wonderful communicator and for a brief 12 years he blazed a trail across the community like a comet. As the *Daily Telegraph* said in its obituary years later: 'An eloquent and popular preacher, a sound scholar, and an accomplished musician, Dr. Artom was greatly admired and respected beyond the limits of his own community.' The new *Jewish Chronicle* didn't see it that way at the beginning: 'It will take some time before a congregation of Englishmen, citizens of a nation singularly unimpressed, will get accustomed to his lively gesticulations.'

Certainly, when the members of Bevis Marks first encountered Artom in a pulpit, they had to adjust to a fresh approach. This was no dry-as-dust instructor on DIY ark-building in the wilderness. This was a vibrant, involved, determined, impassioned speaker, very much in the mould in which Italians have been portrayed in literature throughout the centuries. He regularly produced an all-singing, all-dancing performance guaranteed to enthral the most jaded audience.

At the end the *Jewish Chronicle* revised its opinion:

> 'There was in his influence, especially upon the young, something essentially vivifying... The unceasing efforts of an active and intellectual mind to impart to his flock the many lessons to be derived from the Jewish faith... to explain the bearing of Judaism on the most religious and philosophical questions of the day, must have left a deep impression among his Congregation... His noble presence, his burning words, his stirring exhortations will be sadly missed.'

At this distance, reports of Artom's ability in the pulpit would benefit from some valid evidence. Luckily, he published a book of his sermons and reading them, you know you are in the presence of a real professional.

Good public speaking has its own tricks of the trade. One of them concerns how to grip an audience and keep it involved. The answer is that there is only one thing nobody can resist; the speaker who says 'Once upon a time'. If you find the audience's attention wandering, you can bring them straight back with that promise of a story. Thus Artom's installation sermon begins 'Do you see that noble hoary-headed figure rising before our mind's eye from the mists of antiquity? ... it is the historical figure of an aged man who, oppressed by cares and sorrow, and overwhelmed by fatigue, is yet hurrying his steps onwards and onwards to an unseen goal.'

Absolutely classic. Who is this man, what is his goal, what was happening all those years ago? The audience is immediately captivated. If Artom worked that technique out for himself, he was brilliant, and if he was taught it, he had the best of coaching. Artom was, in fact, going to tell the congregation about Elijah.

He was born in Asti, near Genoa, in Italy in 1835, probably to a French family, and his father died when he was a child. Artom always said that when his father was dying he told him to become a rabbi. The young Benjamin was brought up by his maternal uncle and decided early in life to do as his father had asked. Given a wide religious and secular education, he got his *semicha* from Marco Tedeschi, the Chief Rabbi of Trieste and, at the same time, obtained a university degree as Professor of Literature. By the time he was 20 he was teaching Hebrew, Italian, French, English and German.

These were tumultuous times in Italy, with Giuseppe Garibaldi and Camillo Cavour winning their country's independence from the French and the Austrians. Artom's brother, Isaac, was an enthusiastic nationalist. He fought in a student battalion against Austria in 1848 and went on to be private secretary to Cavour. In the new democratic Italy a Jew could have a career as a diplomat and, defended by Cavour against clerical opposition, Isaac was appointed Minister to Denmark in 1862. He reached the level of Under-Secretary of State at the Italian Foreign Office from 1870 to 1876, during Benjamin's period of office in London. In 1877 Isaac became the first Jewish senator in the Italian Parliament. This was the positive side of continental emancipation for the Jews. The Artom clan were destined to be a distinguished family in Italian politics, literature and science.

Benjamin, after gaining his degrees, became, first, the minister of the Saluzzo synagogue near Genoa and then went on to Naples, creating a congregation where previously one had hardly existed. Under the Bourbon rulers, Jews had not been encouraged to settle in the city and, originally, the services had to be held in the home of Baron de Rothschild, who ran the Italian branch of the family bank.

Artom served the Naples community as Haham but, naturally, for a man of his talents, he had ambitions to minister to a larger community. So, early in 1866, he came to London to check out the possibilities. He went home again, but had made such a good impression that the Mahamad invited him to take up the post in London, at a salary of £400 a year plus a house. He was also promised 30 scholars to teach.

Artom was inducted on a Sunday in December 1866, entering the synagogue with Nathan Adler at his side. After a gap of nearly 40 years it was a great occasion with 'about the entire Jewish clergy in London' on parade. It was, indeed, estimated that the congregation numbered nearly 2,000, which would have packed Bevis Marks from floor to ceiling. It was the first time that there had been instrumental music at a Bevis Marks service – Mr Mombach played the harmonium. Artom spoke in French, and his words went down very well, even his criticism that: 'Never was there so much written about religion as in our days, and never so little practised.'

As the best of the contemporary Ashkenazi preachers, Reverend Aaron Green would remember in a stunning eulogy at the Haham's funeral: 'Entranced as we all were by the charm of his eloquence and impressed by his stirring fervour which his own burning thoughts seemed to exercise on himself . . . we all felt . . . this Congregation had fortunately secured the pious services of a gifted man.'

The contents of the induction sermon were not entirely religious. Artom would have known of the arguments between the Mahamad and Meldola, the last Haham. He took the opportunity to spell out to the elders in the congregation that he expected their full support. He didn't forget to get the women onside either: 'It is woman that educates and inspires man and who forms the good genius of the house.'

Within a year Artom was fluent in English, as well as all his other languages. From that time on visitors flocked to Bevis Marks as: 'The eloquence and force of his sermons stirred his hearers and had a powerful effect upon them. The command of ideas and words he possessed was extraordinary. . . and he might have been a born Englishman.'

There could be nothing more flattering at the time than this last compliment. Nathan Adler summed it up well when he said that Artom:

> spoke to you in words which combined the sound sense of an Englishman with the fiery and soul-stirring eloquence of sunnier climes than ours. With words that burned and thoughts that breathed, he set forth the beauties and duties of our faith, to which he was devoted with every fibre of his warm, impulsive heart and every thought of his high intellect.

In a heightened, almost evangelical atmosphere, Artom went out to inspire his audience and, with his considerable musical talents, set out to improve the choral parts of the service as well. He wrote new prayers in Hebrew, including the Barmitzvah prayer which is still in use, and he was in the mould of great preachers like John Wesley. Anxious to spread the word, he spent an immense amount of time and trouble on bringing the message of Judaism to the poor of the congregation. He also reinvigorated the curriculum in the Sha'are Tikvah and Villa Real Sephardi schools, as well as serving on the Education Committee of Jews' College alongside Nathan Adler.

Artom was in the tradition of those rabbis who were stern critics of their congregation. As he said: 'The preacher should lift up his voice like a trumpet and, without regard to person, reprove Israel for their backslidings.'[2] It was easy to recognize the core disease of the times: 'The rabbi has lost much of his former authority. He is less consulted and even less heeded.'[3] Artom also recognized the cause of that. With all the official Jewish disabilities now ended: 'Alas! That firm union of heart and mind, which is a safeguard to the oppressed, vanished with the chains which had bound them in their days of sorrow.'

As Christianity and Islam had discovered, the Jews were the most obstinate people in the world if it was demanded that they give up their faith. They found it much less easy, however, to deal with tolerance.

Yet Artom saw his role as much more than criticism. He took his responsibilities for helping the members of the community very seriously. His own description of his position was as 'a Jewish pastor'.

Artom set out to change the perception of the rabbi, at least among the Sephardim and, besides the spiritual dimension, he recognized the financial plight of the large number of poor Jews in London. He had set out his stall at his installation: 'He [the Haham] must not shrink from the abode of poverty and the house of suffering; he must not shun any spectacle of pain or grief – the pallet of the dying, or the infection of disease.'

In 1875 there was an advertisement in the *Jewish Chronicle* appealing for donations for a soup-kitchen for the Jewish poor and the patrons included both Artom for the Sephardim and Adler for the Ashkenazim. One good way of encouraging support was used, when the list of contributors was published as well. If your name didn't appear, the more sensitive could be guaranteed to believe their neighbours were gossiping about its absence. It wasn't just for Jewish good causes that Artom worked, however. He was a member of the Council of the Metropolitan Hospitals Sunday Fund and preached at the first service on a Sunday in 1873. Over £200 was subscribed and similar services were continued for more than 75 years.

Artom was a great advocate of unity among all the Jewish congregations. Ashkenazi or Sephardi, including the Reform synagogue; he had a great affection for them all. One of his contributions to that unity was to favour the exchange of pulpits between rabbis and he spoke in many Ashkenazi synagogues. He considered preaching to be a form of religious instruction and he used it to counter what he considered the growing scepticism of the age and the growing indifference to Judaism he found in many of his flock. Rallying the troops at the North London synagogue in 1874, he said: 'We are to keep every precept of the law, not to select those which we preferred ... Yet we have been told but the other day that our religion was dying out! Dying out! No, it lives more strongly than ever.'

It is easy to understand the affection held for Artom if you listen to the gentle humour of his response to the vote of thanks after the service: 'Though Jeremiah has said that evil came from the North, this does not apply to the congregation of North London, for the great number of worshippers present and the excellence of your service proves the attachment to Judaism.'

The Mahamad having repealed the *ascamot* against having other synagogues, a new branch congregation had been opened in 1853 in the West End of London. Eventually it was, for a time, located just round the corner from the Reform synagogue in Upper Berkeley Street. Artom took it upon himself to serve both Sephardi communities.

It was also possible in 1872 to plan a new Sephardi synagogue in Manchester, the heart of the British textile industry. Nathan Mayer Rothschild had exported English textiles to Europe at the beginning of the century from his office in Manchester. Now there was a vast market for all kinds of textiles to be exported to India and the merchants dealing with the trade were often Sephardi. So branch offices were needed for the Indian companies and, just like Bristol in Tudor times, trade created a new community. Business was excellent, though not for the native textile industry in India. As a result, company after company closed down on the subcontinent, ruined by the superior Manchester textile technology. Unemployment, followed by malnutrition and then starvation, killed tens of thousands. This was unlikely to be mentioned in Artom's sermon when he opened the synagogue in Cheetham Hill Road in 1874.

In 1875 he was married by Nathan Adler to one of the Cousinhood, the very rich widow, Henrietta David, who was a sister of Reuben Sassoon, a favoured friend of the Prince of Wales. The wedding was at 11 in the morning followed by a concert until 2 o'clock and then lunch. Adler regretted that he couldn't stay for the reception as he had to perform 10 marriages that day! Apparently, the tremulous voice commented upon by the Liverpool journalist at the time could still stand up to a heavy workload. Artom's efforts to create a united community were emphasized by the fact that the Haham was marrying an Ashkenazi. To recognize the fact that two cannot live as cheaply as one, Artom's salary was raised to a very substantial £700 a year, but he no longer needed it.

In 1877, now a married man, Artom admitted a convert to the Sephardi community. It was said at the time to be the first occasion this had ever happened. The marriage of Isaac Abendana back in the 1680s had conveniently slipped from the memories of the archivist and there may well have been others. Artom had never believed in accepting a convert when the main incentive was a forthcoming marriage. He pointed out that, after the community's promise to Cromwell that they wouldn't evangelize: 'No Christian has ever been converted to Judaism here. That was, and still is, the rule.' In the case of Esther Paris, renamed Miriam Paris, he decided that the lady really did want to become a Jewess. There was room for manoeuvre here. Manasseh ben Israel had, after all, told Cromwell that: 'they do not reject him [the prospective convert] altogether if any man, of his own free will, will come to them'.

On reflection, Artom decided it was time to revert to talmudic law. One old Bevis Marks family member who had been converted to Christianity was the prime minister, Benjamin Disraeli. During his term of office the Old Jew, as Bismarck, the German chancellor called him, got a letter from the synagogue. His grandfather's grave – his name was also Benjamin Disraeli – was in a poor condition and the Mahamad sought permission to repair it. Disraeli thanked them for: 'the great consideration and courtesy with which his Grand-father's remains had been honoured'.

It was, as usual, a time for new challenges for all the Orthodox rabbis. Edison had invented the electric light bulb in 1878 and the inevitable question was whether the new wonder could be used on the Sabbath. Even today there is no clear-cut answer. No consensus decision has been reached. The argument against its use is that it might go against two of the Sabbath prohibitions; the one against creating fire and the other about not doing any work. Of course electricity doesn't create actual fire but it can certainly be used for warmth and cooking. Switching on a light can also be classified as work because the circuit is completed and something happens. It may seem nit-picking but, today, with robots, the turning on of a switch might start an industrial manufacturing process which would certainly be work. The rabbis were always concerned about that thin end of the wedge. Today some Orthodox rabbis approve of the use of electricity on the Sabbath but many more still don't.

Another innovation was the growing practice of cremation, although it was a system which had been used by the Greeks and Romans. What was the Jewish viewpoint? Artom laid down the law from the pulpit of the Sephardim's synagogue in the West End of London in 1874: 'Can we find... any support for this practice?...I answer without hesitation, none... God did not say to Adam "Thou shalt become dust"; but "dust thou art, and to dust shalt thou return".'

That's a very simple example of the Oral Law; interpreting the words in the first book of the Bible in order to find a ruling for a modern question.

By 1879 Artom was well established as a valuable voice for Orthodoxy throughout the country. And then, unhappily, he died a few hours after a heart attack in Brighton in the January of that year at the age of 43. His last act was to strictly observe the minor fast of the tenth day of the Jewish month of Tebeth. Like his father, he died much too young: 'The winning smile of Dr. Artom will no longer greet his friends.'

The community's grief was overwhelming. Artom had been really popular and, if he hadn't done anything earth-shattering, he had equally seldom put a foot wrong. *The Times* admired him too: 'None of the Sephardi Chief Rabbis had a higher place for zeal in the instruction of youth.'

Bevis Marks was packed for the funeral, there were 70 mourning coaches, Hermann Adler gave the funeral oration, all the daily papers published obituaries and the *Jewish Chronicle* gave him the ultimate Victorian accolade: 'a scholar and a gentleman'.

In all there were three memorial services but the memory of Artom has faded away. He left little behind; primarily, a small book of sermons and a host of happy memories. One of the best preachers of the time, Reverend Aaron Green, quoted a famous first-century sage, Rabbi Eleazar ben Azariah, that kings leave their crowns to their sons, rich men their wealth to their families, but: 'The scholar and the preacher dies, and he takes with him the genius that is beyond price and leaves none of his own body to inherit fame.'

NOTES

1   Benjamin Artom, *Sermons*, Trubner & Co., 1876.
2   Ibid.
3   Ibid.

18   A Pause for the Right Wing

Some of the practices of Orthodox Judaism are easy to mock. Take *tephillin* (phylacteries in Greek). The invaluable *Oxford English Dictionary* describes them as: 'A small leather box containing Hebrew texts on vellum, worn by Jewish men at morning prayer as a reminder to keep the law.' The black box is worn on the forehead, kept in place by a circle of black leather strap. There is another box on your arm with another black strap wound round the arm and hand. If you're unaccustomed to wearing tephillin, the result at first sight looks faintly ridiculous.

The regulation comes from the Biblical injunction in the most sacred prayer of the Jews – the Shema in Deuteronomy 6:4 – that you should: 'bind them [the laws in the prayer in the box] for a sign upon thine hand and they shall be for frontlets between thine eyes'. Any hand? No, your weakest one. So most men bind them on their left arm, but left-handed Jews (from the tribe of Benjamin?) wear them on their right arm. Why Benjaminites? Because the Bible records that that the military levy from the tribe was entirely left-handed.

And so it goes on; rule piled on rule, tradition overlaying tradition, minutiae fragmenting into smaller atoms. When the laws are obeyed in front of non-Jews it can embarrass the shy, the timid and the conformist. Getting changed for PE at a non-Jewish school involves taking off your tsitsit – a fringed undergarment worn over the vest. Other children can easily make fun of it and many do.

It is easy to snigger at a considerable number of Jewish practices, even though everybody would agree that they are totally harmless. If you don't want to eat pork because the pig doesn't chew the cud (as prohibited in Leviticus 11:7), for the uninvolved it is little different from vegetarians digging into their nut cutlets. The practices of the very Orthodox are also under attack from within the community, as they have been over the years from without. The Executive Director of the World Union of Progressive Jews said in 2003: 'The world needs Liberal Judaism and liberal interpretations as a counterforce to fundamentalism.'[1] Religious terrorists who kill people who don't agree with them are called fundamentalists. Of course, the Reform leader didn't say he was labelling the Orthodox fundamentalists, with all the unpleasant terrorist overtones. The possibility that this meaning could be gathered from his phrasing might well be a surprise to the speaker.

The key point about Orthodox Judaism is that it is lived every day. From first thing in the morning, when you put on your tsitsit, to saying prayers last thing at night, you are reminded of what the religion demands. So what does it demand?

In Biblical times, among a multitude of other things, it demanded no human sacrifice, which many contemporary religions would have considered ludicrous. It laid down a six-day working week, the freeing of slaves, a prohibition against beating your wife (a practice which would be acceptable for centuries in Christian Canon Law) and no cruelty to animals (the prescribed way of killing a cow results in absolute, immediate unconsciousness for the animal). It made giving charity one of the only three ways of avoiding the wrath of the Almighty (penitence and prayer being the others.) Morally and ethically it was light years ahead of the trendsetting and all-powerful Egyptians, Greeks and Romans.

They weren't only, or exactly, laws; they were commandments, called *mitzvoth*. A law is addressed to a community. A commandment is addressed to an individual. A broken law leads to punishment for the transgressor. A broken commandment makes you feel guilty, but there is no ordained punishment. There is no prize for obeying a law, but Orthodox Jews hope for mercy if they break a commandment and hope there is a reward if they keep the commandments; good luck, good health and so forth.

Today, commandments against slavery or beating your wife may seem commonplace in a democracy. So why bother to keep all the rules which remind you of the commandments? Because there are rules for every kind of eventuality; the treatment of old people, business ethics, immigrants, colour bars (forbidden), crime and punishment. It is a densely woven blanket of laws which – if they were all adopted all over the world – would make it a much better and safer universe.

The commandments didn't originate in the ghetto but it was a good setting for the practice of Orthodoxy. Forced to live cheek by jowl with each other, the less observant would be spotted immediately if they failed to carry out any rules. Freethinkers wouldn't have dared to declare themselves for fear of creating outrage in the community. It was the ultimate in small town life where everybody knew what everybody else was doing. The criticism you would attract for backsliding was one way of keeping the Jews on track.

When the ghetto walls were finally breached, first by Napoleon's edicts and then by emancipation in the middle of the nineteenth century, the less observant-minded found themselves in the clear. The Prague scholar, Judah Jeiteles, coined the phrase 'The Haskalah' to describe the movement for spreading modern European culture among the Jews. Now they could escape their ghetto neighbours and it was a tremendously exciting prospect. The destruction of the Berlin Wall in the 1980s was a similar shock to the mindsets of the people of East Germany. Many Jews deserted the faith, many decided to reform the traditional laws, and the Orthodox had another battle on their hands if they wanted to survive.

The right-wing core dug their heels in. They knew what change could do. The early members of the Reform movement in the 1840s wanted to give up celebrating festivals over two days – only one tradition among hundreds. From that tiny beginning, 150 years later you get, as already mentioned: 'A right to decide whether to subscribe to this particular belief or to that particular practice.'

For the Orthodox there is no such right. The commandments are the rules and they are the *mitzvoth*. If a *mitzvah* (singular) causes you inconvenience, that is unfortunate. To begin with, there are 613 of them in the Torah. A whole string of things which are a nuisance are *mitzvoth*; visiting a relative you dislike in hospital is a *mitzvah*. Making up a *minyan* on a freezing cold January morning at seven o'clock – is a *mitzvah*. Using the car on the Sabbath is not allowed because it is forbidden to light a fire, that is start an engine, which is also inconvenient.

The more Orthodox you are, the more *mitzvoth* you try to keep. Everybody fails on a proportion of them, but the Orthodox don't suggest that the more irritating can be safely ignored. Originally there were the 613 *mitzvoth*. As they were defined and redefined, however, they expanded. As we've seen, the *mitzvah* of keeping the Sabbath became 39 separate actions which could not be taken on the day, if the Sabbath was to be properly kept. Again, some *mitzvoth* you may not have to keep at all. If you're not married, the *mitzvoth* dealing with marriage obviously don't apply to you.

The survival of Orthodox Judaism depends on enough Jews feeling that the law is worth keeping – to the best of their ability. Keeping it even if it kills you, as in pogroms. Keeping it even if it makes you destitute; at the end of the nineteenth century an

Orthodox Jewish immigrant in the East End of London, desperately poor, might have a job in a sweat shop. He would leave on Friday before the start of the Sabbath, even if he was supposed to work until nightfall. He would lose another job every Friday if his employer didn't like the employees dictating their hours of work to him. On Monday the Orthodox Jew would have to find another position, and yet a leading United Synagogue officer at the time wrote:

> its members were always paupers and useless parasites in their own country...If accepted as immigrants in England, they remain paupers and parasites and live or starve on the pittance that the Russian-Jewish Committee and the Board of Guardians successively bestow on them to the detriment of the more deserving because more improvable cases.[2]

Now can we hold it right there because here we're discussing my paternal grandfather. Blanket denunciations are, of course, usually unbalanced. My paternal grandfather came over with the rest of the refugees around 1885. He was a skilled tailor and, although he couldn't do more than write his name, he made a living. Indeed, he made some of the robes for the aristocracy attending the coronation of Edward VII. My grandmother could read and write and brought up five children. Two of them became honorary officers of major United Synagogues. But my father joined the army as a private in the Great War in 1914 to earn more money than he got in my grandfather's workshop – and Grandpa Albert, who had escaped conscription into the Russian army by emigrating, didn't speak to him for two years!

The Orthodox struggled on. The miracle of the survival of an oppressed minority, without a country, over 2,000 years, is the result of struggling on. When Jews leave the religion, for one reason or another, they are giving up the struggle. It could be said that they have seen the light, stopped being old-fashioned or used their common sense; but they have still given up the struggle.

The question of using one's common sense is also worth considering. The laws include a set on personal hygiene which would appear innocuous enough today; like washing. Only 300 years ago, however, Frederick the Great of Prussia (1712–86), like the rest of his countrymen, didn't wash. He was a king, so people followed his example, but the Jews washed because it was a *mitzvah*. Frederick didn't wash for 30 years, cut his leg, developed gangrene and, not surprisingly, died.

Thus Orthodox Jews are none too certain of the rationale of so-called common sense. They keep *kashrut*, for instance, which must reduce the intake of animal fat – it is forbidden to eat any dairy products for hours after eating meat. Do cholesterol levels really mean anything, though? Present day medical science says cholesterol clogs blood vessels. Orthodox Jews don't have to work it out for themselves – they just do what they are told. Circumcision prevents penile cancer; Orthodox Jews in biblical times didn't use their common sense on that one either. Common sense implies that we now have sufficient knowledge to make up our minds on any subject; that, intellectually, we have reached the last lap of man's search for knowledge. The Orthodox would say that was rubbish and, of course, they'd be right. The rules they don't understand, they follow with every confidence that eventually they will become as clear as the laws on washing.

Waves of the Orthodox had reached the freedom of England for over 200 years when, after the assassination of Tsar Alexander II, a series of massacres of Jews started in 1881. To escape these pogroms about 3,000,000 Jews fled Russia and Poland, of whom 2,500,000 went to the United States and about 100,000–150,000 came to Britain. A substantial number of the very Orthodox were among them.

Finding themselves in a friendly and liberal society, many of the Jews eventually assimilated and gave up their religion. The very Orthodox, however, were not to be swayed by benevolence, any more than they had been buffeted off course by terror.

As the Anglicization of the synagogues continued, as the level of observance diminished and the assimilation of the younger generation moved into a higher gear, British Orthodox Jewry needed the equivalent of the US Cavalry to turn up, in what was going to become the nick of time. They did, on cue, but it would be difficult to imagine any group of people who looked less like a relieving army; they only possessed the one crucial weapon needed. They were that section of the refugees from the pogroms who were devoted to the Talmud.

They were almost all desperately poor. They were usually unable to speak or write in English, their clothes were shabby, their English manners were non-existent and they were usually pasty-faced because when they weren't working in a sweatshop, they were studying indoors. They didn't look very prepossessing, in a society which had created cricket in the eighteenth century and recently invented and organized the outdoor sports of football and rugby. When Hermann Adler met them, he described them as 'uncultivated and uncivilized'. These were euphemisms because, quite obviously, the right-wing rabbis and many of their friends and relatives, were intellectually more at home with the precepts and literature of Judaism than the vast majority of Adler's United Synagogue members. As they obeyed the Din, if they were uncivilized, then so was the Din – which, for a Chief Rabbi, is an unsustainable position.

Many of the immigrants' children were later educated at the Jews' Free School, which was devoted to making them more English. The school had a brilliant headmaster in Moses Angel, but his view of the families of his pupils was dismissive. He called them: 'the refuse population of the worst parts of Europe'.[3]

The truth was that the right wing had a shortcoming which was far more serious as far as the long-established community of British Jews was concerned; they were common, and they were common in a formal age when books on correct etiquette sold well. This was the time when well-brought-up ladies and gentlemen were expected to crook their little fingers when drinking their tea. Probably 99 per cent of the right wing didn't know that.

There is a picture of the congregation listening to Joseph Herman Hertz making his inaugural speech as Chief Rabbi in the Great Synagogue in 1913. The drawing is dominated by top hats; everybody wore one in synagogue and the wardens would wear morning dress as well. Until the latter half of the twentieth century, every lady would arrive in synagogue in her best clothes – most still do. So, of course, would the right wing, but their best clothes came from another age and another country; they wore the streimel, a long kaftan and often the knee-breeches and buckled shoes of a Polish nobleman of centuries before. It was as upper-crust for them as the English silk hat. They also didn't speak with an Oxford English accent, the only acceptable intonation for 'society'. Even a lot of English regional accents were considered common long after this. Being nouveau riche was considered common and, as the rich and well-established Jews tried desperately not to be seen as common, their new brethren were thought to make them common by association.

The founders of the Liberal and Reform synagogues were decidedly not common. They came, primarily, from wealthy backgrounds. If there hadn't been a major gulf between their religious beliefs, the two communities would have fallen out on class anyway. The original synagogue of the Liberal movement in St John's Wood has massive Grecian columns, giving it more the appearance of one of the wonders of the ancient world than a

Talmud Torah. The architect of the synagogue got his inspiration from pagan civilizations, although the Victorians had reverted to mock-Gothic and abandoned pagan design to emphasize their Christianity. It was an anomaly few seemed to notice.

When the right wing met the Very Reverend, the Chief Rabbi, they thought his views on traditional Judaism bordered, in many ways, on the heretical. They felt that the levels of observance he laid down for his community were not up to the proper standards. So they set up their own Beth Hamedresh, their own study groups, and eventually their own synagogues run by their own rabbis. Not run by the honorary officers or the boards of management, but by the rabbis.

It was no surprise that Hermann Adler was in two minds. He knew very well that the very Orthodox were not his enemy. He belonged to their way of thinking. His father had taught him the same standards. When he studied for his rabbinical certificate in Prague as a young man, it was with the same people. He knew that they were the rock on which the waves of assimilation would crash with least effect. In the time of Chief Rabbi Jakobovits, it would be suggested that he might create a bridge between the right wing and the Reform and Liberal movements. Jakobovits, with no wish to give offence, reluctantly had to make it clear that the problem was that he agreed with the right wing and not with the Reform and Liberal movements.

On the other hand, Hermann Adler had his own agenda, as mentioned earlier. He couldn't hold the United Synagogue members together if he adopted the attitudes of the very Orthodox. In 1891 he wrote to one of the most respected European rabbis, Rabbi Isaac Spektor, to try to get him to make the newcomers understand the facts of life. He pointed out that if the very Orthodox turned their back on the existing British community, the charity the multitude of their poor needed desperately would be likely to stop from that source. Why give money to people who look down on you religiously? When the very Orthodox try to raise money door-to-door for their charities today, the same aggravation is felt by many of those approached, so the very Orthodox usually held their tongues and still do.

One of the earliest questions was how to handle the spiritual needs of this vast influx of Orthodox Jews. One possible solution, favoured by Lord Rothschild, was to build a very large synagogue in the East End. Attempts to raise the necessary funds went on for many years. Even Sir Julian Goldsmid and Arthur Waley, senior members of Upper Berkeley Street, were called in for discussions in the inner sanctum of the United Synagogue council room. It was the first time the two sides had met officially since 1842 and it illustrated the seriousness of the problem, as they saw it. The difficulty was that the newcomers didn't like the typical United Synagogue. It was too large, too formal, too lax and too one-dimensional; it was, effectively, only used for prayer. The newcomers wanted their own small synagogues to be used for study and for socializing.

Chevras – small congregations – were set up all over the East End, most with their own fully qualified, independent rabbis, who were dismissed by the majority of British Jews with the only epithet available – foreign rabbis. Some recognized the geographical origins of the members; the Grodno, the Brothers of Petrikoff, the Kovno and the United Brethren of Konin. Some were named for their main purpose; the Sons of the Covenant Friendly Society and the Holy Calling Benefit Society. Some for ethical principles; the Peace and Truth, the Love and Kindness. They all found a champion in Sir Samuel Montagu, the local MP for Whitechapel and the man whose firm, effectively, controlled the price of silver.

Sir Samuel Montagu was born Montagu Samuel but there was a mix-up when he was entered for school and his father got his name the wrong way round. Montagu decided he preferred it that way. He became part of the Cousinhood by marrying Ellen Cohen, another descendant of Levi Barent Cohen. He was very rich and very Orthodox; a typical example of Orthodoxy surviving happily outside the ghetto. Montagu was the instigator who welded the *chevras* in the East End into a federation in 1887. It was called originally the Federation of Minor Synagogues.

Montagu dealt with some terrible problems. For example, when there was a death in the family, the United Synagogue would reluctantly provide the ground for the burial. What it would not allow was the placing of a tombstone over the grave until the bill for the burial had been paid. It sounds totally heartless, but every Jewish institution had financial constraints. The money had to come from somewhere and the United Synagogue simply couldn't afford to act like a fairy godmother hundreds of times a year. Montagu solved the problem by buying the Federation its own burial ground at Edmonton in North London in 1889. Now for 1p a family, a week, members could be guaranteed a funeral. This swelled the congregations considerably. By 1912 the Burial Society had 5,000 members.

The last thing Montagu wanted was the creation of a rival ecclesiastical authority to the Chief Rabbi. After all he was the president of the London Board of Shechita and deeply involved in communal affairs. So it was agreed that the Federation would acknowledge the religious supremacy of Adler even though they had brilliant scholars in their own ranks. What they refused to do was take part in the elections for the Chief Rabbi. The Federation's quarrel with the election process was that votes depended on how much you gave to support the Chief Rabbi's office and not on how many members you had. Undemocratic, perhaps, but who was supposed to pay the office expenses? Montagu tried to further cement the relations between the federation and the United Synagogue by ensuring that the former's original constitution laid down that the president of the United Synagogue was always to be the honorary president of the Federation.

The Federation members were delighted to have Lord Rothschild as their titular head and his lordship performed the ceremonial tasks with his usual aplomb. When he opened the new synagogue in New Road, it became known as Die Englishe Shool.

There were, however, to be two major right-wing bodies, for some congregations didn't want to acknowledge the Chief Rabbi or join the Federation. So they set up the North London Beth Hamedresh in 1889 and the Machzike Hadath Shomrei Shabbat community in 1891. Individuals from both communities then developed the Machzike Hadath (The Fortress of Orthodoxy) organization to support the growth of ultra-Orthodoxy throughout the country. And the Machzike Hadath eventually begat the Adath Yisroel and the Adath Yisroel begat the Union of Orthodox Hebrew Congregations (UOHC), which is what exists today. To the right of the United Synagogue is the Federation and to their right is the UOHC. Their withdrawal into their own circle of wagons was in line with the German concept of an *Austritt Gemeinde* – a withdrawn community – strongly defended by its isolation from the influences and attacks of the irreligious. The UOHC was founded in 1924 and has never acknowledged the Chief Rabbi's authority over its affairs.

Small provincial yeshivas grew up alongside the communities: Manchester in 1911, Leeds 1912, Liverpool 1914, Glasgow 1936 and others as well. Schools were created. In 1895 the East End Talmud Torah had ten teachers, 500 children and all the teaching was in Yiddish. To have been able to do all this on a shoestring would have been luxury; they were often too poor for a shoestring. A typical school could be in a tiny kitchen in a house where, in the case of a fire, nobody would have got out alive. Time and again efforts were made to declare such premises unsafe, but the teaching continued. What kept them going was their faith; as my Grandma Kate was fond of saying in my grandfather's tailoring workshop at the time, 'God will provide'. The Jewish tailors struck for a 12-hour day in 1887 in the hope that the sweatshop employers might provide a little more as well.

The first war the Machzike Hadath declared was on the standard of United Synagogue *kashrut* and the first battlefield was the sale of forbidden kidney fat. The Machzike Hadath called on Hermann Adler to complain of the existing practices. Adler said he gave the complainants a 'patient hearing'[4] and, while admitting that there were rogue butchers, assured the delegation that suitable meat was easily available. The Machzike Hadath delegation felt they had been dismissed in a patronising way.

They reacted by setting up their own Board of Shechita which the United Synagogue's Beth Din immediately denounced and said that the Machzike Hadath meat was *trefa*. The Machzike Hadath distributed handbills throughout the East End slagging off the Beth Din. Both sides appealed to eminent rabbis all over Europe to support their positions. One of the most eminent was Rabbi Spektor, the Russian sage. He wrote condemning the Machzike Hadath shochetim and supported Adler. He said that the Chief Rabbi was a Posek and he could *pasken* – lay down the law. A Dayan, as a member of the Jewish court, can rule on legal cases. A Posek is a rabbi you go to, as an individual, if you want to be told what the law is. Since the Dayan is one of a group and a Posek takes on the responsibility single-handed, a Posek is more eminent than a Dayan. When Adler's talmudic ability was questioned, Spektor's view should have been very much part of the case for the defence. Adler was so delighted with Spektor's letter, he hurried over to show it to Rothschild. The row then rumbled on for years.

The Chief Rabbi had a point and so did the very Orthodox rabbis. There are rules to obey in making meat kosher. The Chief Rabbi saw that these were carried out. There are also rules, known as *glatt kosher*, that make doubly sure that the rules are carried out. The very Orthodox wanted *glatt kosher*. The Chief Rabbi thought he had enough trouble trying to get more Jews to eat only kosher meat. He couldn't go the extra mile without the danger of losing the support of a percentage of his community altogether.

Not that every member of the Machzike Hadath was a Hebrew scholar. That would be asking too much of any congregation, but none of them questioned the dictates of the religion. As the famous writer, Israel Zangwill, said of the ultra-Orthodox: 'They don't understand a word of what they're saying, but they certainly mean it.'

The dispute over *kashrut* was another example of Hermann Adler's tightrope. Eventually the row finished up in 1904 in the law courts in Liverpool, in 1904, because of a suggestion that the United Synagogue authorities believed there was bribery involved in the working of the ultra-Orthodox Board of Shechita. The ultra-Orthodox sued and Hermann Adler, among other distinguished rabbis, had to give evidence. The case was an absolute disaster for the image of both communities. The patriarchal Rabbi Avraham Aba Werner, for the right wing, was a monumental rabbinic scholar – but after 11 years in the country, he couldn't speak English – his attitude would have been 'Why bother?' when all the people he talked to spoke Yiddish perfectly well. English was useful in pleading a case, though, even if a German-speaking judge was appointed. There was plenty of laughter in court as some of the more esoteric details of Judaism were expounded:

Witness: The rabbi does not grant divorces. It is the husband who divorces.

His Lordship: Oh, really! (Laughter.)

The right wing lost the case but both sides, sensibly, decided that arguing the toss in front of the general public was totally undesirable and likely to be non-productive. They patched up the quarrel by the end of the year. In 1905 it was agreed that the right wing would have their own Board of Shechita but that it should be run, administratively, by the United Synagogue Beth Din. The Chief Rabbi would approve the appointment of all the shochetim and his authority was confirmed, so long as: 'he acts in accordance with the Shulchan Aruch'.

That was a considerable proviso, leaving Orthodox rabbis plenty of room for questioning. Later there was another major cause for disagreement. Adler had appointed two Jews' College graduates as Dayanim. The East End was furious because they didn't believe that the men would have had the necessary training for such an important role. Their idea of a really expert Dayan was Rabbi Avigdor Chaikin. A refugee from Russia with *semicha* from luminaries like Rabbi Spektor, Chaikin, in Britain, was a talmudic thoroughbred in a field of cart horses. It was typical of the fate of so many refugees that when he arrived in England in 1890, the best

Adler could do for him was a job as a teacher in Sheffield. The pay for that would have been a pittance but Adler had dozens of similar cases. The same problem would reoccur with rabbinic refugees from Nazi Germany in the 1930s.

Chaikin had soon proved his worth and became the minister in Sheffield but he was eventually poached by the Federation as their senior rabbi. Paid by Montagu, it was now agreed that Chaikin would serve as a temporary Dayan at the Beth Din, but the rancour of the ultra-Orthodox was not really assuaged until he was given a permanent role in 1911 as an assistant Dayan. He served with distinction from 1911–26.

The right wing finally recognized that their co-religionists back in eastern Europe would not benefit from the alienation of the Chief Rabbi, whose help they needed so badly. By the time Adler died, though, the membership of the Federation of Synagogues exceeded that of the United Synagogue. The United Synagogue had 5,200 members and the Federation 6,500. This did not, however, give them equal or greater representation in the councils of the community; with the Chief Rabbi, the Board of Shechita, the Board of Deputies or anywhere else. The Jewish community power structure had been welded together long before the refugees arrived and those who had the power didn't intend to give it up.

Nevertheless, from a fight over who had the authority, the Chief Rabbis moved to consultation. When Rabbi Avraham Yitzhak Kook was the leader of the very Orthodox during the First World War, Hertz asked his opinion on eating rice during Passover. Food of any kind was getting to be in short supply. Kook diplomatically said that there were lots of learned rabbis in London and his views were unnecessary. So Hertz called a conference of Ashkenazi rabbis who decided that, shortages or not, rice still wouldn't be allowed. The Sephardim begged to differ – they had eaten rice at Passover since biblical times.

The right wing supported the principle of the Balfour Declaration, except for the president of the Federation, Samuel Montagu's son, who joined other leaders in condemning the idea. That was effectively the end of him.

Many of the lay leaders of Anglo-Jewry between the wars were not in favour of many Orthodox practices. The right-wing community had settled down in north London in Stamford Hill and they continued to live their lives in conformity with the laws and customs of the communities they had left behind in eastern Europe. They harmed nobody, they were law-abiding citizens, but they would not conform to the religious norms of Anglo-Jewry.

Their adherence to the strict letter of the law particularly offended those who were trying to be *glatt* English. No Chief Rabbi would wish to criticize them for carrying out the mitzvoth. Indeed, Chief Rabbi Hertz would approve the appointment of two of their number to the United Synagogue Beth Din; Dayan Mark Gollop and Dayan Yechezkel Abramsky. As the Dayanim started to enforce the law, however, the lay leaders became convinced that they were trying to force the community into obeying ever stricter dictates. There was no truth in this; the task of the Dayanim was not to create new laws; it was to carry out the existing ones. If they had been allowed to fall into disuse for many years, that was hardly the Dayanim's fault. Non-observance didn't abolish them; they still existed and the right-wing Dayanim were there to see they were carried out; whether in the field of marriage and divorce, whether in the proper killing of animals, whether in legal disputes or in conversion applications.

The venom which was aroused by the right wing in many quarters of the community was summed up in the official biography of Sir Robert Waley Cohen: 'Thus in Britain there was arrayed against Bob (Sir Robert Waley Cohen) as against nearly all British Jews of his tradition and background, an alliance of alien dogma, custom and superstition which had never before been any part of Judaism except in dark corners deep inside the ghettos of Eastern Europe.'[5]

The fact that such sentiments were the purest claptrap and could very easily be disproved didn't make them less popular with the non-observant. As Dean Swift said in the eighteenth century: 'there's none so blind as they that won't see'. The laws the right wing were upholding had been created over a period of 4,000 years in many parts of the world, not in the ghettos. The dogma wasn't alien, it was authentically Jewish. It wasn't superstition, unless you wanted to dismiss all religion as superstition. It had always been part of Judaism and upheld by every Chief Rabbi since Sasportas.

Sir Robert, himself, had spoken of his view of leadership in Anglo-Jewry during the Second World War. 'The foundations of Anglo-Jewish life are to be found in many of our present Anglo-Jewish institutions and were laid about a hundred years ago by a small number of Jewish financiers.'[6] If that had been genuinely the case, then the foundations of Anglo-Jewish life were now on the softest of shifting sand. If the foundations weren't firmly rooted in the Written and Oral Laws, then the Orthodox community was drifting into assimilation; slowly perhaps, but drifting.

The right wing ignored the criticism. They had survived so much already that the polemics of talmudically ignorant Jewish critics were not going to keep them awake at nights. They seldom fought back in public, unless pushed very hard. There was one occasion when the Sunday Closing Bill was being discussed in Parliament in the 1930s. The Board of Deputies wanted Jewish businesses which closed for the Sabbath on Friday afternoon and Saturday to be allowed to open on Sunday. Their president, Neville Laski, Haham Gaster's son-in-law, held that 'closing on Friday' should mean 'closing at 6 o'clock in the evening'. The right wing said it should mean closing when the Sabbath started, which could be earlier than 6 o'clock. Laski said: 'we don't want your ultra-Orthodoxy superimposed on our Orthodoxy' and was told: 'You mean my Orthodoxy superimposed upon your lesser Orthodoxy.'

That was accurate, but a Dayan who was present at the time was reluctant to give his own view in a non-legal setting; after all, the Dayanim were officially appointed by the president of the United Synagogue. In the reluctance of the right wing to attack their traducers, their critics scented weakness. The criticism became steadily harsher, with continuous accusations in all future generations that the Chief Rabbinate was being taken over by ultra-Orthodox fanatics.

All the answers are never to be found on one side. The Orthodox were almost all poor, largely foreign, secularly ill-educated and playing away from home. Their primary constraint on which knife and fork they used for a meal, was which was only to be used for milk dishes and which only for meat dishes. They were losing badly with the majority community in every contest of a social and materialist kind. They had only one ace: as a body, they knew the *mitzvoth* better than the richer and long-accepted British congregations. Sometimes, to balance the uneven contest for superiority – or even equality – they would play the religious card rather more intensely than was absolutely necessary. From there it is a very long way to 'alien dogma, custom and superstition'.

Ultra-Orthodox Jews didn't just come to London. In the 1870s Zachariah Bernstone, a Lithuanian glazier, emigrated to Newcastle. He found, however, that the local community wasn't strict enough for him and so he crossed the river to Gateshead. Very slowly other Jews with a similar passion for the *mitzvoth* gathered round him, most notably a young Austrian called Eliezer Adler. They managed to hire a room to pray in during 1883, though they didn't even have a Sefer Torah. They asked Herman Adler for help but he told them to rejoin the Newcastle community. A wealthy lace manufacturer in Nottingham came to the rescue. By 1912 they had a small synagogue and they employed a new teacher, Reverend E. Gamzu. Gamzu was an inspiring educationalist and he set about organizing a really first-class Talmud Torah. The school started with about 30–40 pupils, ranging in age from below 5 to 15.

Those children received a normal ultra-Orthodox education. Which meant three hours after school from Monday to Thursday, three hours on Saturday and six hours on Sunday. Twenty one hours a week on Chumash (the Pentateuch) and Rashi (Rabbi Solomon ben Isaac, 1040–1105), Gemara, the prophets and Jewish law and ethics. Where the children of United Synagogue members might go to classes on Sunday mornings, the Gateshead youngsters devoted their childhoods to learning, and stayed with it as adults.

In 1927 Gamzu went off to Liverpool and Reverend David Dryan took his place. On the rock-solid foundation of the Talmud Torah, Dryan could see the opportunity to start a yeshiva. With financial help from the Sunderland community, the first two students were enrolled in 1929. Throughout the period before the war, Jews were fleeing Germany and the most Orthodox recognized that they would be at home in Gateshead. It was only a small community but they never turned down a student. Somehow the money was found to keep them. More than 600 young men passed through the yeshiva between 1933 and 1939.

Where the students were awarded their *semicha*, they became eligible for pulpits all over the country, but they weren't always welcome in United Synagogue communities. The standards they set for themselves, they were inclined to expect from their congregations as well. If they didn't get the right level, they tended to castigate the worshippers from the pulpit. The congregation often preferred to live in blissful ignorance of the size and number of their sins. With most United Synagogue ministers this was achievable, but with Gateshead graduates at the helm it was known it would be more difficult. The United had many problems in obtaining good ministers but the communities tended to stay apart, even though both fully accepted that the other was legally Jewish.

As many of the most famous talmudic scholars fled to England, Gateshead was able to strengthen its teaching staff even more. Leib Lopian, Leib Gurwitz and Naftali Shakowitzky were just three with tremendous reputations as rabbinic scholars. Of course the expanded community also included businessmen and their new firms reduced unemployment in the north-east quite considerably. The most famous demonstration against unemployment at the time was the Jarrow March from the north-east to London and it seems unlikely that, during the slump, anyone would have considered part of the solution might lie with German Jewish refugees.

There were so many brilliant talmudic scholars at Gateshead that it was decided to set up a *kolel*, a postgraduate college for scholars who were already rabbis. Put it all together and Gateshead today, 70 years later, is the greatest talmudic university in Europe. To great centres of learning like Heidelberg, Yeshiva University in New York, Cambridge, Bar Ilan, the Sorbonne, the Hebrew and Utrecht, you can now add Gateshead. The locals remain slightly bemused, but a police chief once said that the only trouble the students gave him was that their lights were blazing at 2 o'clock in the morning as they continued their studies, and this could disturb the neighbours.

The significance of the right wing was that they came to form a bedrock for the Orthodox Jewish community in Britain. They had large families and the majority of their children grew up equally devoted to Orthodox tradition. At the turn of the twenty-first century they accounted for about 40 per cent of the Jews in Britain.

The right wing remain in a difficult position. There might well be issues in the future when they need to make strong recommendations to the government; for example, if the right to practice *shechita* was threatened, as it has been in many countries. The Board of Deputies remains the body the government looks to when it seeks the views of the Jewish community, but the right wing withdrew from the board in 1970. With self-banishment from its committees, the right wing are in a weaker position to influence those views. They have chosen to go it alone and they are still pretty suspicious of many of the standards of the United Synagogue. They have their own Kashrut Authority and they do not acknowledge the authority of the Chief Rabbi. It is likely that there will have to be a considerable emergency before they review their present policy, but if that happens, there is no doubt that they will find sufficient common ground with the other Orthodox members of the community.

NOTES

1   Rabbi Uri Regev, Executive Director of the WUPJ, speaking in Berlin in July 2003.
2   Chaim Bermant, *Troubled Eden*, Vallentine Mitchell, 1969.
3   Gerry Black, *JFS*, Tymsder Publishing, 1998.
4   *Jewish Chronicle*, 27 November 1891.

5   Robert Henriques, *Sir Robert Waley Cohen*, Secker & Warburg, 1966, p. 386.
6   Ibid., p. 397.

19 Moses Gaster 1887–1917

Of the 21 Chief Rabbis from Jacob Sasportas to Immanuel Jakobovits, 13 died in office, five resigned, two retired and one was fired. The one who was fired was Moses Gaster and there is no doubt that this did happen: 'At Bevis Marks a "League of Yehidim" was formed in protest against the Elders' allegedly "unconstitutional" dismissal of Hakham Moses Gaster.'[1]

The League had no effect on the fate of the Haham. He was out of office from 1917 until he died more than 20 years later. It was an unlikely end for this much larger-than-life character because Gaster, for many good judges: 'is still considered "the most formidable figure to have held ecclesiastical office in the history of Anglo-Jewry". '[2]

For others he was a difficult egomaniac, an impossible colleague and a vicious opponent. In such circumstances, it is likely that possibly the fairest assessment will come from an intelligent son, who would know his father better than almost anybody else. Professor Theodor Gaster said: 'He was generous and lavish but he could also be selfish and egotistical…alike in his work and in his life, always restless and frustrated, and this no amount of public acclaim and renown could altogether allay.'[3]

Some people are born like that. They have better brains than most of their fellows but they never entirely believe it. Every day they have to try to slay another dragon to reassure themselves of their ability. Like mediaeval jousting, challenge becomes a drug to reassure them about their own worth. Discussion becomes part of this challenge; the opportunity of winning an argument and making friend or foe admit that their view is inferior to the superior analysis and wisdom of the speaker: 'I never heard my father admit that he was wrong and I remember the consternation that beset us children when once, at a breakfast chat, Jacob de Haas thundered at him that indeed he might be.'[4]

If Gaster's personality needed the intoxication of challenge that badly, the first 60 years of his life gave him plenty of opportunity to assuage his thirst. He was born in 1856 in Rumania, just one of the

European countries which treated its Jews disgracefully, but there even more than most. In the nineteenth century no less than 200 special laws made it difficult for Jews to earn a living in Rumania. For example, they might be born in Rumania but they were not allowed to be Rumanian citizens. There were pogroms the government chose to ignore. Even when Disraeli got better treatment for them incorporated into the Congress of Berlin in 1878, the Rumanians evaded the terms of the agreement.

Gaster came from one of the small percentage of Jewish families the government found it useful to tolerate. They had served both the state and the community with distinction. In 1877, at the age of 21, Gaster got a PhD in Philology at Leipzig. He got *semicha* in Breslau four years later. Breslau's theological aim was always to get the study of Jewish learning onto a scientific basis and that credo was enthusiastically adopted by Gaster. From 1881–85 he was teaching Rumanian language and literature at Bucharest University and he published a history of Rumanian popular literature in 1883 when he was 27. This was a seriously good brain. Cecil Roth, a contemporary, recalled that he had: 'A memory which was already remarkable and became nothing short of prodigious . . . In his prime he was one of the great English orators.'

The Rumanians went on to make him inspector general of schools and he lectured on the Rumanian Apocrypha, the whole of which he had unearthed in manuscript. He also found time to make a Rumanian translation of the Jewish prayer-book and write a short scripture history.

It was the distant past that always fascinated Gaster. It took him until 1891 – ten years – to compile his magnum opus, which was a chrestomathy of Rumanian literature. A chrestomathy is a selection of passages from a nation's literature which enables you to fully comprehend the language. Overall, Gaster's energy and the range and quality of his work were extraordinary.

It isn't surprising that Cecil Roth, the eminent British historian who specialized in Jewish history, said of Gaster: 'If Moses Gaster fell short of unquestioned primacy in any of his multifarious activities, it was for the very reason that his enormous ability was diverted through so many channels and brought him such high distinction in all.'[5]

Like a number of others, Gaster protested against the oppressive and discriminatory treatment of the Jews in Rumania. The government tried to buy him off by including him in a list of several hundred, out of several hundred thousand, who could be granted citizenship, but Gaster wouldn't accept being made a special case. So the Rumanians solved the problem by deporting him in 1885; he'd been born in the country but, as Jews couldn't be citizens, the authorities were able to throw him out like an illegal immigrant.

Gaster decided to come to England and his ability as a philologist was such that he was offered a lectureship in Graeco-Slavonic literature at Oxford in 1886 and again in 1894. His lectures were also published. Among his literary output over the next ten years would be *Jewish Folklore in the Middle Ages: The Sword of Moses*, from an ancient manuscript of magic, *Jewish Sources and Parallels to the Early English Metrical Romances of King Arthur and Merlin* and *The Chronicles of Jerahmeel*. This last was a study of a small clan which lived on the Southern slopes of the Holy Land and are mentioned very briefly in 1 Samuel 30:29; 'and to them... which were in the cities of the Jerahmeelites'.

Nothing was too obscure to attract Gaster's attention. He would become a member of the Folklore, Biblical, Archaeological and Royal Asiatic Societies and between the ages of 26 and 83 he published some 280 books and articles. He was also a world expert on the Samaritans and so highly regarded by that community that they allowed him the great privilege of examining their ancient Abisha scroll. To communicate with them, Gaster managed to produce a typewriter with Samaritan script.

Gaster was readily accepted in the wider community as one of Britain's most versatile scholars. However, he was not just an academic. He had supported Chovevei Zion in Rumania and was an early member when a British chapter was formed. The movement held its first public meeting in 1890 as a reaction to the Russian pogroms, and had as one of its aims the creation of agricultural colonies in the Holy Land. There had been sporadic attempts to create settlements there for a long time. The movement got financial support from philanthropists such as Sir Moses Montefiore and Baron Edmond de Rothschild. Now there was an organization, rather than individual efforts, and today's famous Rosh Pinah was one of the first colonies in which Gaster was involved.

As the 1880s went by, the Sephardim became increasingly anxious to find a suitable replacement for the much-lamented Haham Artom who had died in 1879. Although Gaster was an Ashkenazi, he seemed just the academically brilliant, talmudically expert, charming and Orthodox leader to fit the bill. As one of the Zionist leaders described him: 'A charming man... splendid company, a vivacious conversationalist with an inexhaustible store of reminiscences and a profound sympathy with all that is human.'[6]

On the Sabbath he would walk from his home near Lords to Bevis Marks in the City and it was a treat for those who accompanied him on the journey: 'talking about linguistics, archaeology, folklore and scholars... or about Graeco-Slavonic literature, Byzantine culture, Ladino or Yiddish literature or of Spinoza.[7]

Gaster told the *Jewish Chronicle* in 1912 that, in fact, he had never considered becoming a practising rabbi. His ambition was to fix Judaism in its place among all the other ancient cultures. Still, the Sephardi community was distinguished, he needed a permanent occupation and he was flattered to be asked. In March 1887 he was unanimously elected at the very early age of 31. It was an unusual election because the Yehidim were allowed to vote for the first time. Previously, the elders had had the sole responsibility, but a more democratic approach was felt to be a good idea. Many of the elders would subsequently change their minds.

Gaster's salary was fixed at £750 a year and he was provided with a house. It was to be a classic case of appoint in haste and repent at leisure but to begin with everything was fine. If his sermons were said by some to be magnificent rather than constructive, if he appeared to love the Jewish heritage more than possessing an inner light, he was still totally enamoured by Judaism's historical continuity. It was by breaking that link that he considered the Reform movement had put its members beyond the Pale.

The Sephardim were little affected by the influx of refugees from the pogroms, as they came, primarily, from Ashkenazi communities. Even without the necessity to support a vast influx of the impoverished, however, the Sephardim did not balance their books during most of Gaster's ministry. The reason was partly a question of the community being small and there was also the problem that many of their richest supporters had gone over to the breakaway community. The Sephardim became rich in assets but poor in cash flow.

As a result there was a proposal by the Mahamad in 1883 to tackle the ongoing problem in the most drastic way; by selling and knocking down Bevis Marks. They pointed out that the community had left the City and that there were occasions when nobody came to the synagogue on the Sabbath at all. At a meeting of the Yehidim there was no objection raised, but over the next 18 months it was found impossible to obtain a buyer. Some of the members had second thoughts anyway and they formed a Bevis Marks Anti-Demolition League. The League appealed to the Mahamad to change their minds but they put up the defence that there had been no opposition to the idea at the outset. Eventually, it was decided to put the sale on hold and the money raised by disposing of other assets resulted in the idea being dropped. In 1929 Bevis Marks was declared an Ancient Monument by the Royal Commission on Historical Monuments and the disaster was averted for the foreseeable future.

Even so, the financial situation had been parlous. The accumulated deficit in 1885 had been £2,283 and in 1899, even after the sales, it stood at £2,300. It is a fact, however, that in extremis, there are usually wealthy members of a congregation like Bevis Marks who will come to the rescue.

Gaster was a tremendous personality: 'We who knew him will never forget the impressive figure in the brown velveteen jacket and the red tarbush [a kind of large fez], holding perpetual court; the constant stream of eloquent conversation, in more languages than some could recognize.'[8]

The Tarboosh was an excellent piece of image building. Like Lenin's cap, Sherlock Holmes' deerstalker or the Churchill sailor's peak, it made him an immediately recognizable figure in a crowd of notables. Gaster's reputation was growing and already, by as early as 1891, the Rumanians feared they had made a mistake. There is a distinct difference between a young agitator and an Oxford don. So they cancelled the expulsion order, gave him the Rumanian Ordre pour le Mérite (1st class) and asked him to come back. Gaster naturally refused and became naturalized in 1893 but, typically, what he did agree to do was write a report for them on the British system of education. This was so good it was accepted in Rumania as the basis for their national approach.

On the domestic front, in 1890 he married Leah Friedländer, the daughter of Michael Friedländer, the able principal of Jews' College for 40 years. It was one of the major social events of the year. They were to have seven sons and six daughters and his house became a hive of activity: 'The two dominant characteristics of his home – the endless array of books, overflowing into every room, and its equally endless stream of visitors, men and women of all vocations and types and from all parts of the world, who poured into it daily.'[9]

Gaster's main interest, though, was academia. A party was forming that didn't feel Gaster was a community rabbi. By 1891 there were already senior members suggesting that he was happier running the Judith Montefiore College in Ramsgate. Sir Moses had created the college to train ministers for the Sephardi communities.

It was well endowed, its first principal had been Louis Loewe, Montefiore's able secretary and the teaching should have been good because there were three rabbis and a total of six staff. The college, however, was in a quiet seaside town in the south of England, student enrolment was never remotely adequate and the institution was not really viable. Gaster had said he couldn't be expected to give up a job for life as Haham for one which only offered a one-year contract at a time. He would want to fit in both tasks. The Mahamad had arranged for a report in 1887 which spelt out the original intentions of Sir Moses and then commented:

> Hitherto, it must be reluctantly admitted, the College has entirely failed to give results corresponding with these intentions; and, before proceeding to carry out the present scheme, we recommend that the services of some or all of the present officers of the College be dispensed with, and that suitable retiring allowances be made to them.

Now Gaster was pleased to accept the additional role of principal of the college in 1888. He wanted to create another Breslau. In future he would spend five days a month in Ramsgate and students would only be accepted if they had the equivalent of BA degrees. His philosophy was always to be more vexed at ignorance than at a lack of spirituality, but quantity was the problem as well as quality. Dr Henry Barnstein and Dr William Greenburg did get their *semichas* from Gaster in 1895 but that was to be the sum total of the graduates and the awards were a total disaster.

The ceremony to confer the *semichas* was reported in the *Jewish Chronicle* on 15 November. It had been a major event in Ramsgate and the two candidates had also earned PhDs from the University of Heidelberg for theses on Semitic philology. The only sour note was provided by one of the teachers at the college, Reverend Benjamin Schewzik, who wouldn't attend. Schewzik had started as a student at the college in 1886 and progressed to a position on the staff, teaching Talmud. When it was decided to investigate this 'painful incident', Schewzik, who had been an examiner of the two men, said that in spite of approving the awards at the time, he strongly believed that neither candidate had the competence to be a rabbi nor had they honestly come by their doctorates – they had had help writing them. He added for good measure that they were immoral, ate *trefa* food and broke the Sabbath.

Gaster said that he had investigated the accusations and found them groundless. Did he do so thoroughly enough? That summer had been a bad time for the Haham, he'd lost a child in July. The college committee then investigated and also said Schewzik's accusations were groundless. The trustees of the college, however, decided to set up a special committee to go into all the allegations and the college committee's conclusions were never printed. All six of the special committee members were elders. The affair was public knowledge – certainly the police knew of the accusations. A delegation of 12 non-Jews from the Ramsgate area came to talk to the resident head of the college about the students. Other students at the college made accusations as well. The two new rabbis had been interviewed initially by the college committee and denied all the allegations. They were not allowed to have a solicitor present to cross-examine their accusers. As a consequence, they were advised by their solicitor not to appear before the subsequent special committee when the same ruling was applied. They were told they could sue Reverend Schewzik but this was beyond their financial means and both Chief Rabbi Hermann Adler and Joseph Sebag Montefiore, the president of the elders, asked them in January 1896 not to do so in order to avoid a scandal.

The secrecy in which the college committee tried to act was picked up on by the *Jewish Chronicle* when criticizing the elders the following year for not allowing the press to report their own meetings: 'the opponents of publicity were mainly those who recently supported the condemnation by the Special Committee of the Haham.'[10]

Gaster had hurried to Ramsgate in December to see if he could track down the origins of the story. He and the college vice-principal, Rabbi Hartwig Hirschfeld, a first-class European academic, had talked to the chief constable of Ramsgate, who made accusations he couldn't support. This was not surprising, as a judge in a murder case the chief constable had recently investigated had said: 'In the whole of his experience he had never found in one case, on behalf of the prosecution more impropriety, incompetence and illegality.'[11]

The row continued in the *Jewish Chronicle* every week in the first six months of 1896. Accusations and counter-accusations were made by both sets of supporters. Weighty comment came down first on one side and then the other. If a juicy scandal improves circulation, the *Jewish Chronicle* must have had a great first half year. Eventually the report of the special committee came out in the spring and was highly critical of Gaster and the rest of the academic staff at Ramsgate.

Gaster wrote and distributed a well-argued and massive defence. The *Observations of Rev. Dr. Gaster on the Report of the Special Committee dated 15th March 1896* ran to 26 foolscap pages with another 23 of copies of correspondence. There is no doubt that Schewzik was a liar. The totally independent local doctor wrote in December before the Special Committee began sitting:

> I have never communicated in any way with the Police Authorities about the students at Montefiore College...Mr. Ross (the police superintendent at Ramsgate) authorised me to say that he never received any information from me, but that Mr. Schewzik had told him that I was aware of immoralities on the part of students...I have this evening received a letter of apology from Mr. Schewzik, in which he says that he has written to the Committee today to withdraw the statement that he made about me.

The special committee in their report said that Gaster's criticisms of Schewzik were not backed up by the students: 'they look upon Mr. Schewzik as a worthy man and hold him in high esteem and regard'.[13]

Why were the committee taking the opinions of the students though in such a serious matter? In 1892 Sebag Montefiore, one of their own members, had said in a letter to Gaster about Schewzik's behaviour in another row:

> Had you brought the matter before the Committee and not interceded for him, it seems to me his dismissal would certainly have ensued, and unless you desired it, I could not have said a word on his behalf, so thoroughly am I convinced of the impropriety of his attitude.

Schewzik had that bad a record, yet Sebag Montefiore signed the report which backed Schewzik against the Haham. The new rabbis' accusers were not, however, confined to Schewzik. The special committee homed in on the key question in a letter from E.L. Mocatta to Gaster dated 18 March 1896: 'Would Drs. Barnstein and Greenburg swear to not sleeping with a girl at Mary Ann Willmoth's, of 2, Heathcote Villas, Margate Road, on the 25th February 1895? as she states that they both slept with the girl on that night, and the Committee attach special importance to it.'

The new rabbis again denied everything to Gaster on oath. The police confirmed that no criminal prosecution was being considered against them, but then sleeping with a woman to whom you are not married isn't a criminal offence. It could, however, certainly get you thrown out of a rabbinical college. The accusations weren't exactly from the cream of Ramsgate society. The woman involved was a petty crook. Another witness identified one of the rabbis from across the street as being at the house; there was no kind of identity parade and, as already noted, nobody could be cross-examined by the defence.

So the case against the new rabbis depended on a discredited policeman, a teacher who had been caught out in many lies, and a petty crook. Even so, the question arose of whether the new rabbis could be deprived of their *semichas*. Rabbinic guidance was sought in Berlin and Paris. Both responsa said it was possible to do so. Gaster wouldn't hear of it. He pointed out, quite correctly, that to withdraw them without any charges being laid was to find the men guilty until proved innocent. This was against the Din and contrary to British practice.

Gaster lashed out in all directions. He said that the judgement of the Special Committee: 'reads more like the presentment of a Prosecuting Counsel, who starts from made-up conclusions and is bent on proving his case by right or by wrong'.

On the detailed report he produced in March 1896, it does appear that the flimsy evidence would never have convinced a jury and that the special committee behaved at times like a kangaroo court. Even Sir Francis Montefiore, one of the most senior elders, said it contained 'grave inaccuracies'. It might have helped matters, though, if Gaster hadn't refused to appear before the committee. If he had accepted its procedural shortcomings and simply produced his very convincing evidence to refute the allegations. As usual, everybody was standing on their dignity.

The Scottish verdict of Not Proven was the least the members of the College could have expected but, in fact, although the special committee's report minced a few words, the final message was clear. Gaster should resign or be dismissed as principal.

Gaster's supporters called for a meeting of the Yehidim to hear all the evidence. Gaster was, in fact, being put on trial, and the elders agreed because they felt the evidence against the Haham was overwhelming. Gaster, however, had plenty of support at the assembly, which attracted a larger audience than the one to prevent Bevis Marks being knocked down. Gaster had been the choice of the Yehidim when they had finally been allowed to vote on the appointment of their spiritual leader after 200 years. When the meeting was held, the spokesman for the committee painstakingly made the case for over three and a half hours, spelling out the facts on which they had based their report. All that remained was for a vote of confidence in Gaster to be rejected. To the chagrin of the committee, it was triumphantly passed in his favour by 75–40.

The range of accusations against the aye votes was imaginative. It was complained that Yehidim who were in arrears to the synagogue and who, therefore, couldn't vote, had been paid up by Gaster's supporters. In fact, only 12 had done so and Sir Francis Montefiore wrote to the *Jewish Chronicle* to deny any such thing. It was also said that the root problem was the yeshiva's location in Ramsgate: 'The situation of the college in a city of pleasure and ease was against it.'[12]

The ayes had their own say: 'Mr. Schewzik has made admissions on his recorded evidence which should suffice to obtain his dismissal from any educational establishment in the country.'[13] Even after this, however, the special committee went on supporting Schewzik. They said he had only done his duty in conveying his concerns to Gaster. In a letter to the *Jewish Chronicle*, one of the committee said that Gaster: 'has entirely failed in his performance of those duties and that the sacred office of Haham has grievously suffered while in his charge'.

So whom do you believe? Schewzik subsequently continued to have a poor record. He became the administrative head of the Jewish Self-Help Association, an organization with enormous ambitions to help the poor in the East End and catastrophic methods of doing so. Selling food below cost, for example, and undermining every poor Jewish grocer trying to make a precarious living. Or offering arbitration in legal disputes where their decisions went against those of the Beth Din. One of the community's most respected moralists attacked Schewzik's character and, effectively, destroyed the association. By 1897, Schewzik was a lieutenant in the Jewish Boys' Brigade charged with recruiting. Gaster's reputation was substantially improved by these events. All the evidence is that Schewzik was a two-faced, malevolent charlatan. The final act in the whole sorry tale was the saddest of all. One of the students who had accused Barnstein and Greenburg was called Isaac Plato and he was a grandson of Samson Raphael Hirsch. By 1897, he was reduced to earning a meagre living as a tutor. His ambition to be a great rabbi, like his grandfather, was in ruins. On the night of 26 April he took a revolver and killed himself. For a religious Jew there is no worse crime than suicide. The committee had accused Gaster and his senior colleagues of putting pressure on the students to withdraw their allegations. Is that why Plato died or was it because of remorse? There is no mention of his leaving a note. Reading the enquiry depositions and the evidence, a lot of people were lying; VIPs and youngsters, rabbis and elders, gave totally contrary statements. At the end of the day you have to come down in favour of Barnstein and Greenburg simply because the committee conducted their proceedings in ways contrary to common justice. Perhaps the new rabbis were guilty as charged, but the way the investigation was conducted was unfair to Barnstein and Greenburg.

Lives and careers were hopelessly scarred. The eminent Dr Hirschfeld, who had been the resident academic in charge in Ramsgate, finished up as sub-librarian at Jews' College. The accusations against Gaster that he had harried the students who gave evidence against Barnstein and Greenburg were never forgotten. But the rich and powerful survived. It was the whistleblowers and the small fry who were ruined.

So what happened to Barnstein and Greenburg? What chance would a couple of novice rabbis have with accusations of immorality hanging over their heads in Victorian England? There is, however, another way of looking at it. If you're a hick town congregation in nineteenth-century America and you have the chance of getting a rabbi with a posh accent from Britain, with a proper *semicha* and a doctorate from Heidelburg, no less, it would be riches beyond the dreams of avarice. And if you were a Reform community as well and could get an Orthodox rabbi to come over to your side, that would be the cream on the cake.

By 1900 Barnstein was the minister of the main Reform congregation in Houston and Greenburg of the Reform in Albuquerque. Having found a safe harbour after the Ramsgate gale, Barnstein stayed for 43 years and died Rabbi Emeritus around 1950. Greenburg went on from Albuquerque to Sacramento, but his congregation wouldn't renew his contract in 1919 because of his Liberal views. He went off to New York and became an insurance adviser. He too died about 1950.

The trustees closed Ramsgate on a vote of 17–5 and all the academics were made redundant. Jews' College and Ramsgate were merged, a plan promoted by Frederick David Mocatta, whose ambition was to be a yahid at Bevis Marks while still a senior member of Upper Berkeley Street. Jews' College was represented at the discussions by the Chief Rabbi and also the eminent educationalist, Sir Philip Magnus, a former Reform minister. It made sense to merge. Jews' College hadn't the money to offer enough scholarships to poor students and Ramsgate had the money but not enough applications. It was decided in 1897 that the Montefiore Foundation would donate £1,000 a year, plus funds for books, to Jews' College and this agreement lasted for the next 15 years.

The position had, of course, been complicated from the start by the fact that the whole subject of *semicha* was a very awkward one at the time. Hermann Adler was against giving them to the Ashkenazi clergy and some of the United Synagogue ministers were highly offended by this. So when Gaster started to grant *semichas*, he was challenging the Other Nation's policy and the Mahamad, who normally never wanted to have this happen if it could be avoided, had backed him up.

It was the honour they might all earn from producing rabbis where the Ashkenazi Jews' College didn't, which afforded the great temptation to go one-up on the larger community. Gaster had set out with enthusiasm to build the college. One great achievement was to raise the money to buy some very important collections of books; he was a great bibliophile. The Leopold Zunz collection alone had 2,000 volumes and over 1,000 pamphlets and cost £420, while the Halberstamm library of 412 manuscripts set the donors back £1,000. Today the total value of the collections runs into, literally, millions of pounds. Gaster could have made a fortune as a rare book dealer.

The Ramsgate debacle was bad enough but things then got much worse – as far as the majority of the elders at Bevis Marks were concerned. In July 1896, a few weeks after the decision to close the college, Gaster met Theodor Herzl and found a fellow-believer in the need for the Jews to return to the Holy Land if they were ever to avoid persecution.

The trigger for Herzl had been the Dreyfus Affair in France. A civilized nation had suddenly succumbed to a wave of anti-Semitism as the establishment imprisoned a Jewish army officer on trumped-up charges of treason. Herzl felt that if this was possible in cultured, sophisticated France, then there was no hope for a long-term future for the Jews, except in terms of a national home in which they could settle. Initially, he wasn't terribly concerned where that might be, but for Gaster the choice was always the Holy Land or nothing.

Herzl contacted Gaster when he first came to England to network and gather support for his idea. Having met Herzl, Gaster immediately became an enthusiastic Zionist. Unlike the vast majority of Anglo-Jewish leaders, who simply ignored the Austrian journalist as a foreign romantic, he helped Herzl make contacts in

England and was prepared to support him publicly. Gaster knew that Herzl's Zionism was a nationalist rather than a religious movement. It was one of the reasons why the right wing viewed it with such suspicion. In the end their worst fears were to be realized, but Gaster was optimistic. The philosophy of the movement was in its infancy and there was always the hope that it would change its stance on the religious aspects. What was more, if Zionism was successful, his suffering co-religionists in Rumania would have the possibility of a new home. Indeed, when the state of Israel was eventually established, almost all the remnants of the Rumanian community which had managed to survive the Holocaust emigrated to Israel. Like ransoming the Jews from the pirates in the Middle Ages, unofficial collections were made all over the world to pay the Rumanian dictator, Nicolae Ceausescu, for each exit visa he granted.

If, however, there was one thing the Sephardim didn't need in 1896 it was a Zionist movement. For over 200 years, successive generations of elders and Mahamadim had had an inviolable mission statement of proving to the government that they were capable of being good British citizens as well as Orthodox Jews. From the beginning, they insisted they weren't a nation; they were a religion. All of a sudden, almost out of nowhere, came a movement which said the exact opposite and, to their chagrin, the Sephardim's own Haham became its most senior British spiritual advocate and a senior officer in the organization. The first major gathering of the Zionists was in August 1897 when hundreds went to the Jewish Working Men's Club in the East End to hear Herzl speak. The only leader in the community who would agree to chair the meeting was Gaster.

The Mahamad were appalled. One of the Yehidim, Haim Guedalla – a surname that had occurred among the members of the Mahamad for at least 100 years and who normally had a lot of time for Gaster – wrote to the *Jewish Chronicle*: 'The Spanish and Portuguese are to a man...dead against the Conference, so let no one be deceived by the chair being taken by our Chief Rabbi, Dr. Gaster, at a meeting composed of a few foreigners.'[14] Well, hundreds of, originally, foreigners, anyway.

The opposition to Zionism was widespread in the community. Reverend Simeon Singer, who produced the Singer Prayer-Book, challenged Gaster to stand for re-election on a Zionist platform. Singer said he'd stand for re-election in his synagogue on an anti-Zionist platform and then they could see who would win. Gaster didn't accept the challenge.

The elders, when discussing Gaster's salary in 1897 also tried to apply pressure, advising him: 'to curtail his Zionist activities on the grounds that these were affecting his pastoral duties'.

Hermann Adler would sum up the views of the mass of the Cousinhood when he described the first Congress of the Zionists in 1898 as an 'egregious blunder', which, according to the *Oxford English Dictionary*, meant it was an outstandingly bad and shocking mistake.

You couldn't fault the Cousinhood's thinking, however. At the time they had a major fight on their hands to convince public opinion that over 100,000 refugee Jews from the pogroms could be easily transformed into good English citizens, because they belonged to the Jewish religion but not to a Jewish nation. Everybody was also fighting hard to stave off the likelihood of an Aliens Act which might well deprive other Jewish refugees of a safe haven; they were fighting, literally, for many of those potential refugees' lives. Their thinking was entirely in line with policy since the days of the Resettlement and, for them, Gaster was a loose cannon.

It is also true that, if you simply applied common sense, the idea of the Jews becoming a nation again, back in Jerusalem after 1,800 years, had to seem like cloud-cuckoo land. Other than putting it on the furthest recesses of the back-burner by saying it would happen when the Messiah came. That was spiritually, politically and logically justified and sensible. To suggest, however, that it could happen in the not too distant, twentieth-century future was regarded as ludicrous by the vast majority of the community and would be until the Balfour Declaration.

For Gaster himself, it was highly desirable – remembering that Rumania was totally unlike tolerant, democratic Britain – and it was a challenge of wonderfully impossible dimensions. It obviously couldn't be done and, therefore, it was tailor-made for him to try to achieve. It would also give him the opportunity to act upon a larger stage than his position as Haham warranted. It was true that the Sephardim in 1896 had opened a new synagogue near Lord's Cricket ground in Lauderdale Road. In no way did it enable them to compete in importance with the vastly more numerous Ashkenazi community and Hermann Adler had, without doubt, the senior Jewish spiritual role in the kingdom. This always aggravated Gaster. When the Prime Minister, Sir Henry Campbell-Bannerman invited Adler to dinner in 1906, Gaster suggested to Winston Churchill that he might have confused Chief Rabbis.

Now that Ramsgate was, effectively, merged with Jews' College, if Gaster wanted to outshine Adler – and Gaster always loved the limelight – it would have to be in an allied field. Zionism provided that opportunity. Of course, Gaster profoundly believed in the Zionist programme and fought hard to make sure that the Holy Land was the only acceptable location for a Jewish National Home. For example, he was always firmly opposed to the possibility of setting it up in Uganda, an idea which surfaced in 1903 and was mooted for some years afterwards. For Gaster, Zionism was initially a cultural renaissance more than a purely political movement. Nevertheless, the promotion of Zionism, in whatever form, did have the added advantage for him that he could make his own mark, independent of a much admired but quite small Sephardi community.

The Mahamad, which had legislated the right to proscribe the activities of the Haham from the earliest *ascamot*, were in a dilemma as to how to control Gaster. There might now be two strikes against the Haham, but the Oxford don and world-famous author was not some young graduate from the yeshiva in Amsterdam looking for a post. This was a community leader who would be elected vice-president of the Anglo-Jewish Association, a founder and first president of the newly established English Zionist Federation from 1907–09, vice-president of five International Zionist congresses up to 1908 and president of the newly formed Bnai Brith. The man was a very public figure and both the East End immigrants and a strong party among the Yehidim, loved him.

There was also the problem for the Mahamad that the Jews had prayed to go back to the Holy Land since they were first expelled, so Gaster was hardly preaching heresy. The row was patched up for years on the agreement that the Haham would always say at any meeting that he was speaking for himself rather than the Sephardi community, which was fine, as far as Gaster was concerned, as it left him completely untrammelled to say what he liked.

There were areas where the Haham and the Mahamad had common ground. Within a few months of the decision to close the college, Gaster was opening the new London synagogue. With a new pulpit he was soon engaged in a series of popular lectures on the Samaritans and proselytization. In 1901 Gaster helped mark the bicentenary of Bevis Marks by writing the *History of the Ancient Synagogue* which remains a source book for the history of the Jews in Britain even after 100 years. The bicentenary of the synagogue in 1902 was an occasion which gave both the Sephardi and Ashkenazi communities much pleasure. For a Jewish synagogue to survive 200 years in a new country and to receive such an exceptional degree of toleration from its government over the entire period, was a cause for much thanksgiving.

Gaster never suggested that he was a historian of Judaism in England but he was one of the founders of this, as well as many other forms of neglected scholarship. It may be accurate, but it is damning with faint praise for one modern writer to say: 'Though a man of much learning, Gaster's judgements tended to be impressionistic, unsupported by a rigourous marshalling of supporting evidence but it is to his merit to have assembled material of which more meticulous students have been able to make good use.'[15]

The outstanding thing about Gaster's scholarship was, indeed, his ability to recognize the importance of certain academic fields long before anyone else and to interest other academics in building on the broad foundations he laid.

The second Sephardi synagogue in Manchester was consecrated in 1904 and the third would be established in 1924. The textile industry in Cottonopolis continued to attract Jews from North Africa, Turkey and the Levant. The Sephardi elders in London were happy to help them get started, providing a gift of 300 guineas (£315) for the 1904 Building Fund.

When the long-dreaded Aliens Act was finally passed in the summer of 1905, Gaster was appalled. It was pretty well universally recognized that it was designed to cut down the number of poverty-stricken Jews coming to the East End of London. The Prime Minister, Arthur Balfour, had referred in a speech on the bill in Parliament to: 'the undoubted evils that had fallen upon the country from an immigration that was largely Jewish'. Political correctness and the Race Relations Act lay in the future. Nevertheless, in the event, if the immigrants were not going to be a burden on the state and if they were healthy and, in any way, persecuted, they would still be allowed in. A Jew, Herbert Samuel, a member of the Cousinhood, no less, was Under Secretary at the Home Office, which initiated the legislation. The act would normally be tempered with humanity, though there were local immigration officials who took a hard line in individual cases. As could have been expected, Gaster almost immediately reacted with fury, saying that the legislation combined: 'the worst features of Rumanian hypocrisy with the draconic legislation of Russia'.

That went down very well in the East End where Gaster was far more popular than Adler precisely because of this intemperance in his language. Without Adler's authority as an official spokesman, he didn't have to weigh every word. The future British Prime Minister,

Stanley Baldwin, once said of a more extreme example of this attitude: 'Power without responsibility has been the prerogative of the harlot throughout the ages'

Meanwhile, the growth of Zionism soon led to the winding up of the Chovevei Zion in 1902. Zionism's own development, however, was tortuous in the extreme. In its early stages it was masterminded by Herzl, but the movement lost his guidance when he died in 1904 aged only 44. There were always several battlefields. There was the internal one between, first, those Zionists who thought the prime necessity was to get agreement from some government that the Jews could return to the Holy Land – the Political Zionists. On the other side there were those who felt that the way forward was to start new settlements, to actually emigrate to the barren country – go on Aliyah – and, over the years, to purchase the land. These were the Practical Zionists and the concept of buying a country did not faze them. Gaster was always a Practical Zionist, if an impractical businessman.

Another major area of conflict was between the Zionists and the anti-Zionists. The latter included the Board of Deputies who saw their right to be the only organization representing the community with the government, under threat from the new movement. They hadn't minded allying their activities with the Anglo-Jewish Association, that self-appointed group of wealthy individuals who did much excellent charitable work. With the AJA they created the Conjoint Foreign Committee in 1881; seven representatives of each body, with revolving chairmen, to deal with foreign affairs on behalf of the community. On the other hand, they had no intention of allowing into the charmed circle a small group of mostly foreign-born Jews with no mandate to promote an apparently crazy idea. 'Foreign' was one of the ongoing criticisms of the Zionists and it struck a resounding chord with everybody trying to live down their overseas origins. Gaster became a vice-president of the AJA along with a number of other Zionist members, but they were badly outnumbered at meetings.

More major opposition came when the author and one of the earliest Zionists, Israel Zangwill, broke away to start his own movement, the Jewish Territorial Organisation or JTO in 1905. The JTO didn't mind where a national home was created and thought that many governments would welcome Jewish investment and a skilled labour force.

Gaster and his colleagues could also look to the Reform and Liberal movements for outright opposition. Particularly from

Claude Montefiore, one of their most respected leaders, from whom came constant attacks on the Zionist ideal. Having initially refused even to see Theodor Herzl, Montefiore, as president of the Anglo-Jewish Association in 1898, told the delegates: 'It was of cardinal importance that they should not seem to commit themselves to, or in any way be in relation with, the Zionist movement'. Montefiore remained AJA president for over 20 years and wanted to stress the common ground between Judaism and Christianity, not to emphasize the distinctive nature of Judaism. He was also often the chair of the Conjoint.

The Zionists could not even count on the support of the new immigrants. They had chosen to come to Britain and were fully engaged in settling down. The idea of now moving again to the impoverished Holy Land from streets potentially paved with gold, did not appeal to most of them. They might turn out to hear Herzl or to some other public meeting but, overall, they were apathetic.

The most serious challenge for the Zionists, however, was to work as a team. Gaster was the problem writ large. On the one hand he would travel the length and breadth of the country for years, preaching the message to often tiny audiences; anything to help the movement get more adherents. When he was in full flow on a platform, he was irresistible. Like the chairman of today's great charity, the Variety Club of Great Britain, he deserved the title of Chief Barker. He gave unstintingly of the time he could have spent on his beloved academic studies and he cheerfully suffered the fate of all mavericks that most men's hands were against him. To make all his efforts the more staggeringly remarkable, the Haham suffered from increasingly poor eyesight, so that for the last 40 years of his life, he was almost totally blind.

The other Gaster was the one who was constantly fighting with his colleagues in the movement. He held grudges, he sensed slights where often none were intended, he found enemies everywhere: 'We must eliminate all those objectionable persons who have proved a snare and a curse to the movement.'[16] But then: 'Gaster never forgave, was never wrong, was always the victim of rogues and knaves.'[17]

One of the problems was that his colleagues very seldom had the same mental capacity he had. It wasn't as if he was working in a university where other academic minds could intellectually challenge and, thereby, restrain his impetuosity. His impatience deteriorated into intolerance. 'He was turned into a King among inferiors – and that is a situation which scarcely breeds self-criticism, humility and a sense of fulfilment.' In committee: 'they plodded where he raced'.[18]

Up and down the country, the Zionist leaders were equally argumentative. In many cases they were men of little ability who saw the openings in the ranks of Zionist committees as a way of jumping the queue to community status. Others had their own axes to grind; a desire to compete with the honorary officers of the local synagogue or to achieve a degree of importance by association. The progress of Zionism was peppered by internal dissension of every kind. It followed that, for a project which aimed to lead the Jews back to the Promised Land, if the most prominent Moses in sight was Gaster, outside forces would be needed. By some miracle, at some point in the future, all the necessary elements would have to be in perfect juxtaposition in the international galaxy.

The Zionists decided that their best chance of winning over the community lay in infiltrating the seats of power and getting more supporters. As members of the Board of Deputies or the Anglo-Jewish Association, they would try to influence others, and to a very minor extent, they were successful. Over the years, the topic of Zionism, which was totally ignored at the outset, occasionally got onto the agenda.

For all their shortcomings, over the 20 years from Herzl's first visit to England until the Balfour Declaration, a degree of progress was made, very much because of the efforts of people like Gaster. In England before Chaim Weizmann, the eventual leader, came to the fore, much of the responsibility for flying the Magen Dovid flag fell on a very few advocates. They ensured that there was sufficient noise for at least some people to hear, for some converts to be made to the cause. Gaster was probably their best speaker and, as everybody knew about his eyesight, he certainly had – and deserved – the sympathy vote. His support was very much appreciated and very valuable.

It was no fault of his that his blindness: 'also prevented him from gauging the reactions of people when he spoke with them'. Was he going down well? What was the body language saying? He couldn't tell until the applause came. When it did, it was balm to his ego: 'For years I have not witnessed … a similar outburst of enthusiastic cheering like the one that followed the pronouncement of the election of myself as President.'[19]

The members of the Mahamad were singularly embarrassed when privately asked to explain the lone voice which was not on-message with the official line of the Board of Deputies and the Anglo-Jewish Association. Their inability to curb their Haham was made more difficult by the fact that one of their most distinguished members was on his side. Sir Francis Montefiore, the great man's descendent, the one the queen had chosen to honour with a baronetcy in memory of Sir Moses, the president of the elders for many years, was an early Zionist. It was what Uncle Moses had always wanted; his support for the Jews in the Holy Land had been consistent and he had made many visits to the country. Whatever cousin Claude might think, Francis would be another supporter the Zionists were proud to have. The Mahamad got Francis, like Gaster, to agree to announce on Zionist platforms that he was speaking only for himself.

When the Great War broke out in 1914, the efforts of the Zionists were redoubled. Gaster played his part, but he was nearing 60 and was pretty well sidelined by Weizmann and the younger Zionist leaders. One of the most contentious issues for the immigrant Jews in the East End was whether they should volunteer to fight for an alliance which included the hated Russians. Gaster sprang to their defence and even after conscription was introduced, supported the Foreign Jews Protection Committee which fought against the immigrants being compelled to join up or be deported. He replaced Lucien Wolf as head of the National Union for Jewish Rights and attained a higher profile still in the East End as one of their most effective spokesmen.

When Zeppelins started to bomb London, Gaster was sufficiently concerned to take himself off to Brighton for safety. Like Sasportas before him, he deserted the community, though Gaster did occasionally return to London. When Gaster spoke up for the Zionists in 1917, however, in the teeth of the opposition from the Conjoint Foreign Committee of the Board of Deputies and the Anglo-Jewish Association, a majority of the elders of Bevis Marks were doubly furious. The Haham was forced out of office, though the explanation was his absence in Brighton rather than his crucial support for the Balfour Declaration. As the Mahamad reported to the elders in 1919:

> In view of the state of his health, the Mahamad had found it necessary to grant to the Rev. Dr. Gaster, in Succot 1917, leave of absence for a period of three months and this was repeatedly extended until last Shabugnot [the Festival of Shavuot]. As Dr. Gaster did not see his way to return to London from Brighton... a prolonged correspondence led to his resignation as from 31st December 1918, on a pension of £650 per annum, and £300 to his widow or children under age. A request from

the Yehidim that he be asked to withdraw his resignation was submitted to you, but you did not consider that, having regard to all the circumstances, it would be in the interests of the Congregation that he should resume the office of Haham.

A minor eulogy on his years in office followed, but the deed was done. It was a generous pension, but the Yehidim felt that Gaster had been one of the first Zionist casualties. Gaster continued to have a body of followers and when he visited Sephardi congregations outside London in later years, he was invariably greeted as a hero. If he wasn't, the congregation soon knew all about it. In Manchester one year he was given an honour in the synagogue but was not called up by his full title of Haham Hashalem. He castigated the community for its discourtesy and warned them of the dire events which could result from such behaviour. The very next day a large crack was said to have appeared in the synagogue wall! In future his title was used in full and the congregation sent him a *sukkah* for his home the following autumn![20] Gaster was highly regarded in right-wing circles as well. When the right-wing leader, Victor Schonfeld, died all too young, Gaster was invited to speak at the funeral, but Hertz, the Chief Rabbi, was not.

Gaster was 63 when he stopped being Haham. He was to die at 83 and in his old age his academic studies were his greatest pleasure. In 1923 the British Academy invited him to be the Schweich lecturer on the Samaritans. In 1925 he stopped collecting books and sold most of his magnificent collection to the British Museum. The Rumanian Academy made him an Honorary Member in 1929 and he was made a Fellow of the Royal Society of Literature in 1930. The calm of well attended academic tributes were light years away from the draughty halls where he had preached Zionism before the war.

Now that he couldn't affect Zionist policy, he disassociated himself from the official party line. It made no difference and history moved on. His most open channel to a continuing influence in the community should have come, as it does for many able old men, in the opportunity to guide the new leaders in private. For example, one of Gaster's sons-in-law was Neville Laski, who would become the president of the Board of Deputies in the crucial years between 1933 and 1940.

He continued to expand his enormous literary output; the *Exempla of the Rabbis* came in 1924, *Samaritan Eschatology* in 1932 and *The Ma'aseh Book* on Jewish tales and legends in 1934 when he was nearly 80. His wife and son, Mannie, were devoted

helpers, reading to him the material he couldn't see. In 1939 Gaster
died in a motor car between Reading and Oxford where he was due
to talk to a group of Rumanian students. Even when blind and in his
eighties he could still hold an audience.

What did Gaster achieve? His successor, Solomon Gaon, said of
him: 'He followed the noble example of the Jewish Sages of old, who
maintained that study of the Torah is of true value only if it leads to
positive action.' Gaster aroused strong emotions in both his
supporters and his detractors. His legacy is the State of Israel which
he believed was feasible in the face of all the arguments to the
contrary. He was a Zionist before Herzl and one of those who
fought for the good of the Jews when it was desperately needed.
Whatever his minor failings, he can be remembered and honoured
for that.

NOTES

1 Stuart A. Cohen, *English Zionists and British Jews*, Princeton University Press, 1992.
2 Virginia H. Hein, *The British Followers of Theodor Herzl*, Garland Publishing, 1987, quoting Chaim Bermant in *Troubled Eden*, London, 1969.
3 Theodor Gaster, 'Prolegomenon', in Moses Gaster's, *Studies and Texts in Folklore: Magic, Mediaeval Romance, Hebrew Apocrypha and Samaritan Archaeology*, Ktav Publishing, 1971.
4 Ibid.
5 Cecil Roth, Jewish Historical Society of England, Vol. 14, 1935–39.
6 Harry Sacher, *Zionist Portraits*, London, 1959.
7 Roth, Jewish Historical Society of England, Vol. 14, 1935–39.
8 Ibid.
9 Gaster, 'Prolegomenon'.
10 *Jewish Chronicle*, 15 January 1897.
11 Moses Gaster, *Observations on the Report of the Special Committee*, March 1896.
12 *Jewish Chronicle*, 8 May 1896.
13 Joshua Levy letter in *Jewish Chronicle*, 17 April 1896.
14 *Jewish Chronicle*, 10 August 1897.
15 Werner Mosse, *Second Chance*, JCB Mohr, 1991.
16 Gaster to Israel Moser, 11 August 1913, Gaster Papers, Mocatta Library, University College, London.
17 Eugene C. Black, *Social Politics of Anglo-Jewry, 1880–1920*,

Basil Blackwell, 1988.
18   Gaster, 'Prolegomenon'.
19   *Jewish Chronicle*, 15 February 1907.
20   A story told by Manoel Cansino, whose father, Isaac, was a close friend and supporter of Gaster.

20   Hermann Adler 1891–1911

Hermann Adler had a great deal on his plate. The ambition of his predecessors may have been to study Torah, but the demands on Adler's time must have made such scholarly preoccupation particularly difficult. The Right Wing often compared his talmudic knowledge unfavourably with the standards reached by their own great rabbis, but most of their sages had the time to devote to learning. They were only looking after a single small congregation. Adler had to deal with the community he inherited plus an unprecedented flood of new Jewish immigration; year after year they poured into the country, destitute, unable to speak English, jobless. The 1880 community of probably 60,000 would have to do its best to succour a further 150,000 over the next 35 years, which almost exactly covered Adler's period in office as Delegate Chief Rabbi and then Chief Rabbi in his own right. In a world before council housing, where were they going to live? When there was no dole, how were they going to eat? If they died – and child mortality was very high – who was even going to bury them?

Agreed, they could be sent to the workhouse, but to make them a burden on the state had never been the Jewish way. Furthermore, the conditions in the workhouses were not likely to keep Jewish children within the fold; these were strictly Christian workhouses.

There would be a need for new Jewish communities, which would spread throughout the country, and Adler was also responsible for congregations wherever they existed throughout the British Empire. Interviewed by the *Christian Commonwealth* in 1891, the journalist wrote 'though a learned rabbi, he is not a hermit but a man of business and a busy man.' He asked Adler to detail his responsibilities, and he:

> partially indicated the various duties belonging to that office . . .
> They comprise the spiritual supervision of all the Hebrew
> congregations under my pastorate; all matters relating to divine
> worship and to synagogue discipline; all the ministers and other
> officials whom the congregations elect must be appointed with

my sanction; watching that the various laws enacted by our religion shall be observed, regarding prohibited food, the partaking of unleavened bread on the Passover; the supervision of the various educational institutions for religious instruction; the Presidency of the Beth Din...; consecration of synagogues; the officiating at the opening of new charitable institutions and homes; the issuing of authorisations for marriages...; also preaching regularly...; also regular visitations of the provinces for the same purposes.[1]

If all that wasn't enough, Adler also had the massive task of dealing with many of the results of the influx of Russian, Polish and Rumanian refugees from the pogroms which killed so many Jews in the latter part of the nineteenth century. He had the desperately important duty of trying to maintain the financial viability of a very considerable number of charitable institutions. He was always being asked to help the poor and the sick, the elderly and the disabled. Admittedly, there was much help on hand through the United Synagogue, the lay leadership and the existing foundations – medical, educational, geriatric and devotional – but keeping each of the elements afloat involved the Chief Rabbi to a greater or lesser extent. He often told the story of the Scottish clergyman who advertised for a horse to do the work of a minister.

Trying to ameliorate the worst of the poverty was now the responsibility of the Jewish Board of Guardians. This was an 1859 amalgamation of a number of charities. They were overwhelmed. To stem the flood the Board paid for an advertising campaign in Europe, the theme of which was 'don't come to Britain'. In his old age Nathan Adler had agreed to write to his European rabbinic colleagues in 1888 along the same lines. He asked them to tell their members: 'not to come to the land of Britain for such ascent is a descent'.

The board refused to give any charity to immigrants until they had survived six months in Britain. Where they could, they repatriated them. Between 1880 and 1914 the Board of Guardians paid for some 50,000 Jews to go back. In 1903, out of 450 who asked for help, 80 per cent were sent home – if you could call it home. It was an ideal climate for the Christian missionary societies who were prepared to step into the breach. The per capita cost of conversions should have been very reasonable.

Adler also saw the need to move the community forward in British life as a whole. The disabilities may have been abolished comparatively recently, but considerable pockets of anti-Semitism remained and these would be inflamed by the effects of the mass immigration. Jews could now sit in both Houses of Parliament, attend any university and belong to any profession or occupation. On the other hand there were plenty of public schools which had quotas for Jewish pupils, golf clubs which didn't take Jews, and hotels and restaurants which were 'full' if your name was Cohen. There were chambers and colleges, London clubs and major commercial companies which would have liked to take Jews but, unfortunately, only seemed to have vacancies on the rarest of occasions!

Anti-Semitism remained and would only diminish slowly over the next century, as other, even darker-hued, scapegoat communities emerged with which to frighten the children. Nevertheless, by 1891, British Jews had achieved a great deal. Now, at the beginning of Hermann Adler's delegate Chief Rabbinate in 1879, they stood to have their image changed for the worse by the arrival of so many refugees from the persecution in eastern Europe. These migrants, of necessity, were prepared to work for lower wages than their English counterparts in the few industries, such as tailoring and furniture-making, which they had in common. This made them deeply unpopular with the working classes in the East End. In addition, the need of the Jewish families for housing raised rents in the area and reduced the value for money. They swamped districts, they didn't mix easily with the local population and they didn't drink much alcohol; a combination which bankrupted many East End publicans. Of more moment to the establishment, the migrants had very good cause to hate the Tsar and many were enthusiastic recruits to socialism; they were supporters of the fashionable new bogeyman, the Red Peril.

Where there is poverty, there is also a greater temptation to commit crime and, as the incoming Jews were almost universally poor, they included plenty of criminals. Some were part of the despicable White Slave trade in prostitution: the Yellow Peril. Indeed, those who distorted the wisdom of perils, if not offering pearls of wisdom, were always sure that the Jews were at the root of the problem. Overall, the richer Jews could see the inevitability of being tarred with the same brush as their poor co-religionists.

This was the period when the *Protocols of the Elders of Zion* was published in 1903; a ludicrous claim that there was an international Jewish conspiracy to take over the world, but one which was gratefully seized upon by anti-Semites and took in a large number of the gullible in many countries.

The carefully established image of the Jews as good British citizens, over 200 years, was threatened by all these events. If you add outside factors such as the political and economic turmoil during Adler's ministry – the constitutional crisis with the House of Lords, Home Rule for Ireland and strikes so fierce the navy had to send warships up the Mersey to defend Liverpool – it was only a slight exaggeration for Winston Churchill to remember: 'a nation torn by the fiercest political strife and even...drawing near to the verge of civil war'.[2]

It also has to be recognized that the fight to dismantle Jewish disabilities had been ongoing for that double century. After being recruited to fight discrimination for that long, it is very difficult to demobilize. The thinking is that the battle may have been won but the enemy could always regroup. After all, the final emancipation had only come with the passing of the Parliamentary Oaths Act in 1866, and the barrier of taking the oath as a Christian remained in force for membership of the House of Lords until 1885. The mental approach is, therefore, to stay on your guard, to check and recheck your defences and not to offer hostages to fortune. The influx of poor immigrants could easily become such hostages.

To make matters worse, in 1880 when Adler had just taken over as Delegate Chief Rabbi, the Jews were in danger of falling out with the new Liberal government. The cause was the Balkans. Former Prime Minister Gladstone had triumphantly regained office by his Midlothian campaign, stumping the country condemning the Turks for massacring Christians in Bulgaria. For the Jews, the caveat was that the Balkan Christians, when not otherwise engaged in fleeing the Turks, spent a fair amount of their remaining spare time killing Jews; whereas the Turks had always treated the Jews tolerantly. The Jews were on the side of the Turks and Gladstone wasn't. The editor of the *Jewish Chronicle* and the Prime Minister had words on the subject.

There was also the problem of the 1853 Factory Act which stopped work on Sunday, thereby leaving Orthodox Jewish manufacturers with a five-day week before its time. In addition, the 1870 Education Act introduced government-financed, universal schooling, but the assimilationist possibilities of Jewish children in Christian schools worried the Orthodox a great deal. There was still an enormous amount of work to be done.

Hermann Adler felt deeply for all the oppressed Jews in eastern Europe. He represented the Russo-Jewish community at the conference of Hebrew Congregations of Europe and America in Berlin in 1882 and in Paris in 1890. He wanted the safety of Britain to remain available to them, but they arrived in such numbers that the original community couldn't cope adequately with their needs. Over the years, a growing tide of public opinion continued to insist that the level of immigration had to be halted, even though the problem was very much exaggerated. In the 1901 census foreigners in Britain were a smaller percentage of the population than in any other European country, except Spain and Sweden.

Not wishing to be confused with the facts, the agitation was obviously a serious threat to the possibility of rescuing more Jews from the continuing massacres in eastern Europe. Every year there was another initiative in the direction of legislation. It did, indeed, culminate in the passing of the Aliens Act in 1905 which dramatically cut down the free entry of Jews into the country. Jews who would have been safe had they been allowed to flee to Britain, now died in many pogroms abroad because of the Aliens Act.

To take a modern example, you can imagine what could have happened to the Iranian Jews when the Shah was overthrown in the 1980s and the fundamentalist regime took over. On that occasion the British quietly let into the country those of the Iranian Jewish community who wanted to come, and it enormously strengthened the Sephardi congregation in London. The Iranians had their poor, but most of the community were massively richer than the victims of the pogroms. Very few countries object to rich immigrants, they just dislike poor ones.

To address all the varied problems, Hermann Adler was the absolutely perfect candidate for Chief Rabbi to succeed his illustrious and popular father. He was born in 1839 in Hanover and his great grand-uncle was David Tevele Schiff. On his mother's side he was the cousin of Henry de Worms, 1st Baron Pirbright. So he had one foot in the Orthodox rabbinical family camp and the other in the House of Lords. He came to Britain with his father in 1845 and from his youth he was friendly with the Rothschilds who treated him with great cordiality. He went to University College School in Hampstead and University College, London. He graduated in 1859, doing particularly well in English, German, Classics and Philosophy. He preached his first sermon at the opening of the Swansea Synagogue in the same year.

Then he went off to Prague to study for the rabbinate at the yeshiva of Rabbi Solomon Rapoport and, after only 18 months, got his *semicha* in 1862 from Rabbis Rapoport, Freund and Ausch. He also took a doctorate at Leipzig in his leisure time, writing his doctoral thesis on Druidism. He might have been more of a polymath than a great talmudic expert, but Adler was no slouch in the theological field.

This had to be the case because, in 1863, he became temporary principal of the new Jews' College and in 1864 he became the first minister of the very fashionably located Bayswater Synagogue in the West End of London. In 1867 he married Rachel Joseph and they had two daughters, Nettie and Ruth, and a son, Alfred. Adler served the Bayswater until he was appointed Delegate Chief Rabbi when his father's health worsened. Hermann Adler was always recognized by the community as a very fine speaker and attracted large congregations. Apart from that, he had: 'turned visitation into a fine art'.

He organized teams of his congregation to visit the poor and infirm on a regular basis. As an English minister of religion, he looked the part, he acted the part and he fitted easily into the role: 'Hermann Adler's outstanding characteristic was perhaps his dignity.'[3] The dignity was balanced though by humour in the vein of England's much loved self-deprecation. For example, in 1896, before giving a paper to the Jewish Historical Society of England he told the members: 'For surely we give you adequate value for your money, save and except, of course, in regard to the address to which you are doomed to listen this evening.'

As Delegate Chief Rabbi for his father, he left the halachic authority in the Beth Din to his colleague, Dayan Jacob Reinowitz. He paid him £2 a week out of his own funds until Reinowitz died in 1893. Even so, on his election, he refused to commit himself to consulting the Beth Din if he didn't feel like it. He also said he wouldn't move to the East End to be near the main body of the community at the Great. Nevertheless, with the strong support of the Rothschilds there was no real competition to Adler replacing his father at a handsome salary of £2,000 a year. This was particularly so as neither the Sephardim nor the Reform movement were prepared to take part in the election process. That such involvement would provide the impression of a united community was counterbalanced by the certain knowledge that the United Synagogue would always make sure to keep the majority of the votes in the hands of their own delegates. Periodic discussions over the century always saw the collapse of any proposals for a joint Sephardi/Ashkenazi Chief Rabbi.

Adler was determined not to be a tool of the lay authorities, and not for nothing was he described as a patrician English gentleman. Hadn't the man who nominated him for Chief Rabbi referred to him as 'the head of our church'? On another occasion Theodore Herzl spoke of a dinner at the Adlers being 'everything English with the old Jewish customs peeping through'.

Adler was derided by the right wing for this approach. It was, however, too easy for that section of Jewry to wrap themselves up in their piety and then appeal to the Jewish establishment for financial help and government diplomatic support. Adler was the most senior Jewish spiritual leader in his time to be working in the public arena. He had to represent his religion and his co-religionists in the wider world of an overwhelmingly Christian nation. For example, in 1878 there was a serious attack on the civic patriotism of the Jewish community by a respected academic, Professor Goldwin Smith. Adler produced two articles refuting the accusations and had the pleasure of receiving Gladstone's congratulations. It was just a counterweight to the argument over Bulgaria. From then on Adler was seen as the major apologist for the British Jews, not only in Britain but also in the United States and Europe.

> He represented it indeed superbly well. He elevated the institution to a dignity and position almost unequalled in the history of the diaspora. On all public occasions when it was called for, the Chief Rabbi would figure on the platform by the side of the Archbishop of Canterbury and the Cardinal of Westminster and would be heard with the utmost deference. At State Services in Westminster Abbey, at times of national mourning or celebration, his impressive figure would be seen in the seat of honour...wearing a quasi-episcopal rosette in the ribbon of his top hat as an addition to the clerical garb.[4]

At the 50th anniversary dinner to mark the admission of Jews to the House of Commons, Adler even addressed the question of whether a Jewish state would have given Christians political rights if the shoe had been on the other foot. He pointed out accurately that:

> History enables us to answer this question with no uncertain voice. From the 8th to the 10th century... there existed a powerful and independent kingdom, the Khazars. Both King and subjects had embraced the Jewish faith. Contemporary historians tell us that the... chief authority, next to that of the sovereign, was vested in a tribunal which was composed of seven persons, two Jews, two Christians, two Mohammedans and one Pagan. And we are assured that there was an entire absence of all sectarian animosities.

Hermann Adler has been accused of trying to disassociate himself from the immigrants and instead attempt to create a Jewish church which was a mirror image of the Christian. After all, this was the man who followed the advice of his friend, the Bishop of Bath and Wells, and adopted the title of Very Reverend. Adler, on occasions, even wore a bishop's gaiters. In order to get a more balanced view of Adler, we are fortunate that he collected his favourite sermons into a book entitled *Anglo-Jewish Memories*, published in 1909, two years before his death.

In those speeches he certainly backed the British party line. He eulogised the jubilees of Queen Victoria and took particular pleasure in the fact that Victoria was the first sovereign to include the Jewish community in a call for a national day of prayer. On 15 April 1887 he announced in the Bayswater Synagogue:

> The Chief Rabbi has this morning received a gracious intimation from the Queen, to the effect that her Majesty fully approves of a Public Service of Thanksgiving being held by members of all religious denominations in celebration of the forthcoming Jubilee.

Palace recognition at last for his whole community; there had never been such times. All the same, there was that strong under-swell of demand for legislation to keep the Jews – and other labour capable of being sweated – out of the country.

Adler also supported the dubious case for the Boer War, but he didn't neglect the newly created articles of the Geneva Convention. Indeed, he quoted the Second Book of Chronicles to the government on the treatment of prisoners of war: 'the prophet rebuked everybody for treating the prisoners badly and the prisoners were clothed and shod and given food and drink and anointed'.

The fact was that when 2,000 Jewish men joined the colours, it gave the lie to the anti-Semitic suggestion that the community wasn't loyal to the country. Adler was a recruiting officer for the Boer War army but the inevitable result later was his duty to unveil the war memorial to those 114 Jews who died as a consequence: half succumbed in battle and half of disease. As he said at the ceremony in 1905: 'Here we are spared that most distressful sight, the revival of odious religious prejudice and pernicious racial antipathies.' It was a powerful unheeded argument against the Aliens Act of the same year.

Adler did care for his poor and he tried to get them every kind of support. Many charitable settlements were created in the East End and Adler tried to recruit helpers for them from all walks of Jewish life. In 1895 in Cambridge he told the Jewish students: 'I ardently hope that when your academic career terminates...you will devote some time and thought to our brethren who toil in the East of London.'

Nor was he disappointed, as many idealistic young Jews hurried to play their part. Adler also encouraged the ideal of the Jewish Lads' Brigade to try to help the poor, young immigrants get on in life, based on the model of the Church Lads' Brigade – the right image in a very jingoistic nation which dearly loved its armed forces. On occasions he used exquisite diplomacy to help the impoverished. In the Central Synagogue in 1884 he spoke at a Memorial Service for Charlotte de Rothschild, one of the most generous of an exceedingly philanthropic family. How felicitous it was that he had been told by a 'dear relative' that the good lady's last words were 'Remember the poor.' At the end of the panegyric Adler homed in: 'I can conceive nothing more affecting, naught more solemn, than the admonition which her dying words and acts convey to those who were supremely dear to her in life.'

Any professional fund-raiser worth his salt would have to give that appeal a standing ovation. The Rothschilds would have gone on being generous anyway, but the idea that this would be a suitable memorial to Charlotte was, unquestionably, a beautifully crafted argument.

A judgement on your ability depends on the league in which you're playing. In the eighteenth century Haham Dazevedo didn't seem very high-powered to his talmudic peers, but he set exceptional standards when judged by Christian hebraists. In the same way Adler was less impressive in the pulpit when compared to the best Christian exponents. James Douglas wrote about preachers for the *Morning Leader* and in 1905 he reported on Adler's sermon in the Hampstead Synagogue:

> Dr. Hermann Adler is no orator. He reads his prelection in a husky voice with a strong Teutonic brogue. His personality is invisible...the voice is passionless, remote, aloof. He has no gesture, no trait, no eccentricity.'[5]

The Hampstead was always a congregation that aped its English upper-class counterparts. Douglas asked the pertinent question of Judaism in his article: 'It defied torture. Will it defy tolerance?' If Adler lacked eccentricity, he certainly had immense tact. When asked to explain why Jews always hoped their children would marry other Jews, Adler explained: 'the fact that we intermarry among ourselves does not by any means clash with the duties we owe as citizens of the state. It is what I may term a self-denying ordinance.'

Hermann Adler's bureaucratic policies could also easily enough be portrayed in a negative way. As one right-wing critic has written:

> A social elite, which became a ruling elite, dominated Jewish life, all but displaced spiritual leadership and created a near mediaeval clergy which could not guide or challenge its masters. Instead, the clergy were deprived of the title rabbi, reduced to being practitioners of ritual, religious functionaries who administered appropriate procedures for the management of life-style events.[6]

Does that stand up to examination as far as Adler was concerned? Was it to avoid competition that he was the only Jewish cleric allowed to use the title of rabbi within his jurisdiction? Or was it also that the German experience he knew so well proved that powerful rabbis could lead their congregations into the Reform movement? Adler remembered the difficulties his father had with the Local Rabbi problem in Manchester in the 1850s, with Schiller-Szenessy eventually going over to the Reform. If he could centralize the spiritual authority, he could more easily resist such challenges to Orthodoxy. There were other reasons for the poor showing of Reform recruitment in Britain in the nineteenth century, but part of their failure was due to Adler's ability to keep his communities in line.

How Orthodox Hermann Adler was, though, depended on your viewpoint. The pressure on his father to allow changes in the liturgy had been stoutly resisted. It was hoped that his son would be more malleable. The *Jewish Chronicle*: 'regretted the slow pace of reform under his (NMA's) stewardship because of the "existence of a reactionary section which strenuously opposed even harmless modifications of established ritual practice". To its dismay, however … Hermann Adler … proved to be a conservative influence.'[7]

A typical example of the problems emerged with the building of the Hampstead synagogue in 1892. Here was a very upper-crust community and they were keen on liturgical change. Morris Joseph, their preferred choice for their first minister, was in favour of an organ on the Sabbath, a mixed choir and the abolition of prayers for the congregation by the Cohanim – the members of the old priestly tribe. He insisted on complete freedom in the pulpit to expound his views, which he later described as: 'midway between the Orthodoxy which regards … the Talmud as the final authority in Judaism, and the extreme liberalism which... would lightly cut the religion loose from the bonds of Tradition.'[8]

Would the new Chief Rabbi accept this viewpoint from the minister of a synagogue for which he was spiritually the final authority? No, Adler wouldn't. He refused to give Joseph the certificate he needed to act as a United Synagogue minister. Hampstead had many rich and powerful members who were not used to being thwarted. Nevertheless, Joseph and the congregation had little option but to agree reluctantly to abide by Adler's decision, as the New had when Nathan Marcus Adler put his foot down. When David Woolf Marks retired from the Reform's Upper Berkeley Street synagogue, Adler would have felt vindicated, as it was Morris Joseph who took over. Like Schiller-Szenessy in the past and like Louis Jacobs in the future, the journey away from strict Orthodoxy started with a single step. Sasportas, David Nietto and Hirschell in the past, Hertz and Brodie in the future, would ensure their community avoided the same pitfall.

Adler was also still seeking greater acceptance of the Jewish community in the wider Christian world. The Christian vicars were called Reverend, so the Jewish ministers were told to call themselves Reverend as well. Adler did, in fact, give *semicha* to at least two students at Jews' College – Moses Hyamson and Asher Feldman in 1898. This was after the Ramsgate scandal in 1896. Feldman was made a Dayan in 1902. Other Jewish ministers obtained *semicha* outside Adler's jurisdiction. There was nothing against that either, although Rabbi Sir Hermann Gollancz and Rabbi Simeon Singer both regretted that they had to go to such lengths – Gollancz went all the way to Galicia.

The ministers took to wearing clerical collars as well but, in moving that far towards the Christian clergy, Adler would have said that he was not going against any Orthodox tenet; after all, hadn't eighteenth-century hazanim worn canonicals? There was no specified Jewish clothing for daytime wear except the tsitsit, and many members of the extreme right were wearing the long-forgotten Polish nobility fashions when they put on the streimel (fur-trimmed hat), knee-breeches and buckled shoes every Sabbath.

Adler was also perfectly happy to dress appropriately for the occasion. When invited to the reconsecration of the ultra-Orthodox Spitalfields Great Synagogue in 1910, he readily agreed not to wear his canonicals.[9] By this time, however, with the Great beginning to be referred to as the Cathedral Synagogue, the right wing could be excused for thinking the United Synagogue was itself heading down a slippery slope. It was also quite unnecessarily insensitive for Adler to insist on addressing even eminent rabbis, like the right wing's Avraham Aba Werner and Eliezer Gordon, as Reverend Mr.

Those who denigrated the ministers produced caricatures: 'The Reverend X, whose Jewish studies terminated when he was 18, who dressed like an Anglican clergyman, carried his umbrella on the Sabbath and was very broadminded about the dietary laws, was the real religious guide of his congregation.'[10]

Certainly, the United Synagogue wasn't looking for Jews' College to produce traditional rabbis. In a 1910 report by the US to the college, it was clearly stated:

> The requirements in a Minister were (a) to preach efficiently, (b) to teach Hebrew and religion, (c) to read the prayers in synagogue, including the Law with proper intonation, (d) to help their congregants with advice and sympathy, (e) to engage actively in and to organize the charitable work ... and (f) to aid if necessary the routine administrative work of their congregation ... Academic distinction, while very desirable, is not everything and other requirements should not be sacrificed to the attainment of profound scholarship.'[11]

There were, of course, many scholarly exceptions and the main reason for all this window-dressing was still the desire to be as English as the English, even if the facts didn't measure up to the theory. For example, at the Jews' College Jubilee Festival in 1906, the guest of honour, Sir Edward Sassoon, said: 'I am glad to think that we are free ... of having holy office and clerical positions filled by strangers.' By which he meant clerics from Europe. There were cries of 'hear, hear'. The fact, however, was that the president, Adler himself, had been born in Germany, the principal, Michael Friedlander, was German and half the teaching staff were mid-European as well. Which was because you couldn't find properly qualified British candidates. Which was because the community wouldn't provide the money to sustain a decent yeshiva.

A Jewish education policy was still, primarily, about raising money to pay for it. Aaron Green, one of the brightest Orthodox ministers, said that, far from trying to educate the refugees in the East End how to become English, it might be better to create: 'a Whitechapel mission to convert the West End Jews to Judaism, with a branch at Bayswater and Kensington, Soho and Hyde Park and at least one in Hampstead' where Green had actually become the very popular minister! To raise the necessary money, Adler was quite content to have leading members of the Upper Berkeley Street community on educational bodies which came under his authority. He might criticize the Liberal synagogue when it came into existence, but he didn't ask their members to withdraw from the educational bodies.

Adler's views on not educating students for *semicha* were finally overturned. Claude Montefiore, the future founder of the Liberal synagogue, was giving out the prizes at Jews' College in 1895 and poured scorn on the existing policy:

> I should not mind the stigma attaching to Jews' College that no single student has received the Rabbinical Diploma at its hands. I should not mind the stigma if it be frankly said, the Rabbinical Diploma cannot be given without the acquisition of a mass of knowledge which has now become obsolete.[12]

In 1900 the council of Jews' College grasped the nettle and considered the possibility of awarding *semicha* as a result of examination results from their students, and Adler finally agreed in 1901. The examining board would include the Chief Rabbi, the Haham, the principal and theology tutor of the college and a Dayan. If there was a tie, the Chief Rabbi would have the casting vote. In 1902 it was agreed that four theology exams, taken over six and a half years, would constitute the curriculum leading to *semicha*. Even so it was another six years before Barnett Cohen got his as a result. In 1908 Adler resigned as chairman of the council. The Sephardi elders had accused him of dictating to the council and wanted the press admitted to the meetings. They carried a resolution to that effect and Adler decided to let them get on with it.

One advantage of Adler's acceptability to the wider clerical authorities was that it did give him a licence to be critical. Standing on his paternalistic pedestal as a respected clergyman in the Mother Religion, Adler, unlike most of his predecessors, was not afraid to take issue with the behaviour of the Christian Church. Lamenting the Russian pogroms in the pulpit at the Great Synagogue in 1905, Adler said that the massacres had: 'affixed a deeper stain and a more far-reaching insult upon Christendom. Does it not, then, behove the leaders of Christian thought and action in this country – aye, throughout the civilized world – to arise and offer their solemn protest against atrocities committed and left unrebuked in a Christian country?'

It would have been much more difficult to take that stance had Adler withdrawn the community behind the stockade walls of spiritual isolation from the world, as some of the right-wing communities would. He spoke, moreover, as a member of the most prestigious club in the country – the Athenaeum – for which he had been proposed by the Bishop of London in 1900. When the pogroms began, it was the Lord Mayor of London who led the Mansion House Appeal which raised £200,000 to help the refugees in 1882. It was Hermann Adler's political friends who ignored the clamour for an Aliens Act for the next 20 years.

There were other Jews who were even more important than Adler in politics, but it was Adler who was called upon to give evidence to government enquiries on sweatshops, Sunday closing and divorce. If the Chief Rabbi had adopted the position of the right wing, it would have disassociated him in many ways from those who wielded power in the land.

Of course, Britain didn't do pogroms. Apart from Guy Fawkes Night there were practically no anti-religious demonstrations at all – and anyway few would remember the origins of 5 November as a party to celebrate an unsuccessful Catholic plot to destroy the government all those years ago.

Adler was equally capable of attacking the religious standards of his own community. On one occasion he quoted a Christian essayist:

> The poor Jew fasted or ate dry bread when he could not get meat which had been duly killed; the rich Jew eats meat unclean to his fathers because the other is not served at the Savoy Hotel . . . the poor Jew clung to his heritage, though the world battered him; the rich Jew gives it up to win a contemptuous smile.

It was a crushing commentary, but Adler did try to tread a delicate middle path between the various factions within Judaism. He may not have approved of the Reform synagogue but he turned up for the memorial service to David Woolf Marks. Nearly 100 years later a Chief Rabbi was criticized for not doing so in similar circumstances. The important difference, which was drowned in the late twentieth-century hysteria, was that, in Adler's time, the procedures of the Reform synagogue were nothing like as far removed from the Orthodox position as they are today.

There was certainly a great need for sensitivity, because there was always one faction or another which would take offence at whatever the Chief Rabbi did – plus ça change, plus c'est la même chose. It is true, for example, that spiritual authority within the United Synagogue was totally centralized, and the desire to wield power can never be excluded as a reason for this. It is suggested that this led to breakaways, like the Liberal synagogue on the left and the very Orthodox Federation of Synagogues and Machzike Hadath on the right. In fact, the Liberal synagogue was a schism from the Reform movement, not the Orthodox. Adler clearly recognized the danger the Liberal movement posed to Orthodoxy very early on. He summed up Montefiore's original creation, the Jewish Religious Union as: 'unJewish, irreligious and disunion', and in 1910 when the Liberal Jewish synagogue was founded:

> A new Judaism is being proclaimed, with many essentials of Judaism left out or whittled down almost to vanishing point. With a stroke of the pen the divine authority of the Pentateuch and of the Prophets and the authority of every teacher in Israel is denied... the purpose which actuated the founders of the new faith is no doubt praiseworthy, to prevent Jews by birth from drifting away from Judaism. But what is the method they employ? They annunciate a new Judaism which constitutes a breach with the past, a Judaism with faith and practice omitted. Wherein does the movement differ from Unitarians and from Theistic and Ethical churches? In lieu of reclaiming the drift of us, are they not promoting assimilation and encouraging disloyalty?

The right wing, by contrast, would never have considered the United Synagogue sufficiently Orthodox for them to come to rest under its banner anyway. As one of their leaders commented 50 years later: 'It is impossible for younger members of the community, and particularly for people who have arrived here since, to realize how lax conditions had become in Jewish official quarters and what remarkable changes have taken place during the past few decades.'[13]

Yet the Federation acknowledged Adler's authority and the Chief Rabbi would not have been supported in his own community had he tried to come up to right-wing standards. The latter had even suggested that Dayan Reinowitz: 'was afraid to come out into the open for fear lest it might affect his livelihood'.[14] Against such generalized criticism Adler could hardly defend his colleague.

The refugees from the pogroms were poor, but that did not automatically make them illiterate. Like many of the eighteenth-century Jewish pedlars, they might have appeared insignificant to the world outside, but inside their homes many were good talmudists. The Orthodox hard core of the migrants could field a more observant and knowledgeable team than the vast majority of the United synagogues. The poor, however, often feel themselves patronised by the rich. The proud poor resent the charity they have to accept. Admittedly, this wouldn't have led to the creation of ultra-religious movements, unless the spiritual dimension had been as strong as it was. Just as Europe had provided almost all the Chief Rabbis and Hahamim, so the new migrants came from the same richer Orthodox stock.

Criticism of right-wing Orthodoxy was not confined to its spiritual content. It became standard practice to locate its existence only in the least attractive setting. Even James Parkes, a pillar of the Church of England and a very good friend to the Jewish community, caught the disease. When he was describing it, he said it was for: 'those who seek to maintain unimpaired the traditional Orthodoxy of the East European ghetto'.[15]

Now it is perfectly true that traditional Orthodoxy was practised in east European ghettos – those impoverished, downtrodden, cramped, bedraggled and dilapidated semi-prisons on the continent to which European Jews had been relegated by oppressive Christian regimes. But Moses Montefiore was equally observant on his estate in seaside Ramsgate. In mansions in Mayfair, in brownstones in New York, on fashionable boulevards in Paris and in great homes in India and Persia, the same standards would apply if the owners were sufficiently Orthodox, and there were plenty who were. To suggest that right-wing Orthodoxy only applied in ghettos was a slur which had – and has – no foundation in fact.

The Reform movement said the United Synagogue was too Orthodox and the very Orthodox Machzike Hadath organization said it wasn't religious enough. The United Synagogue members liked the situation pretty well the way it was. As Britain was supposed to be a middle-of-the-road, constitutional democracy, so was the United Synagogue. The Liberal party were to discover, when they had a majority of over 300 in the House of Commons in 1906, that the House of Lords was capable of destroying their legislation. Similarly, as the members of the United Synagogue knew, the important Jewish families had the ability to remain in office and control for very long periods of time, even if they were a tiny minority on the councils. There was respect and deference for both the members of the House of Lords among the public and for the Cousinhood among the Jews. Adler fought against the wish of many communities to amend their religious services against the Din and, like his father, gave way only on occasions, and very slowly indeed.

Adler, in charge of public relations for the community, foresaw another major problem as well – Zionism. For all the anti-Semites with their cries of 'why don't you go back to your own country?' Zionism was a gift from the gods. Here was a body of Jews who were asking to do just that.

For Adler, Zionism was the bad news. He had worked extremely hard – as had his community and his predecessors – to make the case that the Jews in England were loyal Englishmen, not temporary residents until the Holy Land became vacant. He had been trying to bury any question of dual loyalty, a split between Britain and the various lands in which many of his congregation had been born. Now it might be a question of triple loyalty. Theodor Herzl was Austrian and to Herzl, a national home for the Jews was a necessity. Enough was enough; the Jews had been kicked around for nearly two millennia, there was hardly a year in which some community or another wasn't being viciously attacked and something finally had to be done about it. Waiting for the arrival of universal and everlasting brotherly love had been given a fair chance but it was as far out of sight as ever. They had pleaded for justice and begged for equality long enough. They had endured the howling mobs, mourned their martyrs and fled their homes in the hope of finding somewhere better to live, mostly to no avail. The Holy Land, or some national home, was the answer and the Zionists had the dream of converting what had become a decrepit piece of desert into a modern state.

Adler and most of his community wanted nothing to do with such a pipe dream. To make matters worse, Herzl was a self-confessed atheist and his Zionism was equally secular. The majority of the Zionist leaders wanted to dismantle what they considered the shackles of Orthodoxy. If Herzl was, by any remote chance, successful, the leadership in the Holy Land might well end up in the hands of the ungodly. There is a strong body of opinion today which holds that it has; pork can be bought in Israel.

Adler also rejected Zionism because he believed that the Jewish role in world affairs was to press for a higher morality among the nations. He felt that returning to the position of a small nation-state in the Middle East would reduce the possibility of achieving this. Jewish moral influence would be decreased if all the Jews were to be found in the Holy Land.

Adler's objection to Jewish socialists was equally due to the fact that much of their leadership was anti-religion. The main body of Jewish socialists did not see Orthodox Judaism as a useful weapon in the upcoming class war. They rejected its rituals and deliberately held parties on Yom Kippur, which was hardly a practice designed to cement relations between them and their religious brethren. Adler supported those who remained Orthodox, but it didn't take a genius to recognize that the tenets of Karl Marx left little room for the Oral and Written Laws. Under any circumstances, however, Adler was unlikely to have left-wing views. Indeed in 1898 he wrote to the Jewish congregation in Plymouth to ask them to support the non-Jewish Conservative candidate rather than the Jewish Liberal one.

Towards the end Adler tired. In 1911 when he was over 70 he saw that what: 'must press itself on every thoughtful mind is that a measure of decentralization has become requisite'. An energetic successor, however, would be less convinced of the need for such a move. When he was dying, Adler also made a plea that his successor should be able to win the support of the Jews in the East End better than he had.

Adler's only son, Alfred, who was also a minister, died early in 1911. The Chief Rabbi died of heart failure in July of that year. In August, after 250 years, those who had always proclaimed that anti-Jewish riots could happen in Britain were given one and only piece of positive evidence. There were, in fact, two examples in Wales; one in Tredegar and one up the road in Ebbw Vale. In Tredegar, the disturbances took place on the Saturday and Sunday nights of 19 and 20 August. Eighteen Jewish-owned shops were looted. The town had been going through desperate economic times and some Jewish landlords were widely regarded as charging exorbitant rents to their poor tenants. In addition, some of the Jews who owned factories were accused of paying in tokens, which could only be used in company shops, the infamous 'Truck system'. There were probably a few instances where these reports were accurate.

The largest non-Jewish employer in the town had reported to the Home Office: 'I know of no other reason other than this [rack renting] which would give rise to the feeling against the Jews, many of whom are respectable citizens and who have been in business in Tredegar for very many years.'[16] The Chief Constable wrote later: 'The present state of general unrest is too favourable an opportunity to be missed for attacking the Jews. The advance in prices owing to the railway strike has also caused ill feeling.'[17]

During the looting no Jews were hurt. Many Jewish families nevertheless left their homes to shelter in the houses of non-Jewish friends, who were horrified at the disturbances and supportive of their neighbours. Unlike Russia, where the police would often stand by and watch – and sometimes lend a hand – the local magistrates did their duty, read the Riot Act and called out the troops to help the police. The constabulary waded in with their batons, much to the disgust of one councillor, who was a Miners' Federation-sponsored representative and said they were too brutal. But then it had happened before; only that was 30 years before, and then the Catholics were the ones accused of disturbing the peace of the villeins by undercutting wages. On Monday 21 August troops of the Worcester Regiment arrived in Tredegar from Cardiff to keep order. So on Tuesday the looters moved on and started again a few miles up the road in Ebbw Vale. That was stopped by the same force. By the weekend it was all over.

It didn't, of course, prevent one publication – the *Jewish World* – coming out with a blazing headline: 'An All-British pogrom in South Wales'. That wasn't the general reaction, however. Most Jewish and non-Jewish pundits fell over backwards to protest that the riot was not even anti-Semitic; they insisted that it was just a coincidence that all the Christian shops had their windows broken and all the Jewish shops were looted. The Jewish victims received a lot of sympathy locally but at least one of their leaders was less supportive. Lord Rothschild, when asked to approach the government during the riots, said of his co-religionists: 'They are a bad lot and probably deserve what they are getting.'

The Tredegar council agreed to set aside £12,500 as restitution, though only £6,000 was eventually needed. At Ebbw Vale it was slightly more at £7,500. It meant adding 1p to the rates. All the authorities had behaved impeccably throughout. It is no wonder that the Right Wing still refer to Britain as *malchut shel chesed* – the kingdom of mercy.

What did Hermann Adler achieve? Cecil Roth summed it up very fairly:

> One with less learning, less executive ability, or with a weaker personality, could never have held untangled all the threads of Anglo-Jewish life... could never have preserved for the heterogeneous Anglo-Jewish community even a semblance of unity and integrity.

It's all too easy to judge people in history by today's standards or with the benefit of hindsight. Historically, that is a useless and invalid approach. In the wider community, Adler was better known than any of his predecessors. He added lustre to the community in the eyes of the country's movers and shakers. In Marienbad, where they were both on holiday, Edward VII stopped to talk to him. He was made a Commander of the Victorian Order, which is only in the sovereign's gift. Admittedly, there is one small problem for a Chief Rabbi in wearing the insignia of that illustrious body – below the ribbon is a handsome cross! With typical diplomacy, Adler arranged to cut a slit in his canonicals which concealed the bottom arm of the cross.

Adler certainly lost some battles with the lay leadership. He 'asserted his authority when he could and bent with the wind when he could not'. For example, the traditional place from which to conduct a service in synagogue is on the *bima* in the middle of the building, with the Ark at one end. After pressure from the laity Adler approved the placing of the *bima* in front of the Ark in many synagogues. Then again, at the queen's Diamond Jubilee service at the Great Synagogue, a mixed choir was introduced. The reason a mixed choir in an Orthodox synagogue is not allowed is that it is held that the pleasant voice of a woman distracts the men from their devotions. Inevitably, everybody still protests that an attractive aspect of the opposite sex would never put them off for a moment. If, however, the Almighty had not decided to create just such an attraction, the human race would presumably have died out long ago.

Adler remonstrated with the lay leaders of the synagogue, but other *shuls* started to follow the Great's example – the lay leadership overruled the religious. It would take the best part of 100 years to get the *bima* put back where it should be and mixed choirs abolished again. Nevertheless, the situation would return to normal eventually and, in the meantime, the United Synagogue remained united.

Undoubtedly he would have seen his greatest achievement as keeping the vast majority of the British community within the Orthodox fold. The experience of the Orthodox rabbis in the United States was very different. In America 75 per cent of the Jews eventually turned to Reform. Hermann Adler kept 75 per cent of his community Orthodox. He didn't attack the fact that Reform members played a full part in the Anglo-Jewish Association, because membership of that organization involved no belief in Orthodox Judaism. As mentioned earlier, after the death of Moses Montefiore, the Reform joined the deputies as well. They became far stronger in their ability to sway the community than their numerical insignificance warranted. They achieved power with their cheque books, as people of all opinions have done countless times in the past. To Adler, the lack of democracy in the secretive behaviour of the Conjoint was of less importance to the Jewish needy than the support they would get from the resources of the rich Reform families.

Adler was determined not to give an inch on Orthodox practice and he, correctly, preferred to concentrate his moral force on that front rather than trying to take on everybody about everything. If the Conjoint produced no minutes of their discussions with government, that did not affect Adler's total control over the Board of Shechita. If he could not prevent Jewish immigrants from demanding the overthrow of the Russian grandson of the queen, that didn't enable ministers with Reform leanings to take up pulpits in the United Synagogue. He handed over to his successor a community which could have gone the American way, could have adopted the Reform 1885 Pittsburgh Platform, but didn't. Adler, far more than anybody else, kept the community Orthodox.

With Hermann Adler's death there came to an end an extraordinary dynasty of Ashkenazi Chief Rabbis. Each one, since Aaron Hart in 1705, had been related to the others. Adler's father was Nathan Marcus Adler, whose great uncle was David Tevele Schiff. Schiff's great uncle was Zevi Ashkenazi. Ashkenazi's grandson was Hart Lyon and Hart Lyon's son was Solomon Hirschell. It was a dynasty that ruled for over 210 years.

NOTES

1   *Religious Review of Reviews*, Vol. 2, No. 8, 1891.
2   Winston Churchill, *Great Contemporaries*, Odhams Press, 1937.
3   Cecil Roth, *Jewish Leaders 1750–1940*, Bloch Publishing, 1953.
4   Ibid.
5   James Douglas, *The Man in the Pulpit*, Methuen, 1905.
6   Jules Carlebach, *Second Chance*, JCB Mohr, 1989.
7   David Ceserani, *The Jewish Chronicle and Anglo-Jewry 1841–1991*, Cambridge University Press, 1994.
8   Raymond Apple, *The Hampstead Synagogue, 1892–1967*, Vallentine Mitchell, 1967.
9   Bernard Homa, *A Fortress in Anglo-Jewry*, Shapiro Vallentine, 1953, p. 73.
10   Julius Gould and Shaul Esh, *Jewish Life in Modern Britain*, 1964.
11   Albert Hyamson, *Jews' College 1855–1955*, Jews' College, 1955.
12   Ibid.
13   Homa, *A Fortress in Anglo-Jewry*.

14 Ibid.
15 Maurice Freedman, *A Minority in Britain*, Vallentine Mitchell, 1955.
16 Isidore Harris, *Jews' College Jubilee Volume*, Luzac & Co., 1906.
17 Ursula Henriques, *The Jews of South Wales*, University of Wales Press, 1993.

21   A Pause for the Balfour Declaration

The Seder service at Passover was the 'Last Supper' that Jesus was celebrating before his arrest and execution. It tells the story of the ten plagues with which the Almighty devastated Egypt and how the ruling Pharaoh finally had to let the Jews go to wander through the Sinai for 40 years before reaching the land of Israel. When the service eventually had to be held in exile after the expulsion of the Jews from the Holy Land, a small additional prayer was added. It just asked for, 'next year in Jerusalem'. A prayer that next year the exile, which started with the dispersion in 132, would be over. To return to the Holy Land was that important over the 18 centuries. For the Orthodox that was going to be the ultimate achievement, but it was only expected to occur when the end of the world was at hand, when the Messiah came, which isn't surprising since to recover a country after that many centuries, would appear to require a very great deal of divine help.

There were many steps on the road to the Jewish state which was declared in 1948. One of the most vital was the Balfour Declaration in 1917, the Foreign Secretary declaring that: 'His Majesty's Government views with favour the establishment of a National Home for the Jews in Palestine.'

Why on earth did the British government do that? No other government did anything similar. In 1914 when the Great War started, Palestine had been ruled by the Turks since Sultan Selim I defeated the Mamluks in the battle of Marj Dabik in 1516. The British had no say whatsoever in its government and nobody had suggested they should in the future. The nearest the British got to influence in Jerusalem was the appointment of the first Protestant Bishop, one Michael Alexander, who had previously been the minister of the Jewish congregation in Plymouth, and who had converted to Christianity.

If any European power held sway in the area it was the French. The Holy Land was linked by the Turks with Syria and it was the French who had built the Syrian railways and harbours, opened a university and provided capital for the economy's expansion. The

French wanted the Holy Land in their sphere of influence in the Middle East. The British didn't like that idea at all. At Fashoda in the Sudan in 1898 the British and the French had nearly come to blows over what belonged to whom. The French decided to withdraw at that point, but their *amour propre* was severely damaged. Don't bother to look for Fashoda on the map. Its name was diplomatically changed. Even if Britain and France were allies in the First World War, nobody on either side was certain that the entente cordiale would continue indefinitely when peace returned.

The situation changed when Turkey came into the war on Germany's side. Now it was recognized that the Turkish Empire would be split up if the Allies came out on top. Obviously the French would retain their claim to Syria but, as far as the British were concerned, if they got hold of the Holy Land as well, that would put them too close for comfort to Egypt and the Suez Canal. Protecting the Canal against all-comers was a key plank of British foreign policy as it was the route to India. Having an empty desert to its east, rather than French settlements, suited the British very well.

The allied powers tried to resolve their differences when the war started. A secret agreement was drawn up by the Russians, French and British in 1916 to divide up the Middle East after the end of hostilities, but in the Holy Land the British were only allocated the ports of Haifa and Acre. It was agreed that the rest of the country would be internationalized because of the worldwide interest in the holy sites. The settlement – the Sykes–Picot Agreement – was so-called because the British representative was Sir Mark Sykes and the French delegate was François-Georges Picot. The Zionists were not consulted or involved in any way. France would later claim that Syria included the Holy Land and was, therefore, in the French part of the pickings, but that argument wouldn't stand up at the Versailles Peace Conference in 1919.

On the face of it, it wasn't at all likely that Britain would support the idea of the Holy Land as a national home for the Jews. Herbert Asquith, Prime Minister from 1908–16, thought the idea fantastic, as it was. The idea of setting out to reoccupy a country after 1,800 years is the stuff of dreams, although in 1914 there were already 85,000 Jews in the Holy Land. There were also 600,000 Arabs. Most of the Jews were ultra-Orthodox, living there only to study the Talmud. They were supported financially by their brethren outside the country. Since the 1880s, however, about 35,000 Jews, mostly from eastern Europe, had come to colonize the land. 'Petty colonization' was not what Herzl had in mind, however, for the

Zionists had a much more ambitious agenda. Nevertheless, the Jews founded a few agricultural settlements, developed some vineyards with the help of the Rothschilds, and started to try to restore the desert to a land flowing with milk and honey.

In these endeavours, they were helped by many rich Jews, even though those same Jews may have disapproved strongly of Zionism as a movement. As mentioned earlier, the trouble with Zionism in their eyes was that it suggested the Jews should have their own country and were, therefore, not happy to be citizens of the one in which they had been born or settled. This ran totally counter to what Hermann Adler, for one, had been trying to promote for years. As he said in an article in 1878: 'We stand in the same relation to our countrymen as any other religious sect.'

Adler could justly claim that the Jews were persecuted around the world for being a different religion, not a different nationality. They converted over the centuries because they wanted to stop being persecuted because of their religion. Adler insisted: 'Since the destruction of the Temple and our dispersion, we no longer constitute a nation; we are a religious community.'

In fairness to Adler, that had been the perception of the Jewish authorities in Britain since the Resettlement. The lay leader of the American Jews took the same view. In 1907, Jacob Schiff said: 'speaking as an American, I cannot for a moment consider that one can be at the same time a true American and an honest adherent of the Zionist movement'.[1] Such was the opinion of a descendent of David Tevele Schiff and it would have been interesting to read a Responsum on the subject by the former Chief Rabbi. Jacob's great-grandfather might well have seen things differently.

Most of the Jewish leaders in Britain were anti-Zionist because they felt that their traducers could have a field day on the subject of a Jew's potential dual loyalty, which would immediately arise if the Zionists were successful. Zionism was seen as a self-inflicted wound, and a rod with which the anti-Semites could beat them. In 1914, out of a Jewish population of over 300,000, there were only 8,000 members of the Zionist Federation. In the whole world, out of well over 10 million Jews, there were only 130,000 members. The Jewish community, as a whole, didn't want to know.

Edward Montagu, who became Secretary for India, led the opposition in the House of Commons. Montagu was the son of Sir Samuel Montagu, who had created the very Orthodox Federation of Synagogues, but the apple had fallen a long way from the bough and the elegant aspirant to an honoured place in the British

Establishment was not interested in Orthodoxy. He didn't want the government to support a national home for the Jews and the government found it difficult to ignore the views of a Jewish member of their own Cabinet. Even when it was finally decided to make the statement, the original version had a sentence drafted by Montagu to reflect the antis' position. The declaration, it said, should not affect 'the rights and political status enjoyed in any other country by such Jews who are fully contented with their existing nationality and citizenship'.[2] When consulted on the final wording, the Chief Rabbi asked for this to be changed to 'the rights and political status enjoyed by Jews in any other country'.

That was what was finally agreed, but why did the government entertain the idea in the first place? Why could David Wolffsohn, Herzl's successor, say in 1911 'The Jews generally, and especially the Zionists, have more to thank England for than all the other powers put together'? Reasons for making the declaration have been suggested in plenty: that Lloyd George, the Prime Minister, had been brought up on the Bible and favoured a Jewish return to their ancestral home as an end to their sufferings; furthermore, that he didn't want to see the Holy Land in the hands of 'agnostic, atheistic France'. Others said he had a Jewish mistress. Another reason advanced was the debt Lloyd George and the country owed Chaim Weizmann, the Zionist leader. It was Weizmann, Reader in Biochemistry at Manchester University, who discovered a new way of making acetone, which made it easier to produce ammunition for the war. He was the director of the Admiralty laboratories from 1916 to 1919. Lloyd George actually said 'Acetate converted me to Zionism', but the Balfour Declaration couldn't surely just be a way of saying 'thank you' to Weizmann: 'The war years were not a time for sentimental gestures.'[3]

The fact was that Lloyd George was no stranger to the thinking of the Zionists. He had been introduced to Zionism as far back as 1903, when Balfour was the Conservative Prime Minister. Lloyd George was approached by Herzl to draw up a draft charter for the autonomous state for the Jews, which the Balfour government was considering offering them in East Africa. Why Lloyd George? He was only a lowly Liberal opposition MP at the time, but he was a partner in Lloyd George, Roberts & Co., Solicitors, and a coming man. The Zionists became his clients and in many lengthy discussions on the subject of the charter, he learned a tremendous amount about Zionism.

Lloyd George was also being lobbied, after the Turks came into the war, by the first Jewish member of a British Cabinet, Herbert Samuel. Samuel was a politician from the time he left university and, although a member of the Cousinhood, took no part in Jewish affairs. Edward Montagu was his cousin. Where Samuel stood on Zionism was unknown in 1914. What was also little known, however, was that his wife was a lifelong and intimate friend of Moses Gaster's wife, Leah. It was the Haham, a pillar of the Zionist movement, who first persuaded Samuel to take Zionism seriously.

Lloyd George did see similarities between the Welsh he loved and the ancient Israelites. After the Liberal's election victory in 1906 he said: 'For the first time, Wales has become one in the cause of Freedom, and the nation, like the Israelites of old, has commenced its march from the land of bondage, without leaving a single tribe behind.'[4]

Whatever Lloyd George's affinity for the ideals of Zionism might have been, as Prime Minister he was working on the agenda for which he had been appointed, which was to win the Great War. As with Cromwell's readmission of the Jews, the core reason for the government's proposed policy in Palestine was that it was likely to be in the best interests of Britain, which is what the government is – and always should be – about.

The position of Arthur Balfour, the Foreign Secretary, was also a factor. Balfour was not a Liberal, like Lloyd George. He was brought into the coalition government during the war in order that a united country could confront its enemies. Balfour was a great patriot and a great diplomat but he, too, had a guilt complex about the history of the Jews. As he said in 1916:

> Had Continental Europe followed the example set by this country for the last 250 years, its history would not be stained by many crimes and many injustices which now stand on record as a perpetual reproach to Christian civilization. That in this country there is no Jewish question...is due in no small measure to the fact that the Jews have shown themselves entirely worthy of the rights and privileges they enjoy as citizens of this country.

If the interests of the United Kingdom and the interests of the Jews were the same, then Balfour liked the idea of doing something to balance the Judaeo-Christian books. That opportunity came in the spring of 1916 when Britain and her allies stood a very good chance of losing the war. Wherever you looked, Germany and her supporters were winning. The Dardanelles campaign against the

Turks had been a disaster, the battles on the Western Front against the Germans had produced appalling casualties and the Russians were looking more and more like a beaten force. The cost of the war was ruining the country, the French were getting nowhere and the German blockade was biting.

The single event that could turn the tide was to bring the Americans in on the side of the allies. The problem was that the Americans weren't interested. Although there were plenty of them who were Anglophiles or Francophiles, there were also large numbers of German and Austrian immigrants who supported the opposition; and why risk having a lot of your youngsters killed in a war between European powers 3,000 miles away? How would that benefit the United States? In considerable desperation, the allied governments considered every possibility, no matter how remote, which might bring the Americans into the fold. One thought was that the American Jews might be able to influence President Wilson and his congress.

There was, again, just one major difficulty with this – the American Jews hated the Russians and with ample cause. Why then should they take sides with the allies? This led to an even wilder idea. What about suggesting a national home for the Jews in the Holy Land? Might not that tip the Jewish-American balance in favour of the allies? It was a thought.

As time went by, the situation for those allies worsened. In 1917 the Tsar was overthrown. A number of Jews took senior places in the new government. Now it was a question of whether the Kerensky regime could be persuaded not to make a separate peace with Germany. What might persuade the Russian Jewish politicians to vote to continue fighting for the allies? Zionism seemed an unlikely incentive. Most of the Jewish communists would have favoured another organization – the Russian Jewish Bund. This was created about the same time as the First Zionist Congress in 1897. It was anti-Zionist because its founders felt that Zionism distracted Jewish workers from the socialist revolution.

The declaration remained a possibility. As there was no time for a referendum and nobody had produced the results from any focus groups, everybody could voice their own opinion. Sykes, of the Sykes–Picot agreement, was given the job of advising the government. He talked to Samuel and Samuel put him on to Gaster. Not to an official spokesman for the Zionists but to his wife's friend's husband. Gaster, the dynamic communicator, went into overdrive to persuade Sykes that the impossible dream could become a reality. Gaster made the position, as he saw it, crystal clear: 'The claim to be Englishmen of the Jewish persuasion – that is English by nationality and Jewish by faith – is an absolute self-delusion. ' Most Jews remained deluded, but Sykes was converted to Zionism. He soon recognized, however, that the Zionists had sidelined Gaster and that the control of the organization was more with leaders like Weizmann. Furthermore, Gaster hoped for Anglo-German control of Palestine in the future, rather than Anglo-French, which was, naturally, not an option as far as the British were concerned. So Gaster having done the introductions, the others took over the negotiations. Balfour might get the credit for the Declaration, but it was Sykes who was its architect and when he died in the influenza epidemic in 1919, he was sincerely mourned in the Zionist ranks.

In Britain it was common knowledge that there was a minor pressure group, called the Zionists, who advocated that the Jews should go back to the Holy Land. There was also, however, a considerable body of opinion that thought the Zionists were a front movement for the Germans. After all, Herzl was born in Austro-Hungary, Weizmann was educated in Germany, and the movement's headquarters for many years had been in Berlin. As Haham Gaster had felt it necessary to say at the 11th Zionist congress in 1913: 'We are fighting everywhere to make it clear that we feel neither German, nor English, nor French, nor Russian, but that our feelings and thoughts are solely and exclusively Jewish.'

That was totally in line with what Cromwell and Charles II had accepted 250 years before, but the position of the Mahamad in 1664 had changed as the Jews became British citizens. Now the Haham's statement was the total antithesis of their current stance.

So what did the British Jews, as a whole, think about the idea of a Declaration? Lucien Wolf, the secretary of the Conjoint, who would be the AJA's foreign policy spokesman at the 1919 peace conference, summed up the position of most British Jews at the time: 'They [the Zionists] are all foreign Jews, bearing no quality to speak for the native Jews of the UK with whom, for the most part, they do not cooperate in the affairs of the community.' The answer from the heads of the two major lay bodies – the Board of Deputies and the Anglo-Jewish Association – was made clear in a letter to The Times, published on 24 May 1917. It was signed by David Alexander, KC, president of the Board of Deputies and Claude Montefiore, president of the Anglo-Jewish Association. Alexander was 'rigourously Orthodox and uncompromisingly assimilationist'.

He was a very senior barrister and the wording of the letter was carefully measured:

> 'the present claim is...part and parcel of a wider Zionist theory, which regards all the Jewish communities of the world as constituting one homeless nationality, incapable of complete social and political identification with the nations among whom they dwell and it is argued for this homeless nationality a political centre and an always available homeland in Palestine are necessary.

If this viewpoint were accepted: 'In the countries in which they [the Jews] are still struggling for equal rights they will find themselves hopelessly compromised, while in other countries where those rights have been secured, they would have great difficulty in defending them.'

Alexander and Montefiore didn't want it at any price. The only risk they took in voicing these sentiments was that neither president had a remit to put their view forward as the one held by the body they led. There had been no prior consultations. Only the Conjoint had agreed it by 12 votes to 2, the previous week. The Chief Rabbi was there but had no vote. He objected to the statement and walked out of the meeting. The letter was not even on the agenda of a Board of Deputies meeting held just four days before it appeared in *The Times*. This was typical of the treatment of Zionist motions over the past many years. Often they weren't debated or policy was decided at the top, discussions were guillotined on many occasions and a general boycott was frequently applied to the topic.

The Conjoint members were delegates for their two organizations but, in like vein, they did not report back for approval on such a vital matter. They obviously expected their parent bodies to rubber-stamp their decision – particularly if they didn't know about it until too late. What they ignored was that there was a new Lord Rothschild to be considered, as Hertz's mentor, Natty, had died. His son, Walter, didn't like being upstaged any more than his father would have. He wrote to *The Times* on 28 May, protesting: 'our opponents, although a mere fraction of the Jewish opinion of the world, seek to interfere in the wishes and aspirations of by far the larger mass of the Jewish people'.

Hertz also had his say:

> I cannot allow your readers to remain under the misconception that the said statement represents in the least the views held

either by Anglo-Jewry as a whole, or by the Jewries of the Overseas Dominions ... It is indeed grievously painful to me to write this in your influential columns. But I am impelled to do so in the interests of truth, and in justice to the communities of which I have the honour and privilege of being the spiritual head.

The community's strategic dirty linen was to be washed in public a lot more. On 29 May no less than 18 of the Jewish good and great backed up Alexander and Montefiore: 'we, being Jews of British birth and nationality [a dig at Hertz, who wasn't] actively engaged in public work in the Anglo-Jewish community, desire to state that we approve of, and associate ourselves with the statement ... published in *The Times* of the 24th inst.'

Faced with such conflicting opinions, the government finally decided to consult eight Jews on the subject, including the Chief Rabbi. The Chief Rabbi replied to their request for a view:

'It is with feelings of the profoundest gratification that I learn of the intention of H.M. government to lend its powerful support to the reestablishment in Palestine of a National Home for the Jewish people. The proposed declaration of H.M. government that it will use its best endeavours to facilitate the achievement of this object will mark an epoch in Jewish history. To millions of my brethren throughout the world, it will mean the realisation of Israel's undying hope of a Restoration – a hope that has been the spiritual lodestar of Israel's wanderings for the last 1800 years.

The draft declaration is in spirit and substance everything that could be desired. I welcome the reference to the civil and religious rights of the non-Jewish communities in Palestine ... the overwhelming majority of Anglo-Jewry, as well as the Jewries of His Majesty's Overseas Dominions, will rejoice with me at this broad humanity and far-sighted statesmanship of the men who guide the destinies of the Empire.[5]

If there was no consensus, the government now had an even freer hand to make up its own mind in the best interests of the state. Of all the contributors to the argument, however, the fact that both Rothschild and Hertz, the two most senior leaders of the British Jews – three if you count Gaster – made it clear that they did want the Declaration, reassured the government that the official voice of the community was in favour. Important as the Board of Deputies and the Anglo-Jewish Association were, much as their members controlled the community's religious purse-strings and institutions, they were not icons or the spiritual leaders of the community. Even so, the government was neither so much persuaded as grasping at straws. On that basis, Balfour made his famous, if fuzzy, declaration of British support for a national home.

The government issued the Declaration:

> His Majesty's government view with favour the establishment in Palestine of a home for the Jewish people, and will use their best endeavours to facilitate the achievement of this object, it being clearly understood that nothing shall be done which may prejudice the civil and religious rights of existing non-Jewish communities in Palestine, or the rights and political status enjoyed by Jews in any other country.

The results for the British government were disappointing. The Russians still pulled out of the war, the American Jews didn't have the influence the government had hoped for and the Declaration was a serious embarrassment to their post-war Middle East policy, because it upset the Arabs. Events such as the sinking of the *Lusitania* in 1915, with important American casualties, probably had more effect on President Wilson's decision to enter the conflict.

So much for the wishes of the influential Jews who were anti-Zionist. The Board of Deputies met again and voted by 56–51, with 6 abstentions, not to support their president's action, which substantially strengthened the view of the government. It might well be thought that this obviously meant that the Board of Deputies had a Zionist majority, but such was not the case. Many delegates specifically rejected any such idea. As Deputy Simon Rowson, who voted for the Zionist position, against the views in the letter, said: 'I sincerely hope the decision will not be strained to represent support for the principles of the Zionist organization.' There were probably no more than a dozen active Zionists on the board.

What the Board of Deputies did have was a majority of members who felt they should have been consulted before the president acted. It was the lack of consultation which swung the vote in favour of the Zionists. The provincial deputies had been complaining about unilateral decisions in London for years; nobody had paid much attention. Manchester hadn't forgotten Adler *vs* Schiller-Szenessy in the 1850s. Now the provinces finally had the opportunity of getting their own back and they seized it with alacrity. An analysis of the voting shows up the London/Provincial demarcation very clearly.[6]

The attendance at the meeting was very high. 143 deputies were entitled to vote and 113 did. The numbers who voted were the highest turnout since the board's formation 150 years before. Of the 67 new members elected since 1913, most voted against the old guard: 38–16 with 4 abstentions.

Geographically speaking, the split (figures *for* the president first) was:

London congregation deputies and Sephardim	22 : 4
London-based deputies representing provincial communities and overseas	23 : 18 – 1 abstention
Provincial deputies	<u>6 : 34 – 5 abstentions</u>
	51 : 56 – 6 abstentions

Thus, probably the most crucial vote in the history of the Board of Deputies, disavowing the president's opposition to the proposal known now as the Balfour Declaration, was narrowly passed because a large number of deputies were piqued at not having been asked their opinion yet again. Passed, not because of noble aspirations, not because of a far-sighted strategy, but because of pique.

The president fell on his sword and resigned. The Conjoint Foreign Committee, formed from both the Board and the AJA, was dissolved. Among those who voted for the president was Joseph Freedman, a member of the London Brondesbury Synagogue, representing the Chatham community. My maternal great-grandfather never told me what he had against Zionism.

At the peace conference in 1919 a petition signed by 77,000 asked the delegates to approve the Balfour Declaration. Another, half a million strong, asked President Wilson to support it. It was agreed. As the years went by, however, Hertz remained unimpressed by Britain's efforts to create the national home. As he said as early as 1929: 'The Mandatory Government has not only failed to try to implement the Balfour Declaration, but has tried to fail.'

Even so, the Declaration gave a terrific fillip to Zionism because it created the possibility that a totally unrealistic idea might, amazingly, come to fruition.

NOTES

1   Leonard Stein, *The Balfour Declaration*, Vallentine Mitchell, 1961.
2   Samuel Landman, *Essays Presented to Dr J.H. Hertz*, Chief Rabbi, Edward Goldston, 1942.
3   Stein, *The Balfour Declaration*.
4   O.K. Rabinowicz, 'Zionist–British negotiations in 1906', in *Essays Presented to Chief Rabbi Israel Brodie*, Soncino, 1967.
5   Landman, *Essays Presented to Dr J.H. Hertz*.
6   Stuart Cohen, *The Zionists and the Board of Deputies in 1917*, Jewish Journal of Sociology 1977/78.

Dr Joseph Herman Hertz was installed as Chief Rabbi in the Great Synagogue on 14 April 1913. On 30 June, just a couple of months later, he was speaking at the International Congress for the Suppression of the Traffic in Women and Children – the White Slave trade.

This was, on the face of it, a non-contentious subject. Everybody at the congress was against it, although the *Jewish Chronicle* in 1910 had severely criticized Jews who participated in it – and there were a considerable number of them. The brand new Chief Rabbi could well have been expected to be supportive, and slightly apologetic about the fact that a few members of his community did not have clean hands. If that was what the delegates expected, they were soon going to be disabused. Hertz intended to start as he meant to go on.

Everybody who counted had been invited: the Archbishop of Canterbury, the Cardinal Archbishop of Westminster, ambassadors, politicians and all the top movers and shakers. Speaker after speaker denounced the infamous trade and then came the Chief Rabbi's turn. Hertz stood up and started off in the approved manner: 'a pledge of utmost help... for the suppression of this new slave trade'

He then went on and clobbered the life out of the Russians. At the time, almost all the Jews in Russia were confined to a limited area of the country called the Pale. About 200,000 out of 5 million Jews – the rich, the merchants and the professionals – could live in cities like Moscow. Otherwise, the only Jews who could live anywhere they liked were Jewish prostitutes. If a Jewess wanted to go to a Russian university outside the Pale, she needed a Yellow Card. The Yellow Card was provided by the authorities and it registered her – as a prostitute. 'When they find that these students are merely honest women... they are summarily expelled. In recent months, however, the authorities have gone further, and insist that they should justify their Yellow Tickets'.

The Russians in the audience squirmed and this was, after all, a friendly country whose Tsar was the cousin of George V. Letters from Russian apologists to *The Times* in subsequent days protested that

Hertz had not been speaking the truth. Hertz wrote to *The Times* in reply and quoted the leader of the Russian Liberal Party in the parliament – the Duma – plus several reputable authors and the United States Immigration Report for 1892, page 42! The defenders of the Russians beat a hasty retreat and hoped the fuss would die down.

With Hertz, however, fusses seldom did die down. As the biblical prophets had rubbished under-performing kings, as Jacob Sasportas had torn into Sabbatei Tzevi, as Solomon Hirschell had denounced the Blood Libel in Damascus and as Hermann Adler had upbraided the Church for not speaking out universally against pogroms, so Hertz was quite prepared to continue in what was becoming again the grand old tradition. He attacked the Russian government but, like Hermann Adler, this time with the authority which went with being Chief Rabbi of the British Empire.

There were going to be a lot of battles during his ministry. The new challenges would include Liberal Judaism, Zionism, Nazism, two world wars and increasing assimilation. It was a formidable list but Hertz fought like a tiger to keep the Orthodox community's head above water. In all conscience, he did not lack critics, but when challenged on his combative nature, he often retorted that 'he never neglected the peaceful solution to any problem when all other means had failed'.[1] A more charitable assessment came from the most famous founding father of British Jewish historians, Cecil Roth. He wrote: 'A boundless courage and an inability to maintain a tactful silence in the face of wrongdoing.'[2]

That was absolutely correct. Hertz was no respecter of the good and the great and, if he believed his cause was just – which he always did – he waded in with all guns blazing. When, for example, after the Great War, the troops were demobbed and the dust was settling, it was decided that the former soldiers needed spiritual guidance after the horrors they had experienced. Hertz was asked by the United Synagogue honorary officers to give some sermons on the subject of readjustment. By this time, however, he had come to recognize the danger to the Orthodox position which the philosophy of Claude Montefiore and the Liberal synagogue posed. Montefiore wanted to end the animosities between Christians and Jews and, to do so, he was prepared to meet the Church halfway.

Sabbateians, Karaites, science and emancipation, had all posed threats over the centuries, but nobody since St Paul had come up with as poisoned a chalice for Orthodox Judaism as a rapprochement with Christianity. Convert or die, yes! But rapprochement! Hertz started to attack the Liberal movement in the series of sermons he called *The New Paths – Whither do They Lead?*

> In 1926, and again in the following year, the Chief Rabbi
> excoriated the Liberal movement in a series of homiletical
> tirades delivered from a number of prominent London pulpits.
> These sermons – virtual diatribes – were reproduced in the
> pages of the Jewish Chronicle.[3]

Hertz's view of the Jewish Liberal movement was that it was: 'that
German-American mutation of Judaism, which is a strange
compound of dry rationalism, irreverent criticism and empty
universalism'. The honorary officers of the United Synagogue were
not amused, but if Orthodox Judaism needed a fighting champion
for the next 30 years – and it did – it couldn't have chosen a better
one than Hertz.

He was born in 1872 in Slovakia, which was in the Austro-
Hungarian empire, but his parents emigrated when he was 11. His
father was a plum farmer but he also had *semicha* from the
Hildesheimer seminary. Hertz grew up on New York's East Side. The
Big Apple was definitely not a mirror image of Frankfurt or
Hanover. Hertz went to the City College in New York, got a
doctorate from Columbia in 1894, the same year he got *semicha*
from the Jewish Theological Seminary in New York. The JTS was
originally an Orthodox body and Hertz was the first graduate. Over
the years it very gradually moved away from strict Orthodoxy after
Solomon Schechter moved to the United States to lead it. The United
States Conservative Jewish movement emerged from this process. As
with the Reform movement, the drift from Orthodoxy took a very
long time. Until some years after Hertz's death, there were few
visible divergencies. As a consequence, Hertz remained a faithful
alumnus of the college all his life and gave it his warm support.

> Hertz was a short, broadly built man with a purposeful gait.
> His full beard did not hide his firm features or his genial smile
> among his many personal friends or when with young people.
> It was said of him that he had a brusque manner and kindly
> nature... Hertz [did not] always take adequate account of the
> limited value of abrasiveness as an instrument of communal
> debate.[4]

After JTS Hertz served, first, in Syracuse, New York, and then as
the minister of the Witwatersrand Old Hebrew Congregation in
Johannesburg. He was a prominent supporter of the British against
the Boers and fought hard for the removal of religious disabilities for

both Jews and Catholics, which led to the Boers deporting him in 1899. He went back in 1901 and married another Columbia alumnus, Rose Freed, in 1904. They had six children – three boys born in South Africa and three girls born in England. Rose Hertz was highly cultivated and always popular. She was a modern American girl and very conscious of current fashion. From 1906–08 Hertz was also Professor of Philosophy at Transvaal University and a Past District Grand Chaplain in the Masonic upper echelons. In 1911 he transferred to the Congregation Orach Hayim on the rich Upper East Side of Manhattan, and in his inaugural sermon he made his position very clear: 'I will be no hesitating or stammering witness to the truth [of Orthodox Judaism].'

Not surprisingly, because his pugnacious reputation preceded him, Hertz was not everybody's choice for Chief Rabbi of the British Empire when Hermann Adler died. Schechter, who was regarded in England as an Orthodox and revered teacher, gave him a glowing Jewish Theological Seminary recommendation, but there were other candidates. He was fortunate that he was the choice of Lord Milner, who had been Governor General in South Africa and had found Hertz's support for the British position during the Boer War very helpful; Lord Milner had a word in the ear of Lord Rothschild, and Rothschild laid down the law with the delegation of United Synagogue officers who came to inform him of their doubts about Hertz: 'I have made up my mind. The election will take place and unless Dr. Hertz is elected I shall resign the chairmanship of the United Synagogue.'

He then, quite literally, told a group of very distinguished officers of the United Synagogue to get out of his office. The delegation, their *amour propre* in tatters, decided, albeit with reluctance, that they couldn't fight City Hall; for a long time any heavyweight contests among the lay leaders had been conducted according to Lord Rothschild's Rules. Naturally, such cavalier behaviour gave plenty of ammunition to current and future critics.

As a foreigner – he became a British subject in 1915 – Hertz was considered likely to be more acceptable to the East End right-wing communities. He only spoke limited Yiddish but he wasn't part of the Cousinhood and was, therefore, more acceptable than Hermann Adler. Many members of right-wing synagogues transferred their membership to United Synagogue communities. In United Synagogue religious matters, of course, the Chief Rabbi was protected from ever taking second spiritual place by the constitution. Hertz's pre-eminence was also endorsed by the views of Lord

Rothschild himself. At the Chief Rabbi's installation Rothschild handed him a sefer torah and said: 'I give into your care and safe custody our ancient law and our religious guidance.'

Rothschild, like most of his predecessors in both the Sephardi and Ashkenazi communities, was prepared to leave religion to the rabbis. The idea that the lay leader and the Chief Rabbi would have fundamentally different spiritual outlooks was obviously extremely unlikely, until it happened, just a few years after Hertz's appointment.

In those intervening years the whole community had to survive the First World War. Jews joined up to fight loyally on both sides and produced both British and German heroes and casualties. The war memorials at Jewish cemeteries would eventually mark the thousands who died in the conflict. Comforting many of them as they waited to go into battle was Hertz's first literary effort, *A Book of Jewish Thoughts*, which was reprinted 20 times over the years. He visited the Western Front in 1915 and, on one occasion, visited Jewish soldiers accompanied by Sir John French, the commander in chief. His public image grew again. Among the Jewish chaplains to the forces was soon to be a young rabbi from Newcastle-on-Tyne, called Israel Brodie.

When the serious possibility arose that the government might issue a declaration favouring the Holy Land as a national home for the Jews, Hertz's position on Zionism became a crucial consideration. Hertz was an early Zionist and had held office in Zionist organizations in South Africa. On the other hand he was well aware of the antagonism felt toward the movement in Britain by the senior lay leaders. He had wanted to mend fences when he became Chief Rabbi and not exacerbate the tensions.

There was a major difference, however, between the theory of Zionism and the actuality of a possible favourable declaration by the British government. David Alexander, the president of the Board of Deputies, and Claude Montefiore for the Anglo-Jewish Association had written to *The Times* alleging the community's disassociation from the Zionists' objectives. There was no way that Hertz was going to let the founder of Liberal Judaism have the last word on behalf of the Chief Rabbi's flock. The time had come for Hertz to speak out and he supported the Zionist position.

Within five years of the start of his 30-year rule as Chief Rabbi, Hertz had shown that he was perfectly capable of taking on the Jewish establishment, if necessary, single-handed. He 'attacked the trend in Anglo-Jewry to "cringe and fawn" to those leaders. He called for an end of the "dictator parnass"... In some communities the Minister seems to have no rights which the laymen feel bound to respect.[5]

Whether his opposition reflected the example of the prophets, the suzerainty of the European rabbis in their ghettos, or just the independence of Uncle Sam's citizens, is a moot point. For whatever reason, if United Synagogue ministers found it difficult to 'challenge its masters' Hertz certainly did not. Not that he thought a great deal of the English religious scholars either.

> There are few departments of human endeavour to which modern Jewry has contributed fewer men than it has to Jewish learning... and whatever has been accomplished in this field, very little of it indeed has been done by Jews of English birth and training.[6]

Hertz came to realize that something had to be done about making Jewish learning more accessible and digestible to the community. He also wanted to defend the Written Law, which Montefiore's Liberals were attacking. He decided to undertake a monumental task; what became known as the Hertz *Chumash*. Each week a portion of the first five books of the Bible is read in synagogue on the Sabbath. The Hertz *Chumash* covers all five and the accompanying notes are drawn from a very large number of biblical scholars over the centuries, including some Christian ones, and even the ubiquitous Claude Montefiore. It was a little like the advertising for a new play; whatever the critic had said which was favourable, was included in the advertisement's wording. This aroused the ire of the right wing who felt that no endorsement was needed from non-Orthodox sources. They also questioned some of Hertz's views, and the arguments continue. What Hertz definitely achieved, however, was an explanation of what is in the five books which could be understood far better by the Jew in the street than anything that came before.

In addition, the powerful message of the book – there were five individual volumes initially but they were combined in 1938 – was to be that rabbinical Judaism, the Oral Law, was still 100 per cent valid. Without the rabbinical commentators referred to in its notes, Hertz held that the religion could not have continued to be a meaningful way of life. Without them, its teachings would have been permanently anchored in biblical times. Yet, after Hertz had graduated, this was where the Jewish Theological Seminary in New York had started to deviate. Hertz's insistence on the importance of

Bible instruction and Bible distribution aroused scorn in much of the community. 'I deliberately face ridicule and misrepresentation,' he said. Being Hertz, he stuck to his guns.

The problem with such an enterprise was its cost. Generous as the community was in looking after its poor, disabled and old people, it really didn't have much interest in rabbinics. Jews' College was always trying to survive on a pittance, efforts to raise money for Jewish education fell well below their targets and generous donors were few and far between. The financial problems of the *Chumash* were eventually resolved, due to Joseph Freedman, my great-grandfather, whom we last met voting for Alexander in the 1917 row over at the Board of Deputies. Freedman had started his business life as a pedlar in the valleys of South Wales and made his fortune in his later years out of the new-fangled concept of hire purchase. Now he decided that underwriting the book would be a nice memorial for his recently deceased wife. As a result, it was possible to sell the books for one-third of the correct cost.

The project was begun in the autumn of 1920 and the first volume, that of Genesis, came out in the spring of 1929. Although the work is always referred to as the Hertz *Chumash*, most of the initial research was done by a wide range of scholars, mostly British synagogue ministers. They were paid very little, they put in differing amounts of work – some very substantial – and they do not appear as joint authors, which aggravated a number of them. On the other hand they are warmly acknowledged in the Preface and Hertz merely describes himself as the editor of the Commentaries.

Hertz was not an easy man to work with on the project. Few authors enjoy having their work changed in the slightest and Hertz, commenting on the contribution of his collaborators in the Preface, says, 'they allowed me the widest editorial discretion. I have condensed or enlarged, recast or rewritten at will'. What emerged at the finish was a volume which continued to be one of the two standard books in the synagogue, unchallenged for 60 years, the other being Simeon Singer's Victorian prayer book.

It happened that, in later years, Hertz and Gaster did not always get on. Hertz was still in the driver's seat and Gaster was yesterday's man. As they both became more set in their ways, their tough personalities clashed. Gaster, who had produced his own Sephardi prayer book, wrote a particularly damning critique of the Hertz *Chumash*, excusing himself by quoting, inaccurately, the rabbinic instruction: 'Whenever the Divine Name is being profaned, honour must not be paid to one's teacher', which was more than a bit harsh on Hertz. Specifically, he labelled the *Chumash* 'dilettantism' and 'thoughtless sycophantism' and Hertz rightly considered the criticism a personal attack. As Gaster had been out of office for many years by that time, however, the condemnation had little effect. It was, nevertheless, a shame to see a falling-out of the two most senior rabbis, who had stood side-by-side to support Zionism against the massed ranks of the Jewish lay leadership during the war.

Hertz's treatment of the scholars who worked on the *Chumash* with him was typical of his normal approach. They knew that, in principle, he was in favour of working with them, supporting them and improving their lot. Hertz went all over the country visiting communities and was much respected. At the same time he did not produce a great team and his ministerial colleagues were, for the most part, not of a very high talmudic standard.

The immediate post-war period found the Russian Jews suffering massacres again during the Civil War. Between 1919 and 1920 a total of 250,000 Jews died in the Ukraine in nearly 900 pogroms. When Hertz spoke of such horrors, he reported: 'I have been met with surprised incredulity on the part of great ecclesiastics, statesmen, philanthropists and even leaders of our own community.' In 25 years' time there would be more incredulity at a 25-times higher cost; and before there were Holocaust deniers there were pogrom deniers.

On the home front *shechita* was under attack again. A Slaughtering of Animals Bill was introduced in Parliament and Hertz went into action once more. He quoted Lord Lister, a pillar of the medical establishment, as approving *shechita* and Dr W. M. Haffkine, of the Pasteur Institute who had said, 'The Jewish method not only guarantees that the animal suffers no pain but also prevents the spreading of microbes, and in this is a benefit to the human race.' The Bill didn't get very far.

The 1920s also saw Hertz fighting a major battle to save the seven-day week. A very well-endowed US pressure group decided that 51 seven-day and one eight-day week would be better for international commerce and trade. There was a real chance for years that they could get the League of Nations to vote for the idea. Calendar reform was an appalling prospect for Hertz because, if approved, the Sabbath would occur on different days of each week. He joined with other opponents of the scheme, including Cecil Roth, to stop it becoming law. Memorandas on the subject between them were: 'From CR to CR, re: CR.' It was 'The Battle of the Sabbath at Geneva' in the world's press and Hertz's work in this area earned him an international reputation. He organized a petition against the idea and managed to deliver a protest to the League of Nations signed by hundreds of thousands of Jews from all over the world. Eventually, the League rejected the idea after a rousing speech by the Chief Rabbi, whose reputation in all religious circles was enhanced as a result of it.

Hertz took his relationship with the right wing very seriously. He was hurt that 'the ultra-pious tolerate us' but he understood their thinking. One of the most powerful right-wing voices for many years was Rabbi Dr Victor Schonfeld, who created the right-wing Union of Orthodox Hebrew Congregations. Schonfeld's son, Solomon, married Hertz's daughter, Judith, and went on to become a powerful ally of the Chief Rabbi. He also took on the responsibility for improving right-wing Jewish education after the early death of his father in 1929. It is significant, therefore, that Victor Schonfeld said in 1925: 'I do not regard it [the United Synagogue] as a strictly Orthodox institution.'[7]

It wasn't an unreasonable viewpoint. Even Hertz, at a conference on Jewish education in 1919, was seen walking among the delegates without his head covered. As an Orthodox observer at the time commented: 'He had not yet asserted himself against the prevailing laxity.'[8]

In time, the younger Schonfeld, who had film star looks, would play the part of a real-life Scarlet Pimpernel. Until war was declared he continually visited Germany and Austria to try to arrange to get Jews out. It was Schonfeld who led a committee which arranged *Kindertransport*, trains which carried Jewish children out of German territory to safety in Britain. Alas, most of them would never see their families again but at least their own lives were saved.

If Hertz got on well enough with the right wing, the same could not be said of his relations with the lay leadership of the United Synagogue. From 1913 this was always likely to be Sir Robert Waley Cohen. Ever-present, an immensely hard worker, exceptionally well-organized and devoted to the institution.

Waley Cohen was a member in good standing of the Cousinhood. His grandfather, Louis, was a grandson of Levi Barent Cohen. His father, Natty, invented legal aid for the poor, labour exchanges and the Cambridge University Appointments Board. It was a family that had done much for Jewish and non-Jewish causes. As a scion of the Cousinhood, Waley Cohen was accustomed to having most people obey his wishes without question. If he couldn't order them to do so, he could often count on his colleagues having come from the same public school – the Jewish boarding house at Clifton College in Bristol. This was the only Jewish boarding house at a public school which stood the test of time – it managed to offer what Jewish parents wanted, that elusive mixture of Jewish practice and English culture.

Waley Cohen was also an immensely powerful industrialist, ranking about No. 3 in the hierarchy of the Shell Oil company, where he had been recruited at the very beginning of the company's life by the founder, Sir Marcus Samuel. Oil was probably the most ruthless international industry in the world at the time and Waley Cohen thrived in it. He earned his knighthood during the Great War by, among other things, organizing the immensely complicated oil and petrol supplies for the army and navy and for arranging an Inter-Allied Petroleum Council when the Americans entered the conflict. In reputation – and in stature – he was a giant.

A lot of those born into the Cousinhood families believed that their good fortune also involved responsibilities to the Jewish community. Busy as he was, Waley Cohen agreed to take on the office of treasurer of the United Synagogue in 1913, a position formerly held by his father-in-law. From then until his death in 1952 he was a senior honorary officer of the United. He was elected vice-president from 1918–42 and president from 1942–52. It was wondered at the time whether he spent more of his working life at the headquarters of the United Synagogue or in his office as managing director of Shell Transport and Trading, a couple of miles away.

Certainly, he was absolutely devoted to the United but, at the same time, his mother and many of his friends were members of the Reform synagogue. However, when Waley Cohen arrived on the scene the really major theological differences between Orthodox and Reform had yet to emerge. Waley Cohen never pretended for a moment that he was an observant Jew. By choice in 1917 in New York, he spent Yom Kippur at the Liberal Synagogue, Temple Emmanuel. 'I felt it more like an opera than a service...most beautiful and impressive.'⁹

His mother often took the children's services at Upper Berkeley Street but, concurrently, she kept a strictly kosher home. As a member of one of the very rich Jewish families, Sissy Waley Cohen was also highly regarded by Hermann Adler for her charitable work. The Cousinhood favoured the British 'live and let live' philosophy, so Waley Cohen's future desire to mend the breach between Orthodox and Reform, at the very least, reflected his filial love and family affection.

There were many battlegrounds on which Hertz and Waley Cohen waged war. One of the main causes of dissent was, inevitably, that Sir Robert didn't set a good example to the flock; a case in point was that, as a Cohen, he was one of those with the honour of blessing the synagogue congregation where he worshipped on the festival days. This he always tried to do – sometimes driving up from his farm in Somerset in the morning in order to be there on time, something no observant Jew would dream of doing. It was as if the president of the Golf Club was not above lifting his ball out of an inconvenient bunker.

Both Hertz and Waley Cohen were powerful personalities with ferocious tempers. At the same time, their differing areas of responsibility had been clearly defined in the original act of Parliament which created the United Synagogue: 'all matters connected with the religious administration of the United Synagogue and of its subsidiary charities shall be under the supervision and control of the Chief Rabbi'.

Waley Cohen often ignored this. For example, as mentioned earlier, he wanted to welcome the Reform movement back into the fold, irrespective of how far they had strayed from Orthodox practice. While Hertz was away visiting over 40 Jewish communities throughout the Empire in 1920–1, Waley Cohen – without consulting Hertz in advance – opened up negotiations with Claude Montefiore. He wanted to get more pupils for Jews' College by introducing a course for Reform students for the rabbinate. It would kill two birds with one stone; help the finances of Jews' College and achieve his objective of bringing the two warring parties together; Shell would have admired the commercial logic, even as others wondered how anybody could think the Chief Rabbi's position could be undermined with impunity, although it was true that the ex-minister of Upper Berkeley Street, Sir Philip Magnus, had been elected a vice-president of Jews' College in 1915. He would die holding that office in 1933, but the gap between Orthodoxy and Reform was still there. Montefiore, of course, also wanted the status for his Liberal movement which would have come from religious recognition by the Orthodox United Synagogue. Depending on your viewpoint, the gap would narrow or the wedge become thicker.

When Hertz returned home and found out what was happening, as might have been confidently expected by all but the most arrogant, his fury knew no bounds. Jews' College would have become a laughing stock in Orthodox circles around the world had it trained Reform students. He threatened to resign if the discussions didn't end immediately and Waley Cohen, the man whose word was law in Shell, had to back down. He recognized that if there was one thing neither his reputation nor that of the United Synagogue would ever be able to survive, it was the resignation of the Chief Rabbi of the British Empire on religious grounds.

But what was Waley Cohen doing interfering in the religious curriculum of the college in the first place? If the rabbinical seminary wasn't the responsibility of the Chief Rabbi, then the act was a dead letter. In the oil business at the time, however, a great many agreements were valid only so long as it wasn't advantageous to break them. That was the world in which Waley Cohen laboured throughout most of his working life.

Although no minister could be appointed to a United Synagogue without the Chief Rabbi's certificate, the choice of candidate remained with the individual congregation. Waley Cohen tried to ensure that there was a good choice for them. He dreamed of a new Oxford or Cambridge college which would train candidates for both Orthodox and Reform congregations before a period of study at Jews' College, so that they could all absorb secular as well as religious knowledge.

The problem was how to raise the money. Many large projects were proposed after the war to commemorate those who had fallen in battle. Hertz asked for £1 million for Jewish education, but even a powerful committee made up of the good and the great could only raise about 25 per cent of the amount needed. The necessary support was just not forthcoming and Waley Cohen had to be content with nurturing the Jews' College students. Many had good cause to be grateful to him for his paternalism and support. It meant, however, that Waley Cohen's concept of the ideal United Synagogue minister was some considerable distance from a yeshiva-trained talmudic scholar. Yeshivas did not have the time to cover secular curricula; remember there were 63 tractates of the Mishnah alone.

Anyway, the policy of the United Synagogue towards even cornerstones of Orthodoxy could be dismissive. Asked for financial assistance for a community's *mikveh*, the United Synagogue Council said it was not inclined 'to depart from the principle hitherto guiding the United Synagogue, viz: that it is no part of its function to provide or manage *mikvehs* for the London community'. The Din, in fact, is that if you're setting up a community, you provide the cemetery first, the *mikveh* second and the synagogue third. The United Synagogue would have taken the view that few women would use the *mikveh* now that they had their own bathrooms at home and that the money could be better spent in other ways.

United Synagogue ministers couldn't help a great deal. They were also the secretaries of their synagogues and too often occupied with the bureaucratic minutiae involved. As Hertz complained: 'Anglo-Jewish ministers haven't the time to study, like Continental Rabbis, or long holidays like Americans...the scandal of a miserably underpaid ministry must cease.' Hertz, however, would fight a long and basically unsuccessful battle to improve those salaries and also the funding for Jews' College. He complained that: 'Jews' College is still starved and beggared and without bursaries.'

Throughout the country, between the wars, Jewish ministers could be seen becoming even more like Church of England clerics. Not for nothing was the Reverend Isaac Livingstone in London known as the Vicar of Golders Green. Often treated without due deference by the elected lay leaders, Hertz protested against the ruling lay cliques, 'Democracy in the United Synagogue was a method of more conveniently getting your own way.'

Another major source of conflict between the Chief Rabbi and Waley Cohen was that the latter's greatest talent was as a negotiator with governments and of mergers between his and other oil companies. In the process of those, often protracted, negotiations, there had to be give and take. Intelligent compromise produced the desired results. Waley Cohen couldn't cope with a situation where there was no willingness to give and no room for compromise on the part of the Chief Rabbi.

As Waley Cohen was a tough and powerful man and accustomed to rule, it was fortunate for the future of the Orthodox community that he met his match in Hertz, although it got pretty desperate. By 1928 they were engaging in screaming matches at committee meetings. After one particular row, Waley Cohen wrote to Hertz: 'The last time we met I am afraid your – as it seemed to me – inexhaustible powers of destruction exceeded my far too limited patience.'

In reply, Hertz made his position abundantly clear. He did not even want to see the vice-president of the United Synagogue, his official employer, again:

> Unless and until you understand that the Chief Rabbi is the moral teacher and guide of the Community and not the bondsman of any one individual of the community. Threats and invective are of no avail to divert me from any course of action which I deem is dictated to me by conscience, self-respect or

considerations for the welfare of Judaism and Jewish people.

Relations deteriorated to such an extent that, eventually, representatives of both sides had to meet without the principals to try to reach agreements. What Hertz was up against was illustrated in the official biography of Waley Cohen by his relative, Robert Henriques, in 1966. 'The position of Chief Rabbi in Britain has always been very difficult to maintain, except by a high minded, broad-minded man of great personality able by his quality to win respect from all sections of the Community... Dr. Hertz was not one of them.'[10]

To win respect from all sections of the community has, of course, never been the Chief Rabbi's primary raison d'être. His first responsibility is to maintain the laws of Orthodox Judaism for future generations. In particular, he has no brief to win respect from Jews who fundamentally disagree with the tenets of Orthodox Judaism. Within his own community, even if he wanted to – which he didn't – he couldn't change fundamental laws single-handed to please those who found them inconvenient or spiritually questionable. It is worth repeating that to take such action would only have led to communities abroad rejecting the changes, and there is not a shadow of doubt that it would have isolated, and potentially delegitimized, his own members internationally.

From Waley Cohen's point of view, however, Hertz was a stubborn traditionalist who should have appreciated that his Elders in Britain knew best. Then again, Waley Cohen was initially no Zionist, and Hertz was. For Waley Cohen, Zionism raised that spectre of dual loyalty accusations and he was a very proud Englishman. Nevertheless, between the wars, Waley Cohen established the Palestine Corporation which initiated many commercial enterprises in the Holy Land and he also got agreement for the massive Haifa oil refinery to be built. Overall, there is no doubt that the two men brought out the worst in each other. Waley Cohen by patronising the Chief Rabbi and writing to him consistently like a schoolmaster correcting an essay. Hertz by taking offence at too many perceived slights and exhibiting a considerable degree of vanity. At the end of the day, however, the truth was that Waley Cohen had become accustomed to ruling his subordinates with a rod of iron where necessary and Hertz refused to play the designated role of employee.

Waley Cohen can, however, by no means be written off as a total disaster. He supervised the development of the United Synagogue, following the massive influx of Jews from 1880–1910, with skill and immense hard work. He ran the business with all the care and attention he devoted to Shell. He did support the Chief Rabbi on most occasions and he didn't allow anybody, except himself, to criticize Hertz.

Waley Cohen worked tirelessly against the Nazis. A senior member of a coterie called Focus, he was also instrumental in supporting Churchill financially when the future Prime Minister was out of office and in the political wilderness in the 1930s. Without Focus and Waley Cohen the problem of money could have crippled Churchill's efforts. On the one hand Churchill was, no doubt, grateful. On the other, he refused Waley Cohen's offer of help in any official capacity during the war; he might well have thought, however, that to give a role to the head of the United Synagogue would be grist to Joseph Goebbels' Nazi propaganda mill; there were still international neutrals to be won over before that could be achieved.

If the main battlefield for Waley Cohen and Hertz was on the question of the importance of religious observance, they still worked together harmoniously in many other areas. Synagogue education classes, *kashrut* and helping the Jews in Germany were just three examples. It is, perhaps, too little appreciated that 70 per cent of the Jews in Germany managed to get out of the country before the war. The combined efforts of Jewish communities around the world achieved the miraculous logistical result of finding other countries to take in 350,000 of the original 500,000 Jewish German population.[11]

Fifty thousand came to Britain, including 10,000 children given visas at nearly the last minute in late 1938. In still difficult economic times, the government was able to assure the voters that no public money would be needed to absorb the immigrants, who would be financially supported by the Jewish community. Any number of Jewish families agreed to take one or more children into their homes, where they stayed till they grew up. The Chief Rabbi's Religious Emergency Council kept an eye on them and also undertook to find jobs for refugee rabbis.

The six million Jewish victims of the Holocaust would almost totally consume the other European Jewish communities. Ironically, they suffered because they were in no danger in their homelands until the Nazis struck.

The effect of the threat of Nazism was also to draw the various Jewish communities together in mutual defence. Outright fascism did have some support in Britain and the effect of the snobbishness in British society circles was easily translated into mildly anti-Semitic acts. As the Caterer magazine said in an article on the application of a colour bar in a five-star London hotel in 1925, 'After all, we have known both American and English people to leave moderate size hotels because of the acceptance of Jews, and the latter being given tables in the dining room in the immediate vicinity.'[12]

The ability of a Jew to take his seat in the House of Commons didn't mean that he could also take his seat in a snobbish restaurant or in the boardroom of a lot of companies. There were many firms who would never have dreamt of appointing a Jew as a director. The professions were hardly better: well after the Second World War it was difficult for Jewish medicine graduates to get accepted by the best teaching hospitals and many of the best law firms wouldn't offer Jews Articles. Socially, many golf clubs and tennis clubs had quotas or outright bans. British anti-Semitism was a hydra with many heads, even if none of them was venomous. Faced with a raft of minor discriminatory practices and barriers, echoes of some of which continue to this day, British Jews still knew they were well-off compared to their co-religionists in other countries.

There was another result of discrimination by commercial companies. If you couldn't get a job because of your religion, the only alternative was to go into business on your own. Many of the Jewish pedlars ended up founding major companies – John Cohen and Tesco being only one of the more prominent examples. If the higher echelons of High Street banks were closed to Jews, the merchant banks were often founded by Jews. As, of course, had been companies like ICI, Harland & Wolf the shipbuilders, and Lyons. Discrimination did many Jews a favour because it forced them to strike out on their own. It went all the way down to a lot of Jews becoming independent London taxi drivers.

Anti-Semitism might have existed but, even at its peak, the British Union of Fascists never won a single seat in the House of Commons. In the election of 1931 they polled 36,000 votes, the communists 75,000 and the national government 14.5 million. Britain still didn't do extremism. The BUF's largest meeting was at Olympia in London in 1934 when the brutality with which the stewards manhandled hecklers seriously alarmed the government. Stanley Baldwin, the deputy prime minister, had sent one of his MPs to the rally as an observer of this two-year-old movement. He got an anguished report:

I could not help shuddering at the thought of this vile bitterness, copied from foreign lands, being brought into the centre of England. I came to the conclusion that Mosley was a political maniac and that all decent people must combine to kill his movement.

Bernard Levin, the distinguished *Times* journalist, summed up the situation prevailing at the time, when he wrote many years later: 'Decent society in those days was filled with people who had forgotten what anti-Semitism *had* led to, and who could not guess what it *would* lead to.'

For empires to be successful, they have to prove their superiority in battle. They have to defeat their enemies. The upper classes in Britain wanted to prove the superiority of their own institutions as well, and the Jews proved very useful to them. This was because it is almost impossible to maintain the superiority of your club if nobody wants to join it. To be exclusive there has to be somebody to turn down, to blackball, to refuse to acknowledge as good enough. The Jews were ideal for this role and when, eventually, it had to be agreed that they were as acceptable as anybody else, it became necessary to find alternative groups to take their place – colour bars slowly took the place of anti-Semitism. And where the Sephardim had looked down on the Ashkenazim in London in the seventeenth century, so the Ashkenazim would look down on the Sephardim in Israel in the twentieth century. There is, however, all the difference in the world between petty discrimination and massacre. The difficulty is to get people to realize that from the former can easily come the latter – big trees do grow from little acorns.

William Inge, the Dean of St Paul's, was one who could glimpse what would happen. In 1933 he spoke in the pulpit about the new anti-Semitic measures which Hitler, since his election as chancellor, had introduced in Germany. Inge was reported as making a point which Hitler might have reflected upon in the ruins of Berlin in 1945. 'Why the German government should behave in that strange manner he could not even guess. It was foolish as well as wrong, for the Jews had stood by the graves of all their oppressors in turn.'[13] But then it could be said that Zachariah (4:6) had given Hitler the same warning in the Bible: 'Not by might, not by power, but by my spirit, saieth the Lord of Hosts.'

The government acted early in 1937. It passed the Public Order Act. This banned uniforms and it gave the police powers to ban marches. Of even more importance, the government quietly agreed with the BBC that Sir Oswald Mosley, the BUF leader, should never be allowed to broadcast on the radio again. By 1939 membership of the movement had halved. The ban lasted until 1968. Shorn of their publicity, the BUF were, effectively, destroyed as a political movement.

As the recognition of the danger posed by Hitler to the Jews in Germany sank in, Waley Cohen wanted to produce a comprehensive and co-ordinated response throughout the community. This had to include all the divisions of British Jewry and it soon did. Ecumenicalism was, indeed, the flavour of a lot longer than the month. A lot of people wanted a 'fraternization' of all religious communities to create a better environment for working together. Hertz pointed out that: 'a veritable mania for religious "fraternization" is about, that can only bring down the contempt of clear-thinking men on Anglo-Jewry'.[14] The contrary argument was: 'A cry commonly heard was that the Chief Rabbi and the Beth Din had fallen into the hands of the "Ultras" who were exerting in consequence an influence that their numbers alone did not warrant.'[15]

It reached a point where an Anglican bishop was being installed and a representative was invited from among the Jewish clerics. At the end of the service, the Jewish minister said to the canon of the cathedral that it had been a wonderful discourse by the bishop and he could have preached the same sermon, word for word. The canon commented dryly, 'then either you have lapsed into heresy or we have'.

Hertz also recognized the need for co-operation, but felt there was little sense in working together as Jews if it involved sacrificing Jewish observance. He would then be betraying his office and the right wing would become the only flag bearers for the Orthodox approach.

The 1930s brought much personal sadness to Hertz. His wife, Rose, died in 1930 and he lost his son, Dr. Daniel Hertz, at the tragically early age of 26 in 1936. In the same year there also passed into history the Hambro synagogue, which closed its doors as its remaining members rejoined the congregation of the Great after 230 years.

Even with all the theological disputations, the relationship between the Jewish communities between the wars was far more cordial than it was to become later. For much of Hertz's ministry the gap between United Synagogue members and the Reform movement had not widened greatly since 1840. Violently as Hertz attacked the views of Claude Montefiore in public, the two remained on good terms. When visiting Montefiore for tea with Rose Hertz, the Liberal leader warned him: 'Tell it not in Gath, Dr. Hertz, but the milk is not supervised!'[16] So there were even rare occasions when they would occupy each others pulpits and sometimes conduct joint services. In 1934 Hertz was the guest of honour at the opening of the extension to the Upper Berkeley Street synagogue. He said in the pulpit:

> I feel that my presence here requires some words in explanation. It is certainly not due to the fact that I dismiss the religious issues that led to the formation of this synagogue 94 years ago as of trifling importance. I am the last person in the world to minimize the significance of religious difference in Jewry. If I have nevertheless decided to be with you this morning, it is because of my conviction that far more calamitous than religious difference in Jewry is religious indifference in Jewry.

Hertz, together with senior rabbis from the Reform and Liberal synagogues consecrated the new Cambridge University synagogue together as late as 1937. Each conducted an element of the service, sat together and prayed together. Indeed, they were on good terms. When Rabbi Leslie Edgar for the Liberals had completed his part of the proceedings, he returned to his seat next to Hertz. The Chief Rabbi shook his hand, as is the custom, and said to him, 'I didn't know you could speak Hebrew!'[17]

The two major factors which would eventually make the greatest difference were, first, the arrival of Rabbi Harold Reinhart from the United States in 1928. Second, Reform moved much further away from Orthodoxy with the immigration of a large number of German-Jewish Reform refugees in the 1930s, who were accustomed to a far greater emphasis on personal choice in the practice of their faith.

The counter-balance, which divided the community even more, was the arrival of similar numbers of the very Orthodox from Germany, Austria and Czechoslovakia. Unlike the British Jewish community, which had been able to jog along together in a spirit of middle-of-the-road English compromise, the two sides in Germany had been at each other's spiritual throats for nearly a century. The hegemony of the Anglo-Jewish approach was now under threat from both the United States and Europe.

Typical of the Orthodox rabbinic opposition to reform was Rabbi Yechezkel Abramsky who was appointed a Dayan of Hertz's Beth Din. It is easy to assume that modern rabbis lived sheltered lives, spending most of their time in dealing with the minutiae of the Din, and out of touch with the challenges of the modern day. Abramsky's experiences were very different. He was imprisoned by the Russian government and the American, President Hoover, intervened with the Russians to get him released. Stalin allowed him to emigrate, but would only agree to his taking two of his four sons with him. The condition for allowing the others to leave was that Abramsky invented a fifth. That man would be a Russian agent who could work as a spy in Britain under an alias. Abramsky refused to agree to this and, when he came to London, it was arranged that the leader of the Labour Party, George Lansbury, would intervene, together with a minister at the Foreign Office, the future Prime Minister, Anthony Eden. Their joint efforts were successful and the other two sons were granted permits to emigrate as well. Abramsky knew the real world.

One effect of the centralist approach, of Hermann Adler's English minister rather than learned rabbi, was that few great scholars had emerged from the ranks of Jewish ministers or from Jewish graduates at Jews' College. There were no Poseks to compare to men like Abramsky, and a Posek is there to state the law, not to find ways of compromising it. Abramsky set out to tighten up the rulings. The view took hold, for example, that, 'The time has come to restrict . . . the limits within which "matrimonial" conversions shall be permitted.'

To many one of the great attractions of the progressive congregations remained that it was much easier for a partner in a marriage to get converted to Judaism within those communities. As already mentioned, about two per cent of the marriages in the Great Synagogue in the late eighteenth and early nineteenth centuries involved converted partners, but each application involved the same fundamental question. Did the convert believe in the validity of Judaism or did they want to make their partner happy? If the latter, then conversion was not permitted. For the Orthodox, to change your religion was strictly a question of faith and not of matrimonial felicity. The two communities set out along fundamentally different roads and went their separate ways.

Hertz led the community during the Second World War, while the third world war continued to be waged between the Chief Rabbi and Waley Cohen. The biggest furore centred around the Jewish education of evacuated children. Waley Cohen saw this as an opportunity to infiltrate the Liberal Synagogue into a commanding position. He ingenuously suggested that a new committee was needed to tackle the problem as the United Synagogue and the Board of Deputies were too busy. Such a body to consider 'the Future of Institutional Judaism' was proposed – without the Chief Rabbi being asked to attend the meeting – and the chair nominated was – Lily Montagu, founder of the Liberal Synagogue! At the time 75 per cent of the community were Orthodox and Waley Cohen wanted the education of their children to be decided by a committee headed by the foremost Liberal.

Not surprisingly, Hertz blew his top again. How Waley Cohen ever thought he'd get away with such a stratagem can only be explained by an overwhelming arrogance. The Chief Rabbi quickly arranged with the government to set up his own National Council for Jewish Religious Education and then he didn't invite any of the honorary officers of the United Synagogue to become members of it. When, in May 1941, Frank Samuel, a vice-president and future president, asked why not, Hertz told him quite frankly that, in his view, none of them would have replied to an invitation without Waley Cohen's permission:

> the self-appointed dictator in Jewish religious education. I could not invite him because he is inimical to Traditional Judaism... Far more so, for example, than the late C.G. Montefiore, who was open and above board in his attacks on Orthodox Judaism.

And Waley Cohen was supposed to be on the Orthodox side. The Chief Rabbi then went on to make some additional comments on the president of the United Synagogue's style of leadership:

> He is incurably wedded to the Hitler technique, with outbursts of shouting and abuse, whenever he does not get his own totalitarian ways... No-one who was present will ever forget the fury with which Sir Robert greeted... my proposal to make Kosher provisions for evacuee children.[18]

Ironically, the only wartime job that Waley Cohen was given by the government was to advise them on *kashrut*!

Hertz remained in control of the efforts to provide Jewish education for the community. He also comforted the mourners and visited bombed synagogues. On 10 May 1941 the Great Synagogue was destroyed. After more than 200 years the centre of Ashkenazi Judaism was no more. Admittedly, as Jews in the East End left for the leafier suburbs of London, the Great was becoming isolated from the mainstream but it was still held in great affection.

Twice a year, at the New Year and Passover, Hertz broadcast to the community – and the wider world. In April 1942 he spoke at the time of Passover. His voice was Oxford English with a slight Brooklyn burr and the impact gained much from the Churchill school of delivery. For a 70-year-old, the voice remained very forceful, and it needed to be, because his theme was the correct Jewish attitude towards the Germans after the war. It was appropriate for Passover because on all the other festivals the service includes a number of joyous prayers. On Passover only half of them are said. Why so little joy when celebrating the deliverance from Egypt? Because a lot of Egyptians died in the Red Sea. Orthodox Jews mourn the Egyptians, not just those of their own faith who died when enslaved in Egypt. Why the ruling? Because the Egyptians were God's creatures as well. It was, therefore, right to be sorry for them.

Hertz spoke to a community which knew that thousands of Jews were being murdered in the concentration camps, who had lost their own loved ones in the Blitz, and who had every reason to hate everything German with an intense passion. He told them that the atrocities committed by the Nazis: '[did] not justify vengeance on the whole German Nation . . . Wholesale condemnation would be irrational.' Hertz pleaded for understanding and patience: 'remedies being proverbially slower than diseases'. When the Italian Prime Minister in 2003 told a critical German MEP in a television programme that he would have made an ideal concentration camp guard, he obviously hadn't heeded the message of the broadcast. Hertz in 1942 took the positive step, in conjunction with the Archbishop of Canterbury, William Temple, of creating the Council of Christians and Jews to further improve relations between the communities.

After the setback on his education committee, Waley Cohen continued to take every opportunity he could to create a broad Church, which would include the progressive movement as well as the Orthodox. A major row erupted when the Senior Jewish Chaplain to the Forces, Dayan Gollop, fell seriously ill in 1943. It was necessary to appoint someone to act for him in his absence. Jewish Chaplaincy matters came under a committee appointed by Hertz, called the Jewish War-Services committee. This was chaired by Waley Cohen who said that Gollop had suggested that Rabbi Edgar, the Liberal chaplain, should act for him until he had recovered. Why Dayan Gollop should have said any such thing when there were 18 Orthodox chaplains in England at the time, and Edgar was a junior officer and the only Liberal, remains unclear. After all, Hertz pointed out, 97 per cent of the Jews serving in the forces were

Orthodox. As Edgar then started to sign his letters 'Acting for the Senior Jewish Chaplain', it meant that a chaplain representing a minute proportion of the community would be seen to have a very senior role, and that the Chief Rabbi considered him a suitable, if temporary, replacement for the senior Jewish chaplain. The legitimacy that Hertz would be seen to give to the Liberal movement was precisely what he had been fighting against for 20 years.

Hertz heard of the appointment when he read the *Jewish Chronicle* – he had not been consulted – and rejected it. At a meeting of the Jewish War-Services Committee, he was only supported by the right-wing representative. Hertz made it clear, however, that he would dissolve the Committee and act on his own if that were necessary. Waley Cohen had to back down again and Israel Brodie, the First World War chaplain, an Orthodox Rabbi and a future Chief Rabbi, was soon appointed to replace Dayan Gollop permanently.

Perhaps the saddest example of the bitter feuding between Waley Cohen and Hertz occurred in 1945 when Hertz asked the Jewish ministers to preach a sermon in synagogue, pleading for the Jewish survivors of concentration camps to be allowed to obtain refuge in the Holy Land. When he heard of it, Waley Cohen sent out telegrams to the United Synagogue ministers, ordering them to do no such thing. He considered that such a plea would be 'introducing politics into the synagogue' and he was furious that Hertz had not consulted the honorary officers of the United Synagogue before coming to a decision.

By today's standards, Waley Cohen's behaviour is scarcely credible. The newsreel pictures of the horribly emaciated survivors of the camps, with mounds of unburied human remains behind them, had been the most appalling image of pure barbarism most people had ever seen. Common humanity demanded a home for the wretched remnant who were still dying from the effects of malnutrition, tuberculosis, dysentery and the like. How could the dignity of the United Synagogue honorary officers take precedence over the plea of the Chief Rabbi?

Nothing is that simple. The Jewish lay leadership still trod warily. They thought that discussions with ministers in private might be more productive than hoping the government would succumb to public pressure. The situation in Palestine resembled the conditions which existed in Northern Ireland for so many years. Patriots/terrorists – depending, as always, on your outlook – killing and being killed by the authority – which in this case was Britain. The Jewish lay leadership was concerned about an anti-Semitic backlash in their back yard. They didn't want to give anti-Semitic propagandists anything to feed on. They were pragmatic where Hertz was emotional, but if ever emotion could be excused it was at that time.

After 30 years the relations between the lay and spiritual heads of the community had sunk to an all-time low. Waley Cohen could say in his defence that he was being entirely traditionalist. He believed, as had the Mahamad in the seventeenth century, that Jews should support the government through thick and thin. It was a freer country two centuries later, however, and the right to oppose your government without fear or favour is a key element of democracy. After the decades of intermittent conflict between the two: 'gradually Sir Robert had come to personify all the various tendencies in Anglo-Jewry which Dr. Hertz had most feared'.[19]

Certainly, it was spiteful of Waley Cohen to use his power to humiliate the Chief Rabbi. Hertz was now 73 years old and an approving king had appointed him a Companion of Honour in 1943. The order is restricted to only 65 holders and is a very signal recognition of eminence. If Waley Cohen didn't rate the Chief Rabbi, the government certainly did. Hertz died in 1946 at the age of 74.

What did Hertz achieve over 33 years? As Lord Rothschild had instructed him in 1913, he kept the ancient law in safe custody. He stopped Waley Cohen sabotaging the United Synagogue's position as a bulwark of Orthodox practice. He ensured that Orthodox Judaism would continue to be home for at least 75 per cent of the British Jewish community. In this he completely reversed the American experience, where Orthodoxy became as much a minority sect, as Reform and Liberal Jews remained in Britain. If Hertz hadn't prevented Waley Cohen and Montefiore from introducing the Reform syllabus into Jews' College in 1921, it is likely that the Reform theology would eventually have become acceptable within the United Synagogue. Having drawn up the battle lines at that point, Hertz never surrendered a scrap of Orthodox ground in later years. He was up against one of the ablest and most powerful businessmen in international commerce and, like Horatio, he held the bridge.

NOTES

1   The comment is often attributed to Rev. Ephraim Levine, but the Hertz family say that the Chief Rabbi coined the phrase first.

2   Cecil Roth, *Essays and Portraits in Anglo-Jewish History*, Jewish Publication Society of America, 1962.
3   Harvey Meirovich, *A Vindication of Judaism*, Jewish Theological Seminary of America, 1998.
4   Israel Finestein, *New Dictionary of National Biography*, Oxford University Press.
5   Joseph Hertz, *Sermons, Addresses and Speeches*, Vol. 2, p. 204.
6   Ibid.
7   Homa, *Footprints on the Sands of Time*, n.p., 1990.
8   Ibid.
9   Robert Henriques, *Sir Robert Waley Cohen*, Secker & Warburg, 1966.
10   Ibid.
11   W.D. Rubinstein, *A History of the Jews in the English-Speaking World*, Macmillan, 1996.
12   *Caterer & Hotelkeeper*, February 1925.
13   *Jewish Chronicle*, 5 May 1933.
14   Hertz, *Sermons, Addresses and Speeches*.
15   Newman, *The United Synagogue*.
16   Hertz, Sermons, *Addresses and Speeches*.
17   Rabbi Edgar in conversation with the author.
18   Letters from Chief Rabbi Hertz in the United Synagogue Archives in the London Metropolitan Archives.
19   Aubrey Newman, *The United Synagogue*, Routledge & Kegan Paul, 1976.

23　Israel Brodie 1948–65

Israel Brodie was only the second Chief Rabbi to be born in England; his birthplace was Newcastle-on-Tyne in 1895. Like Hermann Adler and Joseph Hertz before him, he became very much part of the British establishment, but his origins were far humbler than those of Nathan Marcus Adler's son. He was the second of the five children of Aaron and Sheina Brodie. His father was a pedlar, selling sponges in Newcastle. Father Brodie had come from Kovno in Lithuania about 1890 and Brodie always said he was half Kovno and half Oxford.

The boy was taught Hebrew and Talmud both before and after school, and then went on to Jews' College at the age of 17. By now, taking the course meant he was automatically enrolled at University College, London and in 1915 he got his BA in Hebrew, Syriac and Arabic. He also won a scholarship to Balliol at Oxford, a college whose alumni Prime Minister Herbert Asquith characterized, when he referred to 'the tranquil consciousness of effortless superiority which is the mark of a Balliol man'. Brodie never acted as if he thought he was in that league, but some of the prestige of being at Oxford would have bolstered his confidence in the years to come.

Although he was exempt from military service as a theology student, Brodie wanted to do his bit and became the youngest chaplain to the forces in 1917. He was sent to France and remained there till 1919. He was to be one of only three Jewish clergymen who were chaplains in both world wars. After the guns fell silent he went back to Balliol to finish his studies and got his *semicha* in 1923 from Jews' College when he was 28 years old.

He went on to do a lot of work with the clubs set up in the East End to provide social centres for young Jews. One of those most deeply involved in the pastoral work of the East End was a local minister called John Stern, whose synagogue was one of the largest in the area. Stern said of Brodie: 'He has shown that a minister could exercise very great influence if he came into close touch with the young people.'

Soon after this Brodie agreed to serve as rabbi to the Melbourne community in Australia, where his ability as a fine hazan was very much enjoyed. He was a witty man. At a farewell dinner on leaving for Australia he commented 'Judging by some of the accounts I have received about Melbourne, it is like the Red Heifer [a biblical reference to the basis of a key element in *kashrut*] – there is no blemish in it.' But, in fact, the average level of observance in Australia at the time was not very high and Brodie decided he had to take a stand; he refused to attend any function where the food wasn't kosher. On one famous occasion, assured that all was well and that the meal would be fish, he did accept the invitation. The waiter came up to him during the banquet and said, 'Sorry sir, but the oysters are off.' The rabbi replied 'So am I' and left.[1]

Brodie grew to be highly regarded in the wider community in Australia. In Freemasonry, for example, he reached the high rank of district grand officer. Back in Britain he would eventually be appointed a past grand chaplain in the English Grand Lodge.

Brodie came home to Britain in 1937 and took a part-time post as lecturer in Homiletics (preaching) at Jews' College. He was, indeed, an inspiring speaker as well as a great hazan. He invariably spoke extempore, and he could move a congregation to tears. He had a strong, mellifluous voice and his thickset frame with a large black beard commanded respect. His future wife always addressed him as 'Chief Rabbi' in public, producing the affectionate suggestion from his equal as a speaker, Reverend Ephraim Levine, that in bed she probably said, 'Chief Rabbi, would you mind turning over.'

Clerics do not, automatically, take everything in life seriously. Ephy Levine, a Cambridge man from Jesus College, for example, loved playing the horses. Talking to Brodie one day, he explained his philosophical position: 'If you can keep two days for Festivals, I can keep four days for Goodwood.'[2]

A typical example of Brodie's skill in the pulpit was the sermon he gave as Chief Rabbi on the occasion of the centenary of the London Board of Jewish Religious Education. The Central Synagogue was packed that night and the procession was led by a phalanx of rabbis whose appearance was indistinguishable from the Victorian portraits that hung on the walls of the synagogue conference room; top hats, morning coats cut square at the back in the nineteenth century manner, and razor creases in the trousers.

They marched in with the precision of the Brigade of Guards and made their stately way through the synagogue. The ceremonial was typical of Britain at its best. It was, therefore, a much needed reassurance to those who saw the prospect of imminent assimilation looming up that, when the procession reached the pulpit area, its members had no idea where they were supposed to sit. Everything stopped in traditional Jewish organised chaos as they milled gently round in circles, while a harassed minor official in a bowler hat that had seen better days, rushed up to try to sort them out, Many of the congregation breathed a small sigh of relief.

Brodie never used a note and this enabled him to hold his congregation's unwavering attention. He spoke that night of visiting a concentration camp after the war. The pathetic survivors of the Holocaust remained in the camp as they had nowhere to go. Some passed the time by learning modern Hebrew. As they gathered round the blackboard on the parade ground, Brodie could see the class was learning the future tense in *loshen kodesh*. On it was written: 'I *will* go to Israel. You *will* go to Israel. He *will* go to Israel.' There wasn't a dry eye in the house.

During the Second World War he had become a chaplain again. Once more he was sent to France and was evacuated from the Dunkirk beaches in that epic rescue of the British Expeditionary Force in 1940. Later, in the Middle East, he switched from the army to the Air Force with the rank of Squadron Leader. At the time Jews weren't permitted to pilot RAF aircraft – probably the government was anticipating the danger they might pose after the war in an Israeli air force – but Brodie got the rule changed. He was a dignified man with great presence and an establishment manner. With all this, plus his official clerical dog collar and his Oxford antecedents, he was persona grata in any officers' mess. After time with the RAF he went back to the army with the rank of Lieutenant Colonel. In March 1944 he took over from Dayan Gollop as senior Jewish chaplain to the forces and was in Germany for the final stages of the war. That was when he visited the concentration camp at Belsen. He was mentioned in dispatches and remained the senior Jewish chaplain until 1948.

Brodie returned to Jews' College after the war. It was still a comparatively small centre of learning after nearly 100 years. In the 27 years between 1926 and 1953 there were only 114 students in all, but 48 of them took ministries thereafter and many a Jewish congregation benefited greatly. One change which made a great difference was the appointment of Rabbi Kopul Kahana to take the *semicha* stream. Kahana was a refugee who arrived in Cambridge not speaking a word of English. He was short, nondescript and he had thick, pebble glasses. He also had a colossal brain and soon took a degree in English literature at the university. In his first year at

Jews' College, 18 students applied for the *semicha* course, of whom 15 were already ministers. By 1947 there were 30 *semicha* students. Kahana went on to train a considerable number of the present rabbunim in Britain and the Commonwealth.

When Hertz died in 1946 Brodie became a candidate for the Chief Rabbinate. He was English, he was impeccably Orthodox, a Balliol man with a distinguished war record and overseas empire experience in Australia. He had an excellent rapport with young people, a new wife in his old friend Fanny Levine, whom he married in 1946 at the age of 51, and he was a stunning speaker. If you asked for anything more, he was entirely acceptable to the British government. This was even more important than usual, for the British were the mandatory power in the Holy Land, struggling with insoluble problems.

The lay power in British Jewry remained in the hands of Sir Robert Waley Cohen, still president of the United Synagogue and vice-president of the Board of Deputies. He was in a sufficiently influential position that he would, effectively, be able to choose the next Chief Rabbi. If he regretted the passing of the old chief, he was unlikely to remember with much pleasure his working relationship with the spiritual head of the community. In choosing a successor to Hertz, the ageing Waley Cohen was definitely looking for a quieter life. So was everybody else after six years of war. Brodie fitted that bill and he was appointed Chief Rabbi in May 1948 to general acclaim, even if it was agreed for the first time that there would be a retiring date for his period in office.

Waley Cohen died in 1952 and was replaced by, first, Frank Samuel and then Ewen Montagu; the Cousinhood still supported the institution their ancestors had helped create. The two presidents got on very well with the Chief Rabbi and there were few areas of disagreement.

Brodie was, above all, a safe pair of hands. He knew when to put his foot down on specifics and when to be less abrasive, but he walked a tightrope. In June 1950, for example, he was given the opportunity to speak on South African radio and the temptation to denounce apartheid would have been difficult to resist. It would, however, have also affected the delicate relationship between the South African Jews and the South African government, and nothing would have changed. Brodie, diplomatically, kept right out of trouble: 'I earnestly pray that all who love their country and believe in its greater destiny, will be inspired with wisdom and judgement – supported by the spirit of religion – to tackle and solve those problems and so win the approbation of heaven.'

Presumably, such approbation was accepted as lying many years in the future. In 1963 the future looked as bleak as ever but, in an overseas broadcast, Brodie now followed up Harold Macmillan's 'Winds of Change' speech to the South African Parliament. The Prime Minister had warned that things had to alter in South Africa and Brodie had the opportunity to lay it on the line as well: 'Policies of segregation, apartheid and anti-Semitism could never be consistent with those human and spiritual values which some countries declare the standards by which they are guided.' The time would come when the future South African Chief Rabbi, Cyril Harris, one of Kahana's pupils, would be able to be even more positive.

Brodie took office when the relations of the Jewish community with the mass of the population were at their most sensitive since the Resettlement 300 years earlier. The years before Israel's emergence as a separate state in 1948, after the end of the British mandate, were marked by killing on both sides. British troops were often caught in the crossfire between Jews and Arabs and suffered casualties as well. On occasions, they were the targets of one side or the other. Pictures of British sergeants/oppressors killed by Jews in retaliation for Jewish terrorists/patriots executed by the British, made for gruesome newspaper front pages. Whatever you labelled them, the victims of the violence were often indisputably dead. Along with local Arab freedom fighters/extremists. The largest casualties occurred when Jews blew up the British military base in the King David Hotel in Jerusalem. The death toll, compared to the Holocaust, was infinitesimal but that was little comfort to the mourners. The editor of the *Jewish Chronicle*, Ivan Greenberg, supported and excused the Jewish extremists, so that the majority of the directors concluded that the: 'presentation of news was frequently lacking in objectivity... had ceased to be an independent forum for the expression of all shades of opinion'[3] and eventually fired him.

Even under such extreme provocation, the vast majority of the British public remained totally tolerant to its Jewish minority. The only rioting was over the August Bank Holiday weekend in 1947: 'Although no one was injured, crowds of youths destroyed and looted Jewish-owned property, synagogues were attacked and cemeteries were desecrated.'[4]

Britain's interests in Arab oil were naturally greater than its commitment to the Balfour Declaration. Britain was trying to recover from the devastating effects, economically and structurally, of the war. It simply could not afford to be a nanny for a fledgling Jewish state, when Middle East companies, like Iraq Petroleum, were British-run but potentially subject to nationalization. The oil industry was a vital part of Britain's fragile economy and, from that point of view, the need for the mandatory power to ensure fair play between the Jews and the Arabs in Palestine was an embarrassment.

What the anti-Zionists had most feared before the Balfour Declaration was now coming true; the question was being asked whether the Jewish community in Britain was loyal to the United Kingdom or loyal to its co-religionists in the Holy Land. The truth was that the overwhelming majority were totally loyal to both, which worked perfectly well as long as the two were allies. Nobody questioned Winston Churchill's loyalty because he had an American mother; America was our ally. On the other hand, a large number of Germans and Italians had been interned during the war because their loyalty was suspect, even though many of them had been in Britain for 30 years or more.

In 1946 the Jews in Palestine were not allies of the British mandatory government. The single most serious source of contention was the immigration of Jews into the country, particularly those remnants of the slaughtered who languished, effectively stateless, in the liberated concentration camps. The British wouldn't let them emigrate to Palestine because the Arabs would be incensed and revolt. They still considered Palestine their country because they had lived there in those centuries since the Jews had been expelled by the Romans. The idea that the Jews, with the support of the West, could come back and play a part in running the country after more than 1,500 years, seemed grossly unfair, and the bigger the Jewish population, the more likely it was to happen. If you take out the religious aspect, nobody is in favour of giving Britain back to Italy because of the Roman Conquest, or to France because of the Norman Conquest.

Of course, you cannot remove the religious aspect but, in Brodie's early years as Chief Rabbi, the newspapers had a field day, with lurid stories coming out of Palestine on a regular basis. One of the most heartbreaking was a rust tub of a ship called the Exodus which had illegally brought hundreds of extermination camp survivors to Palestine and then wasn't allowed to dock. The world's press was there in force as fruitless negotiations continued. Eventually, the ship was sent back to Germany.

In 1965 Brodie recalled his own encounter with the passengers when they had been returned to a former concentration camp. They were battered, bowed, but still demanding to be allowed to follow the Din:

> I visited the notorious camp outside Lubeck in Germany and came across those men, women and children who had been on the ship, Exodus, had been turned back from Palestine and were transferred to an awful place in a hated country. In the camp they agitated for a *mikveh*.[5]

The British reaction at home to the casualties inflicted by Jews far away, remained restrained in the extreme. It was normally confined to the occasional act of vandalism. For instance, the smashing of a large window in a dress shop in London's Oxford Street, in protest. There was a frisson of horror in the community because there had been a lot of window breaking of Jewish premises by the Nazis in Germany before the war. Except that the Oxford Street shop wasn't actually owned by a Jew – vandalism and intelligence are often complete strangers to each other. Otherwise the British were stoic; the whole Western world had been stunned by the horrors of the Holocaust and there was immense goodwill toward the Jewish survivors. There was also, however, the rule of international law and the need to keep order in a steadily more volatile situation in Palestine.

When the British finally gave up the mandate as a thoroughly bad job and left Palestine in May 1948, the Jews faced no less than five, fully armed, invading Arab armies; Egypt, Syria, Transjordan, Lebanon and Iraq attacked on all fronts. If that didn't make for a sufficiently one-sided fight, all the major arms-exporting nations of the world embargoed the sale of weapons to both the Arab and Jewish sides; except the Arabs had the weapons they needed already!

The Jews won against all the odds. If there was a single reason, the Jews had their backs to the sea and knew what they were fighting for. The Arab armies were poorly led and didn't care overmuch. One of the results of the war was that 500,000 out of 750,000 Arabs fled the Holy Land and when they arrived in the neighbouring Arab countries, they were put into refugee camps where most of their families still are today. Why did they flee? Sir Mark Sykes, creator of the wording of the Balfour Declaration died in 1919 but his son, Christopher Sykes, had a distinguished career in the British Foreign Office and became an author. His book *Crossroads to Israel*, published in 1959, offers an unbiased view. Sykes says that there were atrocities on both sides. The Jews spoke little about them but: 'the Arab radio-propaganda dwelt on atrocity stories and exaggerated them ... the aim was to inflame men with hatred of the

Jews; the effect was to fill them with terror of the Jews.'⁶ The Zionists were, obviously, pleased the Arabs fled but where the Arabs had good leaders, their communities stayed and were unharmed. This was particularly true in towns like Nazareth where the mayor kept the people in the town together.

In Haifa, on the other hand, the Jewish mayor tried to get the Arabs to stay and the Arab National Committee said they: 'proudly asked for the evacuation of the Arabs and their removal to the neighbouring Arab countries'.⁷ Unfortunately, the help provided to Jewish communities over the centuries by their brethren was not the policy followed by the Arab nations. As attempts were made to rewrite history in later years, it was stated by Arab apologists that the National Committee had not rejected Jewish overtures. If they had not, a huge amount of human misery could have been avoided, because the Arabs who remained were not in any physical danger from the infant state.

Israel also came into existence as the result of a vote in the United Nations approving it. The Holocaust led to a majority vote in favour, which would have been impossible under any other circumstances. Enough countries decided to recognize the state of Israel for the Jews to regain control of the Holy Land after 1,900 years. Strictly Catholic countries voted in favour. Historic enemies of the Jews, like Russia, voted in favour. Countries which had never had a Jewish community voted in favour. The total horror of the Holocaust moved the world to pity for a downtrodden minority for just long enough.

Thus, Israel was established and Britain stopped suffering casualties from Jewish guns and bombs. The loyalty of the British community ceased to be an issue, if it ever had been. Brodie was later invited to the coronation of Elizabeth II. Of more importance to the British left-wing government now was the fact that the party in power in Israel was Labour and the collective farms, the kibbutzim, were the finest examples available of pure socialist ideals; Marx and Lenin would have been proud of them.

On the question of dual loyalty Brodie was the perfect image for the community; still half Kovno and half Oxford. Twice a year, before Passover and the New Year, like Hertz, he was invited to broadcast by the BBC. His audience would not be confined to his own co-religionists as, to all intents and purposes, would be the case in the pulpit or in the Jewish press. He would be speaking to anybody who had the radio on. His broadcasts started in 1948 with relations between Britain and the Jews of Palestine at their nadir, and were well received. As the years went by Brodie tended to slip into his talks the case for the loyalty of British Jews to the crown. For example, in an overseas broadcast in September 1950 he said 'I hope I will be heard by our sons who are serving in His Majesty's Forces Overseas.'

As in the Napoleonic and Boer Wars, as in 1914–18 and 1939–45, the allegiance of British Jews to the United Kingdom was there for all to see; it just needed highlighting on occasions. In the same broadcast he attacked on his other front; the denigration and false accusations which came from the tiny minority of anti-Semites in the country. On this occasion Brodie dealt with the stereotyping of Jews as only interested in money.

> To me it is a matter of great rejoicing...that there are hundreds of thousands who are prepared...to leave factory, shop, office, study, laboratory or studio for a period in order to dwell in the courts of the Lord...moreover, most people are not self-employed, and real sacrifice in pay and risk of loss of employment are sometimes involved...despite the usual suggestions which are made that the Jew is exclusively addicted to material gain, so many of the House of Israel testify practically that the things of the spirit still have sway over their lives.

It was true. In the time of the five and a half day week, most organizations worked on Saturday morning. To be excused to go to synagogue meant breaking the terms and conditions of employment. Where the bosses were not prepared to do so, the organization was effectively out of bounds to an Orthodox Jew. This still applied to literally thousands of companies.

It also applied to Jewish MPs who visited their constituencies and talked to their electors on Saturday morning at 'surgeries'. The Brodies had no children but the Chief Rabbi's niece, Myra Janner, had married Greville Janner, now Lord Janner. When Janner became an MP in 1970, after Brodie had retired, he talked to Brodie about the problems of a Jewish MP in serving his constituents and his faith. The Din is that you should do your very best to serve both God and your country. Ideally, a Jewish MP would attend service and then hold the surgery, without breaking the Sabbath rules. The emphasis on correct behaviour in the outside world is certainly no trivial matter. There is a rule, for example, that if you earn all your living from gambling, you can't be a member of a *minyan*. Ten good men and true constitute a *minyan* and you debar yourself by that way of life.

Making allowances for others was often possible within the Din, but it had its limits. In the wider world the recognition that the Holocaust was the appalling result of anti-Semitism had come home to the Church with sickening force. Devout Christians had enthusiastically supported the massacres of Jews during the Crusades, approved of the Inquisition and put up with the pogroms, but nothing could begin to justify the Final Solution. Appalled, the Church of England rallied round the Council of Christians and Jews and, in 1956, the organization received the patronage of the queen. Brodie, in speaking to the Council, often emphasized two points; first, that *parents* must have the right to teach their children their religion, rather than a non-Jewish school. Second, that any religious body would be treated with courtesy in Israel. In fact, the Church, throughout the Middle East, didn't always find that to be the case.

In 1956 the Archbishop of Canterbury gave a garden party for 1,000 guests in Lambeth Palace to mark the tercentenary of the Resettlement. Chief Rabbis, Archbishops and Cardinals would, hence-forth, be firm friends, united against the flood of indifference which was beginning to affect the membership of all religions. As Brodie said at the party: 'Anglo-Jewish history of the past 300 years affords a distinctive example of the growth of the spirit and practice of toleration in England during the period.'

So it did. It was during the tercentenary celebrations that a dinner was held at the Guildhall and the Duke of Edinburgh represented the queen. In giving the toast to Her Majesty's ministers, Brodie expressed the community's gratitude for the way in which it had been treated over the 300 years. He quoted a circular from Palmerston to British consuls at the time of the Smyrna blood libel in 1841, as typical of the British attitude to the Jews:

> Whenever a case is brought to your knowledge in which Jews resident within your district should have been subject to oppression or injustice, you will make a diligent enquiry...and will report fully thereupon to Her Majesty's Ambassador at Constantinople...Upon any suitable occasion you will make known to the local authorities that the British Government feels an interest in the welfare of the Jews in general, and is anxious that they should be protected from oppression.

Of course, that was typical Palmerston. In threatening Greece when the authorities had roughed up a Gibraltan Jew called Don Pacifico, Palmerston delivered himself in the House of Commons in 1850 of the classic British position on all the citizens of the Empire.

Like the Romans, it was 'Civis Romanus sum'. In this regard, Palmerston was quite prepared to make the Jews all over the world the equivalent of British citizens. As an apposite quotation for the tercentenary, it was, perhaps, a trifle excessive but it went down very well at the Guildhall; as did Brodie's comments on the Jewish contribution to the country: 'The sons and grandsons of emigrants... have made notable contributions in industry, in the arts and sciences: they have vied with their fellow citizens in the display of civic virtues in the time of peace and war.'

The creation of Israel, however, raised a question which had not been relevant for 2,000 years. What was the the role of the Diaspora – the Jews outside Israel – to be in the future? Did they have a role? Naturally, their financial support for the infant state would be very welcome but, equally obviously, they would have no say in the country's political agenda; they had no votes to influence the Israeli government but their support, under all circumstances, could be counted on, as Israel looked down the gun barrels of enemies on every side. The Arab armies might have retreated but none had suggested a peace agreement. In those conditions, a policy of support for Israel, right or wrong, was inevitable among the vast majority in the Diaspora communities. It's invariably the same whenever war threatens. If the government in Britain decided in the future to fight in the Falklands or Kuwait, the Opposition would come onside.

Brodie's generation of Diaspora Jews was now in limbo. The Israeli position was that the Jews should now emigrate. Israel needed a larger population to develop the country and *aliyah* was the answer. In the 20 years after 1948 about 10,000 British Jews did leave for Israel, but the vast majority were perfectly happy as British citizens. As their ancestors had always protested, they loved Britain, believed in its way of life and would support it through thick and thin. If their religion was of paramount importance, their support for their local football club, the MCC, their university, old school, trade association, political party and neighbourhood mattered to them as well. They remained 100 per cent British and in a nation that was going to become more and more multi-ethnic, this position became steadily more acceptable.

Brodie had too much experience of war to be blinkered to the needs of only his own community. War is no respecter of religious or ethnic backgrounds. In 1949, when there were few blacks living in Britain, Brodie flatly laid down the Jewish law: 'the continued discrimination against fellow-citizens on the grounds of colour, race and creed... disturb our trust in the reality of the charters, declarations and treaties to which governments have formally and solemnly assented'.

That was Judaism at its best, fighting for the underdog because the equality of man was the Almighty's law. Whatever happened, no matter how the powerful might bridle, even if there was no benefit of any sort for the Jews, for Brodie the Din was the Din was the Din.

The relations of the government with Brodie were invariably extremely cordial. In 1958, for example, when the Slaughter of Animals Act came into being, Brodie was appointed permanent chair of the Rabbinical Commission. It took a lot to affect that relationship on Brodie's side, but there were limits again. What was guaranteed to arouse the ire of every Chief Rabbi were cases of Jewish children being separated from their parents and then brought up as Christians. The Mortara case in Victorian times had been an example. Now, in 1949 there were much larger problems, as many Jewish children were refugees, had lost their parents in the Holocaust and were being looked after by non-Jewish organizations. Brodie wrote in the *Jewish Chronicle*: 'Jews in this country were painfully surprised at the extraordinarily negative position taken up by the representatives of the United Kingdom.'

Did the Foreign Office do enough? Did they care enough? It had been generally accepted by the community since the 1920s that the Foreign Office was on the Arab side because of the oil. The halcyon days of Palmerston always being prepared to go on the warpath for persecuted Jews around the world, were difficult to maintain when you ceased to be a major power. The truth was that the Foreign Office was on the British side and would, one must hope, have been fired had they not been. The huge amount of human debris left in Europe after the war was horrifying and heartbreaking. The sheer size of the problems was always likely to lead to accusations of negative thinking and individual obstruction, but Brodie's job was to try to get the problems of the Jewish children further up the priority list and he worked hard at it. At least, unlike the days of the Restoration, he could attack the government without fear of the consequences, but the downside was he didn't have the advantage now of being able to call on the monarch and get it sorted that way.

Of course, in the Cold War the interests of the government and the Chief Rabbi often coincided, as the case for the superiority of democracy was fought in the world's media against the opposing claims of communism. One occasion was the accusation brought against a number of Russian Jewish doctors in 1952 that they were plotting against Stalin. Brodie broadcast on the European service of the BBC in January 1953: 'It is idle sophistication, born of fear and quibble, for apologists for Communism to maintain that the reference to their Jewish origin of those now accused in Moscow of murder and treason...[has] nothing to do with anti-Semitism.' Fortunately, Stalin died and the accusations were dropped.

If he proclaimed the British position as impeccable, Brodie was to have his concerns about the new state of Israel. The problem was that the behaviour of a small nation state, surrounded by enemies, was unlikely to always measure up to the ethical demands of the religion. The stall had been set out by Israel's first Prime Minister, David Ben Gurion, in 1948 and it led to hopes being raised which were extremely difficult to fulfil:

> The State of Israel will be based on the precepts of liberty, justice and peace taught by the Hebrew Prophets, will uphold the full social and political equality of its citizens, without distinction of race, creed or sex, and will guarantee full freedom of conscience, worship, education and culture.

It was a little like Hertz broadcasting in 1942 that the whole German nation shouldn't be held responsible for the behaviour of the Nazis; correct, but a tall order, particularly in the years to come in Israel when the community had to deal with the intifadas. That it became almost the only – and certainly the most – democratic state in the Middle East, was admirable, but the spiritual belief that it could achieve political and ethical perfection, become a nonpareil among nations, was asking an awful lot. On the radio in 1955 Brodie said:

> We hope to see more from Israel than the normal practice and policies based on the possible, the expedient, the relatively moral – characteristic of many other nations, great and small...
>
> It is understandable where the people of the Bible are concerned, that Israel should be measured by strict prophetic standards and by messianic idealism...Here is a literally heaven-sent opportunity to work out to the full the implications of the comprehensive rules of social conduct and righteousness which are demanded by Judaism.'

Brodie could see the core problem in all this very clearly:

> The Israelites when established in their own country, were required to treat the alien who sought to settle among them with justice and with love...They [the Jews] ought to know the

feelings of degradation which filled the hearts of men treated with contempt and cruelty.

Fifty years later the modus vivendi of both Arabs and Jews living together in the Holy Land would still need to be fully worked out, but institutions such as the Supreme Court and the Knesset (Parliament) in Israel would always ensure that the rule of democratic law prevailed.

Many eminent rabbis fled the Nazis before the war and brought their scholarship to Britain. Some joined the United Synagogue and a few became Dayanim. In Hertz's time their totally Orthodox views hardly came into contact with the easygoing nature of the United Synagogue communities. The European Orthodox leaders were happy just to settle in a safe country and Hertz controlled his religious colleagues very firmly.

After the war, when Brodie was appointed, the situation started to change. The very Orthodox Dayanim had the responsibility for enforcing the law and they started to do so in the correct minute detail and in some delicate and contentious areas. The most sensitive was conversion and those who wanted to convert to Orthodoxy when they married a Jewish partner found it almost impossible. The rules of *shechita* were tightened as well. The community, as a whole, began a long journey towards a more Orthodox, a more right-wing, approach.

For generations the level of observance had been slowly declining. The immigrants from the Pale of Russia had been very *frum*. Their children and grandchildren, however, had abandoned many of the rules. These were the days when if a key football match at Highbury or White Hart Lane took place on Yom Kippur, you could see swathes of season ticket holders' seats empty. They were filled on the Sabbath, however.

As was to be expected, Brodie was accused by the progressive movement of being a puppet in the hands of his Dayanim. It was true that Brodie seldom used his authority to overrule their decisions, but then he was just as Orthodox as they were. When the jockeying for a new Chief Rabbi was at its height, the Orthodox Federation of Synagogues said they would like to take part, and only withdrew when their own nominee wasn't on the short-list of candidates. Their official reason was that they believed the Chief Rabbi should be bound by the decisions of the Beth Din. If there was a crunch, however, the Chief Rabbi had always been independent of that body and the rules didn't change.

Certainly, there was a great gulf growing between the United Synagogue and the progressive movement. What had begun in the West London Synagogue of British Jews a century before as relatively minor differences in the application of the Oral Law, had now developed into the wholesale abandonment of much of traditional Judaism as irrelevant in 'modern' post-war times. If there had ever been any chance of the two communities coming together again, they were hopelessly compromised now. Naturally, members of each community had friends within the other, but the Orthodox spiritual leaders had their roots in the right wing.

It was only natural that the Reform and Liberal Jews would resent the attitude of the Orthodox authorities. One area of contention was the need to have the Chief Rabbi's approval for a Liberal synagogue to be able to issue Marriage Certificates under the 1835 Act. Following pressure from Waley Cohen, Hertz had given his approval to the main Liberal synagogue in London in 1935 and the one in Liverpool in 1939. At the time the Chief Rabbi of Ireland wrote of his disquiet. The future Chief Rabbi of Israel wrote:

> The certificate which the President of the Deputies [the actual authority came from the Board of Deputies on the advice of the Chief Rabbi] issues to the government authorities is the Certificate of the Board of Deputies, which means the certificate of Anglo-Jewry. It would be testifying that marriages which are prohibited by the Law of Torah are in accordance with Jewish law and usage!

The problem was finally resolved by the Liberals getting an Act of Parliament in 1959 authorizing them to issue certificates, as the breakaway synagogue had done in 1856.

The accusation against the Orthodox by the Reform was that Orthodoxy was totally concerned with ritualistic practices. Nothing annoyed Brodie more. The point about the law was that the Orthodox *mitzvoth* were indivisible. There was no ranking, no priorities; it was no more and no less important to the Orthodox to help the poor than it was to put on tephilin every weekday morning. You couldn't eat dishes containing milk and meat and you couldn't abuse your children. It was the law, not a series of pious hopes.

Within the Orthodox community a new challenge was the need to come to grips with the growth of feminism. That Judaism valued its women every bit as much as its men was, of course, easily proved by the fact that it was the status of the mother rather than the father which decided whether a baby was actually Jewish or not. The popular image of the Jewish mother ruling the roost was an affectionate recognition of her importance in the home. It was true, however, that the woman's place in running the synagogue was limited normally to producing the flowers or the refreshments. In 1954 the first step to changing this came when it was decided that a woman who was a member in her own right, should have a vote in the elections for the synagogue board of management. Progress was to be a very slow process but, in non-spiritual settings, women eventually won total equality and Jo Wagerman would be elected president of the Board of Deputies at the end of the century.

The yeshiva the very Orthodox immigrants had set up before the war in Gateshead was flourishing. In that small industrial town a powerhouse of talmudic study had slowly emerged. In time it would produce many more rabbis than Jews' College, and the very orthodox would become a far larger percentage of the Jewish population in the country. This was, in part, a question of demographics. The Jewish community, as a whole, was increasingly middle-class and the two-child family was becoming more normal than the eight- or ten-child unit which characterized earlier days. The middle-classes started to have difficulty in reproducing themselves and, as more married out of the religion, the total numbers in the Orthodox community declined.

In contrast, the very Orthodox had a strong wish to raise large families. They were motivated by the law that parents should continue to have children until they had at least one of each sex; some religious authorities said two of each sex. Even more pressing than that, they were absolutely determined that the intention of the Final Solution should be thwarted. Within their capabilities, they wanted to replace the six million Jews who had been massacred. Large families was the answer.

The Gateshead yeshiva could count on Brodie's support. Among other reasons, it was just down the road from where he was born. He got a fund started to support it financially and, like so many religious bodies, that was very necessary. The students in Gateshead, no matter how long they stay, believe their job is to study and uphold the Torah and everybody else's job is to uphold them. Wherever there is a Jewish district, there is likely to be a gentleman with a long beard and a continental accent outside your door, raising money for a yeshiva somewhere in the world on a Sunday morning. You may not know the organization, your receipt may be somewhat indecipherable to non-Hebrew speakers, but you know your contribution will be going to a good cause.

Brodie might have preferred the future spiritual leaders of the community to come from the graduates of Jews' College; after all, that was his alma mater. Under Rabbi Isidore Epstein it was in safe academic hands and Brodie made sure that diploma classes were continued to enable graduates to get *semicha*. The community, however, continued to be niggardly in its support for the institution. When the centenary of the college was celebrated in 1955, Brodie was less than sanguine about the prospects:

> Were we to have a continuation of the chronic apathy, the niggardly common yawn...the spate of carping criticism and puerile suggestions which created difficulties and anxieties which harried – but did not wear down – the devoted band of illustrious men who administered the affairs of the College over the last hundred years? [Jews' College critics] confidently predicate our apathy and stagnation, and surely predict our assimilation.

Even without the benefit of hindsight it must have seemed highly likely that this would be the case. The enthusiasm for studying and the love of the Talmud that permeated the right wing, could not be found in anything like the same quantity or quality anywhere else. The Anglicization of the community over the years had sapped its spiritual energy and focus. Brodie knew that, if the community was to survive, it would have to get back into talmudic training.

After the war, the Jewish community in England, by size, had moved up to be the third largest in the world; America, Russia and then Britain. This led to responsibilities which would never, historically, have fallen to the British Chief Rabbi. The British Jews had been important because of their domicile in the land of a major international power, but as far as their talmudic contribution was concerned, they were way down the list compared to the great centres of learning in Europe. Now all these had gone and it fell to Brodie to try to repair what little he could of the damage.

In 1957 he founded the Conference of European Rabbis and the first meeting was held in Amsterdam, with Brodie presiding. Long before Britain tried to join the Common Market, Brodie was a European; when he addressed the conference in Paris in 1961, he spoke in French.

With the increasing speed of air travel, Brodie was able to undertake more pastoral tours of the empire and Commonwealth and made his way round the world on a number of occasions. He was away on a pastoral tour of the Commonwealth for six months at the end of 1961. He met many old friends in the dominions where most of the clergy had come from Britain and many from Jews' College.

The 1960s had yet more new challenges for Judaism to face and it was up to the Chief Rabbi to lay down the law. The problem now was the 'new morality'. A combination of revolt against the remnants of the stuffiness of Victorian society, the justified case for more tolerance for homosexuals, the discovery of 'the pill', the relaxation of artistic censorship, the Beatles, and the need for the Labour Party, newly in power, to live up to Harold Wilson's promise of a fresh start. 'Swinging London' in the 1960s was the flagship of the newly acceptable, more materialist, hedonist, liberalized society. And what did Judaism think about all that? The rabbis didn't have to look far for guidance; they'd heard many of the same arguments from the Greeks in biblical times. Brodie pronounced: 'Licence is never identical with freedom – the latter is controlled by law and implies social responsibility. Judaism lays strong emphasis on the sanctity of marriage, on chastity and self-control and on the importance of family life.'

The Catholics would have agreed wholeheartedly, but the Church of England was the spokesman for the nation's moral stance. Over the years it tried to find common ground with the new thinking and to see how the modern aspirations might be incorporated into traditional teaching. Orthodox Judaism would have none of it. It was axiomatic to the Orthodox that the road to hell was paved with good intentions.

In 1962 the United Synagogue made a radical change. For the first time, the office of president went outside the founding families. The appointment went to Sir Isaac Wolfson, who was definitely not one of the Cousinhood – very few Glasgwegian Jews were. Sir Isaac was a power in the land of mail order and his catalogues could be found in the remotest houses in the country. To some extent it was the modern version of the Jewish pedlars 100 years before and nobody did it better than Great Universal Stores.

Wolfson was both Orthodox and generous. Apart from Jesus and Christ, the only other name colleges at both Oxford and Cambridge have in common, is Wolfson. His bounty to good causes was immense and if he could also be a ruthless businessmen on occasions, he had not had the advantages of birth of the later offspring of the Cousinhood. Wolfson left spiritual matters to the Chief Rabbi; as in his own company, if a first-class director could be found, Wolfson didn't ride shotgun.

Brodie was not a confrontationalist by nature but it was a mistake to consider him a soft touch. The Hampstead Synagogue had voted to abolish the blessing of the priests (*duchaning*) in Hermann Adler's time. Attempts to reverse the decision had come up regularly because a member – Elsley Zeitlyn, had done so in 1913, 1914, 1927, 1938, 1954 and 1955. Every time the community had voted not to change, even though abandoning *duchaning* (which is done by Jews from the biblical priestly tribe – the Cohens) was to go against 1,000 years of Ashkenazi practice. After the vote in 1955 the subject was discussed in the *Jewish Chronicle*. Brodie then flatly ruled that: 'any Cohen present who wishes to do so, be permitted to pronounce the Priestly Blessing during Divine Service at the Hampstead Synagogue on all occasions when it is the English *minhag* to do so'.[8]

End of story – after 60 years. Brodie was, however, normally prepared to defer to the superior knowledge of his Dayanim. It was this which led to the row which disturbed his last years in office; the 'Jacobs affair' which temporarily split the community into pro- and anti-Jacobs parties.

The rabbi of the New West End synagogue was Dr Louis Jacobs. He was recognized as a probable head of Jews' College and a likely future Chief Rabbi. He was a product of the Manchester and Gateshead yeshivas, he had a doctorate from University College, London and his first post was as assistant to Rabbi Munk, one of the pillars of the right wing. Jacobs had the support of luminaries such as the former head of the United Synagogue, Ewen Montagu, the chairman of the Jews' College Council, Alan Mocatta, who was also the leading Sephardi voice, and William Frankel, the editor of the *Jewish Chronicle*.

Jacobs had, however, written a book in 1956 called *We have Reason to Believe*. It was admired as a defence of Orthodoxy by Orthodox organs such as the *Jewish Review*. It sold nearly 1,000 copies but it did query whether everything in the Bible had actually happened. For example, had Jonah really been swallowed by a whale?

When it was published Jacobs sent a copy of the book to Brodie and heard nothing more. Brodie had listened as one of his Dayanim, Dr Isidore Grunfeld, had gone through the book with him, pointing out what Grunfeld considered was heresy after heresy. Brodie decided that the book was just an example of youth having its say.

Jacobs had obviously not given up a senior position, like the New West End, for the job of a Jews' College lecturer unless he had been promised Jews' College when the incumbent, Dr Epstein, retired. Three years later, however, when Jacob's probable appointment to head up Jews' College was being mooted, a member of the United Synagogue suggested to Brodie that the views in the book were, indeed, heretical. Brodie had to take notice. The Beth Din agreed.

As the affair rumbled on, Brodie finally decided not to confirm Jacobs' appointment after Epstein retired. Jacobs resigned from Jews' College. When the New West End Synagogue invited him in 1964 to return as their minister, Brodie refused to grant him the certificate to practice unless he recanted. This Jacobs wouldn't do, and so he couldn't take up the office. The New West End invited him to come anyway but then the United Synagogue moved in to support the Chief Rabbi's authority; they dismissed the board of management of the synagogue and put in a caretaker committee to run it.

Outraged, the majority of the New West End congregation left the United in a body. They set up a new community, first in the Sephardim's communal hall at the nearby Lauderdale Road Synagogue, and then, when Brodie had objected to his friends in the Mahamad about the perceived support, eventually in St John's Wood, under their old rabbi. From this in time would come the Masorti movement in Britain, an Orthodox congregation who, like the Reform in 1840, would start to slowly move away from some Orthodox Jewish practices.

The Jacobs affair hurt the community. The story was all over the pages of the press and on radio and television, which distressed everybody. Keeping a low profile remained almost the eleventh commandment for Orthodox Jews. What few could work out was why Brodie had taken such a hard-nosed position: 'He was adamant. He was warned that the issue would be splashed across every page in the country! He still refused. The community would be torn asunder! His mind was made up.'[9]

At Jews' College, Jacobs' resignation was followed by those of the chairman, the joint treasurers and the honorary secretary. Brodie didn't move. As one of the keenest observers of the Jewish scene wrote at the time:

> He came to believe that the continuity of Jewish life could not be assured by compromise, and by the easy-going tolerance which had characterized the United Synagogue throughout its history. As an Anglo-Jewish institution it had become more English than Jewish and the real repositories of Jewish life, the

truly Orthodox congregations, the Yeshivot, were outside the organized community.[10]

To this could be added another possibility. Jacobs had written his book before the permissive society was in full swing, but now, in 1964, the writing was on the wall. It was increasingly the world of 'do-your-own-thing' and anything goes – the Swinging Sixties. The British winds of change were becoming howling gales and Brodie's stance was that anything doesn't go. A line had to be marked in the sand and Louis Jacobs was the public demarcation point. Like so many Chief Rabbis before him, Brodie had been faced with another new challenge to Orthodox teachings. In the tradition of Sasportas, Nietto, Lyon, Meldola and Hertz before him, he stood his ground.

The personal cost was considerable. The stress was immense and as the *Jewish Chronicle* attacked him every week, he grew to dread Fridays when it came out. There were attempts to call off the war. The owner of the *JC* met with Brodie and then wrote to him to defend the paper against accusations that it was devoted to the position of the Reform and Liberal movements: 'It stood for "Progressive Orthodoxy", typified by J.H. Hertz, a product of the Jewish Theological Seminary in New York with which, "ethically speaking" the paper was "basically in harmony".'[11]

What David Kessler, owner of 80 per cent of the shares in the paper, chose not to recognize was just how far the JTS had moved towards Reform since Hertz graduated. He was a member of the Liberal Synagogue and had married a convert. It was precisely this drift that Brodie feared would emerge from Jacobs' views.

The United Synagogue lost valuable members, Brodie was strongly criticized by those who felt Jacobs was hard done by, and the ability of Jacobs himself was lost to the mainstream of Orthodoxy. Support for the Chief Rabbi suffered; in 1963 there were 25 communities in Manchester but only 12 paid their dues for the support of the Chief Rabbi's office. That figure was down to only five in 1964. A resolution to renounce the authority of the Chief Rabbi needed a two-thirds majority at the Garnethill Synagogue in Glasgow; it was only defeated by 27 votes. To make matters worse, Jacobs and the Masorti movement appealed to many Jews who questioned the rigidity of Orthodox rulings. As has been seen so many times, though, if one thing could be changed, why not others? The split slowly widened over the years.

The community was, indeed, losing ground. From 1941 to 1950 there had been 73 marriages in Orthodox synagogues per 10,000

Jews. From 1961 to 1965 this number was down to 40. The situation would continue to deteriorate but, ultimately only the right wing could be counted upon to keep the army in the field indefinitely, and Brodie would remain on the side of the right wing.

In spite of all the drama, Brodie's successor, Immanuel Jakobovits, pointed out that in 'the most violent religious warfare in Anglo-Jewry's history' Brodie didn't lose a single congregation or one minister. Well, he lost Jacobs and it was regretted by a lot of people. The New West End synagogue, however, certainly continued to operate after the defection of most of its members.

When Brodie retired in 1965 he was knighted. It was the first time a Chief Rabbi had received this particular honour, and it marked a further step in the integration of the Jewish community into the fabric of the nation. To 'For services to the Upton St. Marks Urban District Council' could now be added 'For Services to British Jewry'. The community beamed. Brodie was very pleased as well but the disadvantage of retirement is that you stop earning money and Brodie had nothing except an inadequate pension. Where some former Chief Rabbis had regretted that their income from conducting weddings was going through a bad patch, this wasn't Brodie's way. He would accept whisky or cigars but he disliked being offered money.

A number of his friends rallied round. He was looked after until he died of cancer in 1979 but, years later, Fanny ended her life in an old people's home. As Brodie lay, terminally ill, in St Thomas' Hospital, he could look out of his bedroom across the Thames at night to the Houses of Parliament. He told his nephew, Greville Janner: 'I look out on the Palace of Westminster lights. It looks like the Torah. Every time you look, you see something different.'

What had Brodie achieved? As the Jew who was best known to the wider community, he epitomized dogged devotion to crown and country. Before Britain gave up on Palestine, that was important as an image. He also helped the European Jewish sages to come to life again after the war. As religion became less important to vast swathes of society in Britain as a whole, as divorce rates shot up, as family life declined and as the attractions of a materialist society grew ever more desirable to the population, Brodie dismissed the soft option as being a danger to Orthodox Judaism. After all, the religion isn't only concerned with the ritual and the law, it is also about eternal truths and these become less important to people when organized religion has less moral effect on their lives and behaviour. As a Bishop of Brentwood said at a Cambridge University Union Society debate in the 1950s: 'Right is right even if nobody's right.

And wrong is wrong even if everybody's wrong.' Brodie would have said 'hear, hear'.

It is perfectly possible that the non-Orthodox branches of Judaism would have agreed as well but, as the years went by, it would be the much criticized right wing who grew in numbers and continued to have the manpower and womanpower to confidently 'troop the colour'.

NOTES

1   *Essays Presented to Chief Rabbi Israel Brodie on the Occasion of his 70th birthday.* Biographical sketch by John M. Shaftesley, 1967, Jews' College.
2   Reverend Levine's son, Kenneth, in conversation with the author.
3   David Cesarani, *The Jewish Chronicle and Anglo-Jewry, 1841–1991*, Cambridge University Press, 1994.
4   Ibid.
5   Chief Rabbi Brodie addressing the 15th Conference of Anglo-Jewish Preachers in 1965.
6   Christopher Sykes, *Crossroads to Israel*, Collins, 1959.
7   Ibid.
8   Raymond Apple, *The Hampstead Synagogue 1892–1967*, Vallentine Mitchell, 1967.
9   Chaim Bermant, *Troubled Eden*, Vallentine Mitchell, 1969.
10 Ibid.
11 Cesarani, *The Jewish Chronicle and Anglo-Jewry.*

24 Solomon Gaon 1949–77

The arguments between the lay leaders of the Sephardim and Moses Gaster, their Haham, had flared up regularly for more than 20 years. His departure from office in 1917 had also been contentious and the elders and Mahamad were in no hurry to risk any replay of any of the disputes. Gaster died in 1939 with his successor not even a gleam in the community's eye. It was another 10 years before Solomon Gaon was offered the position.

The spiritual leadership of the community after Gaster was put in the hands of the hazan, Reverend David Bueno de Mesquita, who was charming, debonair and the perfect English gentleman. He represented the community effectively in public life and worked with Rabbi Shemtov Gaguine, who combined the role of Ab Beth Din with the position of principal of the yeshiva in Ramsgate. In difficult financial times this relieved Bevis Marks of Gaguine's salary which could come from the Montefiore Endowment. Gaguine was a great talmudic talent, de Mesquita was a great front man, but neither was appointed Haham.

In 1931 the Mahamad recognized that they were particularly short of potential hazans for their Sephardi communities and they dispatched an elder to the Balkans to see if there were any likely candidates who could be trained for the positions. It was in the yeshiva at Sarajevo that he found Eliezer Abinun. There had been Jews in Sarajevo since at least 1550 and most of them were Sephardim. They looked to Istanbul for ultimate leadership, as the Sephardim in New York looked to London, but their eastern culture was different in one important way from the traditional English Marrano approach. Like the right-wing Lubavitch rabbis to the north, a rabbi could earn the complete obedience and reverence of his congregation, and he did have to earn it – it wasn't automatic. There were plenty of examples: the Vilna Gaon, the Seer of Lublin, the Kulisher Rebbe – saintly men whose word was law. It was every ambitious rabbi's dream to reach such eminence.

It was Abinun who recommended his friend, Solomon Gaon.

Abinun came from a middle-class family but Gaon came from a humbler background, which mattered in the Balkans and wasn't an insignificant factor in Britain. Gaon was born in Travnik, in what is now Bosnia, in 1912 and he went with Abinun to the yeshiva. He was a very small fish in a little pond and he was delighted when it was arranged that the two young graduates would come to London and enter Jews' College. He found himself in very different surroundings; a great capital city, a community full of highly influential personalities, many with very considerable wealth, and spiritually presided over by the elegant de Mesquita.

Transportation from the simple life of a small town in the Balkans to the sophistication of the capital of a great empire was a major step for Gaon. He was boxed in by lay leaders, some of whose families had served the community for nigh on 300 years; by City bankers, stockbrokers, lawyers and even Knights of the Realm. Gaon was entranced and intimidated; he did as he was told by his elders and – in no way – betters, as far as religious knowledge was concerned. His natural charm over the years endeared him to the community and, unlike Gaster, he gave every appearance of being the last one likely to rock the communal boat.

Both Abinun and Gaon qualified as hazans, but Abinun had by far the better voice. Before the Second World War the idea of training for *semicha* still wasn't really on the agenda for the average Jews' College student in Britain. They wanted to be ministers and that was the height of their ambition. Gaon got a lower-second class degree at London University. That is perfectly respectable but not the mark of a top-class academic brain. Eventually he produced a doctoral thesis on the influence of Alfonso Tostado on Abravanel, and that was well received. Abravanel was a great fifteenth century talmudic scholar, but he was also the financier for King Ferdinand and Queen Isabella in Spain before the Expulsion. Both Abinun and Gaon took up positions at the Lauderdale Road Synagogue before the war. Married to Regina Hassan, a Gibraltar evacuee, Gaon eventually became the senior minister at the synagogue and continued his studies at Jews' College, but now for *semicha*. Abinun was meanwhile happy singing the praises of the Lord. Gaon finally got the rabbinical diploma in 1948 from the charismatic Kopul Kahana, the first achieved at Jews' College by a Sephardi.

The power in the land of the British Sephardim before the war was Neville Laski. Laski was married to Cissie Gaster, the old Haham's daughter, and Gaster only died in 1939. He remained part of the community and, during Gaon's early days in London, he and

Gaon were on friendly terms. They had in common their origins in the Balkans and Gaster was always a powerful and charismatic teacher.

It had taken a long time for Gaon to get *semicha* and it made him academically superior on paper to his boss, de Mesquita. This kind of achievement is not always welcomed in commercial circles, any more than it is in the world of the synagogue. Many senior executives do not welcome the pressure brought on them by up-and-coming youngsters, well-trained, full of energy and ready to argue with the establishment. There is only so much limelight available and if their progress can be hindered, the position of the older man can be maintained more easily. Gaon suffered from this syndrome and yet, in his turn, would eventually be accused of behaving in the same way. It was very much like the Isaac Nietto–Moses Cohen Dazevedo position 200 years earlier. Gaon's eventual appointment as Haham was also regretted by de Mesquita because he said he would have preferred a British successor. He said he was sorry to leave the congregation in the hands of two foreigners – Gaguine and Gaon. Such a hurtful comment, because nobody at the time objected to foreigners like Einstein, de Gaulle or Eisenhower. 'Foreign' was still really a euphemism for 'common'.

The war was a terrible tragedy for Gaon who lost many members of his family in the Holocaust, including his parents. It strengthened his determination to work for the rest of his life to try to repair the vast damage which had been done to the Jewish community throughout Europe. He was passionate about this work and, like Brodie, had to make the extra effort to take a leading role because there were so few other European spiritual leaders left alive.

After the war the elders and the Mahamad felt it was time to appoint a Haham again and they invited Gaon to take up the position. He would be Haham of the British Commonwealth and at the very early age of 37. It was a risk for the community but the war had left the Jewish world in turmoil and there were very serious problems that had to be addressed. It wasn't only the disaster in Europe. For example, the Sephardi community in India was in the middle of a war zone, as Hindus and Moslems committed horrific atrocities against each other when the British pulled out prematurely from the subcontinent. The likelihood of the Sephardim being caught in the crossfire was very real and much of the community got out. Many came to London and were welcomed and given aid to recreate their congregation in the capital. Gaon did a fine job in helping them to settle down and rebuild their self-confidence.

When the State of Israel was proclaimed in 1948 it was the Sephardim who had dominated the Jewish communities in the neighbouring Arab countries since the Jews spread out after the Roman expulsion. It was this smaller branch of the Jews who were now in the most danger and, over the next few years, it became necessary to get their communities out as well and, as near as possible, in one piece.

It had always been the case with Jewish congregations under threat, that their co-religionists would try to help, whether they had been kidnapped by pirates, subjected to expulsion orders, or threatened by pogroms. Jewish congregations all round the world would rally round, just as Moses Montefiore had with the Smyrna blood libel 100 years before, and this time it was, again, a particularly Sephardic problem. There were substantial numbers of Sephardim, for example, in Syria, Egypt and Iraq. With their armies humiliated in the 1948 war by a cobbled-together Jewish militia, the Arab leaders looked for scapegoats, and their own Jewish communities were, as usual, ideally suited for that role.

As far as the Israeli government was concerned, there was a great need to build up the population and they welcomed every Jew who would come. It was not only a humanitarian position for the hundreds of thousands of refugees but a sensible demographic move to avoid being outnumbered so badly by their non-Israeli neighbours.

The major problem in the exodus was that the majority of the Sephardi leaders were wealthy enough to withdraw to London, Paris and New York. The impoverished masses of the congregations went to Israel where they were perceived to be mostly settled in border areas and employed to do the jobs which were unattractive to the more industrialized Ashkenazim. Lacking their VIPs and with the Ashkenazim holding a substantial majority in the country in 1948, the latter had all the power and the Sephardim could do little about it. The Sephardim certainly had members of the Israeli parliament but this Knesset was dominated by the Ashkenazim. Where the British Sephardi congregation had always been the aristocracy, looked up to by the Ashkenazim as the older community, the position was reversed in Israel, even though there were over 1 million Sephardim in the country by 1970.

Gaon welcomed every Sephardi who came from the Middle East. As Britain retired from running an empire, there were periodic additions. When they pulled out from Aden, for example, there was a considerable influx into London. Although not everybody came to

Europe; communities were set up for Sephardi refugees in countries like Rhodesia and Australia for those who wanted nothing more to do with the bloodstained lands of the European continent and the Middle East. There were, in fact, few Sephardi communities remaining in the world who had been left undamaged by the events of the last 20 years. Without a real effort, the possibility did exist that the Sephardim might be swallowed up by the Ashkenazim, unable to stand on their own feet.

When Gaon was appointed, Israel Brodie was the Chief Rabbi and the two always got on very well. The position of vice-chairman and vice-president of any number of Jewish organizations was always set aside for the Haham; the Sephardim retained the respect of the entire British community. They were a small minority but the Haham usually occupied an honorary or advisory role. In the Jacobs Affair, for example, Gaon was an early supporter of the charismatic rabbi but, on that occasion, he was unable to bring peace to the eventually warring parties. The best he could try to do, with the support of the Mahamad, was to offer Jacobs and his supporters a temporary home in Lauderdale Road. Even this proved impossible within a week as a member, Rabbi Solomon Sassoon, pointed out in no uncertain terms how the rest of the rabbinic world would react to a community succouring what they perceived to be a heretic. Jacobs moved on, the arguments continued to rage, but Gaon preferred to keep his head down anyway and wouldn't be seen to take sides in the quarrel. Moreover, Gaon, like many of the Hahamim before him, was always tolerant when he could be. For example, he was in favour of adding Israel's Independence Day to the religious calendar. The Ashkenazi Chief Rabbis at the time were not, disapproving of the secular society which Israel was increasingly becoming.

When Gaon took office, the Sephardim in Britain were very different from those who lived in North Africa. Along that coast the majority were very poor. There were things that Gaon could do to improve the situation. He realized that he could rescue a number of them from poverty and, at the same time, solve the problem of future spiritual leadership for Sephardi congregations around the world. The yeshiva at Ramsgate had sheltered a number of able Hebrew scholars after they had retired from their British congregations, and also some eminent pre-war refugees. Much good work was done, but it really became a yeshiva in name only. In co-operation with the Torah Department of the Zionist Federation, the college at Ramsgate was reinvigorated in the 1950s by the arrival of a number of youngsters from North Africa.

In 1960 there was a controversial decision to transfer the college to London. The suggestion was that Ramsgate, unlike the perception in the late nineteenth century, was not a sufficiently attractive location for young students. It has to be said that the glamour of the town of Gateshead, as a successful alternative for the right wing, was not obvious to everybody. Anyway, the college was closed and the buildings were demolished. It was the end of a noble effort by Sir Moses Montefiore but all was not lost. With the help of the Smouha family who had arrived from Egypt, a new centre in London was bought and about 20 students came onto the school roll. (In addition, a new school, Kisharon, was started.) The students were given both a secular and religious curriculum. This policy was not the same as that adopted by the right wing, who still believed that there was never enough time to learn the Talmud so it was impossible to spare some for secular subjects.

The students came on scholarships at about the age of 14 and the college became a boarding-school. Many of the children were, naturally, homesick but they were made very welcome and Gaon was a doting father figure to them, supporting them and encouraging them at all times. Many grew up to become rabbis and synagogue officials all over the Sephardi world. As they didn't speak English, Hebrew was initially the first language of the school, which gave them an advantage over almost any other Jewish educational establishment.

Many of the students from overseas went on to Jews' College to qualify as rabbis and teachers for the Sephardim around the world. There was the occasional good English Sephardi candidate as well, but the accusation started to circulate that they were discouraged if they looked likely to become threats to the spiritual leadership in the future. Their career prospects were portrayed to be brighter overseas. Some who would become very distinguished in the future in religious and academic circles, joined a Sephardi brain drain.

Even so, some former students, like Rabbi Professor Alan Corré, who went to the United States, speak very highly of the teaching of Hebrew grammar he received from Gaon, and many others are complimentary as well. It seems to be a case of so far and no further, but this could reflect the genuinely limited opportunities there were for Sephardi religious leaders in Britain. Youngsters were certainly given every chance and if they didn't want the posts they were eventually offered overseas, Gaon would tell them that they were entitled to make their own careers.

Gaon carried out his responsibilities to the British community in the early days in an exemplary manner. He got his feet firmly under the table and reinvigorated the community. He was enormously encouraging to youngsters and an excellent teacher of Hebrew. He did, in fact, speak English, Hebrew, Ladino, German, Spanish, French and the Slavonic languages. He also had a working knowledge of Arabic. The problem eventually was that the larger international stage provided him with a far more glamorous and exciting environment than the problems of a conversion in Manchester, a Speech Day at a Jewish school in a London suburb or a discussion about a hotel's *shechita* licence. The demands of the British community were not so great that Gaon's considerable talents in public affairs could be continually in gear. He began to hanker after greater challenges.

For instance, Gaon was always fascinated by the contribution the Sephardim had made to Spain before the expulsion in 1492. When the Second World War ended in 1945 it was discovered that the Isle of Man had been at war with Germany for 31 years, because nobody had included the island as a participator in the peace treaty in 1918. The Jews, for their part, hadn't been involved in a peace conference with Spain for 450 years. Gaon thought the time had come to end hostilities and heal the breach.

Even after all those years, the love of the Spanish culture was still alive and well and living in Lauderdale Road. Gaon first visited Spain in 1959 for an exhibition of Sephardic culture at the Madrid National Library. The Spanish were entranced with the charm and warmth of the Haham and by the fact that he could speak the mediaeval Castilian language which they had long forgotten. Even General Franco, the Spanish dictator, was genuinely moved to hear the ancient tongue in the mouth of a descendent from the Expulsion so long ago.

Both Franco and, later, King Juan Carlos, wanted to make what amends were possible for the sins of their forefathers. The 1492 Edict of Expulsion was formally repealed in 1968 after 476 years. The embarrassment of it still remaining on the statute book should have matched the horror of the Scottish Law Lords who, in 1948, found that the penalty of hanging, drawing and quartering was still part of their criminal law. The Scots immediately blamed its very existence on the English for insisting on introducing it, but the Spanish had no such excuses.

It was now agreed that the first synagogue since 1492 should be allowed to be built in Madrid and Gaon went along to the opening. The Spanish took no chances with their solitary synagogue. In the

1970s the entrance to the building was guarded by a Spanish army sergeant carrying a machine gun. A fine museum was also created in 1971 at the magnificent El Tránsito synagogue in Toledo, built in 1365. To finally bury the hatchet, in 1992 Gaon proclaimed an act of reconciliation at a historic ceremony in the synagogue in the presence of the king and queen and the president of Israel. It was the 500th anniversary of the Expulsion and Gaon always said it was his proudest moment.

In London, however, the Mahamad had their ups and downs with the Haham. In the case, for example, of the purchase of a house for Hazan Abinun in the same street as the Haham's, all roads did not lead to Rome. The Haham strongly objected to sharing even part of his address with his old friend and colleague and the Mahamad had to go to the lengths of offering to buy Gaon a different house elsewhere. In the end it finally became necessary for the Mahamad to overrule his misgivings and buy the home for Abinun anyway. When there were disagreements, Gaon had a fiery temper and the causes he occasionally espoused were not as important as those which had exercised the minds of Hertz, or even Meldola.

In 1963 came the event which was to affect the rest of Gaon's life. He was invited to spend three months in New York. In a city which had the maximum concentration of Jews in the world, the *New York Times* didn't go out of its way to upset the community. So if a headline at the time read: 'Sephardic Jewry on the Brink of Extinction', things were not going well. What was needed was a charismatic Sephardi leader. A man who portrayed an upmarket image of the Sephardim, far removed from the unattractive poverty of so many of their ancient communities in the Middle East, North Africa or the Balkans. A good fund-raiser who came from a historically famous Sephardi community would be ideal. Gaon fitted the bill wonderfully.

The top-hatted British Haham, the latest in a line which stretched back 300 years to the Resettlement, was a mature and charming internationalist and a better scholar than the vast majority of spiritual leaders in the Sephardi communities in America. It was exactly what was needed. What was more, the New York Shearith Israel community had been asking the advice of the Haham in London since its conception, when England still ruled America. There was no need for innovation; it was simply carrying on a great tradition. Even better, the Sephardim in America were split into Syrian, Spanish and Portuguese, Ladino, Iraqi and North African communities, all of whom treasured their independence from each other. As Gaon could speak all their languages and had either roots or a first-class track record, or both, all over the Sephardi world, he was persona grata everywhere. He was also 51 and at the height of his powers.

Yeshiva University (YU) couldn't produce the courses they considered necessary for the Sephardim on their own. The Sephardim would never be led by the Ashkenazim. They could, however, provide the back-up to the development of the courses and a wealthy Sephardi, Jacob E. Safra, provided a great deal of the money that was needed. Gaon was the acceptable face of the modern Sephardim and he agreed to become a visiting professor. Then he went to work with the enthusiasm of any man who is welcomed with open arms. An additional result was that Sephardic studies could be recognized as continuing under Orthodox auspices, rather than at the Jewish Theological College. This had become Conservative, a creed which was eventually nearer the Reform movement.

Gaon visited Sephardi communities of every kind and called on them to send students to YU. He was always brilliant with young people and, as he was thousands of miles from London, there was no question of who was in charge. As a man from humble origins, he was the best example of a self-made spiritual leader and he attracted a great deal of hero-worship from his students. They saw him comparatively fleetingly and he was perceived as an excellent role model.

He was also able to reproduce the success of his training of new spiritual leaders, which he had started at Ramsgate. Only now it was on a far larger scale. He might only have started with five students in America but the numbers in the department swelled until, by the 1990s, there were 350 Sephardim studying at Yeshiva University, of which the 250 undergraduates were one in seven of the student roll. Over 1,000 students have now covered the appropriate curriculum. It has been a massive achievement.

The regard in which he was held was well illustrated by a letter from the president of Yeshiva University, Samuel Belkin, in 1965. He refers to Gaon's 'calibre of outstanding international rabbinic leadership', 'the love, respect and admiration of his colleagues', 'his untiring and dynamic efforts' and 'selfless and consecrated service.'

Initially he had the Mahamad's blessing and the American congregations took their genial and approachable transatlantic visitor to their hearts. They were a generous community and, recognizing the financial sacrifices inherent in any decision to be a man of the cloth, many tried to make up for it to Gaon with handsome gifts as well as extravagant praise. His reputation was soon sky-high in America and it was a heady atmosphere. After all, in London he still didn't even get the minutes of the meetings of the Mahamad. He took no salary for his work in the United States which, effectively, meant that the British community were subsidizing it. In 1968 he was elected president of the American Society of Sephardic Studies and in 1976 was given the chair of that discipline at the Yeshiva University.

To further cement the international world of the Sephardim, Gaon was also a strong supporter of the grandly-named World Sephardi Federation (WSF) and in 1978 became the Haham for all the congregations affiliated to the organization. Even if the WSF seemed more of a public relations exercise than a serious player in determining the future of Jewry, the position made Gaon an even more highly regarded figure throughout the Sephardi world.

He was far less important in London. For three months a year in America he was a spiritual prince, and in London he was, in many ways, Cinderella. Over the years, the comparison between the key role he played in America and the secondary role he played to the Ashkenazi Chief Rabbi and the Mahamad back home, must have made the latter position seem ever more anachronistic.

Gaon slowly started to feel agitated by the lack of respect with which, on occasions, he perceived himself to be treated by the lay leaders in London. He became easily slighted but, of course, such instances primarily occurred in his dealings with the Mahamad. With the Yehidim, Gaon's public persona was genuinely admirable and admired. He was the most approachable of men, always anxious to help, to comfort and to sustain. He was brilliant at persuading the richer members of the congregation to support worthy causes and he was excellent at representing the community in public. He was a hero to the Yehidim, practically revered, just as Gaster had been, and just as those oriental community rabbis had been from whose stock he came. Gaon had worked hard to earn the reverence and the Mahamad were certainly most reluctant to disturb this vision by advertising disagreements to the community at large. The reputation of the whole Restoration congregation was always at stake and if an argument could not be settled amicably, it needed to be decently interred before the *Jewish Chronicle* tried to dig it up for the front pages. The problem was not the show – it was what was going on backstage.

It was also a factor that the old Sephardi families who had ruled the roost for so many years, were slowly dying out. A new set of leaders was emerging and, as Gaon said, they were, 'a generation that knew not Joseph'. The last time that had happened was in the Book of Exodus, and the Jews finished up enslaved to the Egyptians. Gaon contemplated something similar with his own position, vis-à-vis the Mahamad.

From the Mahamad's point of view, all kinds of communities and organizations benefited from the hard work Gaon put into their affairs. Undoubtedly, however, the one organization which suffered was the Sephardi community in Britain, which paid his salary. It wouldn't have been so bad if Gaon had been happy to delegate some of his responsibilities in London to his assistants, but he wanted to maintain his control of all the details even when he was 3,500 miles away. When one of his congregational rabbis issued an invitation to the Chief Rabbi to visit the synagogue one Sabbath afternoon while Gaon was in America, the Haham was so upset by the idea that the invitation had to be withdrawn.

Eventually the question of how to deal with the juxtaposition of the Haham's role in Britain with the Chair of Sephardic Studies in New York became less important than the problem of avoiding lengthy arguments over administrative minutiae within Lauderdale Road. By the end of the 1960s Gaon was no longer a young man and he see-sawed between a desire to retire and a determination to keep going. He had not recommended his chosen successor to the congregation. In commercial life it would have been different, because one of the main tasks of a senior executive is, indeed, to groom his successor and Gaon should have worked on the same basis; there were obvious candidates.

Sometimes the Mahamad and the Haham still worked well together but that could also lead to a mess. He was certainly very helpful to them on the question of the Nuevo cemetery, the second plot of ground the Sephardim had bought for their burials. The land had suffered from bombing during the war and had become surrounded by Queen Mary College, part of London University. The college very much wanted the cemetery area for a new medical school. The land was worth a lot of money if it was developed. The question was whether the bodies could be exhumed and the land sold. In normal circumstances and according to the Din – and this was the advice London had given to the Sephardi community in New York in the late nineteenth century on the same subject – no, it certainly and definitely couldn't.

The Din changes, however, if there is *force majeure* – that there is nothing the community can do to stop it happening. Gaon persuaded the college that if they said they were going to apply for a compulsory purchase order, that would constitute the *force majeure*. Furthermore, it mattered that the subsequent use of the land would be to save life. Mind you, had there been concerted opposition, the college's chances of getting the order might have been slim. The reputation of an academic body, opposed by a Jewish community in its efforts to uproot an ancient monument, and a 200-year-old cemetery at that, was not likely to be enhanced.

So the Sephardim's honorary surveyor negotiated the deal with the district valuer. Cemeteries cannot be deconsecrated in Britain until the last body has rested 100 years in the grave and as that did not apply to part of the cemetery, that part of it was excluded from the agreement.

The resulting settlement was sanctioned by a private Act of Parliament and then it had to be decided what happened to the money. The Din is that it can't be spent on anything the synagogue ought to provide its members with anyway. Happily, it could be used for a new old people's home and a spanking new building, Edinburgh House, was put up at Wembley, replacing the old eighteenth-century Beth Holim hospital building in the East End.

Unfortunately, exhumations in an old cemetery create many difficulties – the bones aren't always where they are expected to be and start to appear in public view. There was a great deal of understandable anger at the whole operation. Many of the international Sephardi rabbis were also at odds with the validity of the Haham's decision. The Sephardi senior citizens benefited far more than the reputation of the Sephardi Beth Din. Ironically, Queen Mary's College subsequently merged with Roehampton Hospital and the school was built at the latter location.

The disputes rumbled on. Small events get blown up when there is a core problem that is almost impossible to solve; the Mahamad were not going to give up their authority and the Haham wanted to be in full control. Delegation is not the easiest of managerial skills.

The 300th anniversary of the Sephardi synagogue in Amsterdam, whose community had played such a large part in the early days of the Marranos in London, took place in 1975. Gaon also visited Spain and Australia, besides spending long periods in America and the Mahamad made a tentative suggestion that perhaps there should be a Sephardi council established, headed by the Haham, but divorced from the congregation. The congregation could then concentrate more easily on its own business. This did not go down at all well with Gaon, who still wanted to continue acting on both the national and international stages. He would have had to take into account that much of the international work was performed without payment.

After Bevis Marks celebrated its 275th anniversary in 1976, the Mahamad announced that the Haham had decided to retire at 65. This was said to be news to Gaon and in 1977 a major communal split emerged. The Haham had many supporters among the elders and Mahamad, but both sides came together in January 1977 when the Board of Elders decided unanimously that the Haham should retire in December on his 65th birthday. At a Yehidim meeting called by his supporters to settle the issue of the Haham's retirement, there was a resolution calling on Gaon to remain in office which resulted in a tied vote. Another calling on him to stand down was equally 50:50 but passed on the casting vote of the elected chair of the meeting.

The last important occasion on which a Sephardi chairman had exercised the casting vote was when Moses Montefiore blocked the admission to the Board of Deputies of Reform representatives in 1853, 124 years earlier. Where the 275th anniversary of the synagogue had been an occasion for communal joy, the 124th anniversary of the Board of Deputies meeting was almost equally regretted. The side favouring the Haham were not satisfied. They threatened to bring up the whole matter again at the next Annual General Meeting. With great regret the Mahamad told them that, if they did, it would have to be announced that the lay leaders were unanimous in resolving that the Haham was no longer fit to remain in office and give their reasons. The Haham's support went on the back burner.

Gaon had waited out the conclusions in New York and decided he wasn't going to come back. Basically, he had two options. To put up with the aggravation and demotion in Britain or to move more or less permanently to New York, where he would be welcomed with open arms and treated with the affection and respect he had richly earned in that country. He chose New York. He had either retired, as he had suggested was his wish on a number of earlier occasions, or he had been forced out of office. The excuse of his forthcoming entry into the ranks of senior citizens was certainly not credible, because it wasn't any part of his original contract that he should resign when he reached that point in his life. The original contract had, in fact, only one stipulation: that he read the prayer for the Royal Family; under the circumstances, a somewhat limited brief.

The parting was not amicable. Initially, there was even a move to deny Gaon the title of Haham of the congregation and the use of the Haham's chair in the synagogue, though both suggestions were swiftly dropped. The chair stood mutely empty for years as Gaon stayed in New York. When Gaon came back to London, he often chose to worship at an Ashkenazi synagogue rather than one of his own. It was as if nothing had changed since the stormy days of Isaac Nietto 200 years earlier. The elders voted not to appoint a successor 'for some years to come'. Twenty-five years later the position remains unoccupied.

Gaon spent some of his retirement being honoured in many different ways. He remained the president of the World Sephardi Federation for some years and received a number of awards in Israel. He was involved with three Israeli universities and produced learned works, such as *Minhat Shelomo*, which was a commentary on the daily prayer book of the Sephardim. He died in New York in 1994 just after his 82nd birthday.

What had Gaon achieved? He played a major role in keeping the Sephardi world a meaningful part of international Jewry. He ensured that there would be sufficient Sephardi rabbunim to service the communities. He inspired large numbers of his flock, but left a divided Sephardi community in Britain. It is for the international contributions that he will be remembered rather than the sad and bitter disputes of his latter days in office in London.

25   Immanuel Jakobovits 1967–91

There was one enormous difference between Immanuel Jakobovits and all but one of his predecessors as Chief Rabbi since the Resettlement. Like Hart Lyon 200 years before, he honestly and sincerely didn't want the job. When Sir Isaac Wolfson, the president of the United Synagogue, asked him to allow his name to go forward, he wrote:

> I have repeatedly and consistently stated, privately and in public, as well as in my informal discussions with you, that my personal preference would be to remain in my present office in New York ... the opportunities here offered to me are practically unlimited to pursue my communal and literary interests.

Jakobovits was the rabbi of the Fifth Avenue Synagogue at the time. The congregation was intellectual, rich, Orthodox and committed. To move from such an environment to a community divided over the Jacobs affair, inclined to nominal rather than committed Orthodoxy and with fringe groups ready to attack you if they disliked your policies, could easily be construed as an inability to know when you were well off.

In view of his rejection of even his candidature for election going forward, Wolfson and the electoral college, which included London, provincial and overseas congregations, chose Jacob Herzog instead; Herzog was an Israeli diplomat and a fine talmudic scholar. He had served in the Israeli government and had a very good reputation as a diplomat; a virtue in the candidate which was seen as highly desirable, as the fallout after the Jacobs Affair in Brodie's time continued. So, all was agreed, a date was set for the Herzog installation and then disaster struck. A health check identified that, unfortunately, he was seriously ill and, in fact, he died in 1972 at the early age of 50. Faced with a limited life-span and uncertain of his ability to carry out the onerous duties of Chief Rabbi under the circumstances, Herzog decided he couldn't go on.

A crisis is a problem with a time limit. The United Synagogue had to find an alternative candidate quickly; the community needed a spiritual leader to start repairing the wounds of the Jacobs Affair. Wolfson reopened negotiations with Jakobovits, which put the rabbi in a very difficult position. It was still a fact that he and his wife weren't happy with the Jewish schools in Britain and knew they would have to leave their two oldest sons behind in America to finish their education. They still had all they wanted in New York, which had the largest population of Jews in the world. On the other hand, Jakobovits felt a great debt to Britain. He had first come to the country in 1936 as a refugee from Germany, at the age of 15. On many occasions in the future he was to pay tribute to Britain as the nation which, by allowing him into the country, had saved his life. He had studied at the Jewish school of Dr Solomon Schonfeld and gone on to Jews' College and the Yeshivah Etz Haim, where he had gained his *semicha*. He had taken posts at the Brondesbury and Great Synagogues and served ten years as the Chief Rabbi of Ireland. So a great deal of his upbringing and career had been in Britain and Ireland.

What finally convinced him to accept the call was the advice of his wife Amélie's father, Rabbi Elie Munk of Paris. If there was a need, said Munk, then it was his son-in-law's duty to undertake the task.

To the great relief of Wolfson and everybody else, Jakobovits said he'd do it, but – and it was an enormous 'but' – there would have to be conditions. And he laid down a programme of objectives, duties and responsibilities for the Chief Rabbi which gave him far more power than any Chief Rabbi had had before him. It was a strategy document on which there would be no vote. If they wanted him, then those were the terms. It was a vision of a far more inclusive regime than in the days of the Adlers. Jakobovits wanted to use the talents of the rabbis in the community and to give responsibility for specific communal fields to the best of them. He also did not want to spend too much of his time on minor ceremonial occasions. In addition he wanted to rely on his Beth Din more.

Wolfson was perfectly relaxed about the conditions. He was a powerful businessman and the first head of the United Synagogue not to be born into the Cousinhood. He was delighted to have broken into the charmed circle but, basically, he just came from an Orthodox Glaswegian family and wanted to delegate the responsibility for the community's spiritual welfare to a first-class executive. Once such an executive had been found, it was common practice in business life to let that individual get on with it; the chairman of a company as large as Great Universal Stores couldn't run his business by trying to do all the top jobs himself. Only if Jakobovits ran into trouble, would Wolfson be available to come to his aid. He never interfered.

Jakobovits reminisced in later years that he would have occasionally welcomed a good argument, but Wolfson knew his limitations. The hidden agenda was that the United Synagogue held the purse strings and, over the years, it was expected that even a Chief Rabbi could come round to their way of thinking. There were also two specific agreements in the final contract which did not materialize: that there be a new Chief Rabbinate centre to replace the antiquated headquarters, and that a newspaper be published to put an alternative viewpoint on occasions to that voiced in the columns of the *Jewish Chronicle*.

So Jakobovits it was and he was installed in the presence of the Jewish good and the great in April 1967. He was a tall, imposing figure who spoke very well if, normally, at considerable length. Almost everybody breathed a sigh of relief, though it always amused him that the *Jewish Chronicle* hadn't wanted either him or Nathan Marcus Adler.[1] Throughout his ministry Jakobovits did not regard himself as a posek and left the final word on difficult religious subjects to Dayan Ehrentreu, his Ab Beth Din. His own game plan was crystal clear, however, and he followed it without deviation for the next 25 years.

First and foremost, he recognized that the future of the community depended on producing a hard core of committed Orthodox youth. That meant more Jewish schools, which involved the two traditional problems which had defeated his predecessors. First, to find the money for them and, second, to make an education at a Jewish school a respectable alternative to the allure of the public schools. On both grounds, Nathan Marcus Adler had failed. His community wouldn't provide him with enough money and they considered Jewish schools as a step backwards in their efforts to become more British than the British.

Jakobovits would come to live in a different era. Since the creation of Israel, the community had become more confident about identifying themselves as Jews. One illustration of this is the commandment to cover your head. This is done with a small cap called a yarmulke. Before Israel, unless you belonged to the right wing, the yarmulke was never worn in public. It was too distinctive. It was felt it could attract the attention of anti-Semites. It could be dangerous on a dark night. Now, in the Jakobovits years, instead of cowering at the thought of anti-Semitism, the community took heart from the Israeli victories over massive odds in 1948, 1956, 1967 and 1973. The fear – though it never vanished – started to diminish. More Jews wore yarmulkes in the street.

Jakobovits set out, with Wolfson's enthusiastic support, to form the Jewish Educational Development Trust (JEDT), with the objective of massively increasing the provision of Jewish school places. Wolfson contributed a lot of money but the United Synagogue dragged its feet. It had many demands on its income and there were many charities in need of support. Most of the money raised from the community at the time was earmarked to support the infant State of Israel anyway. The fund-raisers of the Joint Israel Appeal were expert and highly persuasive, while those few spiritual leaders who wanted more Jewish schools were not trained in the techniques of the hard sell; though the Haham, Solomon Gaon, had a natural talent for it when in New York.

In the late 1960s the idea of diverting a portion of the Ashkenazi community's disposable charity income to the creation of Jewish schools in Britain was never going to get the support it needed. It seldom had, and the wealthier members of the community still gave the public schools the nod. Even though the schools normally made scant allowance for the Jewish pupils to practise their religion. Many still taught on Saturday morning and refused permission for the Jews to take time off to go to synagogue for any festivals other than Yom Kippur and Rosh Hashonah. Naturally, many of the children grew up to feel that, if their parents could let them give up synagogue on Shavuot or Sukkot and ignore *kashrut* at boarding school, then little was sacred. Why not give up the whole thing later to marry the perfect girl – even when she wasn't Jewish?

Not much change there from the nineteenth century. Two of the three Jewish boarding houses which had existed at public schools had closed; only Clifton was left and the new Carmel College, which owed its success to the devotion of its headmaster, Rabbi Kopul Rosen. The United Synagogue, for its part, wanted to concentrate on its traditional synagogue religion classes. By the end of the 1970s the JEDT was only making very slow progress.

Setting the highest standards in Jewish education at the time was the right wing's Rabbi Dr Solomon Schonfeld, whose Jewish Secondary School Movement (JSSM) was continuing to produce amazing academic results, but was constantly on the verge of bankruptcy. Dr Schonfeld was, astonishingly, able to make Moses Gaster and Joseph Hertz look like pussycats to deal with, by comparison with his own approach. For Schonfeld there were no rules if they got in the way of his objectives for his schools. He drove his local authorities to distraction, year in and year out, by breaking any number of their regulations. For example, the Hasmonean School resources were, for years, so inadequate that if a boy got a chair in his first class, he might well decide to carry it around with him all morning to make sure he had something on which to sit. The local council had to admit, however, that Schonfeld derived no personal benefit from any of his activities, and his results from schools with no entry exams were the best in the borough.

Enraged middle-of-the-road educationalists within the community appealed to Jakobovits to help stop Schonfeld making waves with both Jewish and government authorities. Jakobovits was extremely half-hearted about intervening. First, because Schonfeld was running schools which were exactly what the Chief Rabbi wanted, in terms of a full Orthodox curriculum running alongside the state secular programme of study. Second, because he was, himself, a JSSM alumnus. Schonfeld was unstoppable anyway. In the latter years of his life, he suffered a very severe stroke, but he hardly let it slow him down. His schools remain his monument.

Jakobovits had been out of England for 18 years when he took on the Chief Rabbinate. Moreover, he was always more European than British. He fitted the British role admirably, but he never lost a slight accent and he relied a great deal on the bubbly personality of his wife to help him with his own natural shyness. He was secure in the mastery of his spiritual activities, but he also had to be good at building his own team among the general community. Among his best choices to help him there had been the invaluable Moshe Davis, the executive director of his private office.

In the late 1970s Jakobovits decided to try to move the objectives of the JEDT along rather faster. He turned to Davis who knew all the major Jewish big business players, or was expert in rooting them out and dealing with them. Davis was accepted as a member of the outstandingly upper-crust Athenaeum Club and, when asked how a simple ex-sergeant major had reached such eminence, he was able to point to the Athenaeum's supporters sheet on the proposal for his membership. This in 1977 included the signatures of the Archbishop of Canterbury and the Cardinal Archbishop of Westminster.[2]

Now Davis approached Stanley Kalms (later Lord Kalms) to chair a new committee. Kalms was a major retailer – his company was Dixons – and both he and Davis were members of the same North London synagogue. Kalms and Davis managed to gather round them a high-powered committee of very able Jewish company chiefs – men such as Cyril Stein of Ladbrokes, Trevor Chinn (later Sir Trevor) of Lex and Alan Sugar (later Sir Alan) of Amstrad. They weren't high up in the councils of the United Synagogue but they were very highly regarded by their bank managers. They agreed to build the schools and, extremely generously, they found the millions of pounds it would cost. After all the setbacks suffered by the Chief Rabbis over the centuries, it finally came to pass. It was agreed that each JEDT member would take an area he knew well and see to the needs of the Jewish school children in that vicinity. The United Synagogue's backing wasn't needed, though it continued to finance the Jewish part of the curriculum in the schools.

All of a sudden Jakobovits was free of the financial restraints which the lay synagogue authorities had imposed on so many Chief Rabbis in the past. The businessmen provided him with the funds he needed. New schools were constructed in areas like Ilford in Essex and the Michael Sobell School in Kingsbury, money was found to train teachers, to refurbish buildings and to build a fine new school in North London, to be called Immanuel College. Today it is one of the best public schools in the country. The work was immensely detailed as many of the schools sought – and later became – part of the state education system. Negotiations with the Department of Education were often protracted, but Jakobovits lived to see his dream come true. At the end of his ministry about a third of Orthodox Jewish children went to their own schools.

It was a remarkable effort and, again, Jakobovits was lucky with his timing. The 1970s and early 1980s were a period of severe inflation and the fees of public schools went through the roof. Many parents who would have preferred that kind of education for their children, found it economically too much of a burden. The far cheaper, often free, Jewish schools emerged at just the right time.

To educate the children with the right curriculum and emphasis on religious subjects was only one of Jakobovits' objectives. He also recognized, like David Nietto 250 years earlier, that the whole community had to understand that the tenets of Orthodox Judaism were still relevant to the challenges of modern life. It was Nietto, 250 years before, who tackled the relevance of Judaism in working in harmony with science. Jakobovits followed in his footsteps. His chosen field was Jewish Medical Ethics. He took his PhD in the subject at University College, London and became one of the world authorities on the Jewish approach to such difficult moral issues as abortion, transplants, euthanasia and drugs. He had no difficulty in identifying the Orthodox position but, of course, it was not always the answer sought by popular opinion.

This was, indeed, a fundamental of Jakobovits' approach to life. He did not see himself as a leader who listened to the vox populi and then won acclaim by agreeing with the majority view. He always looked to see what the Din was and then stated it. If Jewish law didn't sit comfortably with the latest foibles and trends, then that was tough. It hadn't with the Greeks and Romans either, and that had been tough too. The Chief Rabbi was into eternal truths, not passing fashions.

There was one occasion when he could not only advise on the Din in medical ethics but also, as Chief Rabbi, tell the community to obey that instruction immediately. The Yom Kippur War of 1973 led to large numbers of casualties in the Jewish armed forces. The president of Israel appealed to Jews around the world to give blood, as the Israeli national blood bank was likely to become exhausted. The appeal came on the eve of the Festival of Sukkot when everybody was preparing to stop work and go to synagogue. Jakobovits homed in on the Din which says that to save human life, all other laws can be suspended.

He gave instructions that rooms were to be set aside in synagogues immediately for blood donors – even if it was Sukkot – and asked Jewish doctors and nurses to carry out the transfusions.

It was an extraordinary experience. Rabbis found their festival congregations shrinking as their members filed in to the hastily set-up adjacent surgeries instead. Jews who wouldn't have dreamed of attending the synagogue to pray, arrived to offer their blood. It was not only a remarkable demonstration of solidarity but also showed the flexibility, the humanity and the good sense of the Din in facing up to a contemporary problem. The official instruction to break the rules was the acceptable face of strict Orthodoxy.

When Jakobovits arrived in 1965 he found a divided community. To bind up the wounds he gave his approval to marriages held within Louis Jacobs' community; it was an endorsement of the Orthodoxy of the community, even if there had been differences in the past. He also made an agreement with the right-wing Federation of Synagogues to work together with their spiritual leaders. This, however, soon broke down. The right wing continued to be suspicious of any authority outside their own community. Jakobovits was never able to resolve this problem. He belonged himself to the right wing, and was just as critical of the standards of observance of the majority of Orthodox Jews as they were in Gateshead or Stamford Hill. Nevertheless, he saw his task as improving the situation, not retiring behind high walls and barricades in glorious isolation. The fact was that, as long as the children's parents had an Orthodox marriage certificate, the offspring could always grow up more observant than their paterfamilias.

The increased feeling of security in the Jewish community was enhanced by the fact that other communities were confronted with the cancer of racialism instead of them. The new Indian, Pakistani and West Indian communities were faced with the same prejudices that had needed to be overcome by the Jews. They were more easily identified as well, because they were black and brown instead of pink. The spotlight of racialism turned away from the Jewish community, who were even considered to be more likely to be allies against the new strangers. It was the same in religious matters; as the churches declined in membership, the need for the religiously committed to stand together against the atheists and the agnostics made for easier relations between Christians and Jews. Even the Roman Catholic Church, under the leadership of Pope John XXIII, markedly softened its historic hostility to Judaism.

With the Reform and Liberal synagogues, Jakobovits tried to create a co-operative atmosphere on anything which wasn't actually theological. He was anxious to work with them on the problems of raising funds for charities, on the ongoing efforts to get the Russians to allow their Jews to emigrate to Israel, on political issues in Israel itself. What he wasn't prepared to do was give an inch on the din. When asked to create bridges between the Right Wing, the United Synagogue and the Progressive movement, he pointed out that, theologically, the Orthodox and the progressives were a long way apart and he was on the side of the right wing.

The Orthodox continued to withhold recognition of the legitimacy of the conversions carried out by the Progressive movement. To be rejected in this way by the authorities speaking for 75 per cent of the total community in Britain, was very frustrating and hurtful for the progressives. They, naturally, made every effort to achieve equality of representation wherever it could be won, and, in 1970, the Board of Deputies agreed to consult Progressive religious leaders if the subject under discussion was one which affected their members. The right-wing representatives on the Board of Deputies walked out at this point and have never returned, though the Federation members didn't follow suit. The right wing's position was that, under no circumstances, would they grant any recognition to the Progressive movement's rabbis. Of course, the presidency of the Board of Deputies had been held by Reform Jews in the past, but in those days the two communities could at least cover-up their differences. One could ignore the moment in the meeting of the Board in December 1932 when the Reform president ended the proceedings by wishing all the members a Happy Christmas!

Jakobovits waited to see if the agreement really made any difference and in 1984 the Board of Deputies bowed to Orthodox pressure and produced a Code of Practice: 'which makes the guidance it receives from the Orthodox Ecclesiastical authorities absolutely mandatory, which had not been the case previously'.[3] Even so, such guidance might be overruled by a simple majority of the votes of the board. There hasn't been a crunch situation yet to find out.

The area where the Chief Rabbi's views caused the most consternation in the community was his very qualified support for the policies of successive Israeli governments. By the time of Jakobovits, most Israelis had totally stopped following most Orthodox practices. The vast majority went to the beaches on the Sabbath rather than the synagogue, they were not particularly concerned about the dietary laws and a wide gulf had grown up between the right wing and most of the rest of the population. Where in the immediate aftermath of 1948 and the creation of the state, the question could be asked of what future use was the Jewish Diaspora outside Israel, one answer increasingly seemed to be to defend the Orthodox tradition.

Naturally, Jakobovits bitterly regretted the way the Israelis, themselves, had moved away from Orthodoxy. He also totally rejected their approach to the problem of Arab refugees. Time and again, he insisted that Israel should make efforts to see that these poor people were better treated by the Arab nations and by Israel itself. He recognized that the perpetuation of the appalling conditions of the refugee camps, created by the Arab states, would only ensure the increased production of an even larger number of bitter enemies of Israel. There was a stark distinction in the Jewish and Arab treatment of refugees. Israel would accept Jews from anywhere in the world, offering no obstacles to their immigration, and integrate them into the general population. The Arab states filled refugee camps.

The position adopted by most of the British Jewish community was to defend the policies of the Israeli government under all circumstances, at least in public. The core problem, of course, was that the pragmatic behaviour of a small secular nation state under constant threat from its neighbours, was always likely to be very different from the ethical standards laid down in the Bible. When Jakobovits attacked the actions of the Israeli government, he created for himself wave after wave of criticism right across the Jewish world. He even favoured compromise with the Arabs on the single point on which most Jews would never compromise; the inviolability of Jerusalem as the property of the Jewish people. In the 1948 war it had only been possible to capture half the city, and great was the rejoicing when the other half was taken in the 1967 conflict. To hold on to Jerusalem was one of the few issues where almost all Jews were in agreement. Except Jakobovits who insisted on recognizing reality, and the sacred position the city held in the religion of the Arabs. He went on record:

> While the Jewish part should be put under Jewish municipal control, the Arab areas should also be self-governing. If they want to fly the Palestinian flag there, then they can. And they can call it the capital of whatever entity they make.

Criticism simply did not concern him. As he told his wife, he was only responsible to the Almighty, so the obloquy was unimportant. The Din was the Din and, as a refugee himself, he knew that the community would take a very different view if they were victims in the camps rather than onlookers on the other side of the border. As he said: 'The task of a rabbi is to speak for Judaism and not necessarily for Jews.'

Atrocities often take place in war on both sides and leaders normally make excuses for the excesses of their supporters. Jakobovits wouldn't ally himself with Israeli Jewish extremists under any circumstances. He warned the British community not to do so either. In 1994 Arab worshippers were assassinated by members of an extremist right-wing Jewish group while they worshipped in a mosque in Hebron. The activities of suicide bombers today often bring Arab crowds into the streets to celebrate the carnage. Jakobovits dealt with the position of the extremist killers of the Arabs in crystal-clear terms: 'Its active supporters may be few, but those who are at least ambivalent in denouncing it as utterly un-Jewish are not so insignificant.'

The Chief Rabbi always regretted the politicization of the right wing in Israeli life. He would have preferred to leave Israeli politics to the politicians. He pleaded for, 'the gradual disengagement of religion from political parties and of the rabbinate from state control'. Fighting for political power often involved powerful temptations to take short cuts with the Din.

Where Jews all round the world were in full agreement – an infrequent situation – was in their wish to get the Russians to allow those Jews who wanted to emigrate to leave the country. The communists frowned on all religion. It was proscribed in many ways. As far as Jews were concerned, the publication of Jewish literature was forbidden and it was an offence to teach Hebrew. You could teach 150 other languages, but not Hebrew. Emigration to Israel was forbidden. Just to apply for permission to do so could lead to imprisonment. When eminent scientists applied, they would, automatically, lose their jobs. The Russians did all they could to stamp out Judaism.

They had a great deal of success. When the Marranos came to London in 1660 they had been almost totally ignorant of Judaism because they had been divorced from Jewish teaching for 170 years. The communists had only had 50 years to achieve the same result but to a large extent they had managed it. The tiny right-wing Orthodox had hung on somehow but they needed world-wide help to get the Russians to move towards granting the freedom promised in the United Nations Charter: the right to live in another country. Help was available from all over the Jewish world but often the Russians wouldn't allow it to be provided, even in comparatively minor areas. For example, when matzo was sent to the Russian Jews for Passover, the Russians confiscated it. They believed that to give way to demands for visas to emigrate would be to succumb to Western pressure and this they were not prepared to do.

Jakobovits went to plead for an amelioration of the conditions in 1970. He saw ministers from the Russian government but there was no further progress. If anything, the adverse rulings became more stringent. Demonstrations were being held in many countries, highly embarrassing to the Russians, but they wouldn't let the people go. Jakobovits was one of the few who realized that permitting emigration wasn't the whole answer. If there had been no attempt in advance to re-educate the Jews involved, the majority would still be lost to the faith. They wouldn't keep to what they didn't know. As with the Sephardim who arrived in Stuart times, he was right to a considerable extent. They, too, would have benefited from more tuition after 1492. Both waves lost a lot of their potential, but both communities have survived. In senior ranks, Jakobovits was almost a lone voice. The Jewish Agency, which was responsible for encouraging immigration, concentrated on *aliyah* to Israel and not on observance. They would not provide funds to provide Jewish education in Russia and Jakobovits couldn't persuade them otherwise.

When it was finally possible to get a visa, the majority of those who left Russia went to countries other than Israel; though 200,000 did go to the Holy Land and only 3 per cent subsequently left it for other destinations. Most Jews, of course, remained in Russia and Jakobovits got his synagogue communities to twin with Russian ones towards the end of his ministry. For example, the Hampstead Garden Suburb synagogue in London twinned with Lvov in the Ukraine.

Jakobovits considered the loss to Judaism of the vast majority of the Russian émigrés was a major failure. Under the circumstances, however, it would have been fairer to consider the overall results a considerable success. The communists, like the Tsar before them, like the Inquisition and the Nazis, had done their worst and a lot of Jews had survived. As on so many previous occasions over the centuries, the very Orthodox started to build once more.

Trained rabbis arrived in Russia from all over the Jewish world to help reconstruct communities and to teach the faith again. While it was quite impossible to find all the money the congregations needed, every year since the collapse of communism has shown a level of improvement. The Russian Jews who went to Israel were integrated into the country's mainstream and a proportion picked up where their Orthodox ancestors had been forced to leave off. Recall Dean Inge's words that 'the Jews had stood by the graves of all their oppressors in turn', and communism is just the latest example.

Jakobovits always had the warmest personal relations with both the primates of the Church of England and the Catholic Church and, of course, they found a great deal of common ground when addressing current ethical and moral problems. However, he never attended a Christian religious service unless invited by the queen to celebrate some momentous event in the nation's life. Then he would attend as the representative of the community but never in clerical dress. Not for Jakobovits the bishop's gaiters of Hermann Adler.

His diplomatic skills were well illustrated when he received an invitation from the Archbishop of York to unveil a memorial to the Jews who had committed mass suicide, rather than fall into the hands of a Christian mob on the Sabbath before Passover in 1190. The setting was Cliffords Tower and, in memory of the martyrs, the Jews had always believed that the rabbis had put a curse on the city and forbidden them to ever again sleep in York overnight. As the Archbishop and Jakobovits waited for the ceremony to begin, the prelate said how pleased he was that there would be a memorial at last and asked whether it was true that the city had been cursed. Jakobovits, absolutely straight-faced, said that he had looked into the records and could find no trace of it. At any event, he had now cancelled any curse there might have been. Eight hundred years the

Jews had slept elsewhere and all of a sudden nobody could find any evidence of why.

It was true, however, that no *herem* had been put on Spain for the Expulsion of 1492. As Haham Gaon pointed out in a sermon in 1960:

> Jacob Sasportas...was also for a long time the diplomatic representative of the Sultan of Morocco at the Spanish Court. Had there been any such ordinance in existence, it is inconceivable that [he] would have found his way into Spain and stayed for a considerable time.[4]

Where there were spiritual differences, however, Jakobovits spoke out. The Canon of Southwark Cathedral called the Bible 'fables'. The Chief Rabbi put the alternative view which had motivated Orthodox Jews over the centuries:

> I do not rely on the fickle human conscience to guide me on what is right and wrong. I rely on external revelation and on the law. And so I wouldn't call that fables . . . It is for the sake of this that all our martyrs gave their lives – to maintain the primacy of a teaching that gives meaning to our very existence.

In 1987 he was awarded the Lambeth degree of Doctor of Divinity by Archbishop Runcie. It was the first time a Lambeth degree had been awarded to a Jew since the See of Canterbury had been given the right to do so in 1533. It was a long way from Sasportas trying to avoid the 1664 Conventicle Act prohibiting dissenters from holding services.

There were differences between the Christian and the Jewish approaches to the problems of poverty, and it was these differences which transformed the last ten years of Jakobovits' life. In 1986 the Church of England produced a report called *Faith in the City*. In it the responsibility for the plight of the poor and the unemployed was firmly placed at the government's door. They were criticized for having failed in their duty to their fellow citizens. The report was sent to the Chief Rabbi for his righteous endorsement – and he couldn't do it. In a number of key aspects the views of the Church were not those of Orthodox Judaism.

It wasn't that he didn't feel he should attack the government. Or that he believed that religious authorities in Britain should stick to spiritual matters. That wasn't the Jewish way at all. As he said in his response: 'The biblical prophets were history's supreme Leaders of the Opposition.'

It was just that the Jewish approach to the problem had always been different, and Orthodoxy is nothing if not consistent. When the eighteenth-century Chief Rabbis and Hahamim were grappling with the influx of poverty-stricken Jews from the European continent, the question of how best to help them had been addressed. It was agreed that the Din was clear all the way back to biblical times. The law was that it is the responsibility of the rich to help the poor to stop being poor. If, in the eighteenth century, they wanted to go to work as pedlars, then they should be given a little money and then left to fight their way out of the gutter by hard work. They should not subsist on begging for charity. As the nineteenth-century Haham, Benjamin Artom, had said: 'But when he helps the poor, he should discourage idleness, and urge self-reliance and industrious exertions.' Jakobovits followed the party line. Except for the handicapped, he was not keen on the welfare state taking on all the responsibility.

He pointed out that, according to Jewish teaching, 'all manner of labour was deserving of esteem.' That artificial distinction in status between white- and blue-collar workers shouldn't exist. Furthermore, 'Cheap labour is more dignified than a free dole.'

These views were entirely in line with the thinking of the Prime Minister, Margaret Thatcher. She had first met Jakobovits when she was the Secretary of State for Education in the Edward Heath administration. Jakobovits had told her that she wasn't the minister for education; she was the minister of defence! She never forgot that moment. When Jakobovits declared that everybody should try to resolve their own problems and not just depend on the government, he was not voicing Conservative views. If the Jews had relied on governments for their survival, they would have disappeared without trace many centuries before. What was the Jewish community's approach? Jakobovits explained:

> Above all, we worked on ourselves, not on others. We gave a better education to our children than anybody else had. We hallowed our home life. We channelled the ambition of our youngsters to academic excellence, not flashy cars.

Thatcher was delighted and decided that Jakobovits was more down-to-earth than either of the current archbishops. In 1988 she took the unprecedented step of asking Jakobovits if he would accept a peerage. The letter from the Prime Minister absolutely staggered both rabbi and rebbetzin. They were in shock the whole day. A Chief Rabbi in the House of Lords! And with a safer seat than an Archbishop, who had to step down when his period of office expired!

Jakobovits hesitated. He was concerned that his appointment might upset his ecclesiastical friends in the other religions. He felt that he was ignorant on any number of subjects which would be debated in the Upper House. He also knew that a minority of his community would hate the high profile he would have, because they still preferred to keep their heads below the parapet for fear of upsetting their neighbours. Thatcher reassured him on all three points. She explained that she had already consulted the other religious leaders who said they were entirely in favour of the honour. She explained that no peer was an expert on all the subjects debated in the Upper House and, if some of his community didn't like the idea, she suggested he ignore them.

The vast majority of the community were, naturally, thrilled. They had recognized over the years that they had a resolute spiritual leader, but a peerage! It was riches beyond the dreams of avarice. Jakobovits took his seat in the House that year. He reflected in his maiden speech soon after:

> I began to feel at home when I was robed in the Moses Room with its painting of Moses, the law giver, holding the Decalogue – presumably as the foundation of laws enacted in the Mother of Parliaments. And since Jews traditionally regard Moses as the first rabbi, I am clearly here as the second rabbi, still upholding the same Ten Commandments.

Jakobovits' peerage had another massive effect as well. Logically, Orthodoxy could no longer be labelled common. It couldn't be equated with 'common' if its leader sat in the House of Lords. As a result, if you admitted to Orthodoxy, it was far more difficult for the assimilationist to pour scorn on your practices. A lot of Orthodox, but mainstream, Jews stopped trying to hide their background when socializing in the general community. For example, in some large City legal and accountancy practices, there was now the introduction of *shiurim*, religious discourses, during the lunch hour for Jewish partners.

The media were not sure how to deal with Jakobovits. They were unaccustomed to a spiritual leader who had no doubts about the right stance on any ethical or moral subject they threw at him, and who immediately stated the answer clearly and unequivocally, with the authority of thousands of years of identical advocacy. A situation developed almost as unbelievable as the achievement of the original aims of Zionism. The media and members of the government actually started to look to a Chief Rabbi for guidance. It was again a far cry from the seventeenth-century *ascamot* of the Sephardim, instructing the Haham to keep his head well down in a Christian country. It certainly wasn't that Jakobovits sought the role of British spiritual adviser, but when he was asked questions, he didn't hesitate to give chapter and verse on what Orthodox Judaism held to be the right answers.

In the House of Lords, Lord Janner, the Labour peer, says that he was liked and respected. He considers him a Tory though he sat on the cross benches. If, however, the rulings of the Din were in line with a Labour Party manifesto, Jakobovits would have been seen differently by the Conservatives. His speeches were listened to with respect, though many Jewish peers would have preferred him not to criticize the Israeli government outside Israel.

Immanuel Jakobovits broke the mould of British Chief Rabbis. For a period of years he was able to be not just a guiding light to his community, but also a light unto a nation; the nation being Britain. Where The Times had published letters by Hertz or Brodie, they now asked the Chief Rabbi for articles. When the Secretary of State for the Department of Education and Science was wondering about a school video which, among other aspects of sex education, advocated condoms to prevent AIDS, he asked what Jakobovits thought about showing it in the classroom? 'Grossly objectionable and offensive to millions of parents' he was told forthrightly. Jakobovits went on to lecture the Secretary of State for Defence on the arms trade and took on law lords and archbishops when he felt their views were mistaken; mistaken that is, according to the teachings of the Torah.

As Rabbi Jeffrey Cohen said when editing some of Jakobovits' responsa: '[he] has become, by sheer force of character, the conscience not only of his own community, but of a large segment of the Western world'.[5]

It was a remarkable outcome for a boy born in East Prussia in 1921 and not even the first choice for Chief Rabbi when Brodie retired in 1965. He also played his part in helping to replace the millions lost in the Holocaust. He was blessed with two sons, four daughters and over 40 grandchildren. In 2004 there are also more than 40 great-grandchildren. His predecessors would envy his riches.

What Jakobovits couldn't halt was the decline in the numbers in the community as a whole. Intermarriage, apostasy, agnosticism and atheism made considerable inroads, thinning the ranks of the Orthodox. Jakobovits was up against the breakdown of family life and parental influence, the growth in divorce and one-parent families, the materialist society and the permissive society. He could neither stop them dead in their tracks when he took office, nor substantially halt their progress as the years went by. What he could do was raise a small army to protect the citadel of Orthodoxy within the mainstream community. Those committed youngsters were the result of his Jewish schools policy and they form the bedrock on which the survival of the community depends today. With the growth in numbers of the right wing, the Orthodox share of the community at the beginning of the twenty-first century is over 70 per cent.

When, after his retirement in 1991, Jakobovits was asked to list his failures, he regretted his inability to get the right wing and the United Synagogue to work together more closely. He was also disappointed that the efforts to reach agreement with the Progressive movement on marriage, divorce and conversion had not been successful. The pain, for both communities, continued and the atmosphere often soured. What Jakobovits did not regret was his consistent stating of the Din, irrespective of the view of important segments of his own community: 'There were occasions when even our Board of Deputies publicly disassociated itself from my views – as if I had ever claimed to speak in its name.'

To the best of his considerable ability, Lord Jakobovits spoke in the name of the Almighty – as had all his predecessors in the office.

NOTES

1. Immanuel Jakobovits, *The Evolution of the British Rabbinate since 1845*, historical essay to honour Dr Israel Porush, 1988.
2. Information provided by the Athenaeum Club to the author.
3. Bernard Homa, *Footprints on the Sands of Time*, 1990.
4. Haham Solomon Gaon, Lecture to the World Sephardi Federation, January 1960.
5. Rabbi Jeffrey Cohen, *Dear Chief Rabbi*, Ktav Publishing, 1995.

26   Jonathan Sacks 1991–

In 1967 Jonathan Sacks was a 19-year-old, first-year Cambridge student wrestling with the problem of what to do with his life. He came from a family that could trace its ancestry back to Zevi Ashkenazi, but he had been blessed with a brilliant academic brain and the option of staying within a university's ivy-covered walls was an attractive option. It was the Six Day War between Israel and the Arabs that first inspired him towards the rabbinate.

The period leading up to the war was terribly worrying for all Jews. The Egyptian leader, Gamal Abdul Nasser, had said, 'We shall not enter Palestine with its soil covered in sand. We shall enter it with its soil saturated in blood.'[1] The Syrians threatened 'a battle of annihilation'.[2] Facing the armies of Egypt, Jordan and Syria, vastly outnumbered, and with another arms embargo cutting off supplies to Israel – but not the Arabs – Israel's sheer existence looked perilous in the extreme. Jewish students who would not, normally, have been seen within miles of the small Cambridge synagogue in Thompson's Lane, found themselves drawn there to stand with their brethren. There was a great deal of solidarity and it was an inspiring time.

The Israelis won the ensuing war in six days and Sacks had been deeply moved. He decided to go off to the United States, determined to talk to the finest rabbis in the country about their contribution to the future of Judaism. Which brought him eventually to Brooklyn and Menahem Mendel Shneersohn, one of the most gifted and influential rabbis of the twentieth century. It was Shneersohn who told Sacks that his future ought to be as a religious leader. He got a First at Cambridge and a PhD at Oxford, but Shneersohn's words stayed with him. He went on to get *semichas* from both the Yeshiva Etz Haim and Jews' College. He was married at 22, at 23 he was teaching Moral Philosophy at Middlesex University, at 25 Jewish Philosophy at Jews' College, and by the time he was 36 he was the principal of Jews' College. He also has a PhD from London University on *Collective Responsibility in Jewish Law and Thought*. He is a much better scholar than his only twentieth-century English-born predecessor,

Israel Brodie, and in illustrious competition with a great exponent, he was also just the better speaker.

Nineteenth- and twentieth-century Jewish history are well documented. There are plenty of books and the nearer you come to the present day, the more likely you are to find eyewitnesses of the original events. There are photographs available, films, radio recordings and television videos. Recording the recent past might, therefore, seem easy, but the writer runs into a serious problem: not all the facts are in the public domain. There are meetings where the minutes are still confidential, discussions and agreements which have taken place in private. There are strategies and hidden agendas where it would be unhelpful or unconstructive to disclose all the information at the moment. You also can't see into the future. In time, what really happened will emerge and become clear – burying history is almost impossible – but the whole truth isn't yet available.

So, as we come to the latest Chief Rabbi, it's important to realize that making any kind of judgement would be grossly unfair. Jonathan Sacks, hopefully, still has a third of his tenure as Chief Rabbi of the United Hebrew Congregations of the Commonwealth to go. He will be 59 in 2007.

Sacks took over at Jews' College when the institution was in a parlous position. In spite of the scholastic excellence of his predecessor, Rabbi Nahum Rabinovitch, the institution was deeply in debt and had very few students. By the time he moved on, the college had been transferred from the West End to a sensible site in north London and the courses had been revitalized. At its peak under his leadership there were some 150 students and the college was concentrating on rabbinic in-service training, improving the standards of every aspect of their responsibilities from leadership to time management.

Sacks was very strong on developing occasions when truly newsworthy events would appeal to very large numbers in the community. An early example was a conference in 1989 called 'Orthodoxy confronts Modernity'. Where David Nietto had written *Matteh Dan*, or Jakobovits covered Jewish Medical Ethics, Sacks utilized modern communications and brought ten rabbinic sages to London from all over the world to lecture for a day to more than 1,000 delegates. The second conference attracted 1,000 delegates again and another 1,000 had to be turned away. The conferences were dazzling successes, achieving one of Sacks' permanent objectives, to create the right climate in which Orthodox Judaism can flourish.

When Lord Jakobovits retired in 1991 at the appointed age, he was succeeded by Sacks who could offer the total package the United Synagogue members had sought for in vain over the previous 100 years. It wasn't that they had any complaints about the outstanding performance of Lord Jakobovits; a CV without parallel. Their former Chief Rabbis had also all had excellent qualities. It was just that they had always wanted an English gentleman, impeccably Orthodox, but also equally at home in an ancient university or writing columns for *The Times*.

Sacks fitted the bill to perfection. He was undoubtedly an absolutely outstanding preacher. Like Artom and Brodie, at an early age he could dazzle an audience with the content, enthusiasm and power of his delivery. He had the ability to simplify complicated philosophical points and to move a congregation to tears or joy. He was lean, handsome and charismatic, with a ready smile and an outgoing personality. He inspired young people and he had, for some years, been growing into one of the acceptable faces of religion, in a Western country which, typically, appeared to be ever more interested in pop stars and footballers than in the complexities of faith. With his wife, Elaine, and his children, Sacks reflected the values of family life in British society, even if the whole institution of the family was under serious threat.

It was understandable that, with these qualifications, he would become a star in the Jewish community, but the Jews were instructed to be a light unto the nations and, perhaps more to the point, the media had become accustomed to getting a lot of their moral input from Jakobovits. As a consequence, Sacks would automatically be given the opportunity to be a public figure and, when he proved well up to the task, he was made welcome. In 1990, even before he became Chief Rabbi, he was invited to give the Reith Lectures on the BBC. His predecessors included Bertrand Russell, the philosopher, J.K. Galbraith, the economist, Bernard Lovell, the astronomer, and Nikolaus Pevsner, the historian; all world-famous. If the BBC thought he was that good, then, as far as the establishment was concerned, he was 'one of us'.

Sacks also set out to become a good writer and in the ten years between 1986 and 1996 he produced no less than 12 books. Writing was always very important to him and he would always make sure that his timetable gave him the opportunity to regularly take himself off to a study without the distractions of office.

Had there not been such a good candidate, it is quite possible that Jakobovits would have been asked to continue in office, for he was certainly quite capable of doing so. Strike when the iron is hot is a good maxim, though, and the United Synagogue made the change when the opportunity arose.

As Chief Rabbi, Sacks set out to burnish the image of Orthodoxy. He created the awards scheme to tell the good news about the achievements of individual Jews and to promote role models for the community. The judges included two Jewish lawyers, Lords Taylor and Woolf, who would both become Lord Chief Justice, and the distinguished academic, Sir Isaiah Berlin. When Sacks waxed enthusiastic, few would gainsay him. If not everybody could win the top prize in the award scheme. many hundreds got their certificate of nomination by their friends and colleagues.

Sacks often acted as a tug; he took the ship safely out of harbour and then left it to continue on its voyage. The Jewish Association of Business Ethics (JABE) is a good example. The Din sets out business ethics in great detail but if there is one lasting, centuries-old accusation against Jews, it is for sharp practice in business. Here was an opportunity to encourage a higher standard of ethics and, at the same time, to distance malefactors from any suggestion that they were not violating the Din; the truth was that Jewish merchants had, historically, based their international trading on the Din and on the vital ingredient of integrity to it. The JABE still exists and sends speakers into schools and sixth form colleges to lecture on the subject and to set out the right code of conduct before the youngsters start their own careers.

Another major initiative was Jewish Continuity where Sacks set out to act on Dr Johnson's advice: 'Depend upon it, Sir, when a man knows he is to be hanged in a fortnight, it concentrates his mind wonderfully.' In a series of pamphlets and in his book *Will We Have Jewish Grandchildren?* Sacks set out to arouse the community to a consciousness of the real danger that the answer might be 'No'. Apostasy was growing and religious indifference in a materialist society was undermining every religion. The support for education of the United Synagogue had been severely reduced by the financial difficulties in which that body was floundering and Sacks became deeply involved with the new team which sorted out the mess.

Talking to Sacks, he never misses an opportunity to give credit to others. If the name isn't in the chapter, that doesn't mean he forgot to mention it. Dr Irving Jacobs and Lord Stanley Kalms at Jews' College, Lord Levy and impresario Harvey Goldsmith with the awards scheme, Lord David Wolfson and Michael Sinclair with Jewish c ontinuity. Sacks' aim is to draw others into the work, not to hog the limelight.

Throughout his ministry Sacks has argued the moral and ethical case with the nation, and the community were proud that their leader was to be found in the prestigious *Times*, writing alongside the heads of the larger denominations. When he was awarded honorary doctorates and important prizes they basked in the reflected glory. In the outside world Judaism was equally as well championed as it had been in Jakobovits' time.

It is questionable, however, whether it is easier to be a public figure on the world stage or the head of a large Jewish community. Not for nothing is it said that three Jews are perfectly capable of forming four political parties. What is more, the greater your eminence in that wider world, the greater the internal scrutiny of those who do not hold the Orthodox views of the United Synagogue. Disagreements with the Progressive movement on the one side and with the right wing on the other, were always going to be inevitable. Sacks was there to be shot at and the only problem for his critics was to find suitable opportunities.

The most contentious occasion, as far as the Progressive movement was concerned, came with the death of Rabbi Hugo Gryn. The Reform rabbi was a fine human being and an inspiration to his members. He was a concentration camp survivor, a good writer, broadcaster and preacher. When he died, Sacks didn't go to the funeral. The progressives were furious and pointed out that Hermann Adler had been to the funeral of David Woolf Marks. Why was Sacks failing to show respect for such a great man? The answer was simple: the Chief Rabbis no longer attended the religious services of the Progressive movement. The crisis days of Hertz pre-war were long gone. It was no longer a question of papering over the cracks between Orthodox and Progressive thinking, as had been possible for so many years after 1840. The cracks had become chasms as the Progressives moved further away from the Orthodox position, and the religious differences were now unbridgable.

There is also the point that, while it was perfectly true that Gryn was a great man, he had inspired any number of Orthodox Jews to become members of the Progressive movement. It was not like the MCC being represented at Don Bradman's funeral; competitors on the sports field united in grief at the passing of a great cricketer, and with all the mourners equally opposed to changes in the rules of the game. The Progressive movement seriously undermined the Orthodox position and, in that posture, was injurious to the continuity of Orthodox communities all over the world. These were not the arguments on which the critics of Sacks' absence focused.

Sacks was also criticized by the right wing for having anything to do with the Progressive movement at all. Unwisely, he responded in writing to one of their eminent rabbis, assuring him that he equally recognized the danger the Progressive movement posed to Orthodoxy. This letter was promptly leaked to the press to undermine, in its turn, the efforts of the Orthodox and Progressive communities to find common ground where they could. If nothing else, the furore surrounding Gryn's passing reinforced the advice Sacks would have had – that there were many totally visible agendas which were antipathetical to the views he held.

Whatever Sacks' position, the critics on the right and the left stood ready to take offence. The right-wing agenda remained to build the walls of their Orthodox defences ever higher. The gales of the outside world they believed were best dealt with by remaining safe in harbour. Sacks felt that the world would be a better place if every religion was tolerated by every other. If secular evils were combated by the united efforts of those who stood for the higher standards of their deity. In reaching out to other religions, Sacks was in danger of attack by the right wing, believing that only their faith was the true one. He had to clarify some passages in one of his books, *The Dignity of Difference*, when the right wing protested that his views on the subject could be construed as heretical. Sacks needed the quality of defence that David Nietto had received from Zevi Ashkenazi on the 'God is Nature' sermon.

Within the Orthodox community as a whole, the centre ground was being steadily eroded. On the one hand, Orthodox Jewish weddings continued to decline in number. Divorce rates continued to rise, although they remained lower than the average for Britain. There were more one-parent families and there was more apostasy. On the other hand, the size of the hard core of committed Orthodox Jews continued to rise. The Jewish education at Jewish schools was far better than anything produced by minor efforts in synagogue classes on Sunday mornings in former years, though these too were far more professional than in the past. Sacks saw the position in terms of concentric circles. That those inhabiting the outer limits might well be lost in the future, but that the hard core of the committed would receive the most attention and grow and strengthen. By insisting on circumcision, Sasportas had taken the same view at the Restoration.

Numerically, the community is declining. Apostasy and small families are the joint causes. There has been no major influx of Orthodox immigrants in recent years and the total community is probably only about half the number it achieved at its peak 100 years ago. Nevertheless, the number of the committed Orthodox is far greater than 50 years ago, due to the far better religious education available and the large families of the right wing. There is sometimes talk on the left wing of a need for a second Chief Rabbi to have the community more broadly represented but, demographically, any second Chief Rabbi should be justly drawn from the right wing, whose membership far outnumbers the Progressive movement.

The community continued to withdraw into two main geographical bases; concentrated in London and Manchester. Smaller congregations had increasing difficulty in surviving, as their young people headed for the greater opportunities of the three major cities. In London the Orthodox community moved further out of the centre as inner-city property prices rose. Among other things, this led to the amalgamation of the Marble Arch synagogue with the Western; a post-war community with one that had been in existence for over 200 years. The largest congregations now became those of north London, such as Stanmore and Hampstead Garden Suburb. The whole community became more middle class but it also became older. The charitable support which was needed for its poor, its handicapped, and its elderly was beginning to fall on the shoulders of a dwindling number of younger people.

When the community looked at its prospects for the twenty-first century, they hadn't done so badly in 350 years. Admittedly, the Cousinhood was a thing of the past. Occasionally the great Victorian names were still to be found in their pews, but it would be the exception that proved the rule. The lay leaders of the Ashkenazi community could normally trace their ancestors to refugees from the pogroms in the late nineteenth century.

They weren't, primarily, tailors any longer or furniture makers. Considerable numbers of them still followed the traditional occupation of doctors and often the exceptionally detailed study of the Talmud by their forebears had bequeathed them an ability to thrive as lawyers; the Talmud, among other things, is a vast law book. There were large numbers of accountants and self-employed businessmen. Many of the companies formed by Jews had long ceased to have any Jewish representation in the boardroom as the founding families disappeared. There was still, however, a strong Jewish representation in retailing as the millennia-long tradition of trading continued.

The amount of virulent anti-Semitism in Britain remained as low as it had always been. There was a good deal of vandalism and a small number of extremists, but the *Jewish Chronicle*, in most years, had to seek photographs of defaced gravestones in some other part of the world if they wanted to suggest that anti-Semitism continued to flourish. It certainly did in many countries outside Britain, but it was, basically, negligible in the United Kingdom. The fear was still there, though, even after 350 years and, too often, it was passed on from generation to generation. The general population would have thrown up their hands in amazement and frustration if they had ever considered the subject. What more could they do? The vast majority had been good neighbours and voted for the manifestos of tolerant governments for more than three centuries.

Yet the community still worried about anti-Semitism, no matter how many deposits the racist party candidates lost in elections. Security at synagogues and Jewish schools was extensive and public figures, like the Chief Rabbi, had a team of security guards who looked after them. As an Israeli ambassador had been shot and seriously wounded at a West End hotel, and as there had been spasmodic attacks on synagogues and cemeteries over the years, the security was warranted. Whether the actual high level of security was necessary is, of course, impossible to say, but it certainly achieved the success that there were comparatively few incidents. A negative effect was, however, that it strengthened the views of those who thought that the number of their enemies was far greater than was really the case.

In Britain the institution of the strong Jewish family was widely admired by the general public, as was the lack of delinquency among Jewish young people and their continuing effort to work hard to make the grade. Of course, there were Jewish criminals; no community is totally free of them, but as the American comedian, Woody Allen, once pointed out, you do not cross the road in order to avoid a Jewish accountant.

The Jews had slightly more than their fair share of MPs and members of the House of Lords. The British community also illustrated the fact that it was possible to retain your own culture in a multi-cultural Britain, while still being recognized as loyal to the state. The question of dual loyalty was not an issue because Israel was the only Western-style democracy in the Middle East and a loyal ally of the West.

The enormous upsurge of pity after the Holocaust lasted for half a century, but slowly dissipated as memories faded and Israel became quite capable of taking care of itself in military matters. Israel came to be seen as bullying the Palestinians, even though vastly out-numbered by hostile Arab states whose public intention was to destroy it. As Palestinian suicide bombers were followed by Israeli military strikes, which also killed many innocent Arab civilians, peace in the Middle East remained seemingly unattainable even after Israel had been in existence for 50 years. One thing which did become clear was that the maintenance of Orthodox Judaism was still the responsibility of the Diaspora communities outside Israel. The likelihood that the state of Israel would become a bastion of Orthodoxy looked ever more unlikely.

One powerful segment in Israel with no interest in Orthodoxy was the majority of the Russian Jews who had finally been able to leave the Soviet Union after the collapse of communism. Jakobovits had been absolutely right in foreseeing that, without any prior Jewish education, they would be impossible to integrate into the Orthodox fold.

Sacks makes his contribution to the debate in Israel in an academic role. He doesn't believe it is possible or correct to try to dictate to the Israelis but, as a teacher at the Hebrew or Bar Ilan Universities, he tries to bridge the gap between the secular and the religious. There are, however, few more exposed positions you can adopt than as a bridger of gaps. It is all too easy to be hit in the crossfire.

The problem is that three centuries is a short space of time in Jewish history and Britain is, by world standards, a small island. As the Irish remember the massacres of Cromwell which took place at the same time as the Resettlement of the Jews, so the Jews remember the far more recent events of the Holocaust and the pogroms. The Portuguese have just about been forgiven for the Inquisition. The scars take centuries to heal.

Relations with other Christian religious bodies remained warm and friendly and a better understanding was achieved with the Moslems as well. Although there was a good deal of anti-Jewish rhetoric among Moslem extremists, within 24 hours of the Twin Towers atrocity on 9/11, Sacks joined the Moslem and Christian leaders at Lambeth Palace to condemn the outrage. In April 2002 Prince Charles became the patron of Respect, a movement for which he gave the Chief Rabbi the credit of suggesting. Respect is supported by all nine major faiths in Britain. It is dedicated to getting its congregants to perform acts of kindness for people of the eight religions they don't belong to themselves.

Sacks is seen by the media as the spokesman for all the Jews in Britain, whether they recognize his authority or not. He was knighted in 2005. He is the acceptable face of Judaism and resembles a Victorian illustration of a biblical prophet. The community is left in peace to get on with its business. As Charles II told them, they could 'promise themselves the effects of the same favour...so long as they demean themselves peacably and quietly, with due obedience to his Majesty's laws'. God save the Queen.

NOTES

1   Howard Sachar, *A History of Israel*, Alfred A. Knopf, 1979, p. 616.
2   Isi Leibler, *The Case for Israel*, Globe Press, 1972.

Bibliography

Abrahams, Beth Zion, *Jews in England* (Robert Anscombe, 1946)

Adler, Elkan, *History of Jews in London* (Jewish Publication Society of America, 1930)

Adler, Chief Rabbi Hermann, *Anglo-Jewish Memories* (Routledge, 1909)

Alderman, Geoffrey, *The Federation of Synagogues, 1887–1987* (Federation of Synagogues, 1987)

American Jewish Historical Society Proceedings

Angel, Rabbi Marc D., Haham *Gaon Memorial Volume* (Sepher Hermon Press, 1997)

Apple, Rabbi Raymond, *The Hampstead Synagogue, 1892–1967* (Vallentine Mitchell, 1967)

—, 'The Emergence of the Anglo-Jewish Pulpit 1656–1855' (2000)

Barnett, Arthur, *The Western Synagogue Through Two Centuries* (Vallentine Mitchell, 1961)

Barnett, Lionel D., *El Libro de los acuerdos* (Oxford University Press, 1931)

Bell, Walter G., *The Great Fire of London in 1666* (Greenwood Publishing, 1971)

Bermant, Chaim, *Troubled Eden* (Vallentine Mitchell, 1969)

—, *The Cousinhood* (Eyre and Spottiswood, 1971)

Black, Eugene C., *The Social Politics of Anglo-Jewry 1880–1920* (Basil Blackwell, 1988)

Black, Gerry, *JFS* (Tymsder Publishing, 1998)

—, *Jewish London* (Breedon Books, 2003)

Brasz, Chaya, and Yosef Kaplan, *Dutch Jews as Perceived by Themselves and Others* (Brill, 2001)

Brodie, Chief Rabbi Israel, *A Word in Season* (Vallentine Mitchell, 1959)

—, *Strength of My Heart* (G.J. George, 1969)

Cardozo, Jessurun, and Paul Goodman, *Think and Thank, the Montefiore Synagogue and College, Ramsgate, 1833–1933* (Oxford University Press, 1933)

Carmilly-Weinberger, Moshe, *Censorship and Freedom of Expression in Jewish History* (Sepher Hermon Press, 1977)

Carr, John Dickson, *The Murder of Sir Edmund Berry Godfrey* (Longmans, 1936)

Cesarani, David, *The Jewish Chronicle and Anglo Jewry, 1841–1991* (Cambridge University Press, 1994)

Churchill, Winston, *Great Contemporaries* (Odhams, 1937)

Cohen, Stuart A., *English Zionists and British Jews* (Princeton University Press, 1982)

Colley, Linda, *Britons* (Yale University Press, 1992)

Colson, Percy, *Lord George Gordon* (R. Hale & Co., 1937)

Da Silva, Haham Joshua, *Discursos Predacaveys* (Amsterdam: 1688)

da Sola, Abraham, *David Aaron da Sola* (Wm. H. Jones, 1864)

Defries, Harry, *Conservative Party Attitudes to Jews* (Frank Cass, 2001)

Douglas, James, *The Man in the Pulpit* (Methuen, 1905)

Duschinsky, Charles, *The Rabbinate of the Great Synagogue* (Oxford University Press, 1921)

Emanuel, Charles, *A Century and a Half of Jewish History* (George Routledge, 1910)

Endelman, Todd M., *Radical Assimilations in English Jewish Literature* (Indiana University Press, 1990)

Faber, Eli, *Jews, Slaves and the Slave Trade* (New York University Press, 1998)

Ferguson, Niall, *The House of Rothschild, 1798–1848* (Viking, 1998)

Finestein, Judge Israel, *Jewish Society in Victorian England* (Vallentine Mitchell, 1993)

—, *Scenes and Personalities in Anglo-Jewry, 1800–2000* (Vallentine Mitchell, 2002)

Fletcher Jones, Pamela, *The Jews of Britain* (Windrush Press, 1990)

Freedman, Maurice, *A Minority in Britain* (Vallentine Mitchell, 1955)

Freely, John, *The Lost Messiah* (Penguin, 2001)

Gaster, Haham Moses, *Observations of Rev. Dr Gaster of the Report of the Special Committee dated 15 March 1896* (Judith, Lady Montefiore College, 1896)

—, *History of the Ancient Synagogue* (Spanish and Portuguese Jews' Congregation, 1901)

Gould, Julius, and Shaul Esh, *Jewish Life in Modern Britain* (Routledge & Kegan Paul, 1964)

Gubbay, Lucien, and Rabbi Abraham Levy, *Ages of Man* (Darton,

Longman & Todd, 1985)

Harris, Isidore, *Jews' College, Jubilee Volume* (Luzac & Co., 1906)

Hein, Virginia H., *The British Followers of Theodor Herzl* (Garland Publishing, 1987)

Henriques, H.S.Q., *The Jews and English Law* (Oxford University Press, 1908)

Henriques, Robert, *Sir Robert Waley Cohen* (Secker & Warburg, 1966)

Henriques, Ursula, *The Jews of South Wales* (University of Wales Press, 1993)

Hershon, Cyril P., *To Make Them English* (Palavas Press, 1938)

Hertz, Chief Rabbi Joseph Herman (ed.), *The Pentateuch and Haftorahs* (Soncino Press, 1938)

—, Sermons, *Addresses and Speeches* (Soncino Press, 1938)

Hibbert, Christopher, *King Mob* (Longmans Green, 1959)

Hirschberg, J.W., 'Jews and Jewish Affairs in the Relations between Great Britain and Morocco in the Eighteenth Century', in *Essays Presented to Chief Rabbi Israel Brodie* (Soncino Press, 1967)

Homa, Bernard, *A Fortress in Anglo-Jewry* (Shapiro Vallentine, 1953)

—, *Footprints on the Sand of Time* (n.p., 1990)

Hyamson, Albert, *The Sephardim of England* (Spanish and Portuguese Jews' Congregation, 1951)

—, *Jews' College 1855–1955* (Jews' College, 1954)

Jakobovits, Chief Rabbi Lord Immanuel, *Journal of a Rabbi* (W.H. Allen, 1967)

—, *If Only My People* (Weidenfeld & Nicolson, 1984)

—, *Dear Chief Rabbi* (Ktav Publishing, 1995)

Jewish Chronicle, Sketches of Anglo-Jewish History (*Jewish Chronicle*, 1873–74)

—, *Anglo-Jewish Historical Exhibition 1887* (*Jewish Chronicle*, 1888)

Jewish Encyclopaedia (United States: 1901)

Johnson, Paul, *A History of the Jews* (Weidenfeld & Nicolson, 1997)

Jung, Leo (ed.), *Jewish Leaders* (Bloch Publishing, 1953)

Katz, David S., *The Jews in the History of England, 1485–1850* (Clarendon Press, 1994)

Kershon, Anne and Romain, Jonathan *Tradition and Change* (Vallentine Mitchell, 1995)

King, Gregory, *Natural and political observations and conclusions upon the state and condition of England, 1696* (1801)

Kochan, Lionel, *Jews, Idols and Messiahs* (Basil Blackwell, 1990)

Krausz, Armin, *Sheffield Jewry* (Bar Ilan University, 1980)

Landman, Samuel, *Essays Presented to Dr J.H. Hertz* (Soncino Press, 1967)

Leibler, Isi, *The Case for Israel* (Globe Press, 1972)

Levy, Rabbi Abraham, *The Sephardim: A Problem of Survival* (1972)

Lipman, Sonia, and V.D. Lipman, *The Century of Moses Montefiore* (Littman Library, 1985)

Lipman, V.D., *Social History of the Jews in England, 1850–1950* (Watts, 1954)

—, *Three Centuries of Anglo-Jewish History* (Jewish Historical Society of England, 1961)

Magnus, Lady Katie, *Jewish Portraits* (Routledge, 1988)

Margoliouth, Moses, *History of the Jews in Great Britain* (London: 1851)

Meirovich, Harvey, *A Vindication of Judaism* (Jewish Theological Seminary of America, 1998)

Milman, Henry H., *History of the Jews* (Everyman Library, 1939)

Mosse, Werner E., *Second Chance* (J.C.B. Mohr, 1991)

Nahon, Gerard, *Dutch Jews as Perceived by Others* (Brill, 2001)

Newman, Aubrey, *Migration and Settlement* (Jewish Historical Society of England, 1971)

—, *The United Synagogue* (Routledge & Kegan Paul, 1976)

Olsover, Lewis, *The Jewish Communities of North-East England* (Ashley Mark, 1981)

Persoff, Meir, *Immanuel Jakobovits: A Prophet in Israel* (Vallentine Mitchell, 2002)

Petuchowski, Rabbi Jakob J., *The Theology of Haham David Nietto* (Ktav Publishing, 1954)

Phillips, Olga Somech, and Hyam A. Simons, *The History of the Bayswater Synagogue 1863–1963* (London: 1963)

Picciotto, James, *Sketches of Anglo-Jewish History* (1875; repr. Soncino Press, 1956)

Pollins, Harold, *Economic History of the Jews in England* (Littman Library, 1982)

Porter and Harel-Hoshen, *Odyssey of the Exiles* (Israel: Ministry of Defence Publishing House, 1992)

Roth, Cecil, *A Life of Menassah ben Israel* (Jewish Publication Society of America, 1934)

—, *Jewish Contribution to Civilization* (Macmillan, 1938)

—, *Jewish Chronicle, 1841–1941* (Jewish Chronicle, 1949)

—, *History of the Great Synagogue* (Edward Goldston, 1950)

—, *Essays and Portraits in Anglo-Jewish History* (Jewish Publication Society of America, 1962)

—, *A History of the Jews in England* (John Trotter, 1964)

—, *The Standard Jewish Encyclopaedia* (W.H. Allen, 1966)

Rubinstein, W.D., *A History of the Jews in the English-Speaking World: Great Britain* (Macmillan, 1996)

Ruderman, David B., *Jewish Enlightenment in an English Key* (Princeton University Press, 2000)

Sachar, Howard, *A History of Israel* (Alfred A. Knopf, 1979)

Sacher, Harry (ed.), *Zionist Portraits and Other Essays* (London: 1959)

Sacks, Chief Rabbi Sir Jonathan, *One People* (Littman Library, 1993)

Samuel, Wilfred S., *First London Synagogue of the Resettlement* (Spottiswoode Ballantyne, 1924)

Saville, J., *Chartism and the State* (Cambridge University Press, 1987)

Schindler, B. (ed.), *Gaster Centenary Publication* (Royal Asiatic Society, 1958)

Scholem, Gershom, *Sabbatai Sevi* (Routledge & Kegan Paul, 1973)

Shaftesley, John M. (ed.), *Remember the Days* (Jewish Historical Society of England, 1966)

Shire, Angela, *Great Synagogue Marriage Registers, 1791–1850* (Frank J. Gent, 2001)

Simons, Hyman A., *Forty Years a Chief Rabbi* (Robson Books, 1980)

Singer, Steven, *Orthodox Judaism in Early Victorian London, 1840–1858* (UMI, 1987)

Stein, Leonard, *The Balfour Declaration* (Vallentine Mitchell, 1961)

Susser, Bernard, *The Jews of South West England* (University of Exeter Press, 1993)

Swetchinski, Daniel, *Reluctant Cosmopolitans* (Littman Library, 2000)

Tovey, D'Blossiers, *Anglia Judaica* (1738)

Vital, David, *A People Apart* (Oxford University Press, 1999)

Williams, Bill, *The Making of Manchester Jewry 1740–1875* (Manchester University Press, 1985)

Index